Applications of
Systemic Family Therapy
The Milan Approach

Applications of
Systemic Family Therapy
The Milan Approach

edited by

David Campbell
and
Rosalind Draper

published for
The Institute of Family Therapy (London)
43 New Cavendish St., London W1

Volume 3
in the series
Complementary Frameworks of Theory and Practice
edited by
Arnon Bentovim, Gill Gorell Barnes, and Alan Cooklin

Grune & Stratton
(Harcourt Brace Jovanovich, Publishers)

London   Orlando   San Diego   New York
   Toronto   Montreal   Sydney   Tokyo

GRUNE & STRATTON, LTD.
24/28 Oval Road
London NW1 70X

United States edition published by
GRUNE & STRATTON, INC.
Orlando, Florida   32887

Library of Congress Catalog Number
International Standard Book Number 0-8089-1696-3

Printed in the United States of America

85 86 87   10 9 8 7 6 5 4 3 2 1

Contributors

AMANDA ACWORTH *Hill End Adolescent Unit, Hill End Hospital, St. Albans, Hertfordshire, England*

JOHN BERRY *Community Psychiatric Nurse, Holmesdale House Health Centre, Hastings, Sussex, England*

ALEXANDER BLOUNT *Clinical Director, Crossroads Community Growth Centre Inc., Holyoke, Massachussetts, USA*

LUIGI BOSCOLO *Co-Director, Centro Milanese di Terapia, Studio della Famiglia, Milan, Italy*

PAULA BOSTON *Family Therapist and Counselor, The American Embassy, London, England*

RICHARD BROWN *Assistant Director of Residence Training, Department of Psychiatry, Cornell University, Medical College and Payne Whitney Clinic, New York, USA*

JOHN BURNHAM *Senior Social Worker and Family Therapist, Charles Burns Clinic, Birmingham, England*

BRIAN CADE *Family Therapist, The Family Institute, Cardiff, Wales*

DAVID CAMPBELL *Supervisor and Teacher, Institute of Family Therapy, London NW3, England, Department for Children and Parents, The Tavistock Clinic, London, NW3, England*

ANNA CASTELLUCCI *Psychologist, Presido Psichiatrico 27 USL, Bologna, Italy*

GIANFRANCO CECCHIN *Co-Director, Centro Milanese di Terapia della Famiglia, Milan, Italy*

STEPHANIE CHRISTOFAS *Social Worker, Islington Family Service Unit, London*

JANE CONN *Acting Centre Organizer, Orford Road Centre, London Borough of Waltham Forest, Raven House, London, England*

EVAN IMBER COPPERSMITH *Associate Professor and Training Co-ordinator, Family Therapy Programme, Department of Psychiatry, University of Calgary, Canada*

MAX CORNWELL *Family Therapist, Private Practice, Sydney, Australia*

VERNON CRONEN *Professor of Department of Communication Studies, University of Massachusetts, Amherst, Massachussetts, USA*

DANIELA DOTTI *Psychiatrist, Servizio di Igiene Mentale e Assistenza Psichiatrica Modena, Italy*

ROSALIND DRAPER *Supervisor and Teacher, Institute of Family Therapy, London W1, England. Senior Social Worker, Department for Children and Parents, The Tavistock Clinic, London W1, England*

ROSSANA FERRARI *Psychiatric Nurse, Servizio di Igiene Mentale e Assistenza Psichiatrica, Modena, Italy*

LAURA FRUGGERI *Assistant Professor, Instituto di Psicologia, Universita de Parma, Parma, Italy*

FREDDY GAINZA *Psychiatrist, Hill End Adolescent Unit, Hill End Hospital, Hertfordshire, England*

ANN GOLDSMITH *Social Worker, Islington Family Service Unit, London, England*

QUEENIE HARRIS *Consultant Child and Adolescent Psychiatrist, Charles Burns Clinic, Birmingham, England*

CHRIS KNIGHT *Social Worker, London Borough of Camden Social Services Department, London, England*

PETER LANG *Member of The Kensington Consultation Centre, The City Centre, London, England*

CAROLINE LINDSEY *Consultant Psychiatrist, Department of Children and Parents, The Tavistock Clinic, London, England*

MARTIN LITTLE *Principal Officer (Social Work), London Borough of Waltham Forest, Raven House, London, England*

JULIETTE LUSTED *Community Psychiatric Nurse, Holmesdale House, Holmesdale House Mental Health Centre, Hastings, Sussex, England*

JOHN MANGAN *Senior Nurse Manager, Holmesdale House, Holmesdale House Mental Health Centre, Hastings, Sussex, England*

FREDA MARTIN *Director, C. M. Hincks Treatment Centre, Toronto, Canada*

PHILIPPA MARX *Social Worker, Islington Family Service Unit, London, England*

BARRY MASON *Principal, The Rownhams Centre for Families and Children, Enfield, London, England*

MAURIZIO MARZARI *Research Assistant, Dipartimento di Sociologia, Universita di Bologna, Bologna, Italy*

MASSIMO MATTEINI *Psychiatrist, Servizio de Igiene Mentale e Assistenza Psichiatrica, Modena, Italy*

LAURA NITZBERG *Senior Psychiatric Social Worker, Cornell University Medical College and Payne Whitney Clinic, Department of Psychiatry, Payne Whitney Clinic, New York, USA*

ARTHUR J. O'NEIL *Team Leader, Whitefield House Assessment Centre, Belfast, Northern Ireland*

JEAN PIERRE PARMAINTENY *Community Psychiatric Nurse, Holmesdale House Mental Health Centre, Hastings, Sussex, England*

JOHN PATTEN *Associate Professor of Psychiatry and Associate Director of Family Therapy Program, Cornell Medical College, Payne Whitney Clinic, New York, USA*

BARNETT PEARCE *Professor and Chairman of Department of Communication Studies, University of Massachussetts, Amherst, Massachussetts, USA*

PHILIP PEATFIELD *Unit Organizer, Islington Family Service Unit, London, England*

MARJORIE PIKE *Senior Social Worker, Hill End Adolescent Unit, Hill End Hospital, St. Albans, Hertfordshire, England*

PETER REDER *Consultant Child and Family Psychiatrist, Charing Cross Hospital, London, England. Previously Consultant Psychiatrist Newham Child Guidance Clinic, London, England*

BEBE SPEED *Family Therapist, The Family Institute, Cardiff, Wales*

MARLENE SPIELMAN *Individual and Family Therapist Private Practice, New York City, USA*

EILEEN SUNDARAM *Community Psychiatric Nurse, Holmesdale House Health Centre, Hastings, Sussex, England*

KARL TOM *Professor and Director of Training, Family Therapy Programme, Department of Psychiatry, University of Calgary, Calgary, Canada*

VALERIA UGAZIO *Assistant Professor, Department of Psychology, Università Cattolica, Milan, Italy, Instructor in Systemic Therapy, Centro Milanese di Terapia della Famiglia, Milan, Italy*

Preface

The publication of *Paradox and Counter Paradox* was an important punctuation in the evolution of family therapy theory and practice. The ideas and techniques emanating from Milan, first from the Centre for the Study of the Family and later from the Milan Centre for Family Therapy (founded in 1983 by Dr. Luigi Boscolo and Dr. Gianfranco Cecchin), have inspired much enthusiasm and criticism.

This book attempts to show how systems therapists on both sides of the Atlantic in places like Calgary, Modena and Cardiff are modifying and developing these ideas to suit the context in which they work. We have deliberately included accounts of problems, questions and difficulties as well as tentative solutions and successes. Above all, this book is about the ways in which the Milan approach has been applied in different settings in order to create a therapeutic context in which change can occur.

We appreciate that the book does not represent the work of all the teams using the Milan approach as their orientation. Nevertheless, the work of the teams described in this book shows their preoccupations at this point in time, and how their ideas are a product of their interaction with the wider professional systems of which they are a part.

We hope that the reader will get from each chapter a sense of the interaction between the ideas and the context which led to a particular application of the Milan approach, and that this will contribute to a richer understanding of the meaning of systemic family therapy as well as its applicability to specific settings.

Taken as a whole, the book covers a vast range of ideas and experiences and is a tribute to the creativity and vision of its contributors, and we would like to thank each of them for their efforts in preparing their manuscripts.

We are grateful to the Institute of Family Therapy and the series editors, Academic Press, and our colleagues who supported the idea of this book and gave us enough rope to carry it out. Nick Baker at Academic Press provided the necessary information and guidance for such an endeavour. We wish to thank the secretaries involved for their invaluable help and patience.

Finally, and above all, the hours we spent editing were borrowed from our families and we thank our spouses and children for reassuring us that any scars will heal long before this book reaches its second publication.

Foreword I

The third volume of the series, *Family Therapy—Complementary Frameworks of Theory and Practice*, continues the traditions of exploration and connection established in the first two volumes. Theory and practice are firmly linked throughout this volume by the approach known as Systemic Family Therapy, or the Milan Approach. The Institute for Family Studies in Milan was originally organised by Mara Selvini Palazzoli in 1967. In 1971 she was joined by others creating a research team, Gianfranco Cecchin, Giuliana Prata, and Luigi Boscolo. Their work on schizophrenic families was published in English in 1978 under the title of *Paradox and Counterparadox*. This work has had a powerful impact on the world of family therapy and consultation to networks related to families. Their ideas and the applications of these have created loyalties and controversies about the nature of the work. The ideas that underlie their thinking are firmly based on systems notions developed from Bateson, Watzlawick, and other pioneer thinkers to whom all family therapists are in debt. Many of these ideas underlie the work also described in the first two volumes.

Through the Milan group workshops and teaching throughout the world, the basic ingredients of their work have become well-known: hypothesis-making, circular questioning, and a neutral therapeutic stance in the use of "systemic" interventions and rituals that positively connote family members' actions in the service of family coherence and loyalty. The power and effectiveness of their approach and the changes created by such interventions has been seen and experienced by those who have observed the work of the original Milan Group or who have experimented with the approach.

This volume represents "second generation" applications of the Milan Approach to Systemtic Family Therapy. Inevitably the integration of new ways of working with old ideas, once the shock of the new has been absorbed, throws up further ways of working and thinking. Reading through this volume the reader will discover that the original ideas and concepts have been enlarged and elaborated.

For example, Tomm describes how circular questioning can enable families to demonstrate their beliefs and actions in ways that would be familiar to therapists using various approaches. Cronen's and Pearce's important contribution on the management of meaning focusses on the power of the Milan Approach to create change in rigid families, yet underlines the problem of applying the approach to unstructured and chaotic families and creates a rationale for "structuring" rather than destablising interventions.

As part of a series on complementary frameworks of theory and practice in family therapy, this volume can be seen as a development rather than as a symmetrical challenge to the field. It is not an expression of total difference but of perspective and vantage point, which will affect the stance and actions of the therapist. This is emphasised in the commentary between the editors David Campbell and Rosalind Draper, with Luigi Boscolo and Gianfranco Cecchin of the Milan group. The emphasis is subtly changing from being concerned with the interacting behaviors of family members to concern with the therapist's role as a part of a family system whose action creates feedback and change or evolution. Approaches are described to a variety of clinical problems, theory, and training, and also to a variety of settings. These range from lower income families and multi-agency problems, to day centres for young people, mental health agencies (whether in-patient or out-patient), social services, and family therapy agencies. In all contexts, the effect of systemic thinking and feedback is explored on agencies that habitually organise clients and workers into a neverending dance.

David Campbell's and Rosalind Draper's overview describes the way that they asked contributors to define their own therapeutic context, thereby leading the contributors to present their resolution of the contradiction and confusion into the system of which they were themselves a part. This book will stimulate the reader to do the same.

Arnon Bentovim
London, England

Foreword II

This milestone anthology is being published none too soon. Since the appearance of *Paradox and Counterparadox* in 1979, there has been no further book on the work of the Milan associates. In particular, none has come out describing the evolution of the work of Gianfranco Cecchin and Luigi Boscolo since they split from the original team or the enormous influence they have had on a second generation of systemic therapists in Italy, England, Canada, and the U.S.

This volume, put together by Rosalind Draper and David Campbell, and covering every kind of agency and public service setting, goes far to remedy the situation. Although they are the editors, the other contributors have been equally instrumental in expanding and disseminating the systemic approach in their home locations. The book speaks with diverse voices, yet with a communal voice. True to a central tenet of the Milan Approach, it is a "team" effort.

Although I am not represented in the volume, I feel incredibly privileged to have been in England when the ideas of the Milan group were first taking root. It was there, in the late 1970s, early 1980s, that I took part in meetings with the editors of this book and many of the other contributors. At times we were joined by Drs. Boscolo and Cecchin, who traveled about like a pair of Johnny Appleseeds, planting seeds and tending seedlings. I remember being impressed that they would turn down prestigious invitations in favor of some unknown clinic where they felt their hosts were actively interested in implementing their ideas.

What are these ideas, and why do they represent such an important departure for the family systems field? Let me try to answer this question from my own, admittedly biased, point of view and to go over what I feel are some of the major new concepts contained in these chapters. My apologies to the writers if I do not also single out their names.

First, let me say that the work represented shows an abiding respect for the formulations of the late Gregory Bateson and for the tradition of research carried on by the colleagues he esteemed. I am talking particularly of cybernetic epistemologists Heinz von Foerster, Humberto Maturana, Ernst von Glasersfeld, and Francisco Varela. It is no surprise that the contributors to this volume have attempted to embody this cybernetic epistemology in clinical terms. Draper says in a chapter on training, "We were all to place ourselves under the arch of Bateson's definition of 'wisdom' as 'a sense of recognition of the fact of circuitry.'" Thus, to begin with, there would be less interest in introducing a new technique of family therapy than on finding ways to apply a systemic view to whatever work a professional was already doing.

At the same time, terms are redefined. In the theory section of the book, one finds words like "context" instead of "pathology"; "recursion" instead of "symptom"; "punctuation" instead of "diagnosis"; and "evolution" instead of "cure." These changes suggest some of the differences between the Milan Method and the more traditional models of family therapy.

Instead of a treatment model, in which a dysfunctional system is treated or fixed, this approach more closely resembles a scientific experiment under the New Physics. The influence of the observer is included and there is no such thing as an objective result. It has long been suspected that the usual format in which a professional "treats" a condition in a family or person (whether you call it a dysfunctional structure, a double-bind communication, or a pathologic interaction sequence) feeds into the verification of that condition. We are hearing more and more these days about the constructivist view—the social construction of reality. "Psychiatric problems" may be prime examples of this process. If this is true, one must be grateful to this book for containing such a wealth of ideas for counteracting the observer blind spots that contribute to or even perhaps create these problems.

Another point of difference is the shift from an emphasis on behavior to an emphasis on meaning. This shift seems to be connected to Bateson's expanded definition of mind. Early family therapists focused on interaction patterns and family structures. These items could presumably be reprogrammed from the outside. The Milan emphasis on meaning systems and premises does not make ideas more important than behaviors, but nevertheless creates a subtle change in the position of the therapist. The constructions of the observer are on the same level as the constructions of the observed. The therapist can no longer be considered separate from the unit to be acted on.

A third difference is suggested by the idea of the "meaningful system"—the way a problem organizes people and events. This view is especially useful when one is dealing with so-called multi-agency families. The treatment unit is whomever and whatever the problem encompasses. This, I would add, always includes the treating professional as soon as the family walks in the door. Thus one could say that the system does not create the problem, the problem creates the system. The implications of this position, taken to its logical conclusion, require a profound rethinking of the very notion of the family as a homeostatic system whose malfunctions produce distress.

Another distinguishing mark of this model is its indifference to hierarchy. In a circular epistemology, all elements have equal importance. Thus position is a more useful indicator than status. If you are behind the mirror, you can see differently (not better) than persons in the room. Context becomes a ruling abstraction. The chapters on consultation give precedence to clarity about context—what contexts constrain people in a given family or professional field—and many of the interventions in the book have to do with spelling-out confusions of context rather than revising family structures.

A characteristic belief of systemic therapists is that living systems have self-healing properties and will, with a minimum of help, demonstrate that fact. As a result, the systemic approach is relatively nonintrusive, relatively noninstrumental. While conceding that coercion, seduction, bullying, or force have a place in human affairs, the systemic therapist believes that people find it hard to change under a negative connotation. This book is full of ingenious ways to counteract these connotations. For example, there is the problem of the enthusiastic trainee going back to his or her agency. The book offers a number of ways to deal with the inevitable loyalty bind for the trainee, the potential for escalation between the rival institutions, and the antagonism that could build up against the model.

This brings me to what I think is the overwhelming strength of this book: its attention to the treatment context of the practitioner. Most of the articles in the book are by clinicians who are trying to bring news of the Milan Method to public service settings and social agencies. When this model first appeared, there were doubts that it could be used outside of the protected private institute where it evolved. How could you use this approach with court-referred families, with child abuse cases, in home care settings? How could you use this approach where every case has many professionals dangling from it, none of them likely to be agreeable to a systemic point of view? How, in particular, would you use it in your own setting, where your superiors and supervisors have been trained in diametrically opposing concepts of therapy and change? Early missionary attempts proved many of these objections to be well-founded.

But an amazing thing happened over time. The trainees in the public institutions began to come back with unlooked-for applications of this model. Their efforts provided a paradigm for a project that had less and less to do with family therapy *per se*, and more and more about how to change or correct an ecosystem from within when you are one of the elements contributing to its imbalance. The concerns professionals would have in this situation are very different from those they would have in treating an individual or a family because they could no longer ignore "the fact of circuitry."

This is what makes this book so outstanding. Chapter after chapter presents fascinating and intelligent narratives of life on this new frontier. This type of experience has been written about before, of course, but never within a codified conceptual framework. It is important to state that the authors have distinguished throughout between the technique aspect of the work (the Milan Method) and the philosophical aspect (the Systemic View), which is on a different level of logical type. There is a constant interplay between systemic awareness and the particular method used to set the context for achieving it.

The last section of the book (after Theory, Teams, Agencies, and Consultations) covers Training and Research. Outcome studies are theoretically outlawed by this model, since it forbids prediction or taking credit for change, but this dilemma is addressed with the same aplomb as other areas where the systemic point of view has been declared inapplicable. The chapters on training were of particular interest to me, since they contain a gold mine of specific teaching exercises. I liked especially an application of circular questioning techniques to case presentations by trainees. And I cannot resist mentioning another idea—a role-play for a simulated family based on Kafka's *The Metamorphosis*. The hierarchical view of supervision was laid in the dust when the teacher was chosen to play Gregor.

As a coda, an informal and charming interview is included with the backstage heroes of this book, Luigi Boscolo and Gianfranco Cecchin. One must applaud the actors in this play, and one must applaud the directors of this play, but then one must also remember who "wrote" the play and call "Author! Author!" Applause is deserved for them, too.

In sum, this book bears witness to a near decade of extraordinary work by people from two continents and several countries, and to the originating genius of the Italians who started it all. To everyone, my own devoted, and admiring thanks.

Lynn Hoffman
Amherst, Massachusetts

Applications of Systemic Family Therapy: The Milan Approach

Contents

PART II—TEAMS

PART III—AGENCIES

Applications of
Systemic Family Therapy
The Milan Approach

Chapter 1

Creating a Context for Change: An Overview

David Campbell and Rosalind Draper

I. INTRODUCTION

Since the publication of *Paradox and Counterparadox* (Palazzoli *et al.*, 1978) and the subsequent wave of enthusiasm for systemic family therapy, teams using the Milan approach have been spawned on both sides of the Atlantic. This book is not a definitive statement, but a progress report, a review of their work and the thinking of this particular second generation. It represents one point in time. We see this book as a punctuation which owes a great debt to the past and may contribute to the development of systemic family therapy in the future.

We would like to identify some of the seminal ideas which have contributed to the thinking in this book. Foremost is the notion that the feedback which one part of a system receives from another part affects that first part in such a way that the two parts together may be described as an interacting system. Bateson (1973) describes a system as any unit structured on feedback. Although von Bertalanffy (1950), Ashby (1954) and other cyberneticians introduced these ideas, Watzlawick *et al.* (1967) brought *feedback* and *systems theory* into the family therapy field. Their description of the wife nagging because the husband withdraws and the husband withdrawing because the wife nags is imprinted on many therapists' minds. In such a sequence of behaviour the therapist punctuates the sequence by placing a boundary around certain interactions; however, the notion of a *punctuation* implies that any observable behaviour is part of a larger pattern of interactions. The description of *Paradox* in human communication led therapists to conceptualise the process of change as a relationship between problem behaviour and the attempted solution of the problem. Haley (1963) reframed the therapeutic process as strategic, and encouraged therapists to devise paradoxical interventions to challenge the family's attempts to solve the problem.

Bateson's (1973) contributions have been profound. No idea has had a greater impact on systemic therapy than the idea that there are *different levels of meaning* in behaviour. He confirmed a new epistemology in psychotherapy through his description of the alcoholic's endeavour to fulfil his pride and defeat the weakness of drunkenness. Bateson also developed Korzybski's dictum that *the map is not the territory* and that the behaviour we observe can be usefully conceptualised as *information* about some system of organisation. More recently, Cronen and Pearce (Cronen *et al.*, 1982) have clarified the levels of meaning which may be attributed to behaviour and

APPLICATIONS OF SYSTEMIC FAMILY THERAPY
ISBN 0-8089-1696-3

introduced the idea that the hierarchically organised structure has a downward force whereby the meaning of higher structures, such as a life script, bear upon the way we act in day to day interactions; but also that behaviour at the lower levels may have an *"implicative"* force which moves upward affecting structures such as the life script (see chapter 7, this volume). This process implies a *recursive relationship* between the higher level beliefs and the lower level actions.

The Milan team (Palazzoli *et al.*, 1978, 1980) is credited with the development and rigorous use of several important concepts. Making a working hypothesis is a way of organising data from the family so that the therapist has a starting point from which to investigate the systemic nature of the family relationships. This investigation is carried out using interviewing techniques known as *circular questioning*, by which the therapist prepares questions for the family based on the feedback he receives from previous questions and the direction implied by his hypothesis. The therapist attempts to maintain a *neutral* stance during the interview. He wishes to convey to each family member an appreciation of the dilemma they experience as a member of their particular family system. At the same time, however, the therapist wishes everyone in the system to believe that he, the therapist, is impartial and does not take sides.

The therapist is also neutral with regard to how or whether the family will change. These tools together make it possible for the therapist to develop respectful views of the behaviour and relationships in the family and offer an explanation for the importance of preserving these relationships. Many therapists today regard *positive con-notation* of the relationships which are organised around the symptomatic behaviour as one of the most powerful tools in therapy. Another major step in the development of systemic thinking is to think of individuals as *showing* certain behaviour rather than *being* a certain way. Moving from the verb *to be* to the verb *to show* enables the therapist to consider the effect the behaviour has on other members of the family and encourages an interactional view.

Systemic family therapists are interested primarily in the relationship between the individual and the system. At some time in the life of every family, Johnny will come downstairs to breakfast and announce, "I don't want to go to school today." At the very moment anyone in the family replies to Johnny, an interacting system will be formed. Mother might say, "Alright dear, why don't you stay home", or she might say, "We all feel like that at times, now run along and get dressed". These different types of feedback create different patterns and the patterns generate beliefs about how and why individuals should behave.

Families may run into trouble, however, if some of these patterns do not change with the times. As Johnny grows up he will make new announcements at the break-fast table and will thereby invite new responses and new relationships. If Johnny's invitations are seen as a threat to other important relationships, they will be refused, Johnny's growth within the family will be inhibited and someone may develop symp-toms. The relationships which are related to symptoms are maintained by beliefs about their importance, and it is here, at this level of the family's experience, that the systemic therapist tries to help them change. He aims to change their beliefs about relationships by first identifying and respecting their beliefs and then introducing new ideas to confuse the old belief system. In the vacuum created by this confusion, the family finds its own, new set of beliefs.

The Milan approach to systemic family therapy captures people's interest because it is an ecological view of human problems. It promotes the individual by looking at his place in the system. The primary tool of the therapist is the belief system of the family, and therefore the therapist uses his "self" differently. Rather than making strong relationships with family members and moving them in a particular direction, the therapist using this approach uses his "self" to reorganise information in such a way that the therapist and family as a co-evolving system create new meaning for behaviour.

Perhaps more than anything, however, this approach has represented a discontinuous leap for people feeling ineffective in their own work settings. An application of systemic thinking to a worker's own context often allows the worker to see his position and find alternative ways of proceeding.

However, effectiveness and ineffectiveness are connected by a delicate recursive relationship. If an ineffective therapist is able to understand his system and create a context which allows for effective work, there is always a danger that the therapist will attempt to hold on to this view and deny the evolution of the system through time. Thereby the same ideas applied to an evolved system will lead once again to ineffectiveness. Reifying systemic thoughts becomes nonsystemic.

II. READING THE BOOK

In editing this book our interest has been to contribute to the development of contexts in which change can occur. A therapeutic context will be different in each setting and the process by which the context is created is the result of the interaction between the worker and the wider system which includes the aim and structure of the agency, the client population, the relationships of the staff, etc. For this reason, we have collected the writings of various workers and teams who have attempted to create therapeutic contexts within their own work settings.

In order for the reader to analyse the process described by each author and apply it to his own work setting, we believe the reader will need to see his approach to each chapter as the beginning of a process which leads to an interaction between him and the authors. We would like to facilitate this interaction in a way that enables the reader to create for himself a therapeutic context in his own work setting. The interaction depends on the feedback between the reader, the authors and the context in which the reader works.

Some of the terms used in this book are given many different meanings by family therapists and we would like to clarify for the reader the way in which these terms are used in this book.

Context: A recognisable pattern of events or ideas which is created by an individual in interaction with his environment. Defining a pattern as context gives meaning to the thoughts and behaviour of the individual.

Epistemology: The rules one uses to make sense out of the world; a world view or belief system. It is the way a person organises his perceptions and thus ascribes meaning to his experience. A distinction is often made between a *lineal epistemology*, which categorises experience into discrete segments, one of which may act upon or cause an affect upon another; and *nonlineal epistemology* (often referred to as *recur-*

sive, circular, reflexive or *systemic*), which categorises experience such that any behaviour is simultaneously a cause *and* effect in relation to all other behaviours in that context.

Hypothesis: An explanation based on a hunch about why things are the way they are or why a system is behaving the way it is behaving. It provides a focus for the therapist's exploration of the family system during the session. The exploration of one hypothesis leads to the formation of another based on new information.

Meta: A prefix meaning *changed in position*, "beyond", "higher", used to describe the position (viewpoint) the therapy team seeks to gain of the client system in order to describe the system without becoming enmeshed.

Punctuation: An artificial break into sequences of behaviour in a variety of contexts.

Symmetrical/complementary relationships: Within the context of a two-sided relationship, a *symmetrical relationship* is one in which behaviours of *A* and *B* are seen as similar and the given behaviour of *A* stimulates more of the same behaviour in *B*; and a *complementary relationship* is one in which the behaviours of *A* and *B* are dissimilar but fit together, and the given behaviour of *A* stimulates more of *B*'s "fitting" behaviour (Bateson, 1973).

We acknowledge that you, the reader, may find certain terms and ideas repeated in the text in a way that seems repetitive. However, it seemed important to us that each author describe the important ideas which underpin their work. We believe there are certain ways of thinking which may be helpful in creating the kind of interaction between reader and authors which will enable the reader to redefine his position as an agent of change and be more effective. We would like to encourage readers to keep the following ideas in their minds as they approach each chapter and the book as a whole.

A. All Systemic Family Therapists are Systemic Thinkers But Not All Systemic Thinkers are Systemic Family Therapists

Two categories—thinkers and therapists—are placed at different logical levels. As discussion continues to pore over the differences and similarities between the different approaches to family therapy, it is important to say that all of the "schools" or family therapy approaches can conceivably be placed within the same rubric of "systemic thinking". Anyone who endeavours to pay attention to the pattern of recursiveness in their client's system might be called a systemic thinker. The Milan approach, which is often described as synonymous with systemic family therapy, is one approach to family therapy with its own theoretical framework and techniques. The editors and contributors have been greatly influenced by the Milan approach, and readers who want descriptions of the rationale for this method of family therapy are referred to the following authors: Palazzoli *et al.* (1978, 1980), Hoffman (1981), Penn (1982), Campbell *et al.* (1983) and Tomm (1984). This book is about the different ways in which therapists have attempted to apply the thinking of the Milan approach to family therapy to their own settings.

An important aspect of examining the application of systemic ideas is that systemic thinking can take place in many settings where family therapy is inappropriate or impossible. Since the "doing" of family therapy, just like the "doing" of anything else, is only possible under certain conditions, the interaction between the context and the individuals becomes paramount. But if at a moment in time this interaction is such that family therapy is not appropriate, such as in a residential treatment centre—or not possible due to staff resources—the worker, who is thinking systemically, may nevertheless continue to look at the pattern of interaction between himself and his wider context, and in so doing continue to be a systemic thinker. The implications of being a systemic thinker for mental health professionals are far reaching, and the aim of this book is to demonstrate varieties of theoretical positions and working contexts which have been affected by systemic thinking.

B. Any Action must be Seen as a Response at One Point in the Continuous Evolution of a System

One of the most important considerations for anyone applying systemic thinking is to respect one's place in a larger system which is always evolving in time. All systems must change and evolve, but it is the way in which they change in reply to evolutionary pressures that is crucial. It seems to be a matter of choosing the right moment to begin to do things differently. If a family member moves away prematurely, the family system may react by rigidly holding on to existing relationships; on the other hand, if the same family member does not move away when the system is ready, relationships may drift apart. In either case, the tenuous relationship between the individual and the system must constantly be negotiated because time ensures the relationship is in a constant state of dynamic tension.

A worker who is interested in change must be able to ride the crest of an evolutionary wave; to use the relationship with the client to see which family relationships are blocking progress and then to let go at the right moment so the family can rejoin its own evolutionary course. A therapist can enable a family to change simply by exploring the development or movement in relationships, and this is more easily accomplished if a therapist has a view of the family as a system moving through time. As a worker attempting to apply new ideas in any agency, it is essential to understand the natural history of relationships in the agency to appreciate what new ideas may mean at that particular moment. When the worker has some understanding of this, he is better equipped to know the most propitious way to introduce the new ideas.

Whether we hold a linear or a circular view of relationships depends on our position in the system we are describing. If, for example, one's position is that of a family member, the view of relationships tends to be linear: "She nags me, therefore I withdraw". But if one is observing a system from a different position, say that of a therapist, it is possible to see the recursive patterns of behaviour among the family members. The problem seems to be that since we are members of the system we hope to change it is difficult to see our part in the recursive pattern which contributes to the status quo.

The view we have of our position is largely affected by our appreciation of *time*. When we feel stuck with a family or within our working context we tend to forget that we are a part of a system moving through time. Our relationships lose potential and we feel stuck with circumstances as they are at the moment. An appreciation of time, however, allows for the potential for growth and movement in relationships. When movement becomes a part of the worker's view, of the system around him, it is more possible to see actions and that will lead to change.

C. We Act Because We Believe and We Believe Because We Act

In our view, meaning and action are two sides of the same coin. Our actions are determined by the meaning we attribute to a given situation. Meaning, in turn, is defined by context. Bateson (1973) coined the phrase "context of action" to explain that Pavlov's experimental neurosis was the result of the dog trying to discriminate shapes in a context which was not a context for discrimination. Keeney (1983) makes the point that "if the dog were to change his punctuation and assume that the laboratory situation had become a context for guessing, he might not attempt to discriminate . . ." (p. 35).

Problems arise in families when it is assumed by one part of the system that different members are acting within the same context while another part of the system assumes they are not. During adolescence for example, parents may be relating to an adolescent child in a context of "You must prepare for life by doing what I tell you", whereas the context which the adolescent creates is more like, "I must prepare for life by rejecting what my parents tell me". It becomes imperative for a therapist to understand the different contexts of family members as well as the context of action which the family as a whole create by coming (or being sent) for therapy.

D. The Awareness of Being in Different Contexts Simultaneously can be Both a Constraint and an Impetus for Change

Any one person, or family, or agency exists in many contexts at once and, for example, if a worker is thinking about introducing family therapy into an agency, he must consider that a new idea will be greeted in different ways according to the context. In the context of "We want our agency to be forward looking", a new idea might be welcomed; whereas in the context of "We don't want to threaten our long established relations with the outside world", a new proposal may be soundly attacked.

If a worker wants to change within his work setting, the task is one of clarifying the different contexts in which his behaviour is perceived by the system he is a part of. Often this process of clarification is sufficient to enable the worker to be lifted out of an impossible situation to see clearly how he might act. We hope that the readers of this book will learn from some of the confusion of contexts which are described by the contributors in their efforts to apply systemic family therapy.

E. The Essence of Systemic Thinking is the Appreciation of Recursiveness

The simplest description of recursiveness comes from Keeney (1983). It is that any behaviour is simultaneously a cause and effect in relation to all other behaviours in that context. Many families who are "stuck" with a problem have lost contact with this recursiveness, and the meaning they attach to symptomatic behaviour becomes lineal: "It is bad or it is mad". The family sees only one side of the coin and there is no longer sufficient movement in the system to move toward alternative behaviours. The therapist can change the context which provides the meanings which symptoms have for families, or which problems have for our own agencies, simply by identifying the recursive pattern of the problem behaviour. The identification in itself is enough to introduce the beginning of a change of context.

F. The First Step in Creating a Therapeutic Context is Identifying Redundant Behaviour

We see redundant behaviour as the response of a system which is unable to respond to pressures to change. The pressure to change from one individual or from an outside source may naturally create a recursive loop within the family's repertoire of behaviour or it may not. If the family resists this invitation to co-evolve, then there is a tension between the forces for stability and the forces for change, and the family has no new options for its behaviours and tends to repeat the old ones. Patterns soon become redundant. The presenting edge of redundant behaviour is a "dead-end" statement. When you hear family members or colleagues at work saying, "I can't do that", "I don't understand", or "They won't allow me to do what I want", you can expect that redundant behaviour will follow.

Although this view is part of the conceptual framework, for this model, we appreciate that readers may not be able to recognise their own redundant patterns of behaviour, but there are clues to recognizing these patterns in the way people respond to problems.

G. The Second Step in Creating a Therapeutic Context is Identifying Confused Messages

When a therapist examines the effect of redundant behaviour, he invariably finds that the behaviour is like a metaphor. It becomes an attempt to resolve some confusion of meanings amongst the relationships in the family. It is as though repeating some action over and over will "bring the system to its senses", clarify confusions, and get it on its merry way again. Identifying these confusions creates new contexts in which behaviour takes on new meaning. If you are able to use these ideas to think of yourself in your own system or to formulate hypotheses for your work with other systems, something may happen.

III.   THE ORGANISATION OF THE BOOK

We asked contributors to this book to describe the ways in which they have defined their own therapeutic context. Inevitably, this involved them in explaining how they dealt with contradictions and confusions in the system of which they are a part. Their different preoccupations reflect the differences in the complexity of the feedback which each of the teams has experienced in relation to their work as a team in their system. The complexity of the feedback can be a product of the amount of time people spend working systemically or the amount of interaction that occurs between them and the wider systems. For example, some teams are preoccupied with theoretical ideas, some with creating systemically organised agencies, some with defining a system team working within a larger agency. Other contributors address systemic work with specific clinical problems and others address training and evaluation.

Finally, we would like to thank the contributors for the time and effort spent preparing each paper and for allowing us to edit the book in a way that makes a coherent whole for the reader.

REFERENCES

Ashby, W. R. (1954). "Design for a Brain", John Wiley & Sons, New York.

Bateson, G. (1973). "Steps to an Ecology of Mind", Paladin, London.

Bertalanffy, L. von (1950). An Outline of General Systems Theory. *British Journal of the Philosophy of Science* 1, 134–165.

Campbell, D., Reder, P., Draper, R. and Pollard, D. (1983). "Working with the Milan Method: Twenty Questions". Occasional Paper 1, Institute of Family Therapy, London.

Cronen, V., Johnson, K. and Lannamann, J. (1982). Paradoxes, Double Binds and Reflexive Loops: An Alternative Theoretical Perspective. *Family Process* 21, 91–112.

Haley, J. (1963). "Strategies of Psychotherapy", Grune & Stratton, New York.

Hoffman, L. (1981). "Foundations of Family Therapy", Basic Books, New York.

Keeney, B. (1983). "Aesthetics of Change", Guilford Press, New York.

Palazzoli, M. S., Boscolo, L., Cecchin, G. and Prata, G. (1978). "Paradox and Counterparadox", Aronson, London.

Palazzoli, M. S., Boscolo, L., Cecchin, G. and Prata, G. (1980). Hypothesizing—Circularity Neutrality: Three Guidelines for the Conductor of the Session. *Family Process* 19, 3–12.

Penn, P. (1982). Circular Questioning. *Family Process* 21, 267–280.

Tomm, K. (1984). One Perspective on the Milan Systemic Approach: Part I. Overview of Development, Theory and Practice. *Journal of Marital and Family Therapy* 10 (2), 113–125.

Tomm, K. (1984). One Perspective on the Milan Systemic Approach: Part II. Description of Session Format, Interviewing Style and Interventions. *Journal of Marital and Family Therapy* 10 (3), 253–271.

Watzlawick, P., Beavin, J. and Jackson, D. (1967). "Pragmatics of Human Communication", Norton, New York.

Part ONE

Theory

Chapter 2

The Development of Systemic Family Therapy and Its Place in the Field

Freda Martin

I. INTRODUCTION

Currently many family therapists are attempting to integrate their own position with several if not all of the major models; that is, to create some "meta" or supra model. Liddle (1982) points out that the major models need not be seen as competing but should rather be viewed as complementary systems of thought, the nature of whose complementarity or interconnections are as yet unclear to us. However, he also notes the danger of premature attempts at integration and suggests that before an active and fruitful dialogue can take place there needs to be a prior act, namely the clarification of our own positions on the most essential dimensions of therapy. An attempt at such a clarification with regard to the Milan method is the major aim of this paper.

II. THE DEVELOPMENT OF THE MODEL

The Milan model was conceived, if not yet born, in 1967 when Mara Selvini Palazzoli and her three colleagues, Luigi Boscolo, Gianfranco Cecchin and Giuliana Prata, all four of whom are both psychiatrists and psychoanalysts, organized the Institute for Family Studies in Milan. The four worked together in virtual professional isolation until 1975, focussing on the ideas of Bateson and Watzlawick. During the later part of the 1970s they presented their work in North America and Europe. During 1979 they effected an amicable separation. Palazzoli and Prata remain in Milan, continuing their research and developing new tools, e.g. the invariant prescription. The two men Boscolo and Cecchin travel widely in Europe and North America, training and consulting, maintaining a home base in Milan.

A. The Method

Out of this prolonged incubation based on the "marriage" of psychoanalytic and Batesonian ideas, came not only a clear, brilliant application of Bateson's circular epistemology to family systems but also, and of equal importance, a detailed, pre-

APPLICATIONS OF SYSTEMIC FAMILY THERAPY
ISBN 0-8089-1696-3

cisely described technique or instrument for interviewing and intervening with families. The technique is summed up by the now familiar words *hypothesizing, circularity* and *neutrality*, and is well described in the article by the same name (Palazzoli *et al.*, 1980a). Other concepts or techniques rightly associated with the Milan model are the necessity of a team behind the mirror, positive connotation, the delivery of a systemic intervention in the form of a message at the end of the session, and a relatively long interval, usually a month, between sessions.

B. Hypothesising

Work begins with the formation of a systemic hypothesis based on whatever initial information is available. In their own words, the hypothesis is "an unproved supposition tentatively accepted to provide a basis for further investigation from which a verification or refutation can be obtained" (Palazzoli *et al.*, 1980a, p. 5). The hypothesis is arrived at by a discussion among the team in which numerous, inevitably linear ideas are put together into a set of coherent circular connections describing the family system. What is unique about the hypothesis in the Milan model is the emphasis on its being fully circular and systemic (most of the major models begin with some hypothesis, for example, about the function of the symptom in the system). Again in their own words, "A fundamental point to emphasize is that every hypothesis must be systemic, must therefore include all components of the family and must furnish us with a supposition concerning the total relational function" (Palazzoli *et al.*, 1980a, p. 6).

In general the hypothesis serves at least three functions. First, it acts as a guide for the interview as to what information is needed either to confirm or to disconfirm it. In the latter case, a new hypothesis should be generated. Second, interest in the nature of the feedback being received from the family and its relation to the hypothesis helps keep the interviewer in the important neutral, and thus meta, position to the family throughout the interview. The interviewer is kept on the central task of obtaining information from the family and avoids being sucked into the family script. Third, the final hypothesis forms the basis for the intervention or prescription at the end of the session.

C. Circulatory

Again to quote directly from the Milan group themselves, "By circularity, we mean the capacity of the therapist to conduct his investigation on the basis of feedback from the family in response to the information he solicits about relationships and therefore about difference and change" (Palazzoli *et al.*, 1980a, p. 8). This aim is achieved by a number of specific methods; first, and undoubtedly most importantly and most uniquely, that of triadic questioning (that is, asking one member to comment upon the relationship of two others in their presence). The group themselves state that this method is particularly fruitful in overcoming resistance and in obtaining the instant interest of the family members being talked about. Also it puts all family members in the position of having to communicate willy-nilly, verbally or nonverbally, in the areas of interest to the therapist. Within the context of triadic questioning, the interviewer is directed always to inquire in terms of specific differences in behaviour, who does what to whom, when. Following this who does what, etc., individuals may also be invited to classify or make a scale of the intensity or frequency of family members' reactions or behaviours.

D.   Neutrality

Neutrality is the term used to describe the meta position the therapist and team wish to maintain vis-a-vis the family. Importantly, it describes the therapist's behaviour, not his inner feelings. During the session neutrality is obtained by the therapist siding with each member of the family in turn, that is, addressing each and asking each for his particular point of view. It is also obtained by the therapist not reacting to family input except by further questions. According to the Milan team the net result should be that the family is unable to say with whom the therapist has ultimately sided (Palazzoli et al., 1980a). The final hypothesis and intervention can be considered neutral in that they do not ascribe blame to anyone, and if praise, then to all equally as acting in the service of maintaining the system (positive connotation).

E.   The Intervention

The prescription or intervention results from the final hypothesis for that session. It is delivered at the end of the session and may be read out to all or mailed either to the whole family or to each member individually. The latter is more usually the case when crucial family members are absent. It may take the form of a paradoxical injunction positively connoting and prescribing the entire family system, and therefore also the symptom for the present, or of a simple task or complex ritual designed to break up or interrupt key dysfunctional behavioural patterns (Palazzoli et al., 1977). Hoffman (1981) points out that although the hypothesis is circular the intervention itself is necessarily linear.

F. .   The Time Interval Between Sessions

Another hallmark of the Milan team is allowing a relatively long, usually at least a month, time interval to elapse between sessions. Initially this practise was not intended to meet a conceptual but a practical need, that of families that had to travel extremely long distances to reach Milan. However, the team soon noticed that these families were actually doing considerably better than their apparently more favoured counterparts who came to the centre weekly. For this reason they lengthened the time interval for families with no practical attendance problems and found that these also did considerably better. Palazzoli (1980) gives two main reasons for this. Both are related to Ashby's (1954) concept of the too richly cross joined system and Hoffman's (1975) application of this concept to family therapy. The first reason is that these families need a long settling down period before the major observable changes effected by an intervention can appear. The second is that the long time interval is necessary in order to place a barrier between therapist and family, that is, to keep an effective boundary within the therapist/family system, otherwise, it itself may all too readily also become too richly cross joined and thus ultra stable.

G. Context and Consultation

The Milan team have developed a particular interest in considering the context in which the family itself is embedded. They have described and discussed the necessity of considering and even directing interventions at the dysfunctional loop which often exists between the family and the referring person or agent who has become part of the problem or the ultrastable system (Palazzoli et al., 1980b).

1. Case Example

Here is an interesting example of its consultative usefulness applied to a teaching system. I asked my supervisor's group for help with a family therapy seminar whose members appeared stuck in negative critical behavior both to the material and to each other. They were all psychiatric residents assigned to a Child and Family Unit within a large traditional Psychiatric Institute. In the group we noted the trainee's excellent attendance and serious attention to reading assignments. On a tape of the seminar, my over-central position, and the engagement by various group members in a series of symmetrically escalating patterns leading to little productive work, was evident, as was their noticeable lack of humour and playfulness. Accordingly, the consultant group asked me to inform the trainees that they were impressed by their intelligence and serious attitude to family therapy but that they felt that I needed help. They would therefore send an observer to be behind the mirror. This information had immediate effects on the group. The positive connotation, because felt to be true, settled them down, and the knowledge of an observer gave them also a bit of a meta position to themselves. This allowed them to discuss the group much more systemically and therefore usefully. They then moved on to discuss systemic thinking as it related to schizophrenia, thoughtfully talking about the issue of relationships versus attributes.[1] It is interesting to note that although one rule changed and symmetry was maintained through a demonstration of detailed understanding rather than criticism, the basic pattern remained. At the end of the session, the observer sent in the following message: "The observer is impressed with the earnestness and intelligence of the group. The group understands how important it is for Dr. Martin to raise the status of systemic family therapy in psychiatry. Each member of the group is so intent on helping Dr. Martin in her serious mission, that each is sacrificing fun and group intimacy. Until Dr. Martin becomes secure that the theory and practice of systemic family therapy has equal status with nonsystemic psychiatric theory, the group must continue to sacrifice relaxation, joining, and group cohesiveness".[2] The session terminated immediately. The message had the following (for me) dramatic effect: In the next session the group were positively joined with me. They worked cooperatively at a difficult case, and for the first time that year there was

---

[1] This was especially relevant since half the group were currently working also in the adult service.

[2] I am indebted to the supervisor's group in general and Annette Kussins, the observer, in particular for this example.

genuine laughter and enjoyment. This was so evident that a resident who had been away the previous session asked in astonishment what had happened. The group denied the change was related to the message. Some important aspects of this intervention are discussed in the next section.

H.   Necessary Conditions for Change

Within the frame or punctuation of the Milan method the following appear to be the necessary effective elements: an accurate hypothesis informing a well framed intervention aimed at the relevant system from the correct position. That is, the hypothesis and intervention need to address the key elements in the system or systems in which the symptomatic behaviour is embedded, and they must do so from a position that is both meta to them and felt to be one of power. This last point is not always made and is open to misunderstanding. Being a prestigious centre, a la Milan helps at times, but it is no substitute for the therapeutic power which comes from directing interventions correctly at the points of both systemic pain and dysfunction. These may at times be between the family and its context rather than within the family itself. The Milan team also notes that unless the system seeking help feels itself seriously threatened to the point of crisis, therapeutic leverage is extremely difficult (Palazzoli et al., 1978).

The importance of context and the therapist's own position in formulating a hypothesis that is both accurate and correctly aimed is illustrated by the following cautionary tale:

I was asked to consult to a family therapy team at a prestigious hospital in my network. The family consisted of mother (father had died three years previously after a long illness at home, nursed by his wife), David, aged 15, and Barbara, aged 13. David had been continuously in a hospital in two different centres over the past 18 months, with worsening symptoms. He had been initially depressive, but now he was virtually physically immobile and also mute. A variety of interventions—pharmacological, psychodynamic, behavior modification, strategic (total bed rest had been prescribed in hopes of a recoil) and structural family therapy—had failed to alter this situation.

Somewhat overawed by my surroundings I fell right into the trap and joined the team to work "on the family". Most of the many competent professionals involved over the months had been impressed by the family's isolation, mother's incompetence and uncooperative behavior (despite being well educated), and David's identification with his father. This last was backed by a family legend of his having been left in charge by his dying father. Initial information pointed to a recursive loop whereby mother's behavior maintained David's helpless dependence, which in turn maintained mother's central role, allowing her to avoid dealing with her own depression and loss of centrality after her husband's death. The daughter was thus freed to function fairly normally. However, elegant and creative interventions aimed at this loop simply were ineffective and yet produced feedback which seemed to corroborate the hypothesis. Stuck in the system myself, I failed to identify the dysfunctional loop between the family and the professionals (who, if anybody, had in fact replaced the dead father); I simply experienced a sense of powerlessness behind the mirror. Stubbornness plus a strong but not clearly identified sense of different information, received on the one occasion I was actually in the therapy room, caused me to offer to take the family on in my own setting when the inpatient unit, because of time factors, was forced to discharge them as a therapeutic failure with a dismal prognosis.

Once home the boy began slowly to improve. The family turned out not to be isolated, but overwhelmed with helpers: three doctors, two ministers, two home helps, three sets of neighbors, etc. Father's role had been the gatekeeper to the end. We had, of course, had hints of these pieces of information previously, but turned them into more evidence of mother's incompetent, uncooperative behavior. Interventions now aimed clearly at mother's key role in protecting and monitoring change for both her children created steady improvement, not without some drama, as she systematically got rid of all her helpers and finally reduced her contact with me. One year after discharge from hospital David is moving and talking normally and has obtained a year's credit for school work completed at home. Mother is not depressed, but beamingly in charge.

Perhaps the essence of the situation is fascinatingly revealed by David breaking his 18-month-long silence and describing his belief that the first hospital was incomprehensibly out to destroy his mind and his mother powerless to prevent it. In the second hospital he felt safe, but knew that if he talked he would be thought crazy and sent back to the first hospital.

These points concerning accurate aim from the meta position are again illustrated by noting that much of the efficacy of the single intervention by the observer of my resident seminar can be attributed to her directing it at the correct system, the interphase between my family unit and the rest of the psychiatric institute. Also, she was both outside the institute, even outside the medical profession, and yet powerful because she represented "the supervisors".

I.   What Families Are Suitable

The literature from both Milan and the United States so far contains accounts only of work with rigidly dysfunctional families. The discussions of Palazzoli herself seem to relate virtually almost exclusively to them. MacKinnon (1983) considers that the Milan Team's central understanding of dysfunction is of family rules so rigid that the family can neither negotiate a point of natural transformation or metacommunicate about their rules. Hoffman (1981) addresses this point when she wonders if using the Milan method with less dysfunctional families is like bringing in a cannon to bear on a canary. She raises another interesting point, however, when she also wonders if the Milan method might not be useful for many families initially and that once the major dysfunctional loop has, so to speak, been cleared away or cut across, more straightforward work could then be effective.

A somewhat different question is with what other type of system and in what context are the various specific techniques indicated. For example, triadic questioning, insofar as it successfully bypasses the system and its member's conscious ideas and intentions, can be compared to the specific analytic techniques of dream analysis and free association. This analogy if correct would suggest that while it would be appropriate for a family who have entered into a contract for therapy, it might be expected to have as disconcerting an effect as its analytic counterpart on a family whose understanding was that they had come for an assessment. Problems might also occur if it were attempted on a variety of other organizations, work groups, etc. to which the system's consultant may be invited.

So far, regrettably, no unit has published more than an introductory account of systematic work utilising this model with less dysfunctional families and in different settings.

J.   Goals and Responsibility

In terms of what she expects to achieve, Palazzoli herself is both audacious and modest. If the team is not to receive unwarranted criticism, it is important that the modesty be heard as well as the audacity. Certainly, it is the claim of the Milan model that they are able to relieve longstanding, chronic and severe symptoms. However, they are often misunderstood by proponents of the open growth model and by psychoanalysts to be claiming to produce the same sort of radical changes in "character" at which these models aim. They make no such claim. The issue is well addressed by Prata quoting Palazzoli (Barrows, 1982). Using the analogy of a river dammed by branches and leaves she says, "We are not like the other therapists who like to go with the water until the delta. The family says we have an impediment. We have something that is preventing us from living freely, so we do what the family is asking us to do. We take away the most important branch, the most important thing that gave the problem to the family and then they choose what they do, to go to the delta, to go right, to go left. We don't know what is best for this family . . . They choose what to do afterwards. It is not our responsibility to give directions, only to free when asked" (Barrows, 1982, p. 69).

Similarly, practitioners of the Milan method can be misunderstood by proponents of other models regarding the nature of therapeutic responsibility. Their stance here is thought congruent with their understanding of the nature of hierarchy (to be discussed) in therapeutic systems. Their therapeutic contract is not one in which the therapist assumes, even temporarily, any family leadership role and thus responsibility for some aspects of family functioning. Therapeutic responsibility then does not include, for example, caretaking responses to apparent crises, but remains focussed on working towards effective interventions. Indeed they would maintain that in order to remain responsible agents of change they must be able to remain overtly unresponsive to such crises. This point is important because unless the nature of their role and contract is clear they remain open to criticism from their colleagues and even lawsuits by their clients.

III.   COMPARISON WITH OTHER MAJOR MODELS

In a recent article, Sluzki (1983) discusses the three major models which in his view form the backbone of current family therapy, all of which share a systemic or cybernetic root. They are those that focus primarily on process (the Milan model would belong here), primarily on structure and primarily on world views. Sluzki proposes that these three models are not mutually exclusive in that each is a specific translation of the broad systemic paradigm. I understand him to mean that each has made the shift from a matter and energy paradigm to a cybernetic one that emphasises information, relationships and recursive patterns. For this reason the major concepts found in the Milan model, hypothesizing, circularity and neutrality are in one sense not at all unique. Concern with having a hypothesis, understanding the nature of feedback occurring within the system, and maintaining a therapeutic stance vis-a-vis the system are found in all three. However, several key concepts, specifically the nature of hierarchy and the nature of change, appear to differentiate these models.

A.   The Nature of Hierarchy

A clear difference exists between the Process, on the one hand, and the Structural and World View models, on the other, in their understanding of the nature of hierarchy in the system with which they are working. The first group have looked to the study of mathematics and formal logic for their model—for example, Russell's theory of logical types (Watzlawick *et al.*, 1967, 1974)—the second group to biology. The two models invoke two entirely different types of hierarchy. The hierarchy in biology is one of function, an executive hierarchy of systems and subsystems within it. Hoffman (1981) describes this as a series of Chinese boxes. The hierarchy in communication theory is not so much of function but of logic, the hierarchy of a class and its members. The "supra" system does not subsume the subsystems but is meta to them. Focussing on this difference is perhaps not an entirely arbitrary punctuation. Bateson (1972) himself distinguishes different classes of "differences" and specifically mentions three such classes: differences by which a territory is transformed into a map the rules of which can be spelled out by words or by formal logic; differences contained in a hallucination or dream image, the rules for transformation of which he feels are little understood; and differences biologists call "levels", in which each subunit is part of the unit of the next larger scope. These differences are particularly relevant to family therapy, as the family can be seen to have both a biological and a social (communicational) function. That is, it must meet its member's biological needs for food, rest, sex, etc., and also many of their basic social needs. Considering this dual aspect of the family's function may be fundamental to understanding its complex nature. It addresses the crucial issue of an individual human being's primary needs being both biological, on the one hand, and social, that is to have his existence confirmed by another human being, on the other. At rock bottom this of course is the age-old mind/body dualism.

B.   Practical and Conceptual Implications

What flows from this difference in conceptualizing the nature of hierarchy in a system is not insignificant. It determines profound differences in conceptualizing the nature of change, and therefore resistance, methods of joining, obtaining therapeutic leverage, introducing change, and the therapist's conduct of himself both within the session and between sessions. Those models which are based on biological systems and an executive concept of hierarchy expect change to occur within the session and, utilizing the concept of positive feedback, that small positive changes within the session will be amplified between sessions (Minuchin, 1974). This notion contrasts with those models that are based on logical systems. They hypothesize that the change will usually have to come from outside of the system, i.e., second order changes as described by Watzlawick (1974), basically a change in the rules. Change will not usually occur within the session but rather, as the result of the new hypothesis and thus intervention (prescription), between sessions. Similarly there is considerable difference in the way the two streams conceptualize resistance to change and the therapist's role in the therapeutic system. Those working with a biological model emphasize the therapist's need to obtain direct leadership of the family, i.e., a dominant position in the executive hierarchy, and to work within the session to move the resistant family in the direction of accepting this leadership. Whereas those therapists working with "logical" systems adopt a meta position to the system and have a much more judo-like attitude towards resistance. They do not expect on the whole to create change or obtain specific leverage during the session.

C.   Evolutionary Feedback and Change

The physicist Prigogine (1980) uses the term evolutionary feedback to describe a special way that change occurs in living systems (social systems). Basically, he puts forward the idea that living systems operate ordinarily through small fluctuations around some central point of equilibrium. If the system becomes somewhat off balance, pushed away from that central point, then a small instability, ordinarily of no consequence, can suddenly amplify and, as it were, push it over the edge, thus forcing it into an entirely new arrangement. This explains the observation of sudden or discontinuous change observed in families. Prigogine emphasizes the randomness of this event. It is not possible to predict which fluctuation will create it or what form the new arrangement will take.

A fuller discussion of this interesting concept and its influence on current thinkers as Dell and Elkaim is given by Hoffman (1981). She considers this to be an important way in which families change, either naturally or through therapy. As she notes, the Milan model relates directly to this idea; pushing the family off centre or base and allowing it to reorganize is a central theme of both the theory and the method.

D.   The Too Richly Cross Joined System

Ashby's (1954) concept of the highly enmeshed or too richly cross joined system and its relevance for family therapy is beautifully and brilliantly discussed by Hoffman (1981). She points out that this system can be considered ultra stable because it cannot allow one part to change without all the other parts having to change too. Thus attempts at change are immediately disqualified. This model suggests two entirely new ideas as to how change may be brought about by the Milan method. The first is through the interview technique itself, circular questioning. Both Penn (1982) and Hoffman (1981) suggest that insofar as the questioning focuses on differences and defines relationships and it can enable family members to be temporarily meta to their own system and thus gain important information for themselves. Penn also states that "responding to the circular questions compels them to experience the circularity of their family system, the family current, if you will, and abandon more linear stances" (p. 271). Indeed Palazzoli *et al.* (1980a) also speculate on this idea, and the two men in the team continue to experiment with it. A second and utterly fascinating idea as to how change can be induced in the too richly cross joined system is put forward by Hoffman (1981). It is the concept of invariance, or holding one part still. She points out that if in such a system one can introduce an element of invariance or simply prevent one circuit in the over reactive system from reacting, the system will be forced to find an alternative organization. She considers that the Milan method "(1) by always remaining nonreactive, (2) by the tactic of introducing blocks of time between the sessions, (3) by the use of tasks or rituals that introduce elements that remain invariant, (4) by their circular questioning—which is in itself a kind of invariance—and (5) by their systemic prescriptions which hold one part still . . . have achieved a remarkable methodology for cutting the system to pieces and forcing it to find alternatives" (p. 322).

IV.   THE MILAN METHOD'S EFFECT ON FAMILY THERAPY

This concept of the importance of invariance in the too richly cross joined system may go some way to explaining the revolutionary effect the Milan Method has had on the field of family therapy. A possible explanation, however, lies in the purity and detailed clarity of the method as described and practiced by the Milan team. This has previously been related both to their psychoanalytic background and their initial self-imposed isolation from the rest of the family therapy field. In introducing this element of a detailed, precise and thus invariant method, more compelling because thoroughly congruent with theory, into the family therapy arena, itself a field with an element of "chaotic stability", now familiar as evidence of a too richly crossed joined system, the Milan Method rapidly became part of the forefront of a family therapy revolution. So far, this instrument appears to have had most effect within Sluzki's Process Model. However, hopefully it will also serve to challenge proponents of the World View and Structural models to take up their epistemological cudgels as well.

V.   CONCLUDING THOUGHTS ABOUT SOME NEW DIRECTIONS

The Milan method with its emphasis on circularity and context has undoubtedly provided an impetus for second generation thinkers to carry our ideas further. In particular they implicate our clinical understanding of homeostasis and resistance and also the nature of theorizing or model making. Currently, concepts of homeostasis and resistance are definitely being revised (Dell, 1982; Hoffman, 1981; Keeney, 1982). Just as no one behaviour or part of a family, or indeed the family as a whole, can any longer be considered the "cause", so also homeostasis cannot be branded "the problem" within the family. As Hoffman (1981) notes, we will have to give up the idea of homeostasis as a sort of recalcitrant force for stability and against change or answer to Dell's charge of engaging in a sort of fuzzy animism. Homeostasis can more correctly be understood as that parameter of a system which manages or monitors growth, change and stability. Also, the fuller implications of the recursive loop, therapist/family/context as discussed by Keeney (1982) specify that the therapist is never an outside agent but always a part of the therapeutic system, the ecosystem. Hoffman (1981) notes that "this position offers an alternative to the formulations that place the therapist versus patient in a power struggle or game that the patient is always trying to win" (p. 343). Concepts in systemic and strategic thinking such as the benevolent contest and even the therapist as fighting against the game although not its victims (Palazzoli *et al.*, 1978) may need to be somewhat rethought.

I conclude with a mild concern and nudge towards the future for the Milan method. Hopefully the very characteristics of purity and precision previously described as a reason for its impressive impact on the family therapy field will not become a cause of its evolutionary downfall; that is, will not contribute to ossifying over-rigidity. As our understanding of the nature of homeostasis and thus resistance becomes more complex, and the fascination with the paradoxical prescription fades, systemic thinkers as described become more aware of the manifold implications of evolutionary feedback and a truly recursive model. Perhaps one of the most important questions for the future of the Milan method relates to its capacity to adapt; to follow the example of its founders in their ingenious capacity to conceptualise (hypothesise) and to create new modes of intervention, and thus to become as Bateson (1972) describes, an ideal unit of survival, a flexible organism in a flexible environment.

REFERENCES

Ashby, W. R. (1954). "Design for a Brain", John Wiley, New York.

Barrows, S. E. (1982). Interview with Mara Selvini Palazzoli and Guiliana Prata. *American Journal of Family Therapy* 10, 61–69.

Bateson, G. (1972). "Steps to an Ecology of Mind", Ballantine Books, New York.

Dell, P. (1982). Beyond Homeostasis, Towards a Concept of Coherence. *Family Process* 21, 21–42.

Hoffman, L. (1975). Enmeshment and the Too Richly Crossed Joined System. *Family Process* 14, 457–468.

Hoffman, L. (1981). "Foundations of Family Therapy", Basic Books, New York.

Keeney, B. (1982). What is an Epistemology of Family Therapy. *Family Process* 21, 153–168.

Liddle, H. A. (1982). On the Problem of Eclecticism, a Call for Epistemological Clarification and Human Scale Theories. *Family Process* 21, 243–249.

MacKinnon, L. (1983). Contrasting Strategic and Milan Therapies. *Family Process* 22, 425–437.

Minuchin, S. (1974). "Families and Family Therapy", Harvard University Press, Cambridge, Mass.

Palazzoli, M. S., Boscolo, L., Cecchin, G. and Prata, G. (1978). "Paradox and Counterparadox", Jason Aronsen, New York.

Palazzoli, M. S. (1980). Why a Long Interval Between Sessions. *In* Andolfi, M. and Zwerling, I. (eds), "Dimensions of Family Therapy", Guilford Press, New York.

Palazzoli, M. S., Boscolo, L., Cecchin, G. and Prata, G. (1980a). Hypothesizing, Circularity, Neutrality. *Family Process* 19, 3–12.

Palazzoli, M. S., Boscolo, L., Cecchin, G. and Prata, G. (1980b). The Problem of the Referring Person. *Journal of Marital and Family Therapy*, 6, 3–9.

Penn, P. (1982). Circular Questioning. *Family Process* 21, 267–280.

Prigogine, I. (1980). L'ordre a Partir du Chaos. *Prospective et Sante* 13, 29–39.

Sluzki, C. E. (1983). Process Structure and World Views, Toward an Integrated View of Systemic Models in Family Therapy. *Family Process* 22, 469–476.

Watzlawick, P., Beavin, J. and Jackson, D. (1967). "Pragmatics of Human Communication", W. W. Norton, New York.

Watzlawick, P., Weakland, J. and Fisch, R. (1974). "Change", W. W. Norton, New York.

Chapter 3

Hypothesis Making: The Milan Approach Revisited

Valeria Ugazio

I. INTRODUCTION

Palazzoli *et al.* (1980) of the Milan Group first formulated the principle of hypothesis making (hypothesizing), proposing it, along with the concepts of "circularity" and "neutrality", as the basis for a systemic session. The authors defined the main principle as the capacity of the therapist, on the basis of the information gathered, to create an hypothesis or an explanation for the relational functions of the symptoms presented by a family seeking therapy. Prior to verification, this hypothesis is seen as neither true nor false, but rather as a point of departure for the subsequent investigations. The authors describe two additional functions for the principle in question. The first is to guarantee the active stance of the therapist in the session, and the second is to introduce new information into the system, hence injecting a "negentropic effect".

Palazzoli *et al.* (1980) go so far as to suggest that this methodology in itself could possibly be the source of change in the therapeutic interaction. In the conclusion of their article, they ask the question, "Can family therapy produce change solely through the negentropic effect of our present method without the necessity of making a final intervention?" (p. 12). Since 1980, the principle of hypothesizing and its relation to therapeutic change has increasingly been the focus of attention for the Milan Group, constituting perhaps one of the central topics of discussion and debate within our group.

It is within the context of this debate that the present article is offered. It proposes a revision of the principle of hypothesizing in the light of theoretical considerations suggested by an examination of the issues of intentionality and the inference of meaning.

By "the problem of meaning" this author refers to the processes through which individuals perceive, categorize, interpret and attribute meaning and intentionality to their own behaviors and those of others with whom they interact.

Watzlawick *et al.* (1967), in their classic text *"Pragmatics of Human Communications"*, were apparently influenced by "mind-as-black-box" assumptions of behaviourism when they chose to focus exclusively on observable interactive behaviour, rather than the explicative schemas which social actors utilize to interpret those interactions. This was in contrast with the earlier theorizing of members of the Palo

APPLICATIONS OF SYSTEMIC FAMILY THERAPY
ISBN 0-8089-1696-3

Alto Group, and particularly with Bateson's position (Ruesch and Bateson, 1951; Bateson, 1972, 1979). Bateson, in both his early and later works, concerned himself with the issue of meaning and meaning making. He sought to analyze mental processes in an attempt to propose a new view of mind as an integral part of the larger human (and living) system, the ecosystem. (The clearest example of this argument is found in the 1971 article, "The Cybernetics of 'Self': A Theory of Alcoholism".)

In this paper, it is proposed that by utilising the semantic aspects of communication, and paying particular attention to the schemas of explanation[1] which family members utilize to interpret their own and each other's behavioural interactions, it is possible to view the principle of hypothesizing as having a direct function in the induction of therapeutic change, as well as having a different and more expanded role in the conduct of the therapy session.

II. SYSTEMIC HYPOTHESES VERSUS COMMON SENSE SCHEMAS TO EXPLAIN BEHAVIOUR

As utilized by the Milan Group, systemic hypotheses are defined as explicative schemas produced by the therapist in an attempt to answer the question "why" of a symptomatic behaviour. They offer *reasons* for the symptoms and other dysfunctional behaviours surrounding the symptomatology in a manner which involves *three* or more members of the system. Some simple examples include: "Carl has developed these symptoms in order to save his parents marriage", or "The young couple is having sexual difficulties because they have come to realize that their parents have not yet accepted the reality of their marriage".

It is important to note two aspects of these hypotheses. The first is that, as used by the Milan Group, these hypotheses refer to *reasons* and not *causes*, because they imply the active participation or even an intentionality on the part of the actor, whereas the "cause" of a symptom implies that the patient is a passive victim of some uncontrollable force.[2] The second aspect is that, even if termed "systemic", these hypotheses are not such from a pure epistemological point of view—they do not strictly adhere to the epistemological principles of systemic theory.

In terms of the problem of causality, it is possible to find two different points of view among systemic theorists. In one view, represented by theorists like Dell (1982), the search of the "why" of a behaviour is already in itself an epistemological error. For these epistemologists, the best explanation for the system is the system itself. In other words, "there is no *why*; there is only *is*" (Dell, 1982, p. 27).

The second point of view, of which Morin (1977, 1980) is an exponent, retains that it is possible to pose the question of causality within a systemic perspective. It

---

[1] This expression ("schemas of explanation") refers to the interpersonal perceptions, explanations, interpretations, attributions of meaning and intentionality in regards to one's own behaviour and that of others, given by the persons who are involved in the interactions. It includes a gamut of phenomena which is more inclusive than, but analogous to, that which Watzlawick *et al.* (1967) call "the punctuation of a sequence of events".

[2] For a more detailed analysis of the relationship between these two concepts ("cause" and "reason"), the reader is referred to Harré and Secord (1972).

is, however, a complex circular causality, one which is mutually inter-relational and which Morin (1977) calls "endo-eco-causality".

Whether one is an adherent of one or the other of these theoretical points of view, the so-called "systemic" hypotheses cannot be considered phenomenological explanations coherent with a systemic epistemology. For theorists like Dell, proponents of the first view, these hypotheses are not strictly systemic because they seek to give a reason for the behaviour; for those like Morin, of the second point of view, they fail to be systemic because they are *linear*, i.e. they contain the implication that one part of the system determines the functioning of the whole. The Milan hypotheses come to be termed systemic only in as much as their construction is based on a mental process which is guided by *some* of the principles of systemic epistemology. The therapist, through a process of inference, and beginning from an analysis of the effects (not only behavioural effects) of the dysfunctional behaviors on the various subsystems, begins to construct "systemic" hypotheses about the system utilising principles such as the interdependence of all the parts of the system to each other and to the whole, the concept of reciprocal influence, the axiom in which the most complex defines the simplest, and other principles of systems theory.

These hypotheses, even if not strictly consistent with a systemic epistemology, are nonetheless structurally different from the explicative schemas which are developed in common sense explanations. First and foremost, they are different in that they are developed through an inferential process which is based in large part on principles foreign to common sense. Secondly, they differ in that they utilize forms of explanation which at the least involve three people, whereas common sense explanations are never more than dyadic in nature.[3]

Common sense psychology and traditional psychological theories, however, share a similarity in the way they conceptualize interpersonal relationships. Both use explanations which are either individual in nature, or at most are dyadic. The meaning of communications emitted in relationships are, as a rule, sought within the sender, the receiver, or at most, within the relationship between the two, and *not in the more extended communicative system in which this communication occurs.*

It is in this sense that systemic hypotheses are structurally different from those produced by family members. The latter utilize, at maximum, dyadic explicative schemas, whereas a family therapist can rely on a systemic epistemology and, in particular, on the principle that the most complex explains the simplest, to create hypotheses which are at least triadic, and therefore imply a different level of explanation.

III.   HYPOTHESIS-MAKING AND THE CONDUCT OF A SESSION: A PROPOSAL OF REVISION

Systemic hypotheses are helpful in triggering a process of change in the measure in which they permit the therapist to connect himself to the family system without becoming enmeshed. To succeed in this, the therapist must be able to provide reasons for behaviours that contrast with explicative schemas and the intentionality

---

[3] The reader is referred to the line of research on "naive psychology" or common sense psychology of interpersonal relations. In particular to Heider (1958), Jones and Davis (1965), Jones *et al.* (1972), Kelley (1973), Kelley and Michela (1980), Nisbett *et al.* (1973), and Storms (1973).

assumed by members of the family system, and yet that are as *plausible* to them as their own. This very plausibility allows the therapist to tie into the family system while simultaneously, the contrast of the systemic hypothesis to the family's common sense explicative schemas prevents the coherence or fit of the input into the logical system of the family, thus preserving the capacity for change.

In order to achieve this, it is essential that the therapist be familiar with the model the family uses to perceive, explain, interpret, and attribute meaning and intentionality, not only to the symptomatic behaviours of the index patient, but also in the general range of interpersonal relations within the family. It is encumbent on the therapist to first formulate and verify one or more hypotheses in regard to what might be the family's model of explanation and intentionality ("step 1" hypotheses). Only then can the therapist begin to construct systemic hypotheses ("step 2" hypotheses) and choose which one might be most useful to apply in the therapy.[4]

In accordance with this perspective, the proposed *methodology for the conduct of* a therapy session involves two phases. In the *first phase*, the session should focus on the family's *interpersonal belief system*. The therapist must enquire about family member's explanations, interpretations, and attributions of meaning and intentionality for their own and other member's behaviours, for the pathological situation in the family and all the problems related to it, and also for their relationship to therapy.

The verification of the family belief system hypothesis (step 1) will come about through a process of indirect negotiation within the session, where each member will come to terms with the other's responses regarding perceptions and explanations. The most frequently used method for this sort of negotiation is that elaborated by Palazzoli *et al.* (1980), where each family member is asked to comment on other dyadic relationships in the family. The therapist should also utilize any other questions which will permit him to infer the intentionality of various key behaviours within the relationships. Lastly, in this first phase of the therapeutic process, the therapist must analyze the pragmatic effects of the dysfunctional behaviours within the family.

In theory (and often in practise as well), it is possible to identify as many pragmatic effects of the symptom as there are people in the system being considered, and through inference, one can create a like number of "systemic" hypotheses. The criteria for choosing one over the others must be the degree of "incoherence", or dissimilarity, of the hypothesis from the family's own explicative schemas. The therapist's knowledge of the family's explicative schemas will guide him in making the choice of which "systemic" hypothesis to introduce in the course of therapy to bring about change.

As mentioned earlier, in order to be useful in the process of change, the systemic hypothesis must also have a degree of plausibility. Rendering the hypothesis plausible is the object of the *second phase* of the therapeutic process. In the second phase the therapist is no longer concerned with the analysis of explicative schemas or the way the family views their reciprocal relationship. On the contrary and as previously indicated, the task is now to play down those explanations in favor of ones which are outside the family's reality. A central importance in the conduct of the session is now

---

[4] In this paper, the terms "step 2" hypotheses and so-called "systemic" hypotheses are used interchangeably.

given to what can be termed *informational questions* and *informational comments* which introduce aspects of the systemic hypothesis itself. The family's reactions to these questions will allow the therapist to test the plausibility of the hypothesis. The therapist obviously cannot expect the family to immediately perceive and accept the aspects of the hypothesis introduced through these types of questions. Expressions of surprise or perplexity are likely, and are expectable. Yet, if along with the perplexity, the family reacts with verbal or analogic indications of interest, thought and a certain willingness to question their previous views, the therapist can continue in the process of construction of a new vision of reality as suggested by the "systemic" hypothesis chosen. If, on the other hand, the hypothesis as introduced through the information-al questions and comments is received with a firm denial, or if the family responds with information which is contradictory to it, then it is clear that it must be aban-doned and substituted with another. This is done not because the first hypothesis is *untrue*, but rather because the therapist has not been successful in creating those new perceptions and attributions of meaning which could have made it appear plausible.

The two phases of therapy described above can vary in length from family to family. The first phase can occur all within the first session, or can last for two or three interviews.[5] In this methodology, one important effect of the first phase of therapy is that it facilitates the engagement of the family. The phase of the thera-peutic process that brings about change can thus begin within an established rapport between the therapist and the family.

It becomes evident that with the perspective introduced by this methodology, the so-called "final intervention" loses a great deal of its importance. To be sure, there is still a place in the therapy for end-of-session conclusions, but the ideas contained in such interventions will have already been "seeded" during the session itself. For example, if the final comment is a reframing, it can be considered simply as a more structured summary of a series of meanings previously introduced in the interview. In the case of a behavioural prescription, the final intervention can be seen as an attempt to clarify or to bring to light perceptions, meanings, and explanations of problematic events; perceptions which the family's own game had previously obscured but whose seeds have been sown in the course of the session through the use of informational questions and comments.

A. Case Example

The Rossis are a married couple who are in their thirties, both employed in the same bank, and have a four-year-old daughter, Silvia.[6] The identified patient is the wife, Simonetta, who is presently expecting a second child. Her problems are said to have begun following the birth of Silvia. Simonetta first had what she and Fulvio (her husband) describe as a "nervous break-down", and she subsequently developed a phobia of scorpions, snakes, and vipers. The symptoms disappeared for two years only to return with the new pregnancy, this time accompanied by anxiety, insomnia and, above all, a fear of the devil.

---

[5] It is important to emphasize that the more the therapist prolongs this phase of the therapy, the more he runs the risk of co-developing a "complementary coherence" with the family.

[6] This case was treated by the author and a colleague, Dr. Roberto Pasquino, at the Centro Psicosociale di Corsico (Milano).

Enmeshment of this couple with their extended families is suggested by the fact that Orlanda, Simonetta's widowed mother, and Fulvio's father, also a widower, had married each other. Also indicative is the fact that Simonetta and Fulvio describe their only recreational social relationship with other adults as being with Rosalia and Pino, who are Simonetta's sister and brother-in-law.

From an analysis of the initial information on the intake sheet furnished by the clinic's intake nurse, the therapists form a few "step 1" hypotheses about the way the couple perceives their problems. They combine two pieces of information: that the symptoms became manifest with the first maternity and then again with the current pregnancy, and the fact that Simonetta had harsh words in describing her mother during the intake. From this, they hypothesize that Simonetta may have entered into a symmetrical escalation with her sister to win the approval of her mother and tried to use her motherhood to attain this aim. However, she may have remained disillusioned by Orlanda's lack of the desired reaction, and may therefore have perceived herself as in a losing move. In addition, since Simonetta readily accepted the invitation to bring her husband to therapy, stating that he would be "very glad to come", a second hypothesis is suggested. The therapists theorize that the couple, rather than having a rigidly linear and monadic perception of Simonetta's symptoms as being internally determined, may be likely to perceive themselves as both involved in a dysfunctional relationship, and that the symptoms may be closely tied to the problematic state of this relationship.

In the first meeting with the couple, the therapists' questions center on the couple's perceptions of the problem and the interpersonal relationships in which they are involved. The results confirm and amplify the initial hypotheses. The identified patient blames her difficulties on her mother who, she affirms, is highly anxious but induces others to get sick while enjoying good health herself. Fulvio describes the relationship between his wife and Orlanda as "disastrous", implying that behind these conflicts lies a preference on the part of his mother-in-law for her other daughter, Rosalia. Yet, he also blames himself for his wife's difficulties, as she has judged him to be inadequate for her in every respect. He states that Simonetta, more frequently in the past but still in the present, openly manifests her lack of esteem for him, to such an extent that he often asks himself why she ever married him.

Fulvio also admits to having a low estimation of himself and lists his many personal faults. He describes himself as timid, confused, full of complexes, incapable of showing emotions; in short, a "loser".

One of the effects of the symptoms has been to bring the couple's four-year-old daughter closer to her father and to her aunt, Rosalia, both of whom are preferred by the girl over her own mother. Because of Simonetta's nervous breakdown shortly after her birth, Silvia had been left in the care of Rosalia, who acted as her mother for numerous months. By reason of a hysterectomy Rosalia and Pino cannot have children, and during that period, they fell in love with Silvia, seeing her very much like a daughter. Their relationship with her even now is termed as excellent.

The couple Pino-Rosalia is described by Simonetta and Fulvio as functioning well. Pino appears to be held as the model against which Simonetta measures her own husband's inadequacies. It becomes evident in the course of the session that Simonetta is in strong competition with her sister; a competition in which she feels herself the loser. She describes Rosalia as being more mature and more intellectually capable than she. In addition, although Rosalia can also be critical towards her mother, her relationship with Orlanda is much better than Simonetta's, as the identified patient is always in open conflict with her mother and is said to "mistreat" her.

For her own part, Orlanda appears to have a low opinion of her daughter. There had been a sort of rapprochement between the two women at the time of the first pregnancy. Orlanda was delighted at the idea of having a grandchild. It is said that the value of the stock she had in her daughter "went up from 30 to 100" (this is, it must be remembered, a financially minded family). However, because of the nervous breakdown, and Simonetta's inadequacies as a mother, she had soon completely devalued herself again in the eyes of Orlanda.

At the end of the first session, the husband asks the therapists if he is to blame for his wife's difficulties. He notes, with a hint of sarcasm, that although he is not particularly discerning in psychological matters, it occurs to him that it is significant his wife's fear of the devil is expressed only when they are in the conjugal bedroom. Surely, he says, this must have some connection with him.

From this short synthesis of the elements extracted from the first session, a view emerges of how the couple's perceptions oscillate between a linear monadic and a linear dyadic vision of the problem. It is linear monadic when the cause is within Simonetta's long history of problematic behaviours and inability to be a mother; or when the cause is within Fulvio's ineptness as a mate and his capacity to be a success only at accidental impregnations. It is a linear dyadic vision when the problem is seen in the difficulties of the couple's relationship. In addition there is another related perception which emerges from the couple: the belief in the clear superiority of the Pino-Rosalia couple. Caught within these perceptions and attributions of meaning, there is no escape for the unhappy couple!

At the end of the first session, on the basis of these perceptions and the pragmatic effects of the symptoms, the following "systemic" or "step 2" hypothesis is formed: Fulvio and Simonetta, through the symptoms of the latter as well as through their conflicts as a couple, permit Rosalia and Pino to maintain a one-up position over them, which compensates for the suffering caused by their inability to have children. Other possible "step 2" hypotheses which might have focused more directly on the functional effects of the symptoms on the mother or the husband are discarded because they do not contrast sufficiently with the perceptions of the couple, and with the intentionality of the identified patient, who was quite clearly in competition with her sister.

Consistent with the "step 2" hypothesis they have chosen, the therapists plan to focus the second phase of the therapeutic process not on the couple, but on the couple's external relationship. Nevertheless, the therapists conclude the first session by offering the couple the indication for a couples therapy, which inevitably confirms the perception that the couple itself has of its problem. This acceptance in itself contributes to the creation of a context within which future interventions of the therapists will be rendered more plausible for the couple. In fact, any other intervention which might have attempted to introduce a "systemic" hypothesis so early in the therapy (at the end of the first session) would have been much too premature and scarcely plausible to the family.

In the following session, the couple arrives convinced that they are beginning a couples therapy. Within that context, they are unexpectedly met with an interview whose content focuses on "the problem of Rosalia and Pino in not being capable of having children". The therapists introduce new perceptions and new meanings to explain those same old behavioural patterns and relationships; explanations which are connected to the "systemic" hypothesis which they have formulated.

A critical point in this interview occurs when a series of *informative questions* are asked by the therapist:

Therapist (to Simonetta): Mrs Rossi, you have told us that the value of your active shares traded in your mother's stock exchange went up from 30 to 100 after the birth of Silvia, but that they plunged again when you demonstrated to her that you were inadequate as a mother. Let's suppose for the moment that you had not had the nervous breakdown and that you did not feel constrained to continually mistreat your mother. Would your mother (Orlanda) not have become so close to you, as the daughter who could provide her with grandchildren, that she would have distanced Rosalia, leaving her somewhat abandoned?

Simonetta: Well . . . I don't think so . . . I don't know . . . (*With a perplexed expression.*) But it's true that my mother likes children . . . I wouldn't know . . . In fact, during my first pregnancy my mother was really different with me.

Therapist (to Fulvio): Mr. Rossi, your wife, with her symptoms, which sometimes even make her call her sister in the middle of the night to come to help her, is almost as if she is continuously saying to Rosalia, "Do you see what hell it is to have children; what pain and suffering they can bring". As you see it, does your sister-in-law suffer her childless state even in spite of these warnings?

Fulvio: (*Long pause.*) I don't know. She's never spoken to me about it. Maybe with my wife? To tell you the truth, I've always thought that she enjoyed not having children. Not having children, both she and Pino are much freer than we are, they can go out at night . . . but they like children a lot. They are incredibly attached to Silvia. It's real passion!

Therapist (to Simonetta): Mrs. Rossi, does even Silvia intuit that if she doesn't reassure her aunt Rosalia by letting her know she prefers to stay with her than with her own mother, your sister would feel even more diminished as a person compared to you?

Simonetta: I don't know, she seems still too little to understand these sorts of things . . . though, come to think of it, there was a period, some months ago, that she hounded me with questions of why her aunt didn't have children, why she didn't have any cousins. She sometimes still comes back to that.

The aim of these questions is to impart new information to the couple and evaluate how it is received. The responses as outlined above do not contain a denial of the theses proposed. It is true that, at least on the verbal level, the couple does not explicitly confirm the ideas behind the questions. However, at the analogic level, the couple's responses reveal a degree of perplexity and interest toward the new version of reality that the therapist is trying out on them.

The final intervention states that the therapists have understood that Rosalia is very dependent on her sister, that there is a strong affective tie between the two sisters, and that it is clear that the identified patient has become aware of how her sister has suffered because of Simonetta's pregnancy, as it was yet another reminder of her incapacity to bear children. The therapists also understand that with the first pregnancy there was the risk that their mother, Orlanda, who has always wanted grandchildren, would become more attached to Simonetta than to Rosalia. For this reason, when Silvia was born, Simonetta decided to "donate" her little girl to her sister. Now that she has become aware of her new pregnancy, Simonetta has begun to be ill again, thereby reassuring her hapless sister with the message "You see what hell it is to bear children!"

This conclusion appears to have a significant effect on both Simonetta and Fulvio, although they do not provide the therapists with any additional information at this point. It will only be in successive meetings that the couple will furnish further information which will begin to validate the new vision of reality. Simonetta will remember, for example, that the first nervous breakdown in the family was not her own but Rosalia's, which occurred right after the latter's hysterectomy. Rosalia and Pino, who had previously never expressed regrets about their inability to have children, will confess to Simonetta and Fulvio their desire to adopt a child. Further, Rosalia, who had always given the impression of being fully satisfied with her marriage, will confide with her sister the fact that she is having sexual difficulties with her husband. Even the perfect relationship between Pino and Rosalia has its flaws!

IV.   CONCLUSION

In conclusion, it is important to make two observations concerning the question of meaning in systemic therapies. The first point is in regards to the relationship between the interview and the final intervention. In the therapeutic model initially advanced by the Milan Group (Palazzoli et al., 1978) there was a rather rigid separation of tasks proposed for the therapeutic process. The sole function of the interview process preceding the intervention, was to gather information which could allow the therapists to create a final prescription. It was the role of the final intervention to introduce the input into the system which would begin the process of change.

The result of this separation was to noticeably emphasize the final intervention, at times providing a dramatic flavor to the conclusion of the session. As none of its elements had been mentioned in the interview proper, the final intervention would take on the character of a cryptic message, suited to a therapist with a peculiar charismatic power.

The revised methodology proposed in this article implies a radical change; one which was already hinted at in Palazzoli et al. (1980); one where the central part of the therapy shifts from intervention to the interview itself. By assigning to the interview the role of inducing change, not only does one reduce the importance of the final prescription, but the division of tasks within the session becomes less rigid. One important consequence of this revision is to render the Milan Group's therapeutic model more transferable to other therapeutic contexts which are often characterized by less prestigious therapists and less severe pathologies.

The second observation relates to the attention given to the problem of meaning, which is at the base of the revision of the concept of hypothesis making herein proposed. This attention reflects a move away from the theoretical position implicit in Watzlawick et al. (1967), and it uncovers a realm of complex issues which could not have been confronted while the focus of analysis remained exclusively on manifest behaviour. The reproposal of the question of meaning in a systemic therapy can be seen as a return to certain themes of Bateson's original thoughts. It is just this reference to the original Batesonian epistemology which has characterized the work of the Milan Group.

Acknowledgment

The author wishes to thank her colleague Dr. Sergio Pirotta for the translation of this article.

REFERENCES

Bateson, G. (1971). The Cybernetics of "Self": A Theory of Alcoholism. *Psychiatry* 34, 1–18.

Bateson, G. (1972). "Steps to an Ecology of Mind". Chandler, San Francisco.

Bateson, G. (1979). "Mind and Nature. A Necessary Unity". Dutton, New York.

Dell, P. F. (1982). Beyond Homeostasis: Toward a Concept of Coherence. *Family Process* 21, 21–41.

Haley, J. (1963). "Strategies of Psychotherapy". Grune and Stratton, New York.

Harré, R., and Secord, P. F. (1972). "The Explanation of Social Behaviour". Basil Blackwell, Oxford.

Heider, F. (1958). "The Psychology of Interpersonal Relations". Wiley, New York.

Jones, E. E., and Davis, K. E. (1965). *In* Berkowitz, L. (ed), "Advances in Experimental Social Psychology, Vol. II". Academic Press, New York and London, pp. 220–266.

Jones, E. E., Kanouse, D. E., Kelley, H. H., Nisbett, R. E., Valins, S., and Weiner, B. (1972). "Attribution: Perceiving the Causes of Behavior". General Learning Press, New York.

Kelley, H. H. (1973). The Process of Causal Attribution. *American Psychologist* 28, 107–128.

Kelley, H. H., and Michela, J. L. (1980). Attribution Theory and Research. *Annual Review of Psychology* 31, 457–501.

Morin, E. (1977). "La Méthode, la Nature de la Nature". Le Seuil, Paris.

Morin, E. (1980). *La Vie de la Vie*. Le Seuil, Paris.

Nisbett, R. E., Caputo, C., Legant, P., and Maracek, J. (1973). Behavior as Seen by the Actor and as Seen by the Observer. *Journal of Personality and Social Psychology* 27, 154–64.

Palazzoli, M., Boscolo, L., Cecchin, G., and Prata, G. (1978). "Paradox and Counterparadox". Aronson, New York.

Palazzoli, M., Boscolo, L., Cecchin, G., and Prata, G. (1980). Hypothesizing-Circularity-Neutrality: Three Guidelines for the Conductor of the Session. *Family Process* 19, 3–12.

Ruesch, J., and Bateson, G. (1951). "Communication. The Social Matrix of Psychiatry". Norton, New York.

Storms, M. D. (1973). Videotape and the Attribution Process: Reversing Actors and Observers Points of View. *Journal of Personality and Social Psychology* 27, 165–75.

Watzlawick, P., Jackson, D., and Beavin, J. (1967). "Pragmatics of Human Communication". Norton, New York.

Chapter 4

Circular Interviewing: A Multifaceted Clinical Tool

Karl Tomm

Circularity is one of the three fundamental principles identified by the Milan team as "indispensible to interviewing the family correctly" (Palazzoli *et al.*, 1980, p. 4). In making this comment, the team was referring to the context of conducting a *systemic* interview. The other two principles are hypothesizing and neutrality. All three are inextricably interrelated.

In some respects, circularity represents the "behavioral" or "executive" aspects of the other two. For instance, hypothesizing is described as a conceptual process of "mental effort . . . [to] organize the observations" (Palazzoli *et al.*, 1980, p. 5) so that they are "coherent with the systemic epistemology" (p. 7). The hypotheses thus formulated, guide the therapist's *investigative activity* to ask circular questions. On the other hand, neutrality is defined with reference to the therapist's "specific pragmatic effect . . . [in being] allied with everyone and no one at the same time" (p. 11). The perceived effect of the therapist's questioning guides his *responsive activity* to avoid coalitions, privileged relationships and moral judgements. "By circularity we mean the capacity of the therapist to conduct his investigation on the basis of feedback from the family in response to the information he solicits about relationships" (p. 8). Thus circularity may be regarded as a bridge connecting systemic hypothesizing and neutrality by means of the therapist's activity.

The Milan team drew heavily from Bateson (1972) in elaborating the principle of circularity. In his writings about the mind, Bateson emphasized the notion of cybernetic feedback as a core aspect of mental process. Mind is no "thing", it is a *pattern that connects* an aggregate of components in circular (or more complex) chains of determination (Bateson, 1979, p. 92). Thus the contributions of Bateson were seminal. However, the Milan team also made a major original contribution by operationalizing the concept and applying it to the conduct of family therapy. Circularity became manifest as a peculiar pattern of therapist activity now known as "circular interviewing". A few examples of the types of questions used in this method of inquiry were described in the original paper by the Milan team (Palazzoli *et al.*, 1980). However, it is probably through the many workshops conducted by the team (especially by Boscolo and Cecchin) that circular interviewing came to be regarded as the distinctive feature of the interview part of the five-part-session. Recently various authors have begun writing about this method of inquiry (Hoffman 1981, Penn 1982, Viaro and Leonardi 1983, Tomm 1984). The net result is that an important clinical "tool" has been differentiated.

APPLICATIONS OF SYSTEMIC FAMILY THERAPY
ISBN 0-8089-1696-3

There are two major aspects of this style of interviewing: circular questioning and circular questions. The second entails the linguistic form and the clinical focus of the questions while the first entails the interactive process in asking them. Although both these facets of circularity are being enacted simultaneously during the course of an interview, they will be described separately.

I. CIRCULAR QUESTIONING

The Milan style of circular questioning has at times been referred to as "the Socratic method" (Boscolo, personal communication). This is because of the apparent pattern of incessant questions, but no answers, from the therapist. Like Socrates, the therapist "knows that he does not know" and hence keeps asking. He does not even ask to learn "the facts". The systemic therapist knows that he will never "know". Granted, he asks for information to formulate and test hypotheses, but more fundamentally he asks questions in order to become "coupled" with the family in a coevolutionary process of systemic exploration. The questioning, if carefully conducted, allows a unique pattern of generativity to emerge. The therapist's questions trigger family members to "release" new information into their own and each others' awareness which enables them to develop a new understanding of their own systems of interaction. This generative style of therapist–family coupling is an important feature of systemic therapy. It is a *systemic enactment* in the relationship between the therapist and the family. The attitude of wondering, of not knowing and of exploring, spreads from the therapist to the family. When the family subsequently "uncouples", it may find itself endowed with a greater capacity to "discover" or "invent" solutions on its own.

One purpose of the systemic therapist is to try to understand the circular processes in the system with which he is concerned. Thus, the general question, "What is happening in this family?", guides the formulation of his specific questions. By considering this general question, however, the therapist implicitly sets himself apart from what he has distinguished and assumes the position of an observer. He acts "as if" he is outside of and separate from the entity that is being explored. He regards the family as an "object" of investigation. He then proceeds to identify circular connections in the objectified system in an empirical manner. This aspect of circularity is sometimes referred to as the cybernetics of "observed systems". It is also known as "first order" or "simple cybernetics" (Keeney, 1982).

However, literal objectivity of external entities is an illusion. No object or phenomenon is ever totally separate from whoever is considering it. The observer's own cognitive processes specify or "generate" whatever entities are being considered (Maturana and Varela, 1980). In other words, the systemic entities investigated in therapy are "brought forth" or "constructed" by the therapist through his interaction with the family. When the therapist consciously takes into account his own actions (cognitive and behavioral) in generating and modifying the systems he is exploring, while he is exploring them, *he is observing himself as an investigating observer*. This process is referred to as the cybernetics of "observing systems" (von Foerster, 1981). In family therapy, this means that the therapist investigates the cybernetic feedback loops between himself and the family at the same time as he

investigates the cybernetic feedback loops within the family itself. This level of complexity is referred to as the "cybernetics of cybernetics" or "second order cybernetics".

Circular questioning entails this kind of second order cybernetic process. Needless
to say, it is extremely difficult to carry out well. Our day-to-day conceptual habits
tend to be predominantly objective and empirical, so we are faced with a constant,
covert "drag" towards a first order cybernetic stance. To maintain a systemic perspective of the overall therapeutic process (not just the family process), an expanded
awareness and additional cognitive processing is required. The therapist's team can
monitor the therapist–family interaction more easily than the therapist. As observers
behind the screen they can use their empirical habits to observe him observing and
acting on what he appears to be construing. However, a team is not always available.
Even when it is, there is the problem of getting the team's feedback to the therapist
to be utilized in the ongoing process. Phone-ins and call-outs are relatively slow,
time consuming and very disruptive when used frequently. Furthermore, the team
does not have as direct access to the therapist's thinking as the therapist himself
potentially could have. Thus it behooves the therapist to try to develop the capacity
to operate at this level of cognitive complexity *while conducting therapy* if he wishes
to maximize his effectiveness as a systemic clinician.

A systemic therapist has two general intentions which lead him to ask different
kinds of questions. These are to try (1) to understand the system and (2) to facilitate
therapeutic change. The corresponding types of questions are (a) *descriptive circular
questions* and (b) *reflexive circular questions*. When the therapist asks a question to
elicit information to generate or modify his understanding of the systemic connectedness of the problem, it is a descriptive question. When he asks a question in an
attempt to deliberately trigger a change in the system being investigated, it is a
reflexive question. I have chosen to call the latter "reflexive" because their effectiveness (when realized) appears to be mediated by the reflexivity in a hypothetical
hierarchy of meanings that organises human interaction (Cronen *et al.*, in press).
Thus, depending on his intent at any moment, his questions may be descriptive,
reflexive or both. The intentions are not mutually exclusive and many questions are,
of course, mixed. However, the distinction is useful, as it helps clarify the vicissi-
tudes of neutrality.

At the moment of asking a purely descriptive question, the therapist adopts a
position of maximal neutrality. In the wording and tone of the question he tries to
convey an attitude of genuine acceptance towards each person and a naive curiosity
towards whatever is described. At these moments he even "accepts" the notion of
violence and abuse and remains neutral with respect to change. Contrary to some
impressions of the systemic attitude, this does not mean that he is condoning violence. What the therapist is accepting is the *description* of the violence, not its enactment. If an angry or violent exchange begins to emerge during a session, he cannot
but respond and would do so with a view towards curtailing it, starting possibly with
a reflexive question (e.g. in the context of a marital argument, the therapist inter-
rupts by addressing a child, "When your parents argue at home is it less intense or
more than it is here?"). When using descriptive circular questions the therapist
accepts the family's descriptions of the situation, violent or otherwise, and in a
neutral manner proceeds to explore their systemic connectedness with other relevant
perceptions, meanings and actions. He does this with the attitude of a fascinated

scientist who is trying to understand "why things have to be the way they are" in this particular system at this particular time. Family members will, of course, be extremely sensitive to the therapist's personal position on every issue. The greater the extent to which they perceive him as taking sides or passing judgement, the greater their responses are distorted by his stance.

However, a skilled therapist can often identify opportunities during the course of an interview where he could offer "immediate" therapeutic input. In other words, he recognises a "good moment" or an "opening" for a particular intervention. To intervene in order to effect a therapeutic change is not being neutral. Rather than become directive (in the sense of telling the family how they should think or behave) and abandon his neutral stance altogether, he may take advantage of these openings and employ a reflexive question. For instance, in the context of a father's tirade against his son the therapist might ask the mother, "How long has your husband had such negative thoughts about the boy?", "When did he first begin to think this way?". These questions are intended to interrupt the scapegoating process and realign the focus. This is not the same as telling the father directly to stop blaming the son. To intervene with a question respects the autonomy of the system in a manner that an explicit opinion, directive or prescription does not. For instance, the hypothetical question, "If instead of your father always leaving, your mother left, what would happen?", is generally provocative but still neutral with respect to a particular outcome. On the other hand, the question, "If you became even more severe in your discipline, do you think it would be more or less likely that he would run away again?", could contain an embedded confrontation and reflect a *tactical* move on the part of the therapist towards a specific outcome. Tactical questions can be risky because the residual neutrality (which usually lies in the tone) is quite limited.

When the therapist introduces an intervention in the form of a question, he has no need to remain committed to it and to justify it if the family strongly rejects its implications. Although he is not fully neutral at the moment he asks a reflexive question, immediately thereafter he can revert back to become more neutral without loss of status. The therapist can then utilize the family's response to re-evaluate the issue (and the process) and approach the system from another angle. Thus time and movement are important elements in enacting the principle of neutrality. The therapist and family engage in a mutual "dance" that is led by his intentions.

The notion of reflexive questioning is a very recent development and needs further analysis and explanation. It is introduced here as an important facet of the second order cybernetic process of circular interviewing. It should be noted, however, that the designation of a question as reflexive does not depend on its semantic content or linguistic structure but on the circumstances in which it is employed. Indeed, the same question may be either descriptive or reflexive (or both) depending on the therapist's intent in asking it. For instance, a triadic question may be descriptive when asked to obtain a third person's neutral report of the interaction between another two. Yet when asked primarily to evoke a particular portrayal to enhance the observer perspective in the other two interactants, it should be considered reflexive. Despite the importance of the immediate process, it is possible to distinguish categories of questions that are likely to be utilised reflexively. Some of these are observer perspective questions, future oriented questions, unexpected context change questions, embedded suggestion questions, normative comparison questions, conservative needs questions and process interruption questions (Tomm, in preparation).

Other categories could, and undoubtedly will, be distinguished as these kinds of questions are more widely utilised and discussed.

The intent of a question does not, of course, guarantee its effect. However, it is impossible to ask a question without having some effect. Most questions, both descriptive and reflexive, probably have a very minor or *conservative effect*. The family responds to the "perturbation" with a minor change in order to remain the same. Yet, every question is a probe and a potential trigger for a *generative effect*, i.e. a more substantive change. What actually happens depends on the family's own organisation and structure. A generative effect can never be predicted with certainty and in some instances will not even be known to have occurred. Some questions "stick" in family members' minds and have an impact for far longer than we suspect. Questions asked with a descriptive intent may, of course, also have a generative effect. The main argument here is only that an admixture of reflexive questions is more likely to have a generative effect than descriptive questions alone, and that one is more likely to achieve the desired effect if one's intentions are clear.

What is particularly appealing about the notion of reflexive questioning is that it provides a focus for the therapist to deliberately introduce generativity into the evolving therapist–family system as the interview unfolds. In addition, change that occurs "spontaneously" through the stimulus of a reflexive question intuitively seems more aesthetic and elegant than change provoked by an explicit end-of-session intervention. Nevertheless, reflexive questioning does not come without risk. When the balance is too much in the direction of reflexive questions (e.g. when the therapist gets "trapped" in trying to have a particular effect), the interview may develop an atmosphere of interrogation or examination. The family begins to close ranks and the session becomes "combative" or "frozen". This may also happen when a series of descriptive questions are not sufficiently neutral. When this kind of "closure" occurs, the therapist has lost his systemic stance and needs to regain his neutrality. This difficulty is less liable to develop if the therapist has a solid grounding in the systemic basis of all his questions (both descriptive and reflexive).

II. CIRCULAR QUESTIONS

A. A Theoretical Basis

Why are the questions asked in this style of interviewing, referred to as "circular"? When thinking systemically the therapist is continually oriented towards identifying circular connections. It is assumed that any phenomenon or "entity" distinguished for investigation may be regarded as (1) a system made up of components, (2) a component of a larger system or (3) both. It is also assumed that the organisation of any system is necessarily circular. This "necessity" is a function of the cognitive act of distinguishing an entity as a system (Maturana, 1978). By definition a system is always a *composite* unity. It is composed of component parts or elements. What makes the collection of elements a "whole", a "totality" or a "system" is the *coherent* organisation of the components. This coherence depends on reciprocal or recursive (i.e. circular) relationships between the components. To understand a system is to understand the coherence in its circular organisation. Thus it is the circular connectedness of ideas, feelings, actions, persons, relationships, groups, events, traditions, etc. that is of interest to the systemic therapist. The questions are circular in that they attempt to elucidate these organisational connections.

The therapist's conception of the nature of mental systems is an important issue and it may be useful to contrast two ways of thinking about systems. Whereas von Bertalanffy (1968) is oriented towards identifying systems of mass and energy in his General Systems Theory, Bateson (1972, 1979) is oriented towards identifying *systems of difference and pattern*. Their units of analysis differ. Von Bertalanffy focusses on intact physical organisms (e.g. a person bounded by his skin) while Bateson focusses on cybernetic circuits of information (e.g. a person-in-his-situation). The mechanism of interaction among components in these systems is different. Bateson's example of a man kicking a dog illustrates this point. The dog's movement due to the physical force of the man's kick is a very different phenomenon than the dog's movement due to the "information" in the act of the man kicking. It is the latter type of interaction (in the man–dog system) that is relevant to understanding behavioral or "mental" systems. The *difference* between what the dog "expects" and what happens that it "doesn't expect" activates the dog to run or growl, not the energy of the kick. Von Bertalanffy's orientation is perhaps more useful for explaining physical and chemical phenomena, but Bateson's is more useful for explaining mental and behavioural phenomena. Bateson acknowledges that mental process requires a base for collateral energy (e.g. the dog uses its own metabolism to run), but what he emphasizes is that mental systems are activated by "differences" which do not consist of energy and have no mass. In a sense, mind is a disembodied system of "bits" of information "flowing" in circuits of differences. Thus mental systems consist of patterns that "exist" quite apart from the physicochemical entities on which they happen to depend (for energy).

It should not be surprising then that circular questions are often focussed on exploring *differences*. For instance, the question, "Who is more jealous, Sandra or Bill?", explores a difference between persons. "Who is father closest to?" explores a difference between relationships. "Are they closer now or were they closer three years ago?" explores a temporal difference. There is a common underlying core in these questions. They seek to uncover differences that may be "causal" in triggering specific interactions among components of mental systems. However, "a difference" is not only a potential link in a causal chain of circular interaction (i.e. in a cybernetic circuit), it is circular in itself. Fundamentally, a difference always defines a *relationship* between whatever categories, phenomena or entities are being distinguished. This relationship, in turn, is always reciprocal and hence is always circular. For instance, if he is brighter than she, then she is duller than he. If she is heavier now than she was last month, she was lighter last month than she is now. While the circularity of the differences in these distinctions may seem trivial and are readily ignored, the consequences of overlooking them may be significant. For instance, badness exists by virtue of the distinction drawn between good and bad. To think of one family member as "bad" is to identify a difference between that individual and the other family members who are implicitly being defined as "good". All too often we forget that *we*, the observers, are drawing these distinctions and then drift towards regarding the badness as an inherent characteristic of the person or act. When we come to believe that these characteristics are, indeed, properties of the designated person or act, we are drawn into lineal thinking and tend to become moralistic and judgemental. On the other hand, questions that deliberately explore the underlying basis for the distinctions being drawn by the family strengthen the therapist's systemic stance.

Multiple differences may be combined or "clustered" to form complex "knots" of connectedness. Thus the next step is to identify "the difference that makes a difference". "If father and Bill were not so close, would Sandra be less jealous?" The latter "difference" is at a *different logical level* than the former. This brings us into the domain of *context* which is extremely important because it enables us to grapple with the notion of "meaning". In day-to-day interaction, the meaning of any particular word, utterance, action, object, event, etc., is usually derived from its context. The challenge, in trying to unravel a particular meaning, is to identify the pertinent context. In order to specify Sandra's behaviour as jealousy, a competitive dyadic relationship is required with respect to mutual relationships with a third party. A multiplicity of differences are entailed. The pivotal "difference" in distinguishing context is a *complementary* one (e.g. part/whole, figure/ground, member/class), while the core differences described in the previous paragraph were either/or ones (e.g. good/bad, bright/dull, close/distant, jealous/not jealous). Drawing a complementary distinction, and thus differentiating a context, makes it possible to connect several either/or distinctions. It is in this way, for instance, that the differences in the father's closeness to the various children may be connected to the jealousies among the children, or that the change in his relationships may be connected to a change in their feelings. Furthermore, in any system of meanings there may be multiple levels of context (Pearce and Cronen, 1980). With each new level the number of connections that are possible increases enormously. What is important to bear in mind, however, is that the relationship between any two levels is always circular, it is reflexive. The membership determines the class just as the class determines the membership. Alliances may promote jealous behaviour, but jealous behaviour also promotes alliances. If we forget that *we* drew the original distinction and begin to believe that the context unilaterally determines the meaning of what is contexted (in a lineal hierarchical fashion), our systemic understanding again risks being eroded. By taking cognizance of this reflexivity in contextual relationships, we enhance our systemic flexibility substantially.

B. Types of Circular Questions

Table I provides an overview of some basic types of circular questions. While the core of a difference question lies in an either/or distinction, the content focus may be either on category differences or on temporal differences. By category difference, I am referring to the dialectical contrast of one percept or concept in relation to another percept or concept. (The term "spatial" was used instead of "categorical" in an earlier paper, Tomm, 1984.)

Category difference questions may enquire about (1) differences between persons, (2) differences between interpersonal relationships, (3) differences between perceptions, ideas or beliefs (quite apart from the persons who "hold" them) and (4) differences between actions and events (regardless of who enacts them). The question, "Who gets more upset when she runs away, mother or father?", is a person-oriented question delineating a difference between persons (the parents) on the dimension of reactivity. An enquiry about category differences in relationships is very useful in

Table I. *Types of circular questions*

Difference Questions	Contextual Questions
I. Category Differences	I. Categorical Contexts
A. between persons	A. meaning/action connections
B. between relationships	(i) meaning to action
C. between perceptions/ideas/beliefs	(ii) action to meaning
D. between actions/events	B. meaning/meaning connections
E. category differences in past	(i) content/speech act
F. category differences in future	(ii) speech act/episode
	(iii) episode/relationships
II. Temporal Differences	(iv) relationship/life script or family myth
A. between past and past	(v) family myth/cultural pattern
B. between past and present	(vi) mixed
C. between past and future	
D. between present and future	II. Temporal Contexts
E. between future and future	A. behavioral effects in a dyadic field
	B. behavioral effects in a triadic field
III. Ordering a Series of Differences	C. behavioral effects in larger fields
A. distinctions made by one person	
B. distinctions made by several	

clarifying alignments and coalitions. For instance, when one asks "Is your wife closer to Sandra or to Bill?", the difference being examined is the mother–daughter dyad in relation to the mother–son dyad. These relationships may be pursued further by asking for behavioral evidence, e.g. "Who does she spend more time with?", "What does she do with him?", "And with her?" When focussing on differences among ideas or beliefs, one might enquire, "When people in this family cry, is it because they are whining to get their own way or because they are weeping out of emotional pain?" "What would be seen as most comforting, to leave the person alone, just be there, try to talk or give a hug?" clarifies categories of action. In asking these questions one is triggering the "release" of perceptions of connectedness between various persons, relationships, beliefs and actions.

A series of difference questions may be asked to generate a classification (or an ordering) of family members on some salient dimension. Responses may be sought from one person or from several. For instance, if a therapist were trying to understand the organisation of a family's beliefs about the origins of "hyperactive" behavior in a child, he could address the following series of questions to a paticular family member: "Who in the family (or even outside the family) believes most strongly that there is something wrong with Bill's brain?", "Who believes this the second most strongly?", "Who believes it the third most?", etc., or "Who believes the least that there is something wrong in his nervous system?", "Who believes it second least?", etc. The answers to these questions describe the different "positions" of various members in the "family game" of beliefs about hyperactivity, as seen by that particular respondent. When other family members are asked the same series of questions (or about their agreement/disagreement) and the therapist monitors the nonverbal "commentaries" throughout, he may observe the *enactment* of various positions in the family game. The overall responses may provide a coherent picture of how the belief system operates in the family. The therapist may be able to identify "points" of apparent "stuckness" (i.e. tenacity in retaining a particular view) in the system and then proceed to examine the effects of these positions: "When your father thinks it's his nerves, what does he do?", "What does your mother do?" One could also ask some reflexive questions to imply possible change. "If your father suddenly believed that the hyperactivity had to do with confused discipline, what would he do?", "Then what would Bill do?" Information about family member positions on crucial issues is often useful for specifying the finer details of an end-of-session intervention such as in a ritual.

A categorical enquiry may be taken into the past or into the future. For instance, "Who was closest to Bill before he got caught for shoplifting?" explores a difference in relationships in the past. "After Bill grows up and leaves home, who do you think he will keep in touch with the most?" explores a speculative difference in the future. When these questions begin to trigger comparisons between time frames, they merge with the next category.

Temporal difference questions are somewhat more complex. They focus on a difference between category differences at two points in time, in other words, on a *change*. The comparison is between relationships of certain categories in one time frame and comparable arrangements in another. Time markers are, of course, required in asking these questions. Using the marker of a major medical crisis, the question, "Was there more fighting before or after mother's stroke last year?", explores a difference in patterns of arguing between one period in the past and another period in the past. If a major change had occurred (e.g. with less arguing after the illness), one might hypothesize about the effect that the fear of mother's loss might be having on the system. A difference between the past and the present is being explored when the family is asked "Was father closer to Sandra when she was a little girl or is he closer now?" Questions of this type may clarify shifts in family alignments and loyalties. If a change is reported, the therapist might ask about the events which may have initiated it, bearing in mind that memories of the past lie in the present.

Questions about the future are interesting because they are often used reflexively. The most common future-oriented question is to examine a difference between the present and the future: "If this arguing were to continue, what do you expect will become of your relationship in five years from now?" Families with problems often find it very difficult to speculate on the future. They seem so deeply immersed in thinking only about the present or the past. Thus deliberately asking a series of questions about the future may shake them free of their narrow range of vision. Questions about dreaded consequences often enable family members to become more aware of how catastrophic expectations influence present patterns of behavior. Future questions may also be used to introduce possibilities for change. For instance, "If next week, mother suddenly believed that father really felt sorry for Bill, would she protect him more or defend him less?" This is a hypothetical reflexive question connecting two points in the future.

The core aspect of a context question is a complementary distinction, rather than an either/or one. Once again, the focus may be categorical or temporal, but the complexity is greater. By *categorical context questions*, I am referring to the exploration of category differences across levels of logical type. Thus there are at least three major points in the comparison, one of which is at a different logical level. A common type is to ask about the relationship between meaning and action. For instance, the question, "When you think he's trying to control you, what does he do?", isolates one category of meaning (control) and asks for a connection to a specific behaviour among two or more categories of action. Or one may start with a behaviour and seek distinctions among meanings: "When he walks out of the room, what do you take it to mean?" It is the specific connection between levels of meaning and action that is crucial.

The idealized hierarchy of six levels of meaning in the "Coordinated Management of Meaning" model of communication (Pearce and Cronen, 1980) may be used as a framework for analysing categorical context questions. These levels include (1) the *content* of an utterance, (2) the *speech act* (the utterance as a whole), (3) an *episode* of interaction, (4) the ongoing *relationship* between persons, (5) *life script/family myth* (view of self or family in relation to others in general) and (6) the larger *cultural pattern*. The question, "When he says he loves you at times like that, is it a loving statement or do you take it as some kind of protest or apology?", connects levels of content and speech act. "If he said it when you were being intimate, could you accept it?" connects content, speech act and episode. "Do you have arguments more or less often when you feel distant from each other?" relates episodes to relationship. "How does your marriage compare to that of your parents?" connects relationship to life script or family myth. "Is your family more, or less open about disagreements than most families?" connects family myth and cultural pattern. There can be as many levels and as many connections between them as the therapist and family choose to specify. For instance, the embedded suggestion question, "If you were to bring her a rose after an argument, like some men do in order to heal a relationship, would you be violating your family tradition?", includes aspects of action, episode, cultural pattern, relationship and family myth. Because multiple levels of meaning impinge simultaneously in any situation, categorical context questions may be very diverse and complex.

Temporal context questions explore meaning by examining the location of a particular action or event within a sequence of actions or events. The therapist attends to behavioral effects—the specific linkages in the sequence—e.g. "When he misbehaves, what do your parents usually do?" If we notice repeated conjunction of certain events in sequences, we tend to inpute a "causal" connection between them. However, this leaves us at risk for lineal thinking. To remain circular and systemic, the therapist must identify *recursiveness* in the sequence and thus ask an extended series of temporal context questions. For instance, "When you are at dinner and your sister is not eating, what do your parents do?", (My mother tries to persuade her); "Does she eat then?", (No, she refuses); "Then what does your mother do?", (She yells at her); "Then does she eat?", (No, she just gets more stubborn); "When she yells at her, what does your father do?", (He walks out); "Then what does your mother do? Does she go after him?" (No, she just stops yelling); "And what does your sister do?" (She starts eating); "Does your father come back?", (Sometimes); "When he comes back, what does your mother say?", (She just glares at him); "Does your sister notice?", (Sometimes); "When she notices, what does she do?" (She stops eating); etc. There are at least two circular patterns evident in the responses to these questions: a simple dyadic one between the mother and sister, and a more complex triadic one between the mother, daughter and father. They are obviously interrelated. In attempting to understand the meaning of any particular behavior or pattern it is always useful to keep enlarging the context of observation. For instance, the triadic pattern noted above may be a component of a larger circular pattern including a sibling, the grandparents or a professional deeply involved with the family.

C. Circularity in Ordinary Interviewing

How are these concepts applicable in day-to-day practise? Family therapists do not usually think in terms of difference questions, contextual questions, category questions, etc. They think in terms of problems, family members and their relationships. A brief outline of "ordinary" questions, noting possible links to these circular concepts, may be helpful. The following categories are used for ordinary questions: (1) Problem Oriented Questions—(a) definition, (b) explanation—and (2) Family Assessment Questions—(a) person oriented, (b) interaction centered and (c) interpersonal perception.

Problem definition questions seek to determine the precise nature of any problem. The basic questions are "Who . . . , what . . . , when . . . , where . . . , how . . . and how much . . . ?" Implicitly, each of these questions utilizes the notion of differences: "Who?" (Paul, not Fred or Mary); "What?" (Marijuana, not alcohol, speed or heroin); "When?" (Yesterday after the argument, not last month); etc. These questions may be described as "centripetal", i.e. center seeking. They seek to funnel down to the "heart" of the issue. The process is one of drawing finer and finer distinctions on those already drawn to get a clearer and clearer picture. When the therapist does not realize that he is utilizing the "tool" of circular differences to paint his picture he is more liable to come to believe that the problems he has identified are objective and "real". The more he focusses on collecting "the facts", the more he gathers "data" but loses "information" and along with it the systemic perspective.

Explanation questions operate at a higher level of complexity. The task is to "map" descriptions onto fundamentals (i.e. basic assumptions about human relations and mental process). The essential questions are "Why . . . , how come . . . and in what way . . . ?" These are contextual questions. The major tool for exploration is the complementary distinction. The focus is on the meaning or function of the problem in the context of the system. The therapist may ask family members directly about their own understanding of the phenomena. Most of the time, however, he asks for an explanation indirectly by exploring his own systemic hypotheses as he assesses the family. In both instances, the questions may be described as "centrifugal", i.e. center fleeing. The approach is to enlarge the field of observation and identify the connectedness of the central issue, the problem, to its larger context.

Person oriented assessment questions may be *self*-oriented (i.e. focus on the respondent) or may be *other*-oriented (i.e. focus on a person other than the respondent). Self-oriented questions elicit self-disclosure. Other-oriented questions, in the presence of the person being described, elicit gossiping and mind reading. When the latter are used to enhance the "observer perspective" of the other they are reflexive. Regardless of focus, person oriented questions that are systemic, search for circular connections between thoughts, feelings and actions. For instance, "When you think of failing, how do you feel?" and "When you feel depressed, what do you do?" are self-oriented context questions. "Do you think he prefers to make his own mistakes or have someone point them out for him?" is an other-oriented category difference question.

Interaction centered questions are far more interesting from a systemic point of view. This is because the ultimate locus for the generation of new meanings and for the initiation of change is social rather than intrapersonal. Interaction centered questions may be divided into those that *include* the respondent and those that *exclude* him. For instance, "When you punish her for coming home late, what does she do?" is a behavioural effect question that includes the behavior of the person being addressed. Interaction questions that exclude the self are referred to as triadic: a third person is asked about the relationship between another two. "When your sister comes home late, what does your mother do?", "If your mother tries to get your father involved, what does he usually do?" Triadic questions may be more complicated as when a fourth person is asked about the relationship between another three, e.g. "When your mother and your brother are having an argument, what does your father do?", "Does he go more on your brother's side or your mother's side?" While these happen to be temporal behavioural effect questions, many triadic questions explore category differences, e.g. "Is your husband more distant from your son or your daughter?", "Who between the two of them, wants the most to have a closer relationship?"

Interpersonal perception questions constitute a bridge between person centered and interaction centered questions. They are mind reading questions that are asked in the presence of the other and allow for clarification of misinterpretation and misunderstanding. These questions become increasingly recursive as interpersonal perception is explored in greater depth. For instance, an adolescent may be asked, "What do you think your mother thinks when you get home late?" (first recursion), "What does she think that you are thinking when you stay out?" (second recursion) and "What does she think you want or expect from her when you don't tell her where you were?" (third recursion). The mother may, of course, be invited to validate or "correct" the adolescent's perceptions at any point. On the other hand, the mother may be asked a similar series of questions about her perception of the perceptions of the adolescent. The salient issue here is the difference between the views of the mother and the adolescent and whether clarifying this difference could make a difference in their interaction. The therapist's use of other-oriented questions rather than self-oriented questions is not trivial. His choice depends on his momentary intent. My bias is that as a therapist becomes more aware of his specific intentions in the process of circular interviewing, he will be able to make better choices.

III. CONCLUDING COMMENT

Why has the delineation of circularity captured the imagination of so many clinicians? Two possible reasons come to mind. First, it has reoriented the therapist's "purpose" in meeting with families. What is becoming clearer is that the purpose of a systemic interview is not so much the lineal "removal" of a problem, but the "discovery" of its systemic connectedness and hence its temporal "necessity". Recognition of this necessity makes the need for alternative action self-evident. The systemic nature of the exploration triggers the "effective freedom" of the therapist and/or the family to evolve new patterns of behaviour that do not "require" the problem. As a result, the problem may dissolve "spontaneously". Many clinicians experience this as a more respectful approach to families than directive, problem solving procedures. Second, circularity emphasizes the inclusion of the therapist himself as an active participant in the elaboration of the mental process ostensibly within the family system. In other words, what the therapist "discovers" in his investigation is, in large part, his own creation. He "chooses" what issues he will attend to and what patterns and relationships will be explored. The "realities" that emerge are "relative" to the process of therapeutic interaction, not "objective". Contrary to some impressions of the systemic approach, this relativity *increases* rather than decreases the therapist's personal responsibility. The net effect is that the therapist takes more responsibility for his own conduct and allows family members more autonomy for theirs.

REFERENCES

Bateson, G. (1972). "Steps to an Ecology of Mind", Chandler, San Francisco.

Bateson, G. (1979). "Mind and Nature: A Necessary Unity", Dutton, New York.

Cronen, V., Pearce, B., and Tomm, K. Radical Change in the Social Construction of Persons: A Model and Case Study. *In* Davis, K. E., and Gergen, K. J. (eds), "The Social Construction of the Person", Springer-Verlag, New York, in press.

Hoffman, L. (1981). "Foundations of Family Therapy", Basic Books, New York.

Keeney, B. (1982). What is an Epistemology of Family Therapy? *Family Process* 21, 153–168.

Maturana, H. (1978). Biology of Language: The Epistemology of Reality. *In* Millar, G. (ed), "Psychology and Biology of Language and Thought", Academic Press, London, pp. 27–63.

Maturana, H., and Varela, F. (1980). "Autopoiesis and Cognition: The Realization of the Living", Reidel Press, Boston.

Palazzoli, M., Boscolo, L., Cecchin, G., and Prata, G. (1980). Hypothesizing–Circularity–Neutrality: Three Guidelines for the Conductor of the Session. *Family Process* 19, 3–12.

Pearce, B., and Cronen, V. (1980). "Communication, Action and Meaning", Praeger, New York.

Penn, P. (1982). Circular Questioning. *Family Process* 21, 267–280.

Tomm, K. (1984). One Perspective On The Milan Systemic Approach: Part II Description of Session Format, Interviewing Style and Interventions. *Journal of Marital and Family Therapy* 10, 253–271.

Tomm, K. "Reflexive Questioning: A Generative Line of Enquiry", in preparation.

Viaro, M., and Leonardi, P. (1983). Getting and Giving Information: Analysis of a Family Interview Strategy. *Family Process* 22, 27–42.

von Bertalanffy, L. (1968). "General Systems Theory: Foundation, Development, Application", George Braziller, New York.

von Foerster, H. (1981). "Observing Systems", Intersystems, Seaside, California.

Chapter 5

New Realities for Old: Some Uses of Teams and One-Way Screens in Therapy

Brian Cade and Max Cornwell

"Now, if you'll only attend, Kitty, and not talk so much,
I'll tell you all my ideas about Looking-glass House."

Alice

The field of family therapy, perhaps more than any other, has developed the use of teams and one-way screens to enable the process of therapy to be observed and acted upon in vivo. This chapter traces some recent developments in their use and in the way their use has been conceptualized.

One-way screens were originally used primarily for the observation of patients. Subsequently they were used to allow a trainee's therapy sessions to be observed by a supervisor, and also for the supervisor to demonstrate interviewing and clinical skills to groups of trainees. The mirror was used essentially *as a device to look through*, a relatively neutral piece of technology designed to intrude *as little as possible* in the immediate process of therapy.

I. FROM OBSERVER GROUP TO TEAM

Gradually, the screen began to intrude more directly, initially with the therapist taking "time out" to consult with the supervisor or observing team, then through the transmission of observer messages (Breunlin and Cade, 1981). The one-way screen began to become a more explicit and integral component of the resources available to a family; the observers were increasingly offering expertise, support and alternative viewpoints, and had begun to *intrude deliberately* into the process of the interview.

Because they did not need to make an immediate response, the observers were often in a better position than most therapists to view the overall process of an interview, or a series of interviews, and to discuss possible interventions, and to estimate the likelihood of their success. The more experienced the observers, the less likely they were to become preoccupied with detailed content or the immediate burden of affect in the interview. This enabled them to have a genuinely different experience of the interview from the therapist and to recognise other possibilities; they were less likely to be drawn into the family system. Their work became increasingly task-

APPLICATIONS OF SYSTEMIC FAMILY THERAPY
ISBN 0-8089-1696-3

focused and geared towards helping both therapist and family to articulate relevant agendas and to abandon unproductive ones. It became much more readily apparent how family and therapist negotiated together a "reality" and how the therapist was part of a system of social interactions.

It became common practice for the therapist to come out at any point he or she wished, to seek guidance or to discuss an idea. Where an interconnecting telephone system was available, ideas could be phoned through, thus allowing an almost instant observer response to the ebb and flow of an interview. Suggestions could be made to reach the therapist when they were likely to be most needed or most relevant, and thus could be used with maximum impact. The one-way screen was becoming, in many ways, a two-way screen. Gradually there emerged the notion of a *therapeutic team*.

The relationships between therapist, observers and family began to be used for a special form of triangulation. Typically, either therapist or observers would side with those aspects of the family that appeared to be supporting change, while the other actively acknowledged the resistances and sought to circumvent them, usually through the device of paradoxical and split messages (Breunlin and Cade, 1981; Cornwell and Pearson, 1981). The sources of messages would be attributed either to the therapist or to the other team members. If more than two options were available, new permutations might be created by reporting a split within the team, or even by elaborating a contrived team conflict (Cade, 1980). What was critical here was the degree of coordination among all team members in devising and orchestrating the messages (Cornwell and Pearson, 1981).

It was increasingly recognised that there was scope for varying the style, the emotional tone and the focus of interventions. Alliances could be made and broken; boundaries could be drawn and redrawn in a variety of ways; attitudes such as approval or disapproval, optimism or pessimism, could be focused on any subsystem in the family or in its social network, or divided between factions, or reported as existing within the team itself.

Papp (1980) describes the use of paradoxical techniques of redefining, prescribing and restraining, with the observer team acting as a Greek chorus that could selectively comment on the interaction between family members and between family and therapist. The chorus might support the family in resisting the therapist, take "public opinion polls" among the observers that reflected the nature and degree of family resistance, sow elements of surprise and confusion to shift the family's preoccupations, or form therapeutic triangles, always adopting the stance of remaining outside the interactions between therapist and family.

More recently the implications have begun to appear broader than in the earlier explorations with triangulation and paradox. The context of therapy, through the medium of the screen, had become more complex again. Therapeutic change was increasingly conceived as a phenomenon that grew out of the evolving nature of the relationship between therapist, team, and family. Variation in any one element could bring about change in the other two. The observing team was in a position to create a "reality" by transmitting information about the team, news of events in the team, of shifting alliances, opinions, of conflicts, etc. Such glimpses, combined with what each family member might project from his or her beliefs, could begin to disrupt habitual patterns of thought and behaviour.

The one-way screen became particularly important for working with those families whose skills at incorporating therapists into their systems of both thought and action, and thus rendering them impotent, made it so important for the therapist to retain maximum flexibility and power. Such families often would easily accommodate themselves to a clearly defined, open and consistent relationship between themselves, the therapist and the observers. First the therapist and then the team would find themselves drawn into the family's "game without end". There was now a way of changing the "reality" of the therapy context, thus making it much more difficult for such families to define the rules of such games.

Palazzoli (1981) notes that "People are most influenced when they expect a certain message and receive instead a message at a totally different level. . . . Anything predictable is therapeutically inefficient" (p. 45). Though it is, of course, possible to be unpredictable without using a screen or a team of observers (for example, the idiosyncratic, almost indefinable work of Carl Whitaker; see Neill and Kniskern, 1982), their availability allows for a much wider range of possibilities. The second part of this chapter concentrates on the use of unexpected contexts or therapeutic positions, on interventions in which "changes" in the team's position or in its dynamics are reported or demonstrated to the family. Usually, no connections are made between these "events" and anything the family is doing, nor is any responsibility placed upon it.

The various interventions were initially evolved as manoeuvres to resolve therapeutic impasses or deadlocks and seen primarily as ways of freeing the therapist to allow him then to proceed with the therapy. However, we increasingly found that these interventions were in themselves frequently powerful promoters of change. It began to be seen how they picked up and reflected (or mirrored) important themes in the family system or in the family-plus-therapist system, yet introduced new connections and new meanings and also introduced an important element of unpredictability into a "reality" that had been created between family and therapist and had become stuck. Where therapy becomes stuck, it can be seen that the therapist has become predictable in the way he or she is approaching the problem. As Cade (1985) suggests:

> Where therapy becomes stuck, it can be seen that the therapist has . . . become predictable in the way he is approaching the problem. Through a reciprocal process of verbal and particularly non-verbal negotiations, a reality will have become constructed that reflects the attitudes, beliefs and responses of all participants but that serves to inhibit change. . . . The implication here seems to be that, to change or increase the adaptability of a system, it is necessary to be able to change oneself and the position one takes, to become, as it were, unpredictable. (p. 40)

The important components of these interventions are usually (1) that there should be sufficient isomorphism with beliefs and attitudes of the family such that the intervention arises, as it were, out of "familiar territory" and out of the implications of the family's own frameworks; (2) a different meaning is placed on significant facets of family behaviours and rules through reframing, relabelling, repunctuation and positive connotation; and (3) an unexpected position is adopted by the team on a nodal issue or issues for the family or for the therapy, either directly or through analogy. It is the latter component this chapter goes on to explore; the first two components have been comprehensively described elsewhere (Cade and Seligman, 1981, De Shazer, 1982, Palazzoli et al., 1978, Watzlawick et al., 1974).

II. SOME BASIC INTERVENTIONS

A common intervention involves criticism by the team of some aspect of the therapist's behaviour or apparent beliefs and attitudes as a way of dealing with the development of a symmetrical struggle between family and therapist, or as a way of "correcting" therapist "error". Based on observations of the way the family is dealing with the therapist, and the subsequent pattern of "more of the same" way of intervening that has developed, the team takes a position vis-à-vis the therapist that reflects the position being adopted by the family, or by a particular family member.

The effect of this intervention is often to shift an interview into a more productive direction. Because its position is both "understood" and powerfully expressed by the team, it may be that the family (or a family member) no longer needs to continue adopting and expressing that position; in other situations, perhaps, by making the family's position overt and even prescribing the family's covert agendas, the team exposes and blocks the symmetrical "game" that is developing in the therapy. Again, it may be that some families will defend their therapist against the "attacks" of an unknown team. Whatever the dynamic, this intervention often elicits more cooperation and can resolve an apparent impasse.

For example, a therapist was struggling with the parents of what he had obviously begun to see as a heavily scapegoated young teenage girl. The more the parents perceived him as defending her, the more critical they became as they attempted to convince him how disturbed and disruptive she was. Both sides were becoming increasingly frustrated, though each remained polite and respectful. The therapist was called out of the interview and advised to return and report that his team was angry with him and had accused him of not understanding just how concerned these parents were about their daughter; that he had really not listened carefully enough to what the parents had been saying.

The whole tone of the interview changed instantly as the parents relaxed and soon began themselves to volunteer that their daughter also had many good qualities. Until the observing team's intervention, the parents had rejected the therapist's attempts to suggest that the girl could "not be *all* bad". By the team allying temporarily with the parents against him, the therapist was helped immediately to regain his therapeutic position. Though that position may have appeared to be undermined, the effect of such interventions is usually to reinstate the therapist into a therapeutic role.

Another common intervention is for the therapist to report on the observing team's opinions, advice, etc., but to remain completely neutral in respect of what is being transmitted. This can be done by claiming to be unsure of what was meant, unable to understand, being puzzled or even totally confused. In this way the therapist can avoid any subsequent symmetrical manoeuvres or other attempts to reject or disqualify what has been said. He or she can claim to be unable to explain, substantiate or even to debate the issues, can remain sympathetic to the family's feelings, and can promise to seek further clarification before the next session. Whilst expressing incomprehension or confusion, the therapist might suggest that the observers are very experienced in the family's particular problem and that he or she would normally respect their judgement. However, when making such a statement, it is important to remain neutral about the current message and not seem to be erring on the side of perhaps agreeing with the team.

For example, a couple were aggressively resisting a therapist's attempts to propose an alternative and systemic perspective on their marital struggles and on the husband's manic-depressive "illness". The therapist was becoming embroiled in a symmetrical struggle and finding it difficult to confront the couple. She was backing down from the neutral position required by the intervention and finding herself feeling anxious and reluctant to deliver the somewhat provocative message. Called out of the interview by the team, she returned a little later looking confused and saying that she felt she ought to warn the couple that she did not fully understand what her team was saying to her but that she would try to convey it as best she could. The couple listened attentively and the therapist found herself able then to deliver the intervention. When the couple, a little stunned by a paradoxical message, then began to question the intervention, the therapist regretted that she was unable to clarify or elaborate because she too was puzzled. Unable thus to disqualify the message, the couple left, still looking rather stunned by what had happened. At the following session, the couple reported significant changes (which, of course, were in no way attributed to the therapy).

Though in our experience it is rare for a family to enquire in a subsequent session whether the therapist had been able to clarify what the team had said, if it were to do so, it is, in our opinion, usually best for the therapist to find a way of retaining a neutral stance. To apparently identify, explicitly or implicitly, either with the team's position or with the family's can lead, with the former, to a more easy disqualification of the team's message or subsequent messages, or, with the latter, of the therapist's position. Remaining neutral helps the therapist retain manoeuvrability as the family struggles to deal with the implications of the team's input rather than with the therapist.

If the message is subsequently felt by the team not to have been a useful one, it is possible, if the family remains preoccupied by it, for a change of position to be made in a number of ways. For example, new evidence can be found, either from what the family is presenting ("From what you have now told us, the team realizes . . ."), from research findings "discovered" since the last session ("This research has helped the team to see . . ."), or from a "more experienced" member of the agency from whom advice has been sought by the team. Alternatively, the therapist can claim that he had not understood properly and had therefore not transmitted the team's position accurately, for which he had subsequently been heavily criticised ("What the team had meant me to convey was . . .").

Another useful manoeuvre involves a declaration of impotence by the therapist or by the whole team (Cade, 1982c). For example, a couple were in their tenth session of marital therapy. Over the past few years they had consulted a number of therapists but claimed that, so far, nothing had been of any help. The couple appeared cooperative, yet nothing seemed to change. The team had tried a range of different interventions, even trying approaches that were inconsistent with its normal ways of working. It gradually became apparent that the couple seemed to be enjoying the contest into which they could be seen as having drawn the team. Looking forward eagerly to what the team would try next, the couple would report at the beginning of each session, almost triumphantly but never accusingly, that things were no better following the previous session. The team seemed to be working harder and harder seeking a way to have some impact on the couple.

Finally, the team declared its impotence. "We have tried everything we know and have explored every avenue possible. You have both been extremely patient and cooperative with us, but we have been totally unable to help you. Your case has beaten us. We feel we do not have the right to offer you another appointment". The couple appeared stunned and looked to each other for support. They asked, "But surely there must be some advice you can give us!" The therapist declared that the team had no answers left to offer.

It is important in such an intervention that the "failure" is in no way blamed on the family, even if only by implication. To infer or hint that this may be so can serve to perpetuate the symmetrical escalation that has led to the impasse. No hint of challenge, disapproval, irony or sarcasm must be betrayed, and the therapist's analogic communication should be consistent with a declaration of impotence. The timing of such interventions is important. As Palazzoli *et al.* (1978) observe, "The correct moment occurs, in our experience, when the angry obstinacy of the therapists is a sure sign of escalation, while the family, on its part, reinforces its disqualifications" (p. 149). The authors go on to declare that, in the sessions following their use of this intervention, "more 'secrets' were revealed than in all the previous sessions combined" (p. 150). If, after such a manoeuvre, the family returns demonstrating changes or offering more information, the team must be wary of being drawn back into a resumption of the game.

It is also possible for the therapist to declare impotence in the face of demands or advice from the observing team. For example, "My colleagues have advised me that it would be dangerous for the family to attempt any changes at this time; they have been very critical of my total insensitivity to your understandable caution, and feel you are absolutely right to question or even reject my suggestions. I now do not know what to do or which way to turn. I feel I have been no help to you at all, in spite of your openness and preparedness to cooperate . . ." Such an intervention can have the effect of focusing the family's resistance onto the team, leaving the family to become more cooperative with the therapist, who is thus placed again in a position of therapeutic manoeuvrability.

It is arguably the unexpected aspects of such team interventions that help create the *difference that makes a difference.* The more a family experiences a particular approach or technique, the less it is likely to receive new information through that particular channel. Unexpected interventions, such as have been described, by the way they are presented, will stand out against the background of the session or of a series of sessions. Therefore, if a certain class of team interventions is too frequently repeated, or if an observer too frequently enters the room in order to make an impact, then such interventions will rapidly become part of an expected range of behaviours, thus introducing no new information.

III. NEW REALITIES FOR OLD

A more elaborate class of interventions involves the construction of a "reality" behind the screen which can be reported on by the therapist or, on occasions, demonstrated. Such "realities", as suggested earlier, will, either directly or through analogy, highlight nodal themes or issues from the family and/or the process of therapy.

For example, a man defined as "schizophrenic" was despairing that anybody who was not himself a schizophrenic could ever understand the "real meaning of life" as revealed to him during his psychotic episodes. His agitated and verbose attempts to convey these revelations to his therapist were making it totally impossible for her to seek further information about his wider family context. She was finding herself unable to interrupt the flow of his increasingly disordered thinking. After a consultation behind the screen, during which the man continued excitedly talking to his wife about the revelations, the therapist returned with a look of concern to report that one of her colleagues had just begun to understand what the man had been saying and had become quite disturbed. This colleague had warned that it was vitally important that she ask some questions of him about his family. The man became instantly calm and cooperative, answering all the therapists questions, and showed no further sign of "disturbed" behaviour.

In response to the man's impassioned and urgent pleas for understanding, with his declaration that only another schizophrenic could really understand, the team had constructed a "reality" that included a *disturbed person* who had begun to *understand*. That person also had a sense of urgency that there was something that needed to be understood better.

The "reality" behind the screen was sufficiently isomorphic with, or mirrored, the man's "reality" and pointed urgently to the importance of understanding his family context. (It is here assumed that the "psychotic revelations" can be taken as a metaphor for the complexities of his family context.)

In the following example, the team actively demonstrated an important feature of its constructed "reality". A family was referred following a gradual escalation of marital violence. The wife had been severely agoraphobic for many years. The team had become increasingly aware of a very close relationship between the husband and a fourteen-year-old daughter which had become, in many ways, like a marriage. The team's current hypothesis was that the wife's symptoms had perhaps become the only hold she had over her husband in the face of her daughter's apparently more successful attractions. For years, now, he had acted towards her more as a "doctor" or an exasperated parent, a role he had learned in childhood in respect of a chronically sick mother.

Over the space of a year the team had worked harder and harder seeking the "correct" systemic intervention. The family had always been extremely "cooperative" and had never complained that the therapy was having no effect, though always demonstrating that nothing had changed. The team was concerned that any straightforward verbal feedback to the family of its current perceptions would be met and disqualified in the same polite, bland and affectless manner that had greeted earlier attempts at provocative interventions.

Following a prolonged consultation the team members began to shout at each other behind the screen. The family, which had until then been chatting and laughing together whilst waiting, became immediately transfixed, the father, particularly, showing signs of considerable anxiety.

Finally, the therapist entered the room looking agitated and confused and reported a violent disagreement in the team over which was the most important marriage in the family (something the family had earlier been asked to consider and had done so without any signs of affect). Half the team considered it was the father and daughter, the other half that it was the father and mother. The team had been unable to resolve the issue and, unfortunately, tempers had been lost. The therapist apologised several times that, in spite of the considerable cooperation of all family members, and their preparedness to be quite open with him, he had totally failed to help them. He declared that he needed considerable time to think about things further, and, also, the team needed time to resolve what had been an almost violent argument. The next session was set with a longer gap than was usual between sessions. The family left in a state of shock.

At the next session it was revealed, after a tense beginning, that the wife had found a part-time job at a local school and an evening job serving behind the bar of a large hotel. She had also been making frequent trips on her own to various shopping centres.

As has been observed elsewhere (Cade, 1982b),

> The struggle behind the screen had replicated analogically, a nodal struggle in the family. Though the family was prepared to talk quite openly about the "two marriages", the connection between this and both the agoraphobia and the inexplicable explosions of marital violence would be hidden and denied. By presenting the "affect" first, through a contrived conflict for which the family had no explanation, it was shaken out of its normal controlled and affectless state and its normal patterns of association disrupted. The struggle was then announced as being the team's to resolve, with no suggestion that there was any connection between the argument and any aspect of the family. . . . The family would be unaware that an intervention had been made, and would thus be unable to control any effects it might potentially have. (p. 139)

We have found that interventions such as those described above tend only to be effective where therapy, or an aspect of therapy, has reached an impasse, and that their potency seems to arise out of the experience of deadlock. Where we have attempted early in a therapy to use them as shortcuts, they appear to be largely ineffective. Where a team becomes stuck with a family, we have noticed, as have others, that it will often take on, or mirror, aspects of the family, both affective and behavioural. Perhaps it is out of these experiences, and even out of proprioceptive information derived from briefly adopting aspects of a family member's posture, etc., that we can have the necessary information, albeit unconsciously, to devise such interventions appropriate to the particular family.[1]

IV.   THE DEVELOPMENT OF A TEAM
PERSPECTIVE

Bateson (1979) refers to the "method of double or multiple comparison" (p. 87), invoking as a metaphor the case of binocular vision. By comparing what is seen by each eye, we disclose another dimension, depth. As Keeney (1983) observes, "As two eyes can derive depth, two descriptions can derive pattern and relationship" (p. 38).

Though for a team to be functional certain basic assumptions must be shared by all team members about frameworks for understanding and for intervening, each

---

[1] Proprioceptive impulses are those that send information to the brain from muscles, tendons, bones and joints, giving information about movement and position.

member will also bring a multitude of different ways of experiencing and interpreting family events and their meanings. From this potential richness can emerge a wide variety of overlapping and contrasting perceptions or viewpoints which can provide a depth of understanding not always easily available to any one person. Keeney (1983) observes, "Any effort to study a particular slice of process, form, or recursion will inevitably lead to limited understanding . . . the boundaries of any unit of observation are always drawn by an observer" (p. 47).

One team member may punctuate the events in a family in one way, a second in a different way. Out of the two descriptions can come a more systemic analysis. Keeney uses, as an example, a married couple in which the one can be seen as nagging because the other withdraws, or, alternatively, one can be seen as withdrawing because the other is always nagging. A comparison of these two punctuations can lead to a perception of a relationship *pattern* in which neither description is the true one, though both seem to fit.

It is relatively easy for a single therapist to become "persuaded" by a particular punctuation (though this can also happen to a team) such that he or she unwittingly joins the family's "game" (either by agreeing with, or by disagreeing with, the perceptions and explanations of the family or of a faction of the family).

For example, a man in his mid-fifties had persuaded a therapist that his considerably younger and obsessional wife had become more irrational and disturbed since the previous session. As the husband and the therapist discussed these developments, the wife, who had behaved throughout previous sessions in an adolescent way, sat looking angry and resentful. The team, however, had perceived her as having begun to make considerable moves towards emancipation from her "fatherly" husband, and that it was these moves that the man was desperately attempting to define as disturbed. During a team consultation it took a considerable time to convince the therapist of this alternative perspective, her counterarguments often echoing the indignant position being taken by the husband.

Therapist: So, will we be cautioning her against growing up?

1st Team Member: Excuse me, she already has begun to grow up.

Therapist: Well, you must admit some of her behaviour has been rather strange.

2nd Team Member: Only if you accept the husband's description. For each example of crazy behaviour he brought up, she had a perfectly reasonable and normal explanation.

Therapist: But he found her in the kitchen carving the meat on the floor and in the nude! You can't tell me that's normal behaviour!

2nd Team Member: The way *he* described it certainly made it sound weird, but her explanation was quite reasonable; the side was full of pans and so she put the plate with the meat down on the floor.

3rd Team Member: Besides, the way she has been obsessively cleaning everything, her kitchen floor is probably cleaner than most of *our* plates.

Therapist: But its hardly been a flaming hot June!

3rd Team Member: Why shouldn't she walk around in the nude in her own home? Brigette Bardot used to and nobody thought she was crazy.

2nd Team Member: I've never thought of you as such a prude before.

Therapist: Well . . . O.K. . . . . I'll accept that its possible to see it in that way; so, what shall we do . . . ?

To have adopted either of these viewpoints could have led the team to join in a family "game" around the question of whether the woman was disturbed or not and to take sides in it. Having access to both enabled the team then to, as it were, step back into a *meta* position and to devise an intervention in which both perspectives were included and positively connoted.

In many circumstances, a therapist can be influenced by strong feelings aroused by a family, or a family member, to take a position that leaves him embroiled in the family's "game" and incorporated into its systems of thought and action. This can happen, particularly, where the therapist's level of anxiety is raised by what is happening, where he becomes angry or frustrated by the family's responses, or becomes overprotective and caring of the family or one of its members.

It is important that the observers do not also become embroiled in this way. It is of little use for a "weighed down" therapist to come back behind the one-way screen to find an equally "weighed down" team. A number of devices can be used to distance the team from the burden of affect, though, as Cornwell and Pearson (1981) caution, "A balance needs to be found and maintained that pre-empts undue involvement in affect levels at the expense of task performance (role blurring), and that does not foster dysfunctional insensitivity and over-reliance on cognition (a special form of disengagement or dissociation)" (p. 209).

Such devices include discussion, during which the sound can sometimes be turned down, irrelevant discussions or even humour. Elsewhere, Cade (1982a) has commented, "Many of our more constructive and effective interventions have begun as jokes or as 'silly' suggestions. It is as if the use of humour with its collisions of seemingly unrelated frameworks opens unconscious pathways in the brain allowing access to different perspectives, different associations, to lateral rather than linear patterns of thought" (p. 39).

Palazzoli *et al.* (1980) elaborate a clear set of guidelines for the conductor of a family session such that a working hypothesis can be built up and the various possibilities tested. Whilst such guidelines can be important, it is also vital to be able to trust intuitions that arise in members of the team. It is important to have access to both the analytical and the intuitive, be they invested separately in different members or together in each. It can be out of the tension between these two modes that a team can maximise its functioning, though sometimes differences in ways of thinking and working can lead to disagreements which need to be resolved.

V. AN AFTERTHOUGHT

There is an increasingly fashionable position in the field that seeks to promote the aesthetic above the pragmatic and to elevate the systemic to the level of truth. Discussions that seek to differentiate between systemic and strategic approaches often serve only to obscure the strategic brilliance of the Milan associates and to ignore the systemic underpinnings of most strategic therapists.

Imagine a hypothetical situation where all therapy was conducted with one-way screens and using a systemic perspective. Would it then follow that some intrepid adventurers in the future would deliberately interview *without* a screen, in order to challenge and extend our ways of seeing, and to infuse therapy with a new element of structured unpredictability to enhance change in families?

Acknowledgment

This chapter is an expansion of Cade, B. W., and Cornwell, M. (1983). Evolution of the One-Way Screen. *Australian Journal of Family Therapy* 4, 73–80.

REFERENCES

Bateson, G. (1979). "Mind and Nature", Wildwood Hall, London.

Breunlin, D. C., and Cade, B. W. (1981). Intervening in Family Systems using Observer Messages. *Journal of Marital and Family Therapy* 7, 453–460.

Cade, B. W. (1980). Resolving Therapeutic Deadlocks using a Contrived Team Conflict. *International Journal of Family Therapy* 2, 253–262.

Cade, B. W. (1982a). Humour and Creativity. *Journal of Family Therapy* 4, 35–42.

Cade, B. W. (1982b). Some Uses of Metaphor. *Australian Journal of Family Therapy* 3, 135–140.

Cade, B. W. (1982c). The Potency of Impotence. *Australian Journal of Family Therapy* 4, 23–26.

Cade, B. W. (1985). Unpredictability and Change: A. Holographic Metaphor. *In* Weeks, G. (ed), "Promoting Change Through Paradoxical Therapy", Dow Jones–Irwin, Homewood, Illinois, 28–59.

Cade, B. W., and Cornwell, M. (1983). Evolution of the One-Way Screen. *Australian Journal of Family Therapy* 4, 73–80.

Cade, B. W., and Seligman, P. (1981). Nothing is Good or Bad but Thinking Makes It So. *Association for Child Psychology and Psychiatry Newsletter* 6, 4–7.

Cornwell, M., and Pearson, R. (1981). Cotherapy Teams and One-Way Screen in Family Therapy Practice and Training. *Family Process* 20, 199–209.

De Shazer, S. (1982). "Patterns of Brief Family Therapy", Guilford Press, New York.

Keeney, B. (1983). "Aesthetics of Change", Guilford Press, New York.

Neill, J. R., and Kniskern, D. P. (1982). "From Psyche to System: The Evolving Therapy of Carl Whitaker", Guilford Press, New York.

Palazzoli, M. S. (1980). Why a Long Interval Between Sessions? *In* Andolfi, M., and Zwerling, I. (eds), "Dimensions of Family Therapy", Guilford Press, New York, pp. 161–169.

Palazzoli, M. S. (1981). Comments on P. Dell, "Some irreverent thoughts on paradox". *Family Process* 20, 37–51.

Palazzoli, M. S., Boscolo, L., Cecchin, G., and Prata, G. (1978). "Paradox and Counter-Paradox", Jason Aronson, New York.

Palazzoli, M. S., Boscolo, L., Cecchin, G., and Prata, G. (1980). Hypothesizing–Circularity–Neutrality: Three Guidelines for the Conduct of the Session. *Family Process* 19, 3–12.

Papp, P. (1980). The Greek Chorus and other techniques of paradoxical therapy. *Family Process* 19, 45–57.

Watzlawick, P., Weakland, J., and Fisch, R. (1974). "Change: Principles of Problem Formation and Problem Resolution", W. W. Norton, New York.

Chapter 6

Therapy, Supervision, Consultation: Different Levels of a System

John Burnham and Queenie Harris

I. INTRODUCTION

One of the most important contributions that the late anthropologist Gregory Bateson made to the development of family theory and therapy is the notion that meaning is derived from context.

> I offer you the notion of context, of pattern through time. . . . Without context, words and actions have no meaning at all. This is true not only of human communication in words but also of all communication whatsoever, of all mental process, of all mind. . . . It is the context that fixes the meaning (Bateson, 1979).

Family therapy is noted for the attention it pays to context, and has developed by investigating the meaning of problems manifested by individuals in the contexts in which they occur, usually the family. The variety of contexts that are seen to be relevant in considering a particular problem has gradually expanded beyond the family to include schools, neighbourhood networks, work places, and helping agencies. Now the issue has become not one of which group of people are being observed, but what is in the mind of the observer. As Bateson (1971) says, "The polarisation of opinion will not be simply between practitioners of individual therapy and practitioners of family therapy but between those who think in terms of systems and those who think in terms of lineal sequences of cause and effect" (p. 242). Thus there has been a co-evolutionary process between a new way of doing therapy and a new way of thinking about therapy.

The focus of this chapter is a team approach to issues of therapy, supervision and consultation based on the Milan model. It offers a theoretical schema which distinguishes between these three activities as different levels of system with the consequent implications for practice. Our perceptions have been developed mainly through contact with Drs. Boscolo and Cecchin over a period of five years and our own experience during this time.

Current views differ concerning the meaning of the terms live supervision and consultation. For instance, Speed *et al.* (1982) and Kingston & Smith (1983) seem to share the view that the differentiation between the two terms should be made on the basis of the relative expertise of the therapists on either side of the screen. For example, if the therapist with the family is less experienced than the therapist behind the screen then the relationship is denoted as *supervision*. If the therapist with the

APPLICATIONS OF SYSTEMIC FAMILY THERAPY
ISBN 0-8089-1696-3

family is a peer of the therapists behind the screen then the relationship is called *consultation.* We prefer to refer to this difference as *trainee supervision* and *peer supervision,* and reserve the term *consultation* to signify a change in the level of system. We have found it to be a useful conceptual distinction based on the principle, derived from Russell's Theory of Logical Types that a member of a system cannot observe the system of which it is a part. This idea is a familiar one to systemic therapists and essentially describes our rationale for considering therapy, live supervision, and consultation as progressively higher levels of system. Just as no member of a family can study that family system from a meta-position since they are part of it, similarly no therapist can study a family therapy system since by definition he or she is part of that system, and so on.

Systemic therapists have switched between levels of family system both conceptually and executively when therapy is stuck, by including members of the extended family or a representative from another agency in the session. This strategy provides the opportunity to define clearly relationships between generations and contexts, an important tenet in the Milan approach, and it may be applied to problems in the therapeutic context. Therefore, it seems just as important to define clearly the relationship between different levels of therapeutic system as it is to clarify the levels of family system. This chapter proposes definitions of therapy supervision and consultation as different levels of system and suggests that such clarity can help to maintain the usefulness of each level in relation to the others.

II. THERAPY

As a level of system, therapy is perhaps the easiest to define in space, time and function. A member of the team designated as therapist actively engages the family in direct contact for the duration of therapy. The activity of the therapist is directed towards the family system, and is guided more or less by the supervisory team. The less experienced the therapists are, the more the supervision team guides their activity. The evolving patterns between therapist and family leads to the formation of the family therapy system of which the therapist is seen as a member. This system is of a higher level than the former and therefore has a greater chance of producing change, since the therapist is not subject to the culture of the family system, i.e. the rules which govern the existing system. The proximity of the therapist facilitates access to the family system and the opportunity to perturb it. Simultaneously the danger of being absorbed into the family system is increased, thus reducing the potency of therapy. In this case a system has not been created which can be defined as therapeutic, and the therapist may be seen as part of this impasse. This problem and its solution will be less obvious and less available to the therapist due to his position in the system. In such a situation the function of the supervision team becomes clear.

III. SUPERVISION

Spatially the supervisory team is separated from the family therapy system by virtue of being behind the one-way screen and therefore not in face-to-face contact with the family. In this approach the supervisory team is usually comprised of the same group of people behind the screen for each session.

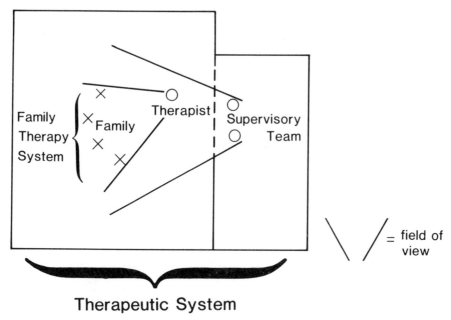

Therapeutic System

Fig. 1.

Figure 1 illustrates the spatial relationship between the family therapy system and supervisory team. Supervision attains its position as a higher level of system by including the therapist in its field of vision and by the way in which the definition of relationship is established between therapist and supervisory team. The supervisory team behind the screen can concentrate on the patterns emerging in the family and the patterns between the therapist and the family. As Cecchin (personal communication, 1983) said, "An important function of the team is to seduce the therapist out of the family's way of viewing the problem".

The main functions of the supervisory team are to prepare the therapist for the interview, achieve a meta-view of therapy, keep the therapist to task, maintain the therapist's neutrality, provide new direction when necessary, and prepare interventions. In essence the supervisory team's function is to maintain the effectiveness of the therapist in disrupting the dysfunctional patterns of the family.

The supervisory team, from their relatively detached position behind the screen, are in a meta-position to the family therapy system and are able to observe processes occurring not only within the family but between the family and the therapist. Their interruptions can disrupt nonproductive patterns and help the therapist regain his meta-position in relation to the family system. The above is not a description of what the supervisory team "does" to the therapist, but is a description of the relationship between the therapist and supervisory team. This relationship is not only based on physical positions but on the acceptance by the therapist and the supervisory team that they have access to different sets of information and that this "double description" can lead to a better understanding. Neither position is "right". At the level of peers the therapist accepts that he or she cannot have access to the same information as the supervisory team no matter how experienced he or she is, and vice versa.

After a period of time the therapeutic system, i.e. the team system plus the family systems with whom they work, will almost certainly develop redundancies (repetitive patterns), some of which cease to be useful. For example, the team will develop "standard" hypotheses, themes and interventions for the family system. Even when these stop working the team appears unable, almost reluctant, to abandon them in favour of creating new ones. At times like these, the team will need to have an input from outside its own system. Thus the practice of *consultation* has grown, which we perceive to be different from supervision in that it is at a higher level and can be distinguished in space, time and function.

IV. CONSULTATION

In order to continue its development a therapeutic system will need new information, for, as Wilden (1972) suggests, "the open system is open to its environment, without which it cannot survive and on which it depends for those aspects of its time-dependent development which are not controlled by the internal rules and constraints related to self differentiation" (p. 360). Live consultation has the most potential for perturbing the therapeutic system and stimulating change and complexity.

In this section we will outline the novel way in which the Milan team consult to a therapeutic system, the impact it can have and the ways in which this type of consultation has influenced our way of working. The mode of consultation is generally in line with the model of therapy. This is the case with a Milan style consultation, which in our experience follows the same ritual as for family interviews.

The Milan team show due regard for the professional relationship that exists between consultants and team. However they also make it clear, in word and deed, that they must regard the therapy team (and their context) as part of the system to be considered both in the interview and in any intervention that is made. Only in this way is it possible for them to be able to achieve a meta-position to the therapeutic system. Their attitude towards a consultation may be represented thus: "A good consultation should leave the therapist free to accept or reject the intervention of the consultants" (Boscolo & Cecchin, personal communication 1979). Therefore consultations are usually organised in the following way:

(1) *Intake meeting*

The consultants meet with the therapy team to gather information about the therapy, the presenting problem, the team's hypotheses and interventions so far, and the family's response to therapy.

(2) *Pre-session*

The consultants, independent of the therapeutic team, hypothesise about the impasse in the therapeutic system, utilising such concepts as complementarity, symmetry, definition of relationships, homeostasis, etc. The separation of the therapy team and consultants at this and later stages is intended as a context marker between systems.

(3) *The interview*

One consultant supervised by the other, "behind-the-screen" interviews the family therapy system, testing the hypotheses made and creating new "maps" for the therapeutic system.

(4) *Mid-session discussion*

The information gained in the interview leads to an intervention which is designed to perturb patterns within the family and those between the family and therapy team.

(5) *Intervention*

If time permits, the intervention is delivered to the reassembled family and therapist or the decision for a report to follow is announced.

(6) *Post-session discussion*

The consultants and therapy team reconvene after the family have left to discuss the session and future strategies in therapy.

A. Case Example I

Drs. Boscolo and Cecchin gave a consultation in July 1980 to a Latvian family, which we shall call the G family, consisting of mother (aged 53 years), father (aged 55 years) and Janis (aged 15 years), resident in England for 32 years. The boy presented with psychotic behaviour of some two years' duration which had proved resistant to various forms of therapy, drugs, in-patient care, etc., before being referred in October 1979 for family therapy. Our therapy based on the Milan approach, produced little change. As Dr. Boscolo began to ask about the extended family relationships, it emerged that each member of this family were in their own way extremely attached to the family of the maternal aunt who also lived in the same town. This family (the W family) were perceived by the G family to have adapted better to the English culture, even though they arrived much later than the G family. Mrs. W was very critical of Mr. & Mrs. G as parents and spouses, and of Janis as a son and a pupil, comparing him unfavourably with her own children. The G family saw themselves as being inferior to the W family. The consultant enquired about the opinion of the W family on the therapy of the G family. For example, "whom is it more important that you please, the W family or the therapist?" "Does your sister ever say that you should withdraw from therapy and take her advice instead?" It transpired that the G family were very attached to the W family in a complementary relationship, i.e. the more the G family failed the more successful the W family seemed and vice versa.

It seemed that the therapist by positively connoting the G family and ignoring this relationship had inadvertently become symmetrical to the W family. The G family were thus seen as triangulated between therapy and the W family, and could not utilise the therapeutic input while still remaining attached to the W family.

Time did not allow for the consultants to deliver the intervention themselves.

Instead the therapist read to the family at the next session their written report which is summarised as follows:

"The consultants were impressed by how much the G family have helped the W family over the years since they came to England—by being good hosts and supportive to them. In addition, the distance they have maintained between each other has allowed the W family to feel better. The happiness and success of the W family since they have been in England is entirely related to the selfless work done by the G family, and as a result the W family has been helped to feel adequate and to feel close. By the G family having problems the W family has been helped to feel successful. One day it will become clear to you all that the W family is quite settled and no longer in need of your help. Until then you should continue to be distant towards each other, Janis should continue to behave in the way he does, and none of you should try to socialise.

"The consultants think that you did quite right to come to therapy and that you should continue to do so—they are concerned that the family might get too attached to therapy, and might interrupt the work of helping the W family—but are relieved and reassured to see that Mrs.G remains doubtful about therapy".

This consultation helped us in three ways. Firstly it enabled us to overcome the impasse with this particular family. Secondly, and perhaps more importantly, it demonstrated the danger of restricting one's interventions to a particular system, in this case the nuclear family. We had always been aware of "important others" in the family's context but now were able to elicit information in a way that revealed the implications of therapy for these relationships and intervene accordingly. This knowledge meant that we were much less likely to become symmetrical to important others, e.g. extended family, other therapists, religious mentors, etc. Thirdly it led us to change the way we dealt with families who were already involved in a continuing helping relationship, e.g. therapist, social worker, probation officer, etc. In such cases we routinely begin with a consultation interview of the family therapy system, which of course includes the other professional. This shift in thinking and practice can perhaps best be illustrated by reference to a case that tested our new position.

B. Case Example II

This was a case referred to us from another hospital in our region where the identified patient, a 15 year old girl, had been an inpatient for the past three months "suffering" from a hysterical paralysis. Various treatments had been tried including behaviour modification, narcoanalysis and individual psychotherapy. The girl had been making some progress and then relapsed. She had begun to expand her "repertoire" of symptoms by adopting those of other patients. The hospital knew of our work, and so on the supposition that the girl's family might be "sabotaging" their treatment programme referred them to our centre for family therapy. The family consisted of a single-parent (divorced) mother and three children, Susan aged 16 years, Barbara (the I.P.) aged 15 years, and Derek aged 14 years. After considering the information available, we decided that our efforts should be directed towards (a) achieving a meta-position to the hospital/family system; (b) exploring the function of the symptom and the nature of relationships in (i) the family system, (ii) the hospital system, (iii) between the hospital and family connected as they were by Barbara; (c) avoiding either becoming symmetrical to the other hospital or being drawn into making decisions about the discharge of the girl from hospital. In order to achieve these aims we followed the consultation format. We do not intend to portray this case in detail, our purpose is to highlight the process of consultation.

The individual therapist was invited to attend the session as a representative of the referring hospital. He was the person said to be most closely involved with Barbara's treatment. Only the family attended the first interview, in which our hypothesis about sibling rivalry was confirmed. An intervention was made which was iso-morphic with the family's religious beliefs and which prepared the ground for a systemic intervention.

The individual therapist attended the next session, in which we enquired about the function of the symptom in the hospital system. We asked questions of the following sort: *To Barbara:* "Who in the hospital do you find most sympathetic and most helpful to talk to?" "Of all the patients in the hospital who do you think the staff find the most interesting and difficult to understand?" "If the problems do not get better, and you remain unable to walk, who would you most like to look after you—someone in the hospital or someone at home?" *To the therapist:* "What would be the criteria for discharging Barbara?" *To the family:* "Do you think the hospital treatment is doing any good?" "What do you think would be most helpful to Barbara—the hospital treatment or prayer?" "If the hospital decides to discharge her, who in the family will give up part of their own life to look after her?"

In the mid-session discussion the team noted the following factors as being most important: (a) The girl's temporary improvement had coincided with the commencement of individual therapy, while her relapses coincided with talk of discharge and losing the individual therapist. (b) Both verbally and non-verbally Barbara showed a great attachment to the individual therapist. (c) The family showed what might be described as utter boredom with Barbara and her condition. Since they realised she was not physically ill and felt she was either "putting it on" or that it was due to the "Will of God".

The intervention delivered at the end of this session systemically reframed Barbara's symptoms; ascribed a positive purpose to her behaviour, thus allowing her to give up her symptoms without "losing face"; and positively connoted treatment so far and took a neutral position with regard to its continuation:

"We have been impressed by Barbara's independence. It may seem an unusual and odd form of independence but nevertheless we see Barbara's behaviour as a kind of independence. At first we wondered how it came about that although you, Mrs. S., see Barbara as making progress towards adult life, perhaps the first to have a boy-friend, maybe the first to leave home, that Barbara should sacrifice her independence by becoming helpless, having so much difficulty in walking that she had to be admitted to hospital.

"We think she makes this sacrifice because she has the idea at an unconscious level that she will not be able to take the place of Susan or even Derek as a companion and friend to you, Mrs. S., when they eventually leave home. She therefore sees a danger that the family may split up, so she makes this sacrifice to keep the family together. . . . While she has this idea, then all the good work that is being done by Dr. W and the staff at the hospital is unlikely to be successful.

"Dr. W, we think that you should not be expecting Barbara to make a lot of progress and in fact Barbara should slow down the progress she is already making.

Whether she stays in hospital or goes home we would anticipate that as long as she has this idea she will not make rapid progress. We recommend further family meetings to discuss this subconscious idea and we would also like to discuss with Dr. W how he can continue to work with Barbara."

In a meeting with Dr. W five days later, he seemed receptive to our ideas as he had already seen some improvement. We offered the following intervention in the form of a report which we suggested he read out when he next met with Barbara in hospital:

"We are impressed by the good working relationship between Barbara and Dr. W, between Dr. W and Barbara. . . . In general we agree with Dr. W, that Barbara could decide to be more outgoing, make friends and live a fuller life. However, we have some reservations about his opinion that she can do these things so quickly. As we said in our meeting with the family, Barbara has decided to behave as she does for her family and, while we agree she could decide to improve any time she chooses, we think that it is premature to think that the time is right now. We think that Barbara will continue to have the idea that she needs to go on doing this work for her family for some time. She will do this work in one way or another: not walking, being depressed, not making friends, etc. Any improvement will probably be temporary. So we would recommend that Dr. W continues to see Barbara on a regular basis, whether she improves or not. We would predict that for some time Barbara will make improvements then relapse and so on. Therefore, Dr. W should not be too enthusiastic or optimistic about the improvements that Barbara makes from time to time. We understand how eager Dr. W is to help Barbara and how keen Barbara is to improve, but advise him to proceed slowly.

"We approve of Dr. W's enthusiastic approach but know from our experience that younger psychiatrists often expect changes to occur too quickly. Barbara's situation is a particularly difficult one and we think that Dr. W is over-optimistic in thinking that he can achieve major changes when other more senior people have failed."

The rationale for this intervention was: (a) to allow for the continuation of the therapeutic relationship between Dr. W and Barbara without the need for symptoms to maintain it; (b) to use our position as experts in criticising Dr. W, thus provoking Barbara into "saving" her therapist by improving, to prove us wrong. There followed a rapid improvement leading to her discharge from the hospital within a few weeks. This progress as is our custom was credited to the combined efforts of the family and the staff of the hospital. We saw the family several months later and noted the continuation of improvement which has been maintained to date.

A consultation should intervene in such a way that it allows the therapeutic system to evolve towards what Wilden (1972) refers to as "an apparent goal of increasing levels of variety or organisation coupled with an increased viability (increased adaptive range) and an increase in the complexity of information transmission" (p. 361). Consultations are probably best done on an infrequent basis since the consultants may become absorbed into the culture of the therapeutic system and their visits cease to initiate sufficient difference necessary to create information.

The above is a description of one way in which supervisors relate to family therapy systems and outside consultants can relate to a therapeutic system. It would be a mistake, however, to think that the influence always flows from the higher level system to the lower levels. Cronen et al. (1982) illustrate the reflexive nature of the exchange of information between levels of context. For example, the feedback that consultants receive from one consultation will influence the way in which they conduct their next.

V. SUMMARY

We have proposed in this chapter that systemic concepts useful in working with "stuck" family patterns can also be used to analyse and intervene in "stuck" therapeutic patterns. In particular we have considered the growth in the practice of live supervision and consultation as means towards effective systemic therapy. We have suggested that the increased proximity between therapy supervision and consultation allowed for by the advent of the one-way screen has many advantages. However if these advantages are to be maximised then it is important to maintain a clear definition of the relationship between these activities. A format has been offered that distinguishes between them as three levels of system in clinical practice.

REFERENCES

Bateson, G. (1971). A Systems Approach Evaluation of Family Therapy. *International Journal of Psychiatry* 9, 242–244.

Bateson, G. (1979). "Mind and Nature: A Necessary Unity", Fontana, London.

Cronen, V., Johnson, K. M., Hahnemann, J. W., (1982). Paradoxes, Double Binds and Reflexive Loops: An Alternative Theoretical Perspective. *Family Process* 21, 91–112.

Kingston, P., and Smith, D. (1983). Preparation for Live Consultation and Live Supervision When Working without One-way Screen. *Journal of Family Therapy* 5, 219–233.

Speed, B., Seligman, P., Kingston, P., Cade, B., (1982). A Team Approach to Therapy. *Journal of Family Therapy* 4, 271–284.

Wilden, A. (1972). "System and Structure: Essays in Communication and Exchange", Tavistock Publications, London.

Chapter 7

Toward an Explanation of How the Milan Method Works: An Invitation to a Systemic Epistemology and the Evolution of Family Systems

Vernon E. Cronen and W. Barnett Pearce

The audacity of the task assumed in the title of this chapter has not escaped us. We are social scientists interested in understanding how social systems in a wide variety of contexts are formed, how they change, and how they function. As part of a wider research program, for the last five years we have, in effect, "looked over the shoulders" of family therapists. We have taken the therapists as our "subjects" and asked what it is that they do which has (or is intended to have) beneficial effects on their clients.

We chose therapists because they are experienced and at least sometimes dramatically effective "change agents". We studied family therapists because this intellectual community is excitingly engaged in an analysis of their own epistemology and because they deal with intact systems. When Karl Tomm of the University of Calgary Medical School Family Therapy Program introduced us to the Milan approach and to Gianfranco Cecchin and Luigi Boscolo, we focused on this approach to family therapy because it is very compatible with our own meta-theoretical assumptions.

The Milan team is neither mute nor inarticulate. Let it be said clearly and early: we are not attempting to pose as "experts" on therapy or on their work, nor do we think that they need help in locating their intellectual grounding. We are reporting and interpreting the results of our observations of planned therapeutic change in families. We have had the opportunity to observe Drs. Cecchin and Boscolo doing work as "therapeutic consultants" and have worked with teams using the Milan method in Canada, Japan, England and the United States.

Our perspective as social scientists gives us a somewhat different vantage than that of therapists, and our own theoretical and research work provides some vocabulary and concepts which we find useful in articulating the connection between therapists and family systems. We hope that our analysis of the Milan method will be useful to therapists who are using or contemplating the use of the Milan method.

APPLICATIONS OF SYSTEMIC FAMILY THERAPY
ISBN 0-8089-1696-3

I. WHAT IS THE MILAN METHOD?

The Milan method is *not* just a collection of techniques which a therapist can *use*. It is a broad-based, sophisticated "epistemology", a way of thinking about and acting in social systems. The Milan method consists of "inviting" in various ways the family to engage in actions consistent with this epistemology. If the invitation is successful, the participation itself in this epistemology brings about changes in the "logic" of the family system and the course of its evolution. Fine descriptions of the Milan approach are available elsewhere (Tomm, 1894a and 1984b) as well as in this volume. We limit our description here to those features most relevant to our analysis.

The "goal" of the Milan method is to facilitate the evolution of family systems in ways which do not cause unnecessary distress. This goal includes some concepts with startling implications. Milan therapists work at thinking of families systemically and dynamically. In this view, the structure of the family resides in the relationships among the members of the family, not in the attributes of each member.

The structure is always in a process of evolution. Even the existence of a symptom for a long time does not imply that the system has stopped evolving, because the reoccurrence of a pattern of action is a different event than its original occurrence. Systems continuously evolve because their "structure" is reflexivly tied to "action". The family must act, and whatever actions they produce both "express" and "recon-stitute" the structure of the system. But this evolution is not always in desirable directions. Sometimes the logic of a family results in pain, and through one means or another the family confronts a therapist. However, the "presenting problem" is often a poor description of the structure and action patterns of the family. Like most of us, families usually think in terms of individuals rather than systems, in terms of linear processes rather than reflexive relations, and in terms of static "states" rather than dynamic "processes".

In our judgement, the procedures which Milan-style therapists use can be seen as "expressing" a systemic, reflexive, dynamic epistemology which is in sharp contrast with that of most families. The therapy session itself, as well as the "intervention" and "prescriptions", is an invitation for the family to participate in patterns of action which reflexively "reconstitute" this epistemology. To the extent that the family engages in these practices, and to the extent that these practices are linked to the family structure, the logic of the family system is changed, sometimes dramatically (Cronen, Pearce and Tomm, in press).

Taken singly and out of context, the procedures used in the Milan method are not necessarily unique. Therapists of other persuasions often (and sometimes rightly) accuse the Milan team of using "intrapsychic" analyses and "structural" interven-tions. Even the "counterparadox" move which is the most distinctive Milan-style intervention is similar to that used by a variety of other therapists. Such observations do not distress the Milan team, however, because they recognise that it is a mistake to pull out particular interventions and analyse their effects as if they were a specific antidote for a particular virus. This kind of thinking confuses the "content" of a communicative act for its "effect" which descends on its place in a larger system.

Taken conjointly and understood as an invitation to participate in actions which recon-stitute a systemic epistemology, the procedures used in the Milan method are distinc-tive. In fact, we have had to invent a new word to describe the way they work. With apologies, we characterize them as "ambifinal".

Any discussion of "effects" or of how things work in a system is difficult using a language whose bias is linear. In a systemic epistemology, "causes" are not distinct from "effects" and the relevant variables cannot be "isolated" without killing the system. An ambifinal cause is one whose "effects" are "context dependent" or "contingent" on the state of the system in which it occurs.

The concept itself seems unobjectionable: a natural expression of the whole notion of systemic organization and "relational" variables. A fluid at a temperature of 175 degrees Fahrenheit is "hot" if a 98-degree hand is inserted to it, but "cold" if circulated in a 1000-degree engine block. The effect of pouring such a liquid into a system depends on the configuration—in this case, the temperature—of the system itself. The procedures which the Milan method uses to invite clients to participate in a systemic epistemology are ambifinal because they have different effects depending upon the characteristics of the system to which the invitation is given. Further, the various effects are sufficiently broad to pose a powerful impetus to change the existing logic of the system.

We suggest that the Milan method "works" to the extent that it engages the clients in patterns of action which imply a systemic epistemology, and that this epistemology changes the existing logic of the family system and facilitates its evolution. To explain this process more specifically, we need to introduce some concepts about family systems, their evolution and communication.

II. THE COORDINATED MANAGEMENT OF MEANING

Our perspective on the Milan approach uses the lens of the theory of the Coordinated Management of Meaning (or CMM). More complete statements of the theory are available elsewhere (Pearce and Cronen, 1980; Cronen, Johnson, and Lannamann, 1982).

Communication is *not* fundamentally an individual problem of "correctly" mapping structure on action, but rather a social process of coordinating action and managing structure. Coordination must not be read as a synonym for mutual understanding among social actors. Research from our team has shown that in some cases the differences in the ways actors interpret messages can facilitate mutually satisfying coordination (Harris *et al.*, 1979), and in other cases the close consonance of interpretations can contribute to problems (Cronen, Pearce and Tomm, in press).

CMM offers a unique set of formalisms for analyzing structure. These formalisms are based on two claims that are well supported: (1) social actors organize meaning both temporally and hierarchically; and (2) all social structures entail ways of managing consciousness of various elements of those structures. The content and organization of structure are by no means "necessary"; they emerge from conjoint action and are always in the process of emergence.

We conceive of social meanings as hierarchically organized so that one level is the context for the interpretation of others. The number and nature of embedded levels of context is not fixed. However, in the analysis of families, we typically employ five embedded levels which can be schematized as shown in Figure 1. The number, nature and order of the levels is not fixed. In the analysis of families, however, we

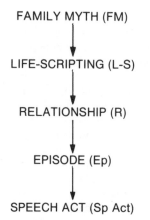

FAMILY MYTH (FM)

LIFE-SCRIPTING (L-S)

RELATIONSHIP (R)

EPISODE (Ep)

SPEECH ACT (Sp Act)   Fig. 1.   Five embedded levels of context.

typically employ the levels shown in Figure 1. Each of the five is a place marker for a complex of information at a particular level of abstraction. The levels of information are defined as follows:

(1) *Speech acts (SpAct)*. These are the relational meanings of verbal and nonverbal messages. Examples include "threat to my worth", "promise", and "conceding the point".

(2) *Episodes (Ep)*. Episodes are conceptions of patterns of reciprocated' acts. For example, "Our usual fight over who gets to use the car".

(3) *Relationship (R)*. Relationship refers to a conception of how and on what terms two or more persons engage. For example, part of a relational concept might be "I'm the initiator; s/he is the follower".

(4) *Life-scripting (L-S)*. This is a person's conception of self in social action. For example, "I am an intellectual and skeptic".

(5) *Family myth (FM)*. This refers to high-order general conceptions of how society, personal roles, and family relationships work.

The patterns in which these levels are actually organized in a specific situation are indicated by symbols developed by Brown (1972) and Varela (1975). When a relationship (R) is the higher order context within which an episode is understood, the structural situation is symbolized $\frac{R}{Ep|}$. This symbolization should not be taken to mean that the only relationship is from the higher level of context to the lower. Even when a clear order of contextual embeddedness can be discerned, there is some degree of reflexivity among the levels. For example, we studied a case in which the wife's structure clearly included the notion that her relationship to her own mother (R–m) was the context for understanding and guiding her relationship with her son (R–s). We express this symbolically as $\frac{R-m}{R-s|}$. Her understanding of R–m was very stable and did not fluctuate with every significant change in R–s. However, there are things which did or could occur in her relationship to her son which would affect her construction of her relationship with her mother.

A structure in which the reflexive relationship is weak would provide problems.

We think here of a student who came to the university from a small secondary school with the reputation of being a "math wizard". This life-scripting persisted even though he repeatedly had difficulties with courses in advanced mathematics, and he refused to change his field to something he could handle better. For this student no set of events could be clearly identified which would unsettle the "math-wizard" life-script.

The degree of reflexivity between any two levels of embedded contexts depends on information at a level of context which subsumes them both, so CMM analysis always employs at least three levels of contexts (see Cronen, Johnson and Lannamann, 1982).

Two levels of context may be organized so that each is equally the context for and within the context of the other. The levels form a loop in which changes in each level affect the meaning of the other. When two persons are getting acquainted, the nature of their relationship is very sensitive to the conduct of a particular episode. Yet, as the relationship has begun to emerge, it also guides the conduct and interpretation of the episode. The loop may be symbolized like this $\square$. If no change in understanding results no matter which context is momentarily viewed as the higher, then they form a mutually confirming, or "charmed" loop, symbolized $\square \heartsuit$. Sometimes contexts are looped so that treating one as "higher" leads to different and contradictory interpretations than if the other is "higher". This pattern is a *paradox* or "strange" loop, symbolized $\square^S$.

The structure which produces the alcoholic's syndrome (of periodic sobriety and drunkenness) may be characterized as a strange loop. The life-scripting context includes two, mutually exclusive possibilities: "I am an alcoholic" and "I am not an alcoholic". The episode context also contains two mutually exclusive patterns of actions: "I refuse drinks" and "I engage in drinking". In the context of the "alcoholic" life-script, one must refuse drinks. If, however, the episode of refusing drinks is the higher context, this implies the salience of the life-script of not being an alcoholic because the person has proven that they can control their drinking. If he now switches to the "non-alcoholic" life-script as the higher context, episodes of drinking are legitimated, and these episodes—and their aftermath—may be used as a context for switching back to the original "alcoholic" life-script, and so it goes. This alcoholic's strange loop is guided by a yet higher level of context, perhaps a family myth to the effect that alcoholism is determined by behaviour rather than physical dependence. A strange loop within a larger context is symbolized $\overline{\square^S}$.

CMM is sometimes referred to as a rule-based theory. More precisely, we use the form of two types of rules as a conceptual device for describing the way actors structure their social reality. Constitutive rules (cR) integrate the hierarchical structure of embedded contexts shown in Figure 1. Constitutive rules indicate: the matter in which two levels of organization are related given the context provided by a third level. Regulative rules (rR) guide action. Their structure is a series of three speech acts all within a set of higher level embedded or looped contexts. Thus a regulative rule specifies a set of contexts and a pattern of action. The three speech acts are: (1) other's antecedent act, (2) an act from one's own repertory, and (3) a desired response from other. Regulative rules also include a deontic operator indicating the moral force perceived to operate on one's choice. When the actor is conscious of structural constraints, the operators are obligatory, legitimate, prohibitive and undetermined. When the actor claims not to be conscious of structural constraints, the operators are caused, probable, inhibited and random. Finally, regulative rule models include the Kantian "I" or the locus of consciousness in structure to which information about structure may be reported. The distinction between the "I" and life scripting roughly parallels Mead's distinction between the "I" and "me".

There are three classes of variables among the elements in the regulative rule model. The first is *PREFIGURATIVE FORCE*. This refers to extant conditions that prefigure the choice of action. These might include life-scripting, the episode in progress, the antecedent act, etc. The second is *PRACTICAL FORCE*. This refers to the shaping of one's choice of action by the response an actor desires. People may report "I had to do that no matter what the other would say or do next", which indicates a very weak practical force. Stronger practical force is evidenced by the report that "I said that to get him to ask me out". The last class is *REFLEXIVE NEEDS AND EFFECTS*. A particular response (C) might be needed to sustain someone's sense of identity, confirm their conception of a relationship, or maintain the course of an episode. The actual response obtained may have the effect of changing, modifying or dramatically altering a context.

Identifying reflexive needs and effects is crucial to understand the "nodal points" of a system. For example, a father may need a response from his daughter to sustain the conception that he is in a struggle to save her from sin. The response she must provide is a sign of resistance to his moralizing, which suggests to him that she might "trespass" and thus needs his strong moral stance. This type of response reconstitutes father's life-scripting and relationship to his daughter which, in turn, prefigures very rigid efforts to control her. Yet these very controlling effects elicit the daughter's resistance. In this kind of situation, the father is often conscious of the prefigurative force and sees his acts as obligations. He is not conscious of the obligation to resist that his acts produce for his daughter, nor of the importance her responses have for him in sustaining his life-scripting as a moral policeman.

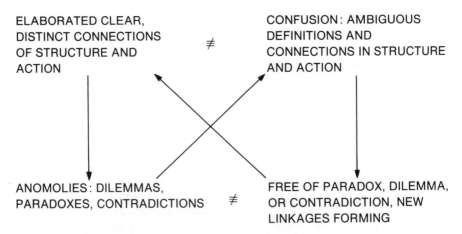

Fig. 2. The evolution of social systems. These elements form a strange loop as shown in the context of a traditional positivist–reductionist perspective. In the context of Kuhn's (1970) evolutionary view, they form a charmed loop of emergent elaborations and paradigm shifts.

III. CLARITY AND CONFUSION IN SOCIAL SYSTEMS

One way of describing the dynamics of social systems is to postulate a dialectical tension between states of "confusion" and "clarity". The crucial relationship is that between the "structure" of the system and the patterns of action which express and reconstitute it. A model we find useful is shown in Figure 2. In the model, "clear and distinct" structure is depicted as incompatible with "confused" structure, and "anomalies" (in the form of inconsistencies and paradox) as incompatible with "clarifying linkages". The pattern of arrows indicates a closed, continuous loop which we think depicts the evolution of systems.

A system whose structure is "clear and distinct" evolves elaborated structures that participants perceive as neatly ordered. The emergent linkages between the structure and the patterns of action seem coherent and clear. It is precisely the clarity and elaboration of a system that makes it vulnerable to anomalies; when a system is ambiguous or ill formed, contradictions do not stand out. As human systems are elaborated in action, clarity breaks down for any of several reasons: the system becomes enmeshed with some other system which imposes different interpretations or performance demands; some component of the system changes, perhaps due to maturation; or some aspect of the system becomes distressed.

This evolution produces a certain kind of disorder; not chaos but "anomalies". The anomalies may take the form of dilemmas in which persons must choose between equally unacceptable alternatives; or of paradox, in which persons must simultaneously act or not act. Social systems may remain "stuck" with their anomalies for quite long periods of time, often with considerable distress. The model thus differentiates two types of confusion. Type 1 confusion refers to anomalies in a clear structure. Type 2 confusion refers to highly ambiguous concepts and relationships between them. To illustrate: the statement made by a Cretan that "All Cretans are liars" can only be perceived as paradoxical if there is a relatively clear understanding of what we mean by "Cretan", by "lying", and by what we understand to be a person's responsibility for their utterances. With these understandings, the statement "all Cretans are liars" uttered by a Cretan is paradoxical and a type 1 confusion. But, suppose a student encountering the Cretan's paradox is wondering "What is a Cretan? A stupid person, someone from Crete, a Martian of dubious parentage, or what? What is lying? Accidental inaccuracies, deliberate deception, or is it a Martian word? And can Martians deliberately speak falsely? Can humans avoid unintended lies—if there is any such thing? This is confusion type 2. In this sort of confusion, no paradox is possible nor can any true anomaly be identified.

Anomalies usually (necessarily?) are "resolved" by a softening of the clear and distinct ideas which comprise structure and produce a kind of confusion in which the relationship between patterns of action and various elements in the structure of the system is uncertain. In confused systems, people often simply do not know what to do or what to make of someone else's actions. In type 2 confused systems, there are "linkages" between ideas or between ideas and actions which provide clarification. As these ideas are developed and refined, they change the system into one in which there are clear and distinct ideas, and so the system goes.

This model, of course, is a heuristic device, and too much should not be expected from it. It does, however, help to show that family systems with different structures can be helped—or hurt—by different things. A family which is "confused" in the sense of type 2 confusion is not helped by a "counterparadox". We saw one family whose confusion was simply compounded by repeated, clever, counterparadoxical interventions. The family was helped by what the therapist thought at the time was a mistake; he performed a simple "structural" move. At the next session, the dys-functional symptoms were dramatically reduced. At the end of the session, however, another clever counterparadoxical intervention was given to the family and the orig-inal symptoms quickly reappeared. On the other hand, a family which is "stuck" in an anomaly because of inconsistent but very clear and distinct ideas can be thrown into confusion by a paradox, and the evolution of the family system facilitated.

Further, the model shows that the cluster of procedures which the Milan method encompasses does not simply "add confusion" or "add clarity". It does both, and in a manner which is importantly affected by the existing structure of the system.

IV.   THE MILAN METHOD AND CHANGES IN THE LOGIC OF SYSTEMS

The relationship of the Milan approach to the CMM perspective was exploited by Kaplan (1984) in a study of multiproblem families. Milan interview techniques were used to generate hypotheses testable with CMM measurement procedures. The highly successful results provide some empirical support for the utility of using CMM concepts in describing family therapy.

In our judgement, the impact of any intervention depends on the state of the family system itself. The Milan method is ambifinal, in that the cluster of procedures which it employs is sufficiently robust to have desirable effects on a wide variety of systems. As a whole, the Milan method attempts to engage the clients in patterns of action which implicate a systemic epistemology, in which many of the problems experienced by the family are changed. Our purposes are not best served by an attempt to list and account for the effect of every type of procedure in the Milan method. Rather, we discuss three topics which seem important and which can serve as a model for the analysis of other Milan-style interactions with distressed families.

A. The Reconfiguration of Logical Force

Several aspects of the Milan method change the relative strength of the various components of logical force. We will discuss "circular questioning" and "positive connotation of the structure of the system".

The "circular questions" are worded in a way which invites the respondants to perceive their actions in terms of practical or reflexive forces rather than prefigur-ative force. Instead of asking some version of "what causes Mother to" perform the symptom, family members are asked "to whom does Mother show" the symptom. By answering a direct question, the family engages in patterns of action which make linkages between actions and their consequence.

In families whose structure is "clear and distinct" or characterized by "anom-alies", prefigurative forces predominate. A common concomitant of "clarity" is "perceived obligation". In these families, circular questioning is a powerful move toward "confusion" by suggesting that troublesome forms of action be thought of in terms of their intentions or effects instead of their "prefiguring" conditions. This introduces uncertainty about the meaning of particular actions, and about attributions of the motives for various actions. To the extent that such families feel compelled or enabled to make choices where before everything was clear and/or obligatory, the course of the evolution of their social system has been productively altered.

In families whose structure is "confused", the subtle suggestions of linkages between acts and consequences may provide a clarifying way of restructuring the system. In some families, the problem is that the parents of the family simply cannot figure out what to do when, for example, their daughter refuses to eat or their son physically threatens them. If this is the problem, some sort of "structural" move is needed which will instill some pattern in the system which allows the members to act.

Positive connotation is one of the most distinctive procedures used in the Milan method. The family is frequently told that the pattern of activity about which they are complaining is really serving an important function for their family. Symptoms are described as so basic to the family logic that they cannot be expected to be alleviated quickly or easily. In fact, it is good if the whole pattern of action continues, although perhaps in a slightly modified form. Therefore, the family should continue to perform the pattern, but perhaps not so often, or perhaps letting someone else take over the role associated with the symptom about which the family complained. Of course, only the family can decide how much longer this pattern is necessary, so every once in a while they should ask whether it has gone on long enough.

This procedure startles many clients—and some other therapists. It creates a complex pattern of thought which simultaneously defines the problematic pattern of action as "prefigurative" (out of control, obligated by external or previous events, etc.) and "purposive" (controllable, purposive, etc.). The pattern is depicted in Figure 3 as a strange loop in the context of the "lifescript" and as the context of action in the problematic episode.

Note that the therapist has said two things: that the problematic acts are prefigured—uncontrollable—*and* that the family should deliberately continue to perform those acts, monitoring to see if they are still necessary. The second statement implies that the problematic acts are purposive and controllable. There is a paradox in the therapist's positive connotation, but it has power only when tied to action: people have plenty and enough ways of avoiding the teeth of a contradiction as long as it is all a matter of talk. When tied to action, paradox is more effective.

Assume that the "episode" containing the problematic behaviour has been initiated, and the "antecendent event" has occurred. The strange loop described in Figure 3 is brought into play when the family engages in the pattern of action which they find distressing. The context has been provided by the therapist: their behaviours are "prefigured" and out of their control. This leads to the comfortable fatalism that the symptom is important and that we cannot simply make it go away, but also to the prescription that they should—for this reason—deliberately perform the problematic act with a high degree of awareness and intentionality. Of course, this type of performance is anything but highly prefigured, and leads to the conclusion that the family is indeed acting in a purposive, controllable manner, and that they could simply make the problem go away. This conclusion is invalidated, however, by the fact that the family did perform the problematic acts again, so—the inference follows—the family's behaviours are highly prefigured, and so on.

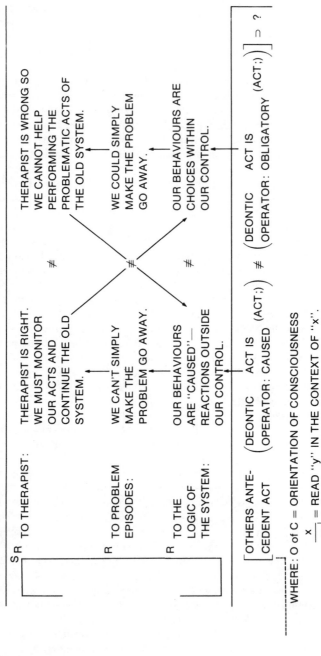

Fig. 3. Type 1 confusion about the relationship of a family to their own logic.

The whole is more important than any given part of this model. As a whole, it introduces a great deal of uncertainty and confusion to the system by bringing into question the relation between any pattern of action and the structure of the system. The family is made to ask "are we in control or out of control of our actions?" Simply to pose that question tends to shift the system away from a configuration of logic force in which prefigurative force predominates.

There is an easy resolution to this strange loop. If the family simply stops performing the problematic behaviour, the confusion—and the problem—is eliminated. This resolution can even provide a good context: that of deciding that the therapist was wrong, that this symptom was not such an important feature of the family's logic; in fact, it was dispensible.

In our judgement, positively connoting a system in which the problem is too much clarity or too many anomalies is a powerful move which facilitates continued evolution. However, positive connotations of systems which suffer too much confusion or are struggling to find explanatory schemes simply adds to the confusion and perpetuates the system in its existing configuration.

B. The Management of Consciousness

Consciousness is a product of the structure of a system and vice versa. One way of inducing change into a system is that of altering the extent to which the person is aware of various parts of the system, or the pattern of that awareness.

One way of discussing the "pattern" of awareness is in terms of the personal perspective. Shotter (1983) argues that each of the "personal" positions—I, you, they—carry with them "duties" and "responsibilities". For example, it is not difficult to transform this discussion of "duties" and "responsibilities" into an analysis of what a person may, must and must not know about the system in which he lives and works.

In circular questioning, family members are asked to "gossip in front of each other" by telling the therapist about the others' behaviours. This changes the relationship between the structure of the system and the pattern of action being discussed. Instead of taking a participants' perspective in an "I/we—you" relationship, a "third party" perspective is created by the form of the question. The answer is invited to be in a "he—they" framework.

Particular "rights" and "duties" accompany each perspective. In a participants' perspective, persons are entitled/expected to be "enmeshed", their actions to be sincere, to be consistent, etc. When various members of the family describe these patterns in an "objective" manner to an "outsider" who persistently refuses to be astonished or to take sides, or hears these descriptions by other members of the family, particularly children, this shifts the form of "consciousness" of the logical force.

In a system troubled by too much clarity and rigor, this shift in consciousness is liberating. It opens new ways of thinking and reduces the high prefigurative force which apparently obligated particular acts and interpretations of actions. In a system troubled by too much confusion, this shift in consciousness is liberating precisely because it provides a way of thinking which can replace unstructured "mush" which stifles thought and action.

Positive connotation of the system also affects consciousness. Families who seek

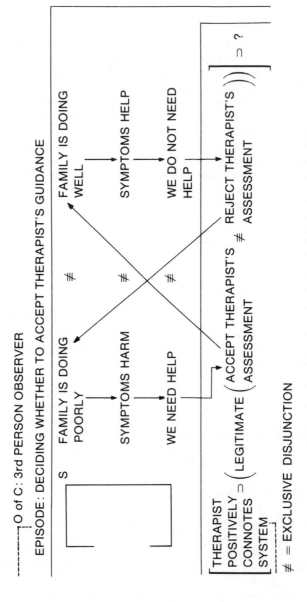

Fig. 4. Type 1 confusion about the relationship of the family to the therapist.

80

therapy usually do so because something hurts. Therapists using the Milan method frequently tell their clients that their family system is really doing well and that the painful symptoms serve important functions in a larger pattern. The combination of these two meanings poses a problem which we depict as a strange loop in the "family perception of itself" in Figure 4. The strange loop in Figure 4 is within the context of any episode during which the family must decide whether to accept or reject the therapist's guidance. The function of the strange loop which is described below is to make the family take an "objective" or third person perspective on themselves. The loop and the change in perspective are tied to the action of accepting or rejecting what the therapist says. This episodic context is sometimes made unavoidable by prescribing a "ritual" which the family is to perform. Whether they perform the ritual or not is not as important as the *decision* they must make about whether to perform it. This decision precipitates the act of accepting or not accepting the therapists' positive connotation and leads into the structure in Figure 4.

Figure 4 portrays lines of thought which go something like this. Granted that we hurt. If we accept what the therapist says, then we are doing quite well as a family, and these symptoms are normal or even positively helpful. If we are normal and doing well, then we do not need therapy, and we made a mistake in coming to therapy and should not accept the therapists' advice. But if the therapist is wrong, then we are not doing so well; these painful symptoms indicate that we need help and we should accept the therapists' advice. But what the therapist says is that we are doing pretty well . . . and so on.

The loop is initiated even if the family decides to reject the therapists' positive connotation. If the family decides that the therapist is wrong, then they define themselves as not doing so well, needing therapy, and put themselves into a position where they should accept what the therapist says, except that the therapist says that they are doing all right . . . and so on.

Either way, this loop makes the family's understanding of itself problematic. Is it doing well, or not? Should it accept the therapists' diagnosis? Should they remain in therapy? What about these painful symptoms anyway? Such questions move the family from the perspective of participants to that of observers, and change the logic of the system by altering their consciousness of it.

In a confused system, this move probably simply adds confusion. In a system which has sufficient clarity that the problems are caused by dilemmas or paradoxes, the introduction of this type of confusion may open avenues for restructuring the system and thus continuing its evolution.

C.   The Unique Potential of Rituals

The use of ritual has particularly interesting consequences in conjunction with other techniques. Recall our example of the father who constantly demanded that his daughter enact a stern moral code and account to him for all her actions. He "must" do this to fulfill his life-scripting while at the same time he needs the resistance he elicits to sustain his life-scripting. After all, who can justify setting themselves up as a moral policeman in a naturally moral order? The therapist might describe the system and give it positive connotation, indicating how daughter helps father to fulfill and live up to his role and how father helps daughter find opportunities to express independence. Laying out this system does several things previously dis-

EPISODE: PERFORMANCE OF RITUAL PRESCRIBED

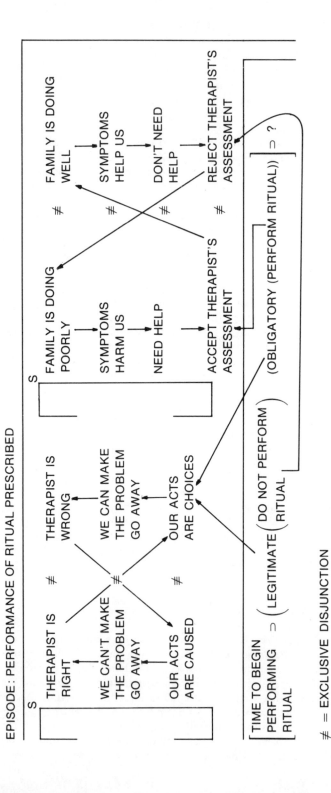

Fig. 5.   Ritual activating two strange loops.

≠ = EXCLUSIVE DISJUNCTION

82

cussed; shift consciousness by providing an immediate static snapshot of the whole system, generate type 1 confusion about whether the acts performed were caused or chosen. In addition, the therapist might prescribe a ritual requiring at dinner time that father, daughter and others in the family, enact a scripted conversation in which each thanks the others for playing their role in the positively connotated system. By so doing, the therapist clearly shifts responsibility for message choices to him/herself. This shift can be very liberating, leaving the participants to make their own assessment of whether they have to enact the system they had created. Simply facing the possibility of actually doing the ritual—getting to the dinner table—and rejecting the therapist's requirements is useful. After all, *"if we don't have to do this, then we can change* (see Figure 3), *so the therapist is wrong"*. If the therapist is wrong, we can reject what the therapist prescribes, but the therapist prescribes the continuation of our old system. To resist the therapist is to reject that system (see Figure 4).

Complicated? Yes. What the ritual does is to initiate both the loops in Figures 3 and 4. This occurs in a concrete moment of social action that the family must anticipate encountering. The initiation of both loops by the ritual is shown in Figure 5. Thus rituals act simultaneously on three aspects of structure: family's relationship to its own logic, family's relationship to therapist, and the orientation of consciousness. The ritual is also capable of another kind of effect. For the family enmeshed in type 2 confusion the ritual provides a way of sorting out elements in a time-extended sequence. In type 2 confusions the ritual may act as the reverse of describing and positively connoting the system. Whereas positive connotation alters consciousness by compressing a time-extended pattern into a snapshot, the ritual can sort out and organize the simultaneity of type 2 confusion into a temporally organized sequence.

V. OVERALL OBSERVATIONS

The theory of CMM and the Milan approach unite in a rejection of certain choices that have dogged social science in general and clinical psychology in particular. Those choices can be listed as a set of four distinctly *unproductive* questions: (1) Are persons basically reactive or purposive? (2) Are the factors that really count conscious or nonconscious? (3) Should the unit of observation be persons or systems? (4) Should the techniques of therapy be structural, strategic or systemic?

Both CMM theory and the Milan approach demand a "both" or "all of the above" response to these questions. Persons construct systems in which they are at times reactive and at other times purposive. These are variables, not exclusive categories of the human condition. Consciousness is an integral aspect of structure. No social system can operate with near total consciousness of its own structure from a third-person position at all times. Try falling in love that way! Yet consciousness can facilitate other aspects of life. Human systems are about persons whose internal life ("mind", if you will) is a social product, but a social product that includes idiosyncrasies at the individual level which count in the emergence of social action. It is social action, of course, through which individuals themselves evolve and change. To Bateson's claim "no context, no meaning", we would add, "no action, no contexts". Finally, the experience of the Milan group indicates that clinical epistemologies are not exhausted—or even well described—simply by listing their "techniques".

Rather, the development and selection of techniques derive from a fundamental epistemology. The way one accounts for human activity ought to suggest the appropriate use of a variety of techniques.

REFERENCES

Brown, G., Spencer, (1972). "The Laws of Form", Julian Press, New York.

Cronen, V. E., Johnson, K. L., and Lannamann, J. W. (1982). Paradoxes, Double Binds, and Reflexive Loops: An Alternative Theoretical Perspective. *Family Process* 20, 91–112.

Cronen, V. E., Pearce, W. B., and Tomm, K. (1985). A dialectical view of personal change. *In* Gergen, K. J. and Davis, K. E.(eds.), "The Social Construction of the Person", Springer-Verlag, New York.

Harris, L. M., Cronen, V. E., and McNamee, S. (1979). An Empirical Case Study of Communication Episodes. Unpublished paper reported in Pearce and Cronen, 1980.

Kaplan, L. W. (1984). The Multi-Problem Family Phenomenon: An Interactional Perspective. Ed.D. dissertation, University of Massachusetts, Amherst.

Pearce, W. B., and Cronen, V. E. (1980). "Communication, Action and Meaning", Praeger, New York.

Shotter, J. (1981). Telling and Reporting: Prospective and Retrospective Uses of Self-Ascriptions. *In* Antaki, C. (ed.), "The Psychology of Ordinary Explanations of Social Behaviour", Academic Press, New York, pp. 157–182.

Shotter, J. (1983). The Renunciation of Theory. Lecture presented to the University of Massachusetts, Amherst.

Tomm, K. (1984a). One Perspective on the Milan Approach. Part I: Overview of Development of Theory and Practice. *Journal of Marriage and Family Therapy* 10, 113–125.

Tomm, K. (1984b). One Perspective on the Milan Approach. Part II: Description of Session Format and Interviewing Style and Interventions. *Journal of Marriage and Family Therapy* 10, 253–271.

Varela, F. J. (1975). A Calculus for Self-reference. *International Journal of General Systems* 2, 5–24.

Von Wright, G. (1951). Deontic Logic. *Mind* 60, 1–15.

Wittgenstein, L. (1953). "Philosophical Investigations", (G. E. M. Anscombe, trans.) Basil Blackwell, Oxford.

Part TWO

Teams

Chapter 8

Setting Up a Systemic Therapy Team in a Local Authority Social Services Department Area Office: How to be One Down and Still Invited to the Ball

Christopher J. Knight

This is an account of the work of a group of four social workers, Mary Barnes, Chris Knight, Anne Mhlongo and Dennis Reid, who began in April 1983 to work systemically in an area office of a Social Services Department in an inner London Borough.

I. DESCRIPTION OF THE AGENCY CONTEXT

Local authority social services departments were established following the Seebohm Committee report (1968) and the Local Authority Social Services Act (1970). The responsibility of social workers, broadly speaking, is to meet the welfare needs of individuals and families in the community, especially those deemed most in need or at risk, and they are accountable to a hierarchical management structure.

Our agency is one of five area offices which were established in May 1971 as part of the movement of services out of the town hall and into the community, and now coordinated by a central office. The area office in which we work has approximately 60 staff. Social workers are organised into four social work teams comprising on average eight social workers and a team leader. Other staff include occupational therapists, a good neighbour/volunteer organiser, home help staff, administrative staff and the area head and her deputy. The area's population is approximately 27,000 and consists of 12,000 households out of a Borough total of 79,802 households.

Referrals to the area office are for a range of social services, and it has been estimated that 50% of such referrals do not require a professional social worker's involvement (London Borough of Camden, 1983). Social work referrals come from a number of sources, either other agencies (e.g. the courts, schools, health services) or direct requests from the public. The area office serves a diverse community as regards housing, class, ethnicity and type of problem. Each social worker has a generic caseload with responsibility for a wide range of casework with individuals and families.

APPLICATIONS OF SYSTEMIC FAMILY THERAPY
ISBN 0-8089-1696-3

II.   FAMILY THERAPY IN THE AGENCY

A family therapy interest group had been established in the agency in 1975, and was seen as a specialised interest group up until the time it ended in December 1982. In 1983, in order to establish a new group, it was necessary to intervene in our own agency system, and reflexively address our position in it. I drew up an unpublished paper entitled "Preliminary statement on the setting up of a focused family therapy team/group". This statement set out the group's proposed aims and orientation, *viz.*, "to apply systems theory with a particular focus on the systemic family therapy model and related skills". It was constructed with a view to mapping out those areas which I felt had made for difficulty in the previous group and needed addressing to ensure success for the new group. Apart from specific information on the size of the group and frequency of meeting times, a list of membership requirements was itemised. The group would adopt a "team approach based on the Milan method and live supervision". Members of the group would be peers. To begin with, however, the group was to be co-convened by Anne Mhlongo and myself.

The statement included an observation that, although the proposed group would be different, it could, in fact, exist alongside a family therapy interest group of the kind that had previously existed in the agency. In other words, I was careful to connote the difference neutrally by allowing for "more of the same" alongside "trying something different" (Watzlawick *et al.*, 1974; Watzlawick, 1978). Furthermore, the statement contained guidelines on accountability which clearly acknowledged the organisational context. It was important that management approve of the group's functioning and that agreement be reached on the issue of team responsibility for the work undertaken. It was proposed that individuals would consult with their team leader about which case(s) they would bring for work within the group. The group would then look at each case to determine the most appropriate approach. Subsequent feedback to the team leader, from time to time, and clear messages on the case file would provide information that might be needed in the event of a worker's absence and a crisis requiring an agency response.

We were careful to connote positively the existing support and accountability structures. So, for example, case conferences involving a member of management, and possibly other agencies, were framed as a "resource for use by the group". One of the aims of the statement, therefore, was to create a balance between group responsibility, wherein ideas and skills would assume an equivalent status to hierarchical position, and the agency context with its accountability requirements. Given the statutory agency context, the statement needed to be sufficiently precise and structured to gain legitimacy as a "well thought out" proposal that would meet with approval from the agency management team.

III.   ENGAGING OUR HIERARCHY

Anne Mhlongo and I had an initial meeting with the area head to whom the statement and guidelines were made available. This meeting was followed by two further meetings, one with the area head and the team leaders, and a third with the team leaders only. There was some initial concern that a small closed group would arouse feelings of envy and that there would be an attempt to alter the membership or the selection procedure. However, this did not become an obstacle and the proposals and membership composition met with management's approval. We anticipated that there would be some anxiety about our method or approach with regard to a conventional understanding that "paradox" was a part of the model and might be used at every opportunity! We took the initiative in addressing this potential worry, as we hypothesised that the understanding of the "technique" was "underdeveloped" and assumed to be a simple prescription indiscriminately applied to "difficult clients". When we met with the team leaders, I raised the issue merely by saying that, for instance, we would not be prescribing non-attendance at school to school refusers, rather than entering into a complicated theoretical discussion on the meaning of paradox (Bogdan, 1982; Dell, 1981; Fisher *et al.*, 1981; Hoffman, 1981; Rosenbaum, 1982). We needed to respond to its conception as "manipulative" and to the anxiety that might be aroused in a public agency that is highly sensitive to issues of competence and public accountability.

The proposed use of live supervision/consultation was a new development in the agency (Bamford, 1982, pp. 58–59). I had recently asked my team leader to supervise live on one of my worrying cases and prepared the situation by giving him some material to read (Smith and Kingston, 1980). The introduction of this new information was a positive experience which allowed for some difference and connected with the change that was being proposed in setting up the new group with the use of live supervision/consultation. Once we had met with the management group, we started meeting as a separate group on a fortnightly basis for one and a half hours, alongside team work in pairs.

IV. CONCEPTUALISING OUR CONTEXT

It would appear from some of the current literature that an assumption is made that social workers, as systemic therapists, will necessarily find themselves in a symmetrical relationship with their own agency system. This assumption presumably is based on the premise that the systemic approach is both "different" and challenges the "status quo". A further assumption that the therapist will be engaged in changing his own context reinforces the symmetrical relationship. This relationship might be characterised by the worker feeling in a bind, since his *thinking* enables his context to be conceptualised systemically at the same time as his *practice* is contextualised by his agency system. Although the worker thinks about his agency as a system, he has, at the same time, to work within it and understand how his practice is organised by his agency. Part of the solution (adopting the systemic model) becomes part of the problem if these assumptions are not acknowledged, on one level, as "part of the problem". Once this happens, it becomes possible to clarify the difficulties that arise and to begin to perceive when and how one is organised by one's agency context and how that reality might be redefined and possibly reorganised. A different position is required of not seeking to change the system whilst working to create the conditions that will allow difference to be introduced. This position seeks to avoid the bind of prescribing to one self a role that seeks to change

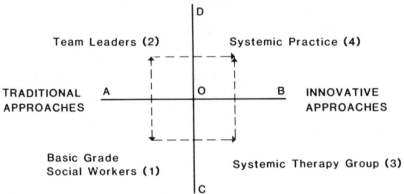

Fig. 1.

the context which one is *a part of* as if one were *apart from it*. It assumes that if change is to take place, it will follow from the introduction of difference into the system which will then allow space for systemic practice.

Figure 1 is a formulation of our group's reflexive position within the agency. The diagram is a heuristic device, mapping the reflexive position of our group within the agency. The axis COD represents the hierarchical structure from basic grade field social workers to senior management. The horizontal axis AOB represents the dimension of practice skills, for example, from traditional casework and indirect supervision to systemic family therapy and live supervision/consultation. The two dimensions identify different parts of the system's organisation and practice. As basic grade social workers (1) we first had to negotiate various boundary issues with team leaders (2) in order to establish a closed systemic therapy group (3). The quadrant COB represents the space wherein the group meets as a closed group and organises itself. The actual direct work with families—systemic practice (4)—will then be identified as taking place in the area DOB. The arrows indicate the possible movement in the system with innovative approaches being open to management as well as the group, for example, live supervision/consultation by a team leader. We conceptualise position (4) as approximating a position of "neutrality", which permits systemic therapeutic work to take place within the statutory agency context.

V.   THE APPLICATION OF SYSTEMIC THINKING

The following case illustrates our initial efforts to use a systemic model and Milan approach since the group was established.

A.   "Learning to Live Apart"

Mr. Smith, a self-employed builder in his fifties, and his son, Peter, aged 12, were referred for social work support by a hospital child psychiatry department. The hospital had assessed Peter as "school phobic" and in their referral letter expressed considerable concern for his welfare. Ms. Smith had left her husband and Peter two years previously with Peter's 14 year old stepsister, and all attempts at re-establishing contact had failed. Since his mother's departure Peter had shared his father's bed and both complained of each other's behaviour.

Our initial hypothesis was that Peter and his father were continuing the marital battle and in conflict over the loss of mother/wife and stepsister/daughter. We, as an agency, were being asked to "supervise" the father–son relationship and thereby become part of the family system and assume statutory responsibility. The referrers, however, were not clear what they were actually asking us to do (Palazzoli *et al.*, 1980a).

At the outset we set various tasks to see what difference they would make (Palazzoli *et al.*, 1978; White, 1980). We consistently positively connoted Mr. Smith's efforts to make a home for himself and Peter, as well as Peter's attendance at school and the sessions (although erratic!). When Mr. Smith, in an individual session, doubted whether Peter was being bullied at school, we suggested he pretend that his son was telling the truth and act accordingly (Madanes, 1980, 1981). After our first three sessions with Mr. Smith and Peter, followed by three with Mr. Smith, two subsequent appointments which were to be joint, were not kept. We hypothesised that we had become part of the problem and that further contact should be contingent on change. We wrote to Mr. Smith putting ourselves "one down" and stated that "only you yourself are able to make the difference that will improve your relationship whereby you can exercise authority over your son". Shortly thereafter Mr. Smith telephoned to say he agreed with our letter, thanked us, and agreed to let us know if things changed, for better or worse.

After a six week period we again heard from Mr. Smith, who had recently contacted the National Society for the Prevention of Cruelty to Children (NSPCC). We saw Mr. Smith and Peter for two further sessions and Mr. Smith once separately. Our last session with both Mr. Smith and Peter explored their triangulation with mother/wife and ourselves, incorporating the concept of distance regulation (Byng-Hall, 1980). Two subsequent appointments were not kept. We responded with a letter conveying the message that we felt that Mr. Smith and Peter had reached the stage where they did not need us to offer them another fixed appointment and that we would be very willing to see them again when they decided it was the right time. Mr. Smith contacted us afterwards to say that one of our letters had gone astray, however things were "pretty generally okay" and he would contact us in the future if the need arose.

Shortly afterwards Mr. Smith contacted us again to ask whether we would be attempting to get in touch with Peter's mother. We offered him an appointment to clarify this question which led to the conclusion that Mr. Smith would assume responsibility for efforts to reach Peter's mother, and that we would convene a review meeting in approximately four month's time. Six weeks later Mr. Smith contacted us to say that Peter had returned to his mother. During the intervening period, contact had been successfully established and, following several weekend access visits, he had agreed to Peter going to live with his mother. However, he said he now doubted his decision as being in Peter's best interests and wished to discuss the changed situation.

We have framed Mr. Smith's situation in terms of the "dilemmas of change". To date, by maintaining a neutral position, we have seen changes take place following decisions made by Mr. Smith and Peter rather than by ourselves, as might have been expected or requested by the family, our own agency or other professionals.

Our initial focus on whether we could help improve the relationship between father and son was contextualised by the assumptions of a statutory agency and the need to be clear about "who's in charge of what" (Reder, 1983). The latter was addressed in this case on three levels. Firstly, in terms of our direct work with the family, we wished to see if we could make a difference in the quality of the relationship between father and son. This meant we had to be clear about our role and not assume responsibility for Peter, but rather support their own efforts to change. Secondly, we needed to address our relationship with our own hierarchy and outside agencies in relation to our statutory responsibility and accountability. For example, we attended two case conferences *as a team*, in our capacity as "working directly with Mr. Smith and Peter", having established with our own team leader, who did not attend, that if the outside agencies were asking that we take charge in the form of statutory responsibility, we would declare our impotence and request another case conference with our team leader present. This contingency has not yet arisen. Thirdly, the therapist–consultant relationship has developed over time, and we had to work hard initially discussing our individual styles, needs and understanding of the Milan method. Our interventions are kept to a minimum and usually in the form of asking for information through circular questioning (Campbell *et al.*, 1983; Penn, 1982; Palazzoli, 1980b).

VI. SOME OBSERVATIONS ON THE RESULTS OF OUR WORK

A feature of systemic therapy is that the therapist should not expect recognition for positive change from the family/client (Hoffman, 1981). Such an expectation runs counter to the prevailing needs and motivation of social workers who hope for some recognition and/or indication of effectiveness—if not from the client, at least from the agency. This observation relates to the question of evaluation and how to assess the results of one's work.

Our group has only been meeting, at the time of writing, for one year. We are interested in our own skills development as practitioners, and in our relationship to our own agency as an autonomous peer group team. One of the questions that we have been asking ourselves is "what kind of information exchange about our work needs to take place with our colleagues at the same level in the hierarchy and management, at what point in time?" Answers to this question help ensure that the group remains a viable entity and is accepted within the system.

We have conceptualised a model involving various stages in an attempt to identify our relationship with our own agency and wider system. During *Stage One* the group is established, having studied the agency context and practice method to a sufficient degree. In the course of *Stage Two* the agency as a whole is informed that the group is meeting. This can take place on a general or specific level. Information about our group was made available to the agency during one of its regular area business meetings, as part of a general feedback about different interest groups meeting in the agency. There was also a short specific feedback to this same forum following a brief presentation by our group at the "Milan in London" workshop in July 1983. *Stage*

Three would involve an exchange of information outside the agency through, for instance, participation in workshops. *Stage Four* is seen as further feedback to the agency and to the group. This stage might involve a different form of exchange from that in Stage Two, such as the holding of a workshop or "open meeting" for those people in the agency who are particularly interested. During Stages Three/Four, feedback on cases would be incorporated.

This four-stage model implies an exchange of information either on an informal or formal level. The feedback to date from our own agency since the group has been meeting has been mainly on an informal level. Newer members of staff have approached individuals in the group with questions about whether the group was open to new members, took referrals or offered consultations. There has been some expression of "envy" that the group appears to be meeting a particular need of its members.

Recently the group has formally presented an account of its work by inviting members of our agency to one of our regular meetings, and we initiated a dialogue in response to the information we gave (Stage Four). Individual response from people who attended this feedback has been positive.

As a group of four, we have reached a position where we can reflect on our practice and use our colleagues in the group for consultations and support. We have over time introduced information strategically into our agency. For example, I asked my team leader to supervise "live" on an interview and provided reading material beforehand, and we gave selective feedback to management in the case of Mr. Smith. Requests for information from outside our agency, such as this chapter, or presentation to an outside forum, have been met with initial positive encouragement from our management. To date this recognition "from outside" has not been matched by any similar request from within our own agency.

As our clients very rarely come requesting therapy, we do not see ourselves as imposing it. We seek rather to respond isomorphically to the family and wider network, for example, by responding as closely as possible to the family's definition(s) of the situation and to their language. We are not a group to whom outside agencies would make specific referrals for "systemic family therapy". The question of our group's relationship with the wider professional network can only be addressed when other professionals have been/are also involved in the group's cases, and if/when we choose to give information about our approach. For example, in the case of Mr. Smith and Peter, the only information we gave the professional network about our work was that we were meeting with the family to see if we could make a difference in their relationship.

The effect of applying systemic thinking has increased our interest and enthusiasm for the work, and as a group we would wish to increase our knowledge of how our practice differs from other groups in similar settings.

VII. CONCLUSION

We see ourselves, as a group, experimentally asking the question: "Is it possible to work/think systemically using the Milan method in a social services department?" While further questions are raised, we answer the question affirmatively in terms of our group's experience to date.

Although a systemic approach might not suit therapists who must be liked at all costs, to work as a team requires those elements of sharing and trust that have been mentioned by other practitioners (Boscolo and Cecchin, 1982; Campbell *et al.*, 1983; Palazzoli, 1983; Whiffen and Byng-Hall, 1982). A parallel level of trust has also to be established in relation to the agency hierarchy.

The method in its questioning and tracking of relationship patterns can be usefully incorporated into the general practice of field social workers and, I would suggest, their supervisors. It can be expected, however, that those workers unfamiliar with the method might at first experience some dissonance due to the discipline involved, particularly in terms of asking or being asked questions.

The Milan method is typified by its assumption of neutrality which, some might argue, is inappropriate for a statutory social services agency context. However, a considerable amount of work within a statutory agency does not lead to the invocation of legal or other powers. The concept of neutrality, moreover, can be used as an overall criterion whereby to evaluate whether work with a family is consistent with the Milan model or not. On the level of practice, circular questioning, for example, can be used as a means of maintaining neutrality.

In relation to statutory work, the use of statutory powers means that work in a particular case can no longer be described as neutral in respect of the Milan model. In the case example described above, were we to have taken Peter into council care, or to do so at some future point in time, our relationship as therapists to the family would change. Nonetheless action that is determined by the requirements of the statutory agency role does not preclude use of systemic thought.

The challenge we face as practitioners in the statutory social services is to clarify the aforementioned differences on the levels of theory and practice with a view to developing our therapeutic skills and effectiveness.

REFERENCES

Bamford, T. (1982). "Managing Social Work". Tavistock Publications, London.

Bogdan, J. L. (1982). Paradoxical Communication as Interpersonal Influence. *Family Process* 21, 443–452.

Boscolo, L., and Cecchin, G. (1982). Training in Systemic Therapy at the Milan Centre. *In* Whiffen, R., and Byng-Hall, J. eds., "Family Therapy Supervision: Recent Developments in Practice". Academic Press, London and New York, pp. 153–165.

Byng-Hall, J. (1980). Symptom Bearer as Marital Distance Regulator: Clinical Implication. *Family Process* 19, 355–365.

Campbell, D., Reder, P., Draper, R., and Pollard, D. (1983). Working with the Milan Method: Twenty Questions. *In* "Occasional Papers on Family Therapy, No. 1". Institute of Family Therapy, London.

Dell, P. F. (1981). Some Irreverent Thoughts on Paradox. *Family Process* 20, 37–51.

Fisher, L., Anderson, A., and Jones, J. (1981). Types of Paradoxical Interventions and Indications/Contraindications for Use in Clinical Practice. *Family Process* 20, 25–35.

Hoffman, L. (1981). "Foundations of Family Therapy: A Conceptual Framework for Systems Change". Basic Books, New York.

Local Authority Social Services Act. (1970). London, ch. 42.

London Borough of Camden, Department of Social Services. (November 1983). Sample Case Flow Analysis for Period 1.4.83–30.6.83. (Data Control: Fieldwork Management).

Madanes, C. (1980). Protection, Paradox and Pretending. *Family Process* **19**, 73–87.

Madanes, C. (1981). "Strategic Family Therapy", Jossey-Bass, San Francisco.

Palazzoli, M., Boscolo, L., Cecchin, G., and Prata, G. (1978). A Ritualized Prescription in Family Therapy: Odd Days and Even Days. *Journal of Marriage and Family Counselling* **4** 3–9.

Palazzoli, M., Boscolo, L., Cecchin, G., and Prata, G. (1980a). The Problem of the Referring Person. *Journal of Marital and Family Therapy* **3**, 3–9.

Palazzoli, M., Boscolo, L., Cecchin, G., and Prata, G. (1980b). Hypothesizing-Circularity–Neutrality: Three Guidelines for the Conductor of the Session. *Family Process* **19**, 3–12.

Palazzoli, M. (1983). The Emergence of a Comprehensive Systems Approach. *Journal of Family Therapy* **5**, 165–177.

Reder, P. (1983). Disorganised Families and the Helping Professions: "Who's in Charge of What?" *Journal of Family Therapy* **5**, 23–36.

Rosenbaum, R. L. (1982). Paradox as Epistemological Jump. *Family Process* **21**, 85–90.

Seebohm, F. (chairman). (1968). Report of the Committee on Local Authority and Allied Personal Social Services. London, HMSO, Cmnd 3703.

Smith, D., and Kingston, P. (1980). Live Supervision without a One-way Screen. *Journal of Family Therapy* **2**, 379–387.

Watzlawick, P., Weakland, J. H., and Fisch, R. (1974). "Change: Principles of Problem Formation and Problem Resolution". W. W. Norton, New York and London.

Watzlawick, P. (1978). "The Language of Change: Elements of Therepeutic Communication". Basic Books, New York.

Whiffen, R., and Byng-Hall, J. (1982). "Family Therapy Supervision: Recent Developments in Practice". Academic Press, London and New York.

White, M. (1980). Systemic Task Setting in Family Therapy. *Australian Journal of Family Therapy* **1**, 171–182.

Chapter 9

Milan in the East End: Systemic Therapy with Lower-Income and Multi-Agency Families

Peter Reder

I. INTRODUCTION

The most detailed accounts of therapy with lower-income families and families variously called "multi-problem", "disorganised" or "underorganised" come from the Philadelphia Child Guidance Clinic (e.g. Minuchin, Auerswald, King & Rabinowitz, 1964; Minuchin, Montalvo, Guerney, Rosman & Schumar, 1967; Minuchin & Montalvo, 1967; Aponte, 1976). This chapter is an interim report by a team experimenting with the Milan method of systemic therapy for such cases. The team is based in an East London child guidance clinic and at the time of writing has been together for about one year and seen over one hundred families.[1]

I shall describe the context in which we work—with special reference to our client population—and how we modify the Milan method to suit these lower-income families. I shall summarise our clinical impressions of families who present a number of problems to multiple helping agencies (for whom we prefer the term *multi-agency* families) and illustrate how our work with them places special emphasis on the interrelationship between the family and their professional network.

II. SETTING

The Borough of Newham lies to the east of the City of London. Its population is approximately three-quarters British-born families long resident in the area and one-quarter families with roots in the Indian subcontinent, the West Indies and Africa. Unemployment, poor housing, high-rise council flats, large families and single-parent families are all prominent features of the Borough, and Newham appears second out of all England boroughs on an index of urban deprivation (Department of the Environment Inner Cities Directorate, 1983).

---

[1] The author and Michael Owen formed the nucleus of the team; we were soon joined by Eduardo Pitchon and more recently by Jennifer Greenwood.

APPLICATIONS OF SYSTEMIC FAMILY THERAPY
ISBN 0-8089-1696-3

The clinic is a multi-disciplinary, National Health Service, district facility offering assessment, advice and treatment for psychological and behavioural problems shown by children. We are a secondary care agency, tending to see families some time after the onset of the child's symptoms and usually after one or more primary care professionals have seen them.

The team is one of three in the clinic. We came together to further our interest in the Milan method by applying it in the majority of our cases. However, the (rightly) reserved response from other clinic staff quickly taught us to offer a service consistent with our context, instead of an apparently specialised and exclusive *therapy*. We needed to redefine ourselves as a child guidance clinic team in which systemic therapy was available as one possible treatment. We also tried to be unselective of cases allocated to the team and this has helped us maintain satisfactory relationships within the clinic.

We now have the advantage of a one-way screen, but before this was installed the observing members of the team sat in one corner of the interviewing room. We had to send the family back to the waiting area during team discussions, and the screen allows us to take many more breaks and to continually revise our hypotheses during sessions.

A. The Continuum of "Lower-Income"—"Multi-Agency" Family Significant Systems

We use the term *significant system* for those individuals who appear to be actors in the symptomatic "game" and are likely to be affected by any changes brought about through treatment. We can identify this significant system extending beyond the nuclear family, because all families show some important relationship with extended family, with informal neighbourhood support, and with professional helping agents (Bott, 1957, 1971; Auerswald, 1968; Erickson, 1975; Palazzoli *et al.*, 1980). Different families show variations in the balance of these relationships, and on this basis we conceptualise a continuum of lower-income multi-agency family significant systems.

At one point on the continuum are the majority of lower-income families who have strong extended family ties and valuable informal helping networks, and only make temporary connections with professionals at moments of crisis. They contrast with the multi-agency families who seem to become locked in with helping agents. In between lie those families who evolve a trusting and close relationship with one or more professional workers, but with mutual flexibility in contact. While the lower-income family appears able to move on in its "spiral development" (as described by Hoffman, 1981), the multi-agency family can be considered developmentally stuck and connected to a wide professional network.

B. The Lower-Income Family System

The findings of Young & Willmott (1957) that East London families maintain the strongest intergenerational bond through the mother–maternal grandmother relationship still seems to hold true today. Frequently we have found that the maternal grandmother lives close by and holds influential views on the problem—including our treatment.

In times of crisis, a Newham family often seeks out one of the children's school teachers who, reciprocally, is prepared to support and advise mothers on parenting problems. Social workers, education welfare officers, school medical officers and health visitors equally may be turned to and, in time, the family and the helper can develop a strong bond. It seems to be families in which the mother feels unsupported by her mother or husband, or the father is absent, who behave as though they are only functional with the help of this professional person (whom I have referred to elsewhere as the "supplementing" worker—Reder, 1983). We have been so impressed by the strength of relationships that can evolve between a symptomatic family and a Borough professional that we always hypothesise that the referring person (and possibly a number of his/her primary care colleagues) is part of the significant system.

C. The Multi-Agency Family System

If a common rule for East London lower-income families seems to be "stay connected to the neighbourhood and extended family network because we can help each other", that of the multi-agency family appears instead as "stay connected to professional helpers". They certainly give the impression of being more mobile as families, developing fewer stable connections in any one neighbourhood, and usually have severed links with families or origin. When developmental crises occur, such as the mother has a new partner or the social worker leaves, symptoms most readily surface around basic caring and controlling of the children: these are amongst the most vulnerable and easily noticed aspects of family life and are a guaranteed communication to concerned professionals in the network.

The special nature of a network of helping professionals is that members have strong emotional reactions to the presenting problem and (commendably) passionate personal investments in attempted solutions. Also, each professional worker has responsibilities and obligations which organise his response to the problem: these obligations may be statutory (e.g. a social worker holding a Care Order on a child), legal (e.g. the need to obtain consent from both legal parents before instituting treatment), professional (e.g. maintenance of confidentiality), assumed (e.g. the belief that he is responsible for the life of his patient/client), or imposed (e.g. the fear of critical newspaper reports).

Therefore, in the circular sequence of events, it becomes impossible to know whether the family keeps the helping-agency network actively connected to it or whether it is the professionals in the network who, once activated, become caught in processes which inhibit changes of their involvement (see Reder & Kraemer, 1980; Reder, 1983).

III. WORKING WITH THE LOWER-INCOME FAMILY SYSTEM

We are still learning how to adapt our language to that of our families (see Bernstein, 1964, 1971) but have noted that the interviewer must avoid using abstract concepts and instead ask about activity: "Who does what to whom?", "What does the next person do?", "What happens in practice?", "How many times has that happened?", etc. Since the children often reply "I don't know" to our questions we pay attention to analogic communication—eye contact, body posture—and any discrepancies between analogic and verbal communication.

We make our interventions as economical, clear and brief as possible using simple language. Because the family tends to see solutions to problems in terms of activity, we end with some concrete advice or specific recommendation. For example, we might suggest "keep a record of the number of times . . .", or "Next time that happens, father should handle it instead of mother . . .", or "Do not change anything for the time being because if you did there's a danger that . . .". The work of de Shazer (1982) has been helpful to us in devising interventions because of his emphasis on positive connotation, simple prescriptions and regular tasks designed to break up a repetitive cycle of interaction. We have had a noticeable increase in reattendance rates by the simple, yet concrete, act of handing the family an appointment card at the end of the session.

Our families anticipate a brief, problem-solving treatment which will take only a few meetings and contain specific advice. We have reduced the length of each session (except the first consultation) to about one hour and we see our families for an average of only four sessions.

Both families and referrers expect specific recommendations from the clinic, including a decision whether treatment is being offered or not. We have felt it important to distinguish between consultation and therapy, and if we are offering family therapy we specifically say so and we only suggest "come along for further meetings", or "for a review of how things are" if there are clinical indications for remaining vague (such as a vague definition of the problem by the family). The need to be clear about a treatment offer prevents the team unwittingly trying to smuggle in an intervention in competition with the help already available from the referrer: a self-made trap we very easily fell into at the beginning of our work.

For example, a teacher referred us an adolescent boy whose behaviour at school caused the teacher much concern. He was already seeing a counsellor and education welfare officer at school, and when we interviewed the family they all showed contempt for the idea of clinic help. However, under pressure of concern from the teacher and our wish to appear helpful we kept offering them appointments to "monitor whether they were ready for therapy in the clinic". The eventual changes in this system were a demoralised team and contempt for our efforts from both family and teacher! We realized that we should have defined further family meetings as inappropriate and turned our attention to the school system's attempts to handle the boy.

Our intervention to families referred by Borough professionals must be sensitive to the relationship between family and referrer. Some families do not believe there is a problem but attend the clinic in order to maintain a loyal bond with the referrer (fearing they will lose his help if they fail to keep the appointment with us). At the end of these consultations we positively connote the family, the referrer's concern and the importance of the relationship between family and referrer.

During an initial consultation with a single mother and her young daughter we discovered that their health visitor had encouraged the mother to seek advice on her handling of her child. The team concluded that the mother benefited from a dependent and a long-term relationship with the health visitor and that both the mother and child showed normal behaviour in the session. We finally said to them, "We feel (the health visitor) has been very helpful to you, including suggesting you come here. We are glad you followed her advice, despite believing there was nothing wrong, because from what we see today we can reassure you all that things are OK. We suggest you let her know our conclusions, and you and she continue meeting in the same way, so long as it is helpful."

Alternatively, the family may have been "sent" against their will by a referrer who is more concerned about the child than are his parents. We try to avoid a symmetrical struggle with any of them about the supposed problem, but if it is impossible to remain neutral we attempt to engage the family through a demonstration of confusion at the referral and questions such as "What do you think (the referrer) had in mind when he told you to come here?" If further work with the family does not seem possible (as in the case referred by the head-teacher), we then reply to the referrer positively connoting his concern and saying we would be pleased to discuss his concerns with him.

Such experiences have led us to start all family consultations with "Whose idea was it for you to come here?", "What was your reaction to that suggestion?" and "What were you hoping for from us?" Increasingly we are inviting the referrer/co-referrers to the first consultation so that we can circular question about the relationship between the family and him/them and we give our final intervention to the family and professional/s simultaneously.

Hoffman (1981) feels that paradoxical interventions are effective when the family finds itself in a "sweat box" and must somehow change to escape the tension. The referrer can act as a back door out of the sweat box and so neutralize our intervention: for example, general practitioners have a direct link in to the clinic through psychiatrists which can bypass the therapist, as do teachers through psychologists and field social workers through clinic social workers. We are always aware of the shadow of the referrer and we only use a paradoxical type of intervention when his role can be satisfactorily explained and addressed.

A head-teacher referred a pupil to the clinic for the third time in four years, this time for aggressive behaviour on the way home from school. The mother was a single parent but her son's behaviour resulted in sustained contact between her and the concerned head-teacher. A series of family interviews led us to an hypothesis that the mother still longed for the positive regard from a man that she felt was lacking from her father. When he had remarried five years ago she had turned to be even closer to her son. Despite adopting many characteristics of his grandfather (e.g. "irresponsible behaviour") the son was unable to satisfy his mother's needs, but through his symptoms he had found a way of bringing her closer to a kindly and concerned man (his head-teacher). We condensed this circular story as the introduction of our intervention, finally advising mother and child to discuss before the next meeting "when might be the right time for the boy to take a rest from his work?"

IV. WORKING WITH THE MULTI-AGENCY FAMILY SYSTEM

In our work with multi-agency families we have learned to assume that the significant professionals include anyone who is likely to take, or influence, a clinical decision in relation to the case. The referrer of a multi-agency family customarily communicates urgency and concern over the care and control of the children. We usually telephone the referrer back and ask "Who else is involved?" and "With whom have you discussed this case?" It is particularly important to gather as much information as possible before seeing the family so that we can prepare a satisfactory hypothesis and we therefore call our own network meeting. We ask all professional members of the significant system to be present at this meeting and ask them about the family's life cycle, the history of professional involvements and the developing pattern of roles and relationships in the family/network system. We are always interested in the nature of the current crisis and everyone's response to it and the recent (or impending) changes in the system. We need to know basic legal information, such as what court cases are pending and who are the child's legal parents (being the legal decision-takers they must be present at future meetings; see Byng-Hall & Bruggen, 1974). Our systemic picture is completed by asking everyone to define his expectations of our involvement.

After we have concluded this information-gathering meeting the team meets to develop a working hypothesis. This hypothesis aims to explain the role played by the various professionals for the family and to arrive at a systemic description of the family/network and its rules. Our hypothesis tries to explain the current crisis and suggest what role the clinic therapist is being invited to take in the system. We believe that the network's referral often contains a covert message to the therapist to "be on the same hierarchical level as the rest of us in this family/network system and help retain the coherence of a changing system". In order to be an effective agent of change we feel we must work from a *meta* position to the family and the network, even if our response is initially confusing to them and discordant with their expectations.

This early phase of our contact with the case, therefore, involves the network and therapist struggling for control of who will define the rules of their working relationship. During these (undeclared) negotiations there is a real danger of symmetry between the network and the therapist and it is vitally important for us to retain a friendly, cooperative and professional relationship with our network colleagues. We strive, as Mara Selvini-Palazzoli counsels, to "never, *never* become indignant!" and we try to treat with respect all communications from the network.

A social worker asked us to see an adolescent boy who had sexually assaulted a little girl, to the concern of his parents, school teacher, education welfare officer, social worker and her senior, and policeman from the juvenile bureau. We invited all of them to a first consultation. The team heard of incompatible "agendas" from different members of the professional network: the social worker hoped to join our prime worker as co-therapist, the policeman needed to consider prosecution and the teacher, education welfare officer and senior social worker suggested removing the boy from home to an assessment centre (which was acceptable to his parents). Eventually all network professionals agreed with this majority view and we decided to hold back offering family therapy, even though we felt it could be beneficial. It seemed that we had helped the extended system reach a common decision and so an offer of therapy from us only would have compounded the original muddle.

It is ideal to invite all members of the significant system to a session (also suggested by Auerswald, 1971; Erickson *et al.*, 1974; Waters, 1983). However, we sometimes try to economise by holding a smaller meeting and reporting our final message to sufficient members that it will have a ripple effect around to the others. We would choose the most significantly connected members of the professional network and write separately to each one to invite him to a meeting with the family. We write separately to the family.

Our experience of working this way is that approximately half of the invited families attend and we can conduct a session using the one-way screen and ending with an intervention to the whole system. When the family fails to attend we hold a brief interview with the professionals who have come, enquire about the relationship between themselves, the family and the clinic and we deliver a final intervention which outlines our systemic understanding of the problem. We end with some variation of the theme that "this does not seem to be the right time for the family to come. . . . It seems that you are the most helpful person to them at the moment and we suggest that you continue with the good work you have been doing.", or "We suggest that all of you hold a series of meetings with the family to discuss when might be the right time for them to come". We try to avoid suggesting that the professional should become *less* involved with the family, feeling that they as a system are best able to decide this together.

A teacher who consulted us had become so involved as a surrogate parent that he had recently spent five hours driving around the neighbourhood looking for a pupil. The boy had allegedly run away from home but had also written to the teacher threatening suicide unless his school suspension for misbehaviour was lifted. We decided to spell out the teacher's dilemma as we saw it. We first outlined our systemic formulation of the family history and current problem, and added, "It seems to us that on the one hand you could continue to offer more of your help, but when would you have time for your real job of teaching and for a life of your own? On the other hand you could become less involved, but you are likely to feel guilty that you are responsible for the boy's life. We do not know how to advise you for sure, but wonder whether, as things stand at the moment, you might consider trying to do more." The teacher nodded acceptance of each part of our message and left the meeting looking relieved but thoughtful.

Usually (as in the above case) the professionals show understanding of our conclusions and express appreciation that we have placed their roles in a new context. In addition, if the family does eventually come to the clinic it is with much less drama and anxiety than was generated in the original referral and the multi-agency network also tends to be less pressingly connected.

V. EFFECTS

While our work changes and adapts to our context, colleagues, referrers and clients are slowly adjusting to the existence of a systemic team. It is premature to assess the long-term effects of our work, but so far we have received positive and negative feedback, including clinic colleagues asking to join the team and Borough professionals requesting us to teach and advise them.

We have seen many examples of the effect new information has on systems. A few families have reacted to our approach with disappointment that we have not provided what they expected and either have contacted an alternative service or returned to their referrer. Some members of the Borough's education system have expressed concern that their hoped-for intervention was no longer reliably provided in the clinic. We take any criticism seriously and try to learn from it and, if appropriate, we modify our technique. Above all, we need to respond to their responses. We try to adopt a low-key stance within the clinic, but our pride sometimes lets us down! We have attempted to make more direct contact with Borough professionals and avoid appearing to be an exclusive and superiorly "meta" team. We are prepared to discuss our work informally with them and have needed to reply to puzzled or critical referrers: "We found this family's problem difficult to deal with and we shall need your help over some time to see whether our work with them will bring results."

VI. CONCLUSIONS

The Milan method is about mapping systemic processes and giving them new meaning. Therefore the team's work would be seriously incomplete without a continual review of the recursive communications between ourselves and our wider systems. We have found it useful to "map our ecosystem", in which we trace the history of the clinic in order to identify major life-cycle events and apparent "rules" which govern roles and professional transactions. We also examine the repetitive themes in the life of the Borough and in relationships among professionals and between professionals and the population. Through this the team has learned to accommodate to existing "rules" and not confront them head-on.

In a sense, the writing of this chapter is part of the review process. In it I have chosen to focus on just a few important features, e.g. the client population and relationships with our referral network. This information has helped the team refine its approach and develop context-appropriate strategies and therefore remain consistent with the basic tenets of systemic therapy.

REFERENCES

Aponte, H. (1976). Underorganization in the Poor Family. *In* Guerin, P. J. (ed.), "Family Therapy: Theory and Practice". Gardner, New York, pp. 220–232.

Auerswald, E. H. (1968). Interdisciplinary vs Ecological Approach. *Family Process* 7, 202–215.

Auerswald, E. H. (1971). Families, Change, and the Ecological Perspective. *Family Process* 10, 263–280.

Bernstein, B. (1964). Social Class, Speech Systems and Psychotherapy. *British Journal of Sociology* 15, 54–64.

Bernstein, B. (1971) Social Class, Language and Socialization. *In* "Class, Codes and Controls, Volume 1: Theoretical Studies towards a Sociology of Language". Routledge & Kegan Paul, London, pp. 170–189.

Bott, E. (1957). "Family and Social Network: Roles, Norms, and External Relations in Ordinary Urban Families". Tavistock, London.

Bott, E. (1971). Families and Crisis. *In* Sutherland, J. D. (ed.), "Towards Community Mental Health". Tavistock, London, pp. 17–30.

Byng-Hall, J., and Bruggen, P. (1974). Family Admission Decisions as a Therapeutic Tool. *Family Process* 13, 443–459.

Department of the Environment Inner Cities Directorate. (1983). "A Census Information Note No. 2: Urban Deprivation". London, HMSO.

de Shazer, S. (1982). "Patterns of Brief Psychotherapy: An Ecosystemic Approach". Guilford, New York.

Erickson, G. D. (1975). The Concept of Personal Network in Clinical Practice. *Family Process* 14, 487–498.

Erickson, G., Rachlis, R., and Tobin, M. (1974). Combined Family and Service Network Intervention. *The Social Worker (Canada)*, **Winter, No. 41,** 276–283.

Hoffman, L. (1981). "Foundations of Family Therapy: A Conceptual Framework for Systems Change". Basic Books, New York.

Minuchin, S., Auerswald, E., King, C. H., and Rabinowitz, C. (1964). The Study and Treatment of Families that Produce Multiple Acting-Out Boys. *American Journal of Orthopsychiatry* 34, 125–133.

Minuchin, S., and Montalvo, B. (1967). Techniques for Working with Disorganized Low Socioeconomic Families. *American Journal of Orthopsychiatry* 37, 880–887.

Minuchin, S., Montalvo, B., Guerney, B. G., Rosman, B. L., and Schumer, F. (1967). "Families of the Slums: An Exploration of their Structure and Treatment". Basic Books, New York.

Palazzoli, M., Boscolo, L., Cecchin, G., and Prata, G. (1980). The Problem of the Referring Person. *Journal of Marital and Family Therapy* 6, 3–9.

Reder, P. (1983). Disorganized Families and the Helping Professions: "Who's in Charge of What?" *Journal of Family Therapy* 5, 23–36.

Reder, P., and Kraemer, S. (1980). Dynamic Aspects of Professional Collaboration in Child Guidance Referral. *Journal of Adolescence* 3, 165–173.

Waters, J. (1983). Giving the Family Credit for Being Experts about Themselves. *Community Care*, **May 12th (No. 460),** 36–37.

Young, M., and Willmott, P. (1957). "Family and Kinship in East London". Routledge & Kegan Paul, London.

Chapter 10

Systemic Family Therapy in a Day Assessment Centre for Juveniles

Arthur J. O'NEIL

I. DESCRIPTION OF AGENCY

Whitefield House Assessment Centre was set up to service the Juvenile Court in the Greater Belfast area to provide assessment for children attending daily. This followed a decision by the Northern Ireland office to remove assessment from Lisnevin Training School (C.H.E.) and replace it with the day assessment facility which began in October 1977. This paper demonstrates that in an agency of this nature, systemic thinking and the Milan model of family therapy in particular can be applied to give an overview of a child (who is attending the centre) and the family, and the therapist, and the nature of the intervention made. The implications of introducing this model to an agency and its effects on clients, teams, referring agents and the wider context of Whitefield House are described.

Three main agencies make referrals to the unit, normally on the basis of a court recommendation. The court also makes referrals in opposition to or without an agency recommendation. The unit will also accept referrals without direction from the court, as long as the client is the subject of some form of statutory order. The agency does not have any statutory responsibility for taking referrals, this is done in court on a contractual basis, with parents and children having the right to refuse referral and seek alternative disposal. In a case where a care order exists, the agent holding that order retains statutory responsibilities.

There is a wide variety of reasons for referrals ranging from seriously delinquent to welfare cases where children are in need of care protection and control. A large percentage of referrals have associated school problems. Research which compares Whitefield population with that of the training schools (C.H.E.'s) demonstrates that there is a significant overlap between the two groups in terms of offences and problematic behaviour (McAuley, 1982).

II. ORGANISATION OF THE AGENCY

Whitefield operates on a team basis. Each team has responsibility for the assessment and treatment of up to 16 referrals at any one time. Over the last three years each team developed its own modus operandi, supported and encouraged by management. This acceptance was encouraged to a greater or lesser degree by team leaders who had an investment in pursuing approaches of their own interest even

APPLICATIONS OF SYSTEMIC FAMILY THERAPY
ISBN 0-8089-1696-3

though they might conflict with the management view of what was an appropriate model of work with families and the agency belief system in general. This distance from senior management enabled teams to have the space necessary to work their chosen way. Relationships within teams are necessarily consensual and team units tend to be cohesive. Relationships within the overall staff group can be tense, however, and levels of conflict are high (McAuley, 1982).

A. Procedure on Referrals

When an agent makes a recommendation to court which is accepted, our intake team is informed immediately. (Whitefield has a court officer in attendance at the Belfast Juvenile Court to expedite this procedure.) They contact the child's parents quickly to allay fears and make reception arrangements. The main intervention is family therapy in our team and we take a systemic overview of each referral prior to contact with family. This is developed from an initial conference, when all the information available is collected and a working systemic hypothesis is created. This hypothesis takes into consideration the identified problem as seen by the referring agent and gives a basis for the first session with the family.

The initial conference can give information regarding the position of the referring agent in the system. Victor was referred for theft and glue-sniffing and the referring agent reported that work needed to be focussed on this aspect of his behaviour. Our hypothesis suggested that Victor (aged 16) needed to stay a child in order to give his mother some responsibility and purpose in life. He could not pass 16 years, since she had a break-up with her own father at 16 and got pregnant. This initial view was accepted by the referring agency. However mother then began to complain to them that enough was not being done with regard to Victor's glue-sniffing.

Another problem, gambling addiction, was then presented by the agent and family as focus for work. Our subsequent hypothesis was that this family needed problems in order to maintain a comfortable distance in relationships. This was not acceptable to the agency system and further negotiation was required at a higher level in the agency in order to achieve a position and space where we could work with the family system, which included the referring agent.

This experience taught us to give greater consideration to views expressed by agents. A lack of regard for their interpretations of the problems tended to encourage them to "sabotage" therapy which conflicted with their own views of the case. The situation with Victor was contained by discussing the addiction problems with him and relating the information to the family system, e.g. "by using your dole money, how do you show your mother that you are still very young". "I can't live on my money, I spend it in one day". "Does your mother agree that you cannot handle money well"? "Yes". After a few sessions the "addictions" disappeared to be replaced by a different problem, i.e. bad temper fits. In effect by dealing with the presenting problem with the client individually and relating it to our hypothesis we were intervening at a level with the client and another level with the family.

Our solution to referrals of this nature is to carefully explore the position of the agent in each referral (Palazzoli et al., 1980a). Some agents when they came to Whitefield expected behaviour modification, individual counselling and re-education for their clients; anticipated control of therapy and were not prepared for the systemic approach. Others expected clear definition of the goals of therapy and since it is not possible to predict the course which changes may take nor to predict the unique solutions which families find, we could only explain the original aim of therapy, which is to challenge or perturb the family system and then step back and allow the family to reorganise itself in its own particular way. The last example given attempts to demonstrate how we managed the referring agent's response in order to avoid symmetrical conflict or rejection by the referrer of Whitefield in general. Other strategies are also used to maintain a balance between ourselves and the referring agency in the form of involvement in case discussion and in some cases in the form of observing family sessions. We also provide progress report either verbal or written and this gives us the opportunity to report a meta-view of the system. All staff in the agency arrange and contribute to seminars and workshops with colleagues outside.

III.   EFFECTS OF MODEL ON CLIENT AND CONTEXT

The introduction of the systemic model has had quite an extensive effect on the clients referred for assessment. It is our view that clients get a better deal as far as therapeutic change is concerned, since the model by nature deals with second order change (Watzlawick *et al.*, 1967) as opposed to symptom removal, which is the nature of brief therapy work. A recent review of the cases in which this model was used reveals that we were better equipped to tackle serious problems and create change than in previous cases whereby established problems were presented when a symptom removal approach was used.

As the model provides an important conceptual framework (Boscolo and Cecchin, 1982) for the understanding of behaviour in a systems context, it is useful in our situation because the presenting problem in the family is usually the child referred by the court and he can come to understand his bizarre behaviour as neither "mad nor bad" but appropriate at that time in the family context. Our experience has been that much of the work done in this way has a longer lasting effect than was previously the case. Contact with children in a family worked with over one year ago has revealed that they had reconsidered many of the ideas and interventions made during therapy and have reported that some began to make sense only after six months or a year. We would suggest that as a result there is a "transfer of understanding" from one situation to another, i.e. from family situation to peer or workmate situation.

In the specific context of Whitefield, attempting to "marry" the two ideologies of psychotherapy and systemic family therapy has not been easy, but the development of a way of taking an overview without oversimplifying a complex picture has been beneficial. It would appear then that if individual interventions such as the psycho-analytic input are considered as information about the system, and their effects on the whole system monitored by the team, then it is possible to maintain a meta-view where interventions based on different epistemologies can co-exist.

As the team became more confident in the use of this model, members became aware of an unusual effect which occurred. It had become much easier to seek consultation elsewhere when faced with "stuckness". Undoubtedly this is also associated with the team feeling more secure and competent, but the fact which has a large bearing on the matter is that it is easier to admit to being inducted into a family's system and therefore to being powerless to affect change, than to admit that as a team we did not know what to do next. With hindsight the freedom to "declare one's impotence" (Palazzoli *et al.*, 1978) to a family has proved beneficial to the team in general in a search for solutions to family crises; thus the resolution of team conflict allows the team to feel that it is not unprofessional or inexpert to be wrong, giving a "framework" to legitimise therapeutic mistakes.

When a report is required for court it is the expectation of the agency that the family see at first hand what is written about them. This caused the team a great deal of concern since by nature, in order to fulfill its purpose, the report needed to show some improvement in the family's functioning; but this interfered with the neutral stance of the team vis a vis the family and the technique of being pessimistic about any improvement. Our initial solution was to delay until near the end of therapy. (One choice open to us was to inform the family that we were writing to the court and explain in vague terms what was being said, but that was considered unethical and not acceptable to the agency.) Recently we have considered the option of writing a report from a meta-view. The report would then contain a systemic formulation and a review of alternative solutions, listing the disadvantages and advantages of each.

IV. CONCLUSION

The most significant aspects of "change" have been the provision of a conceptual framework which now includes many of the previously unrelated aspects of the work and the move from "symptom removal" in the short term to systemic reorganisation incorporating second order change. It would also appear that as this epistemological model changes families' ways of thinking about themselves by widening their context, a similar process has occurred with the team and agency in general! Campbell *et al.* (1983) write that as any new information to a family which would lead to change is experienced as disruptive to the current order, an enthusiastic proponent of the systemic approach to families and referrals is likely to meet equally strong counter arguments. They continue, "The proponent will need to have sufficient experience, confidence and clinical autonomy and be prepared to introduce the ideas slowly and with humility with the message that colleagues should not think of changing their established way of working!" (p. 40). Our introduction has been slow, but perhaps we were a little short on the *humility*.

REFERENCES

Boscolo, L., and Cecchin, G. (1982). Training in Systemic Therapy at the Milan Centre. *In* Whiffen, R., and Byng-Hall, J. (eds.), "Family Therapy Supervision: Recent Developments in Practice". Academic Press, London, pp. 153–165.

Campbell, D., Reder, P., Draper, R., and Pollard, D. (1983). "Working with the Milan Model: Twenty Questions". Institute of Family Therapy, London.

McAulay, M. (1982). A Report on Whitefield House (An unpublished paper).

Palazzoli, M. (1980). Why a Long Interval between Sessions? The Therapeutic Control of the Family Therapist Supra System. *In* Andolfi, M., and Zwerling, I. (eds.), "Dimensions of Family Therapy". Guilford, New York, pp. 161–170.

Palazzoli, M., Boscolo, L., Cecchin, G., and Prata, G. (1980a). The Problem of the Referring Person. *Journal of Marital and Family Therapy* **6**, 3–9.

Palazzoli, M., Boscolo, L., Cecchin, G., and Prata, G. (1980b). Hypothesising, Circularity, Neutrality: Three Guidelines for the Conductor of the Session. *Family Process* **19**, 3–12.

Palazzoli, M., Boscolo, L., Cecchin, G., and Prata, G. (1978). "Paradox and Counterparadox". Jason Aaronson, New York.

Watzlawick, P., Beavin, J., and Jackson, D. (1967). "The Pragmatics of Human Communication". W. W. Norton, New York.

Chapter 11

Systemic Family Work Within a Community Mental Health Centre by a Community Psychiatric Nursing Team: By Tradition...?

Jean-Pierre Parmainteny, John Mangan, Juliette Lusted,
Eileen Sundaram and John Berry

Over the past three years a group of community psychiatric nurses (CPN's) in this South Coast health district have worked part-time as a team treating families. The CPN service is an integral part of mental health services for the adult population, excluding the elderly, and is mental health centre based. Although in the more affluent South of England, the social need indicators of the area are relatively high. A range of treatments and care are provided by the centre to respond to the diverse mental health needs of the local population.

The origins of community psychiatric nursing lie in the advances in chemotherapy and medical treatments for psychiatric disorder and in the drive to reduce bed numbers in the large psychiatric institutions, an objective embodied in the 1959 Mental Health Act. The first CPN's in this country were referred to as out-patient nurses and their role was clearly defined. As registered mental nurses with experience in acute psychiatry they were seen as well qualified to assess the patient's mental state, monitor the effects of medication and to detect and remedy deficiencies in personal care. Nurses worked in the community under the direction of a consultant psychiatrist and remained on the staff of the psychiatric hospital and within its medical/nursing and administrative framework. With an increase in the number of nurses working in the community and with the philosophy of developing mental health services focused on prevention and early detection, so the trend to offer direct referral access to CPN's by general medical practitioners (GP) grew.

The new role for the CPN brought with it new and different demands which were embodied in the change of referral pattern to the service. In 1979 six CPN's received a relatively small number of referrals (150). All of these were known to the consultant psychiatrist, many had a long history of psychiatric disorder and some had a history of hospital admissions. The wording of the referral tended to be prescriptive and focused on individual treatments. In the year ended December 1984 the number of referrals to the service had increased to 800, 75% of which were made by general medical practitioners. Very few of these had a history of long-term psychiatric treatment or hospital admission. The referrer was more likely to request advice or help

APPLICATIONS OF SYSTEMIC FAMILY THERAPY
ISBN 0-8089-1696-3

from the CPN, and the problem, if identified with an individual, was more likely to be stated in the context of a relationship.

In turn the change in the referral pattern has presented major challenges to the psychiatric nurses working in the community; it has challenged their belief framework; it has challenged their determination to achieve an identity in independent practice, and it has focused on the need for the CPN's to apply their understanding of mental health problems differently and to acquire new skills.

Working with families was one area of skills training particularly important to this team. Supported by colleagues in another health authority, the Regional Health Authority's training centre provided a series of introductory courses on family therapy. This provided the foundation from which members pursued more advanced courses of study. The five members of the Community Psychiatric Nursing Service who worked as a team treating families adopted the name "The Family Therapy Supervision Group". All but one member of the team have broadly similar backgrounds in psychiatric nursing in large psychiatric hospitals and in the early development of community psychiatric nursing. The fifth member has a background in psychiatric nursing in a variety of settings other than large psychiatric hospitals.

Except on very rare occasions referrals are addressed to a named individual. When the referral is made by the GP this will generally be to the CPN identified with his practice. Words most often used in referral letters to indicate the expectation of the referrer are "see and offer what help you can". Occasionally, the referrer will have selected family therapy as being indicated, but more commonly this decision is made by the CPN receiving the referral either on the basis of the referral information or at a stage in individual therapy when no progress has been made—when therapy is "stuck". Being identified with the GP gives, and acknowledges, the expectation that the CPN will remain in contact with the doctor, although the nature of that contact may be limited. One of the principal advantages afforded by choosing to refer to the CPN rather than a consultant psychiatrist is that the referring doctor retains medical control. This is manifest by the regular presence of the CPN in the GP's surgery. Developing a successful working relationship is dependent on the nature of such contact. The CPN needs to demonstrate attitudes and behaviours which recognise the nature of general medical practice. This requires a commitment to "the practice" which is measured by the willingness to see all referred persons and a positive feedback to the doctor by those he referred. Most often when one of the team is the CPN identified with the relevant GP he becomes the principal therapist.

Two adjacent rooms connected by a telephone link and one-way viewing screen and equipped for audio-visual recording allow the team to work in a favourable physical environment. The team meets twice weekly. One half day is given to seeing families, and a review meeting takes place later in the week when new referrals are discussed and those in treatment reviewed. Early on the team recognised the value of regular meetings in order to facilitate the development of a common philosophy and to debate the problems occurring in therapy.

By tradition the role of the psychiatric nurse in the community is defined in terms of caring, supporting and administering medication. This is a model which may often underestimate the client's ability to realise his potential for change, and may encourage within the nurse a need to establish a controlling influence. Basic psychiatric nurse education has been, and largely remains, medically oriented. It is concerned with recognising mental disorder, reporting on the patient's mental state and implementing treatment prescribed by other disciplines, principally doctors. The training takes place in an institutional setting and little, if any, community experience is gained by the students. Consequently the values and beliefs of the establishment are enshrined in their education and work experience. The relationship between nurses and doctors is founded on the basis of submission rather than cooperation. However, the introduction to nursing of a more academic and perhaps more adventurous generation, coupled with the extension of the role of the psychiatric nurse into the community, has encouraged the drive for a new identity in practice. However, the ability of the institution as a system to accommodate change remains limited. The system can tolerate new ideas and beliefs but the rules of that system will often prevent development and concretisation of these ideas. Concern and anxiety is raised in the hierarchy so that the nurse who has a different understanding from that generally accepted and seeks to apply it is likely to be rejected, not only by his seniors but also by his peers. Hence, to have an understanding of systemic thinking and to apply it is a significant and traumatic shift of orientation for the CPN and this team.

A. Case Example

Tim was a young man of eighteen when he was referred to our team by one of the psychiatrists in the centre. He had been brought to see the psychiatrist by his mother on the advice of their general practitioner. She was concerned that Tim was stealing money from his father and their guest. With enthusiasm (we had only recently formed as a team) we wrote offering a family appointment. Prior to seeing the family we looked at the data available. We knew that mother was concerned about Tim, who was most reluctant to take part in therapy, and that the psychiatrist had chosen to refer Tim as the identified patient and had also asked for a family assessment. Palazzoli et al. (1980b) wrote of "The Problem of the Referring Person". With this in mind we were determined to include the referrer in our provisional hypothesis. We had to include in our hypothesis that the referrer was known to the team as a very caring psychiatrist who recognised the value of providing support to, and regular supervision of, his patient. His understanding of psychological distress relied much on the use of medication in its treatment. In our communication with him we were cautious not to negatively connote these beliefs by describing our own approach in terms of providing support to the family. From the data available the team made a tentative hypothesis which focused on the issues of leaving home and mid-marriage renegotiations. We also recognised that we should be aware that the team and its new way of working were being tested.

The guidelines used for the three therapy sessions which took place were based on the main principles of hypothesis, circularity and neutrality as defined by Palazzoli et al. (1980a). Tim's parents, Harold and Wendy, arrived on their own for the first session. Harold, since his retirement from the RAF education corps, together with a colleague, has run a language school in the town. Wendy, who described herself as an "army wife", helped with the school's administration. Tim's sister Liz, three years his senior, was away studying at university. She had moved to live with her fiance some months earlier and they had declared their intentions to live in Germany on completion of their studies. This decision was strongly disapproved of by her parents, who had always seen her as "the perfect daughter". Tim lived with his parents and had no permanent employment since leaving school at sixteen. This data helped us to enlarge our field of vision and move away from the mistaken belief that Tim's behaviour might be independent from the context in which it took place.

Focusing on Tim, his parents said that since the age of five he had been seen as different from other children; his academic achievements were poor in contrast with his sister, who had always done well. They expressed concern and anxiety about his past and recent behaviour and kept united in their view that this required the intervention of the psychiatric services. However, Tim had declined to attend this session with his parents. The parents had tried various ways to deal with the "problem" (stealing money for three years). They had recently decided on a system of fines for domestic misdemeanours, and the key to the door had been removed from him. The extended family (some lived in Canada, others in New Zealand) was frequently contacted to seek their help and advice, and here one could measure the amount of concern by the size of the family's telephone bill.

The team felt that the original hypothesis was workable when during the session Harold and Wendy started to talk about their early marriage and in particular the close relationship between Wendy and her mother which developed following the sudden death of Wendy's younger brother. Throughout the session the use of positive connotation and reframing had helped us to maintain some aspect of neutrality. Harold and Wendy were asked to wait whilst the team met for consultation. Our formulation for the session was that Tim's behaviour helped keep the family united in their concern for him. It ensured that he would stay at home preventing open discussion between the parents about their future relationship and also defusing the disapproval of Liz's decision to live with Hans. The team decided on the following intervention. We talked about families who at this stage in their lives experience some difficulties but could not understand why this family had these problems. We also explained that sometimes families get natural urges to make changes following the initial session, and we asked them to resist these urges as best they could, at least for the moment, should they occur. We had no way of knowing how this family would re-organise itself around the intervention but hoped that somehow this would at least relieve some of the pressure on Tim.

The next session was set for three weeks later. Again, Harold and Wendy had tried to bring Tim along but he had declined, saying that it was his mother who needed a psychiatrist. Harold told us that the stealing had stopped, Tim had a new girl friend and was working. Wendy confirmed this and added that Tim was now "telling fibs". Somehow, during the session it was now less important for this couple to talk about Tim and they were more interested in talking about their relationship. After a consultation with the team the therapist was sent back to deliver the final intervention. This was lengthy and verbose and had interspersed within it the following statements: "The team is puzzled as to why things are slightly better. . . . We would like to caution you about moving too quickly. . . . We were impressed with this family's decision and the team has agreed with Tim's request to see you . . . the parents . . . to discuss these parental issues. . . . One member of the team has expressed concern about what Harold and Wendy would do to fill the void created if Tim decided to be well and leave home . . . ."

A further appointment was given for three weeks later. At this session Harold and Wendy confirmed that the situation with Tim was now "fine". He was still working and moved into a flat with his girlfriend. Harold also said that everyone had got on very well. That was two years ago; we understand that Tim is now married.

The contact we had with the referrer during our involvement with the family was crucial. We continuously kept him informed of our decisions and actions, but always reframed this in terms of trying something "slightly different" but without much faith in the outcome. Failure to have done this could have served to reinforce the homeostatic bond which often exists between the referrer and the referree. It is also possible that a declaration of intent by the team would produce a response by the network which could push the system into a spiral of symmetrical battles. All communications with the referring agent was conducted verbally, since he worked in the same building. Due to practicalities, the referrer never attended any of the sessions, although this had been offered. During our contact with this family we took care not to suggest any break in their relationship with the referring doctor. In our last communication with the referrer regarding this family we expressed our lack of understanding of the changes which had taken place. At no time did we express any sense of success, and indeed suggested that should he want us to do so we would "keep an eye on the situation".

A shift of orientation by a CPN team produces news of difference (information) to the system within which they function (the network). This implies that the systemic therapy team needs to handle the network in a systemic way in order to function effectively and still maintain its commitment to be part of the larger context. This was an unusual "case" in as much as we never met with the identified patient, but accepted what the system had presented us, and also accepted the family's decision to resolve their difficulty in the way they choose.

So we can see that a systemic approach involves abandoning notions of linear causality and realising that the "target" is not any family member or even the "malfunctioning" family but the "family game". To take a meta-position enables the therapist to look at the rules and the meta-rules that guide the game. In this instance the game-without-end was fixing Tim as either mad or bad, and the rules were around staying together at all cost. To accept Bateson's (1974) circular cybernetic epistemology and apply it through the Milan method means not only freeing "stuck" family systems but also freeing "stuck" therapy teams.

As we have seen with the above example, to hold a systemic view is more likely to have an outcome which is satisfying to the client. Obviously working with families is only one part of the team's commitment to the service. Each member of the team has to work away from the team setting. However, to have a systemic epistemology is not something which is turned on and off only when working in the context of the supervision group. Thus the growth and development of the team has been exported by individual members of it in their day to day work and has influenced other workers principally within the rest of the community psychiatric nursing team and some other professionals within the Mental Health Centre. When individual clients are seen the CPN views the presented problem in a systemic way and will often deliver an intervention which will target not just the client but his whole system.

In working in the way we do, the majority of clients seen by us have been less likely to embark on a psychiatric career. The process of live supervision and the benefits gained by the team has influenced other members of the CPN team and other professionals within the Mental Health Centre. It is now a more common occurrence for members of different disciplines to supervise one another. This may also, in some small way, have helped a house forum to start and develop. Those attending the weekly forum are largely those who share a common view, not necessarily systemic, that psychiatric problems should not be looked at primarily in terms of an organic causation but more in humanistic and ecological terms. These meetings are often used to discuss the relationship existing between different disciplines. Although our colleagues are now less likely to resist discussion about family therapy, this team remains aware of the possible dangers of being perceived as elitist, and we are now able, more often than not, to put across a systemic argument without having to refer to the term "family therapy".

As the team and its work became established we became aware of some changes in the referral pattern. Initially general practitioners chose to refer individuals, but now the trend is for them to refer more couples and families. It is perhaps that the ways of viewing the problems communicated by the community psychiatric nurse matches more effectively those of the GP's. Undoubtedly many GP's recognise that the origin and solution to many problems presented to them in their surgeries will not be found within pure medical science. Also some general practitioners recognise that they may not possess the necessary psychotherapeutic skills to deal with such problems presented. Equally, some recognise that they do not have the time available to devote to such treatment. To us this indicates that the relationship between the individual member of the team and the general practitioners with whom they are identified is successful.

Recently Palazzoli (1983) wrote of her experience in a small clinic which is part of the District Psychiatric Services on the outskirts of Milan. In this she expressed the opinion that "a psychiatric service of the primary level is the ideal place for an applied family systems view". So far our experience seems to show that if a community mental health centre is not necessarily the "ideal place" for family therapy, it is at least a milieu where a family systems view can be applied successfully.

The team was often unsure to what extent it had support within District Psychiatric Services. We knew we had the support of some key members as this approach provided an alternative understanding and treatment of psychological distress. Our anxiety about being accepted by others has largely diminished due to the team being able to practice continuously and the skills of the team being recognised by the referrer. Within the nursing hierarchy the work can be seen to represent one element of the development of independent practice for the nursing profession as a whole. This was considered by Shapiro (1975) when he wrote that "greater clinical autonomy for nurses is certainly feasible within the field of family therapy". But, of course, nurses *by tradition* . . .

REFERENCES

Bateson, G. (1974). "Steps to an Ecology of Mind". Paladin Books, London, pp. 285.

Palazzoli, M., Cecchin, G., Prata, G., *et al.* (1980a). Hypothesizing–Circularity–Neutrality: Three guidelines for the conductor of the session. *Family Process* 19, 3–12.

Palazzoli, M., Cecchin, G., Prata, G., *et al.* (1980b). The Problem of the Referring Person. *Journal of Marital and Family Therapy* 6, 3–9.

Palazzoli, M. (1983). The Emergence of a Comprehensive Systems Approach. *Journal of Family Therapy* 5, 165–177.

Shapiro, R. (1975). Some Implications of Training Psychiatric Nurses in Family Therapy. *Journal of Marriage and Family Counselling* 1, 323–330.

Chapter 12

An In-Patient Unit for Adolescents—
An Adaptation of the Approach

Amanda Acworth, Fred Gainza and Margery Pike

I. THE INSTITUTION

A. Area and Staff

Hill End Adolescent Unit provides an in-patient psychiatric service for 11 to 16 year olds. Its referrals come from the area of the North West Thames Regional Authority, which has a population of four million. The staff includes psychiatrists, nurses, teachers and social workers who offer consultation and pre-admission pre-ventative work, as well as the in-patient service should admission be decided upon.

B. Admission

Psychiatric disturbance in younger adolescents can often be seen as rooted in ques-tions of authority and family ties. The unit aims to clarify the site of legal parental authority and to work with the holders of that authority. Family members are invited to all meetings in which decisions regarding admission and discharge are made.

In this initial therapy it is hoped that the clarifying of the site of authority and the reasons for the proposed admission may enable sufficient problem resolution to prevent admission to hospital, which is always presented as a last possible choice. The reason for any proposed admission is formulated in terms which are under-standable to all; and minimum positive goals to be achieved before discharge focus the work to be done with the family, the community resources and the adolescent.

Within the unit the structured programme uses limit-setting, group meetings and other therapeutic techniques as part of an environment designed to give care and support and be conducive of change. While this may facilitate a change in the adole-scents, however, the unit does not guarantee families or institutions any more than a breathing space or a break for a short period.

C. Referrers and Professional Network

Referrals are accepted only from professionals dealing with families and adole-scents. The majority of these come from social service departments, child and family

APPLICATIONS OF SYSTEMIC FAMILY THERAPY
ISBN 0-8089-1696-3

psychiatric clinics, hospitals and general practitioners. The unit sees itself as working alongside professionals in the community and invites them to join in any meetings with the family.

As an adolescent service we are therefore seen as an attempt by society to deal with two sources of anxiety. The first is that provoked by the "disturbed" behaviour of a sector of its members, and the second is the "inappropriate" placement of such adolescents in adult psychiatric institutions. The consequence of this view is that admission is seen as the result of the social and family network becoming unable to cope with behaviour presented by the indexed patient. The decision to admit is therefore to be made on the basis of anxieties about behaviour; and made by those members of the network with the legal responsibility for decisions such as placement and medical treatment. A more detailed account of the general development of the ideas of this unit and some of the implications of its beds never being full and it not having a waiting list is given elsewhere (Bruggen and Davies, 1977).

II. THE NEW VIEW

When the ideas from the Milan method began to take hold in the unit these two key concepts were easily reframed. Thus admission was reframed from the commonly held view of it being the latest step in the series of attempts to "solve the problem" to that of "a break from the problem", while at the same time, the unit's neutrality was such that it neither advised nor discouraged admission.

For example, Roberta was referred for admission after repeated episodes of self-injury which necessitated hospital treatment. The view of her divorced parents and of the professionals who had provided individual psychotherapy for several months was unanimous: Roberta was seen as someone in need of more intense psychological treatment and specialised facilities. This view was acknowledged by us as a caring and perfectly "valid" one. However, during discussions about the decision to admit we would negotiate only on the basis of what her father (who had been granted custody after the divorce) could or could not cope with. Eventually, the father stated that he could not cope with the 99% certainty he had to live with that on returning home from work he would find his daughter bleeding or else would receive news that she had been to hospital again. He requested admission to help him deal with this anxiety. We offered the parents a break from the problem but not a solution to the problem. The idea of relief through one member leaving the family was taken up by the family.

Another characteristic of the way of functioning of Hill End Adolescent Unit has been its ready acceptance of a whole stream of new and challenging therapeutic concepts. Ideas derived from Gestalt, Bio-Energetics, psychoanalysis, encounter groups, primal therapy, psychodrama, etc. have always found fertile soil. This resulted in not only extremely valuable and exciting work, but also in a certain resistance to the idea of any disciplined method to work by. The appearance on the scene of the Milan method of family work, with all its emphasis on rigour and disciplined examination of data and thinking ran counter to some of that tradition. An acknowledged sense of rivalry and split developed along certain pre-existing differences between staff. The new method was perceived to be the province of the psychiatric and social work disciplines while the "old" methods that of the nursing staff. Psychiatrists and social workers worked from nine until five and were leaders in family therapy, while the nursing staff worked shifts, were in charge of the group work and had more contact with the adolescents. The rivalries, conflicts and, we think competitive fantasies of "my work is better than yours", have lessened with our more open acknowledgement that the integration of the new method of thinking about families and the rest of the residential therapeutic activities does remain a problem.

The Milan method led us to look at different ways of structuring the family session. Prior to this the members of the team would all sit in the room together with the family and share the work of discussing family issues and the admission decision making. This often produced a degree of confusion unhelpful to both tasks. In an attempt to ease this confusion and to provide for both the family therapy and the decision making, a new structure for these meetings was devised.

In the team of three, one person is responsible for conducting the "family therapy" and another person for the decision-making part of the meeting. They act as consultants for each other. The third person, usually a student, acts as observer/consultant with specific roles.

A. A Family Therapy

Family therapy is a discussion with the family about the presenting problems and will be dealt with by circular questioning, using rating, open gossip, time—past and present—and fantasy. From information the team had received during the telephone referral, an hypothesis or starting point will have been decided.

B. The Decision Making

Part of the session focuses on giving straight information about the unit as well as facilitating a decision from those in legal parental authority. If an adolescent is admitted, a reason for admission and minimum change are negotiated in this part of the meeting.

During the session the team has a break to formulate an intervention which will be presented to the family at the end. This intervention is based on information given by the family during the session; it may include positive connotation and paradoxical statement.

Time at the beginning and end of each session is used to meet with the referring professionals involved. The first meeting with the family is at the referrers' place of work. To subsequent meetings at the unit, if any, the referrer is invited. In some of the cases when social workers are the referring professionals, they are also holders of legal parental authority and have to make the admission decisions; such work is even more complicated.

C. Case Example

Pauline, an active 14 year old, had been in care six months when she was referred for admission to the adolescent unit. Hers was a history of tragic deaths and separation. When she was four her mother left her husband and Pauline went to live with her. After divorce Pauline's mother married again and died in childbirth. Pauline's stepfather, now with three children to bring up, married again, but soon after that he himself died of cancer leaving Pauline and her two halfbrothers with their new step-mother. Pauline's stepmother found it increasingly difficult to cope with Pauline's lying, glue sniffing and stealing from shops. Eventually she approached the Social Services and Pauline was taken into care.

Pauline was placed at a children's home where she continued to sniff glue and began not to go to school. Her professional carers became more and more concerned about the damage she was doing to herself through glue sniffing. She became violent and destructive in the children's home when she was under the influence of glue. At this point the Social Services approached the unit because they felt that they could no longer cope with Pauline.

Pauline was admitted to the unit by her social worker. If she should talk to her social worker and children's home staff for ten minutes on a Friday evening when she returned to the children's home for the weekend, for four weekends, then her social worker would discharge her.

Pauline was convinced that the Social Services Department was keeping her and her family apart; and she believed that being in care was for only a short time, because her young halfbrother had been in care for a few months and was again back with his stepmother. There were six meetings at the unit with Pauline and her professional carers. Pauline's stepmother and halfbrothers were invited but did not come.

With the use of circular questioning Pauline looked at family issues although none of the family members were present. These sessions were fruitful and helpful both to her and her social worker. We also looked at the system into which Pauline was to return. Pauline entered into discussion about her behaviour at the children's home and the problems there might be when she returned. She was articulate and contributed in a mature and sensitive manner in these.

Pauline was very reluctant, however, to enter into any conversation when her social worker was present, though she seemed to have a lot to say about him when he was not there, saying things like "He is too old to be my social worker". "I can't stand his clothes". "He only does things to make it easier for himself". "He doesn't care about me". "He doesn't want me to live with my family". "I don't want to talk to him".

The social worker had also voiced some of his own doubts and worries. He had said he really did not know how to handle Pauline as she was so difficult. He did not seem to have any comfortable contact with her when they were together. She seemed distant and not to want to respond. He said he felt rejected by Pauline. He was sometimes very angry and felt impotent when she rejected all of his suggestions.

We decided to treat Pauline and her social worker as one system and to work with them alone. The relationship between them was a vital one and one that they would be involved with as long as Pauline was in care. We thought that Pauline's behaviour was helpful in that it prevented her social worker and her becoming too emotionally involved. We related this to her previous experience of attachment and loss. We also felt that the social worker's request for Pauline to be admitted to Hill End Adolescent Unit brought in experts to help develop his own skills of working with young people.

The therapist started by making a statement about some of the work that had already been done; work with Pauline's family and the work with the relationships at the children's home.

Therapist to Social Worker: What do you think Pauline thinks about you as her social worker?

Social Worker: I think she thinks I'm too old. (*The social worker gradually became more able to expand feelings and ideas about Pauline.*)

Therapist to Pauline: Pauline, what do you think your social worker might feel about you?

Pauline: I think he thinks I'm being awkward.

Therapist: What do you think he finds the most awkward thing about you?

Pauline: When he decides I've got to do something and I won't do it and then he doesn't decide.

Pauline and her social worker then talked for several minutes voicing their dissatisfactions with their relationship. Although Pauline and her social worker appeared to find it difficult at first, this method of intervention released them from a position in which Pauline was saying "I'm not going to talk to you", and her social worker insisting that she did talk to him. Pauline and her social worker's relationship improved gradually and Pauline did manage to meet the "minimum change" asked by her social worker.

One of the most striking effects of applying systemic thinking in our work has been on our relationship with referring professionals. They are often intrigued by our circular questioning and wonder what we are trying to do. In some cases, referrers have found our insistence on parental coping and stresses within the family—a relief from the problem rather than trying to solve the problem—to have far-reaching consequences, such as someone else becoming the designated patient and going into hospital while the adolescent's symptoms subsided, to be followed by the reuniting of the family and their managing without psychiatric help. Some may regard us as elite, especially when we wish to meet together as a team before delivering the intervention, although we explain that we do this simply because we are a "separate" system and wish our involvement with the family to be seen as a separate one from theirs. We point out that if they are to continue to work with the clients, it might be convenient for them to be able to dissociate themselves from anything we say which may be provocative.

Within our own agency the application of systemic thinking conflicts with the previous models of confrontation and structural family work. Some colleagues have expressed doubts about whether therapists are saying what they actually think or mean, or whether they are behaving paradoxically.

We see circular questioning as another method of confrontation and one which can be used in group work within the unit:

Staff member (to a boy who had previously taken an overdose of aspirin): If you had died, who in your family would be the most upset?

Staff member (to a girl sitting alongside a silent boy): If Alan had answered the question I asked him, what do you think he would have said?

Our experience of applying systemic thinking and the meta-position has been that it has enabled our therapists, in family meetings or ward groups or ad hoc encounters, to feel more liberated. Circular questioning appears to be less provocative and creates less resistance than direct forms of questioning.

C. Training

For most beginner therapists this appears to be a new way of thinking and takes some time to adapt. We have formulated an exercise for practice and to train staff in circular questioning. A group of six or eight people discuss a subject and each person spends five to ten minutes using circular questions. Experience suggests that circular questions promote further thought. The Milan group have given us a base to build our own style of therapy.

III. THE INFLUENCE OF OUR SETTING

The way we apply the ideas and methods of the Milan group is greatly influenced by our own particular setting. Ours is an in-patient unit and we see referrals exclusively from professionals. We see our referring colleagues as the ones who have the problem, at least initially. In all our meetings with families there is a decision to be made or reviewed, namely whether to admit or not; or whether to discharge or not. The decision making clearly divides the members of the family into those with an executive function (the parents) and those who have views and feelings about it but have no vote (the children). We see this as an extension of that systemic work done in an outpatient or clinic setting when there is recognition of a number of facts—some people simply do have to be carried (babes in arms); some people really are the breadwinners (the working and income-drawing father and mother, as opposed to dependent children); some people (parents) are required by law to get other people (their children) to attend school.

Another major difference lies in the composition of our teams. While we try to keep the same team working with one family, in contrast with many institutions, we do not always have the same people working in the same team. Nurses work shifts, our staff change frequently and students work with us. We try to have a team with two experienced members and one who will be doing more learning than contributing. When we have a team of three experienced people then the work seems to us to be more effective. If we did work consistently with a team of the same people we would become more adept at shorthand communication. We had to choose between having as many members of staff as possible doing family therapy and having a few members as elite, consistent teams. We were more anxious about what we foresaw as the implications of the latter.

IV. CONCLUSION

When thinking of the larger context of this kind of work we encounter new difficulties. Traditionally, in-patient facilities and their success and efficacy have been assessed in terms of bed occupancy. Occupied beds and long waiting lists signify successful functioning. At Hill End Adolescent Unit the introduction of ideas from the Milan method appears to have resulted in the reduction in the number of admissions as well as a shortening of the length of stay of those cases admitted. Out of 159 referrals during the first 9 months of 1983 there were 25 admissions. The average length of stay is between 6 weeks and 12 weeks.

Do we carry on our policy to its very end? If we become so "successful" that there are no further admissions and no bed occupancy, will we risk being congratulated on our success and thanked for our services while the unit is shut down? Do we adhere to our principles only until the size of the in-patient group becomes alarmingly small, and then we become less active in our preventative work? Is there a way of assessing the efficacy and funding requirements of this type of work other than bed occupancy? Do we grasp the fantasy of a nil bed occupancy and the closure of the institution as an exceptional opportunity to practice positive connotation?

REFERENCES

Bruggen, P., and Davies, G. (1977). Review Article: Family Therapy in Adolescent Psychiatry. *British Journal of Psychiatry* 131, 433–447.

Chapter 13

The Use of the Milan Approach in Sex Therapy

Bebe Speed

I. INTRODUCTION

The work to be described in this chapter has been carried out over a three-year period at the Family Institute, Cardiff, an agency established twelve years ago and funded by a major British charity, Dr Barnardo's. Currently, there are five full-time members of staff whose original trainings include psychology, sociology, social work, drama therapy, and individual and group psychotherapy. About half the referrals seen at the institute are self-referred either via the local newspaper or on recommendation, whilst the rest are referred by other professionals in the Cardiff area and further afield. The range of problems for which help is sought includes psychiatric symptoms, behaviour problems in children and adolescents, marital stress and sexual difficulties. Besides clinical work, the institute has a heavy commitment to training programmes and courses both within and outside the agency, as well as undertaking research. The use of a video, a one-way screen and one or more colleagues behind the screen is the norm.

Three years ago, the author and a male colleague began working together as a co-therapy pair seeing all couples who referred themselves or were referred specifically with sexual problems. Up until Spring 1983, there were 47 couple referrals: 14 from general practitioners, 25 self-referrals (many at the recommendation of a general practitioner) and 8 referrals from other professionals, including social workers and health visitors. Of the 47, 42 arrived for their first appointment, a "show" rate of 89%. Low sexual desire in the female partner was the problem specified in 55% of cases at referral or during the first interview; with impotence the next most frequent, at 19%; followed by non-consummation, at 9%. Women were twice as likely as men to be initially presented as the dysfunctional partner, though it is common to find on closer questioning that the male partner too has sexual difficulties, often premature ejaculation.

II. USING THE MILAN APPROACH TO THEORISE ABOUT SEXUAL DIFFICULTIES

Traditionally, sexual difficulties have been conceptualised psychoanalytically or behaviourally. Drawing on the Milan approach, we have developed a way of conceptualising such problems as behaviour which is part of interconnected patterns of

APPLICATIONS OF SYSTEMIC FAMILY THERAPY
ISBN 0-8089-1696-3

relating not only between a couple but also within relationships in the wider system. This is not to deny the physiological or individual psychological aspects of such difficulties but to concentrate more on the communicational significance of such symptoms in the relationship context. We would thus focus on how a sexual problem such as a wife's fear of pain of intercourse is part of the interactional patterns between her and her husband and between them and other people in their relationship network. How, for example, is the knowledge that the couple have not consummated their marriage, or had a child, or behave more like children than sexually aware adults, affecting the patterning of relationships in the family system, and how is the patterning of the wider relationships affecting the couple's relationship including its sexual aspect?

Whilst accepting the connectedness of sexual difficulties and relationship patterns, it appears from the work we have done to be necessary nevertheless to distinguish between systems where change in any part of the system is relatively easily accommodated and responded to in a way which enhances that change and those where it is not, where any change or attempted change in part of the pattern is found difficult, threatening and is resisted.

An example may serve to clarify this distinction. A couple referred with the problem of the husband's premature ejaculation, a difficulty since the beginning of their sexual relationship six years previously. Closer questioning revealed that the wife had lost sexual desire following the birth of their second child two years earlier, and it seemed that it was at this point that the premature ejaculation became more of a focus for both of them. In addition, the wife's relationship with her mother had become closer following the birth of this child as the two women moved more together over child-care issues. As the mother–daughter relationship became closer, the wife–husband relationship seemed to become more distant, and this was expressed by a decrease in sexual contact between them as well as by greater complaints by both of them concerning the level of their sexual satisfaction.

We treated this couple mainly with the use of sexual tasks aimed at the husband's failure to acquire ejaculatory control over the years, and opinions and tasks aimed at the couple's relationship with each other more generally. Whilst aware of the mother's position in the relationship context, we did not intervene directly in any way to affect this. One way of seeing the considerable improvements which occurred is that as the couple became closer the mother readjusted to their greater closeness and accepted it, allowing her daughter to alter the balance of her relationships between her husband and herself. But the mother could have responded to any attempt by the daughter to move closer to her husband and further away from her by encouraging the daughter to remain where she was. Such feedback might, for example, have included the mother behaving in depressed ways and indicating that she felt angry with her daughter if the frequency and intensity of their relationship changed. Or the feedback from the mother might have provoked a quarrel between the couple, thus reinstating the former distance between the husband and wife.

Thus, whilst we always make a systemic formulation, because of our awareness that some relationship systems will be relatively accepting of change, we also find it useful to conceptualise sexual difficulties more narrowly. For example, we sometimes use conceptualisations drawn from Masters and Johnson (1970) concerning maladaptive behavioural sequences between a couple. In the case already mentioned, for example, we considered how the husband's premature ejaculation and the wife's lack of desire were in a mutually reinforcing sequence at a simpler behavioural level; that is, the more he ejaculated quickly, the less the wife was satisfied and the more he tried, thus putting himself into a "be-spontaneous-paradox"; and ultimately, the less the wife was satisfied the more she began to encourage her husband to "get it over with", thus reinforcing the problem. We also assessed the couple's relationship with each other more generally and hypothesised that the sexual difficulties were barometers of other difficulties between the couple; for example, the wife's lack of sexual desire was a reflection of anger towards her husband over his perceived inadequacy not only sexually but in many other areas of their relationship as well. Additionally, at the simplest level of all, we were also aware of the possibility of the couple's lack of knowledge, for example, that the husband had simply never learnt to control the ejaculatory reflex.

III. USING THE MILAN APPROACH IN CONDUCTING THE SESSION

When seeing couples with sexual difficulties, we work as co-therapists (unless an individual only is being interviewed and this will then be done by the same-sex therapist). Unlike the Milan team, we do not have colleagues behind the screen as a matter of course. There are rarely colleagues behind the screen at the first interview, an arrangement which partially arose out of an effort to alleviate the clients' and co-therapists' anxieties about discussing sexuality in front of an audience. Having begun to work without colleagues, we discovered that many of the advantages of teamwork were replicated by the co-therapy arrangement. We used each other for the discussion of information, hypotheses and interventions, pre- and post-interview, as well as by taking a break away from the couple during the interview. We also came to rely on the presence of each other as a guard against becoming unhelpfully drawn in, with one or the other of us taking a less active part in the session from time to time as well as challenging each others' perceptions and punctuations of the situation. During interviews subsequent to the first one, colleagues may be behind the screen either by chance (because it is a clinic day and the colleague has time available) or by special request from the co-therapists because they recognise that the therapy has become stuck.

Another difference between our approach and that of the Milan group is that, however widely we might define the significant system in our hypothesising, it is usually only the couple who are actually seen. This is because of the nature of the problem initially specified, i.e. sexual difficulties, and the assumed reluctance of many couples to discuss these openly with other family members present.

When we begin a first session with a couple, we are seeking information on a number of levels, and on the basis of that information we will construct one, two or more inter-related hypotheses. Because of our assumption that narrower as well as wider systemic conceptualisations may be useful, we usually question more closely than do the Milan group about the presented problems. We begin by asking in some detail about the sexual difficulty and the couple's sexual development both individually and together, and often split into same-sex pairs to explore these aspects in more detail. We might thus at this stage be developing a formulation about the sexual difficulty at a relatively simple behavioural level, for example that a young man's inability to maintain his erection to the point of intercourse is maintained by his anxiety and his girlfriend's impatience. The more his girlfriend shows impatience, the more anxious he becomes and the more likely he is to lose his erection.

Having asked about the problem, we then ask questions which will give us information about the couple's relationship more generally and their relationships with others in the wider system. In the context of our example, we might have a hypothesis that the man's inability to maintain his erection is symbolic of a lack of commitment to the couple relationship and the continuing strong involvement of both partners with their families of origin. We would, therefore, ask the usual Milan-style questions to elicit such relationship information and evolve a second, more complex systemic hypothesis which interrelates with the first, simpler, behavioural hypothesis.

With many couples it is common to find that sexual difficulties have existed for many years, but that help has only now been sought. We explore this in some detail, and often find that a request for therapy *now* often seems related not to the sexual difficulty *per se* but to some change in the wider context so that sexual difficulties come to be defined in a different way. For example, we have often seen couples who redefine their previously accepted level of sexual functioning as problematic at a time when their children are beginning to grow up and leave home (see Haley, 1980). Similarly, a non-consummated marriage may only result in a request for therapy at a time when change is occurring in the wider system; for example, one of the spouses is threatening to have an affair or a parent has died and a previous close relationship is no longer available and thus more attention is paid to the marriage and its perceived deficiencies.

We take time out towards the end of a session to further discuss hypotheses about the maintenance of the problem and its place in the relationship context. Sexual difficulties can be seen as one of a number of distancing mechanisms in a couple's relationship, warding off too great an intimacy between the partners and thus protecting stronger loyalties to other relationships, often between the partners and their children and/or between the partners and their parents. It is interesting to note that on occasions when couples become more successful sexually, they sometimes report that other distancing mechanisms have been put into operation.

We are similar to the practice of the Milan team in our use of a neutral stance derived from a circular epistemology which leads away from a tendency to blame and moralise towards seeing a pattern in which people are caught and for which no one can be blamed. This can be used explicitly with the couple, for example the female therapist might say to the male in the couple's presence that she feels he hadn't fully understood the wife's position in the situation or vice versa. Being neutral *vis à vis* the couple's beliefs and goals is also important. For example, we always ask in a situation where a couple are complaining about the loss of desire in one spouse, whether loss of desire in the other spouse would be as good a solution for them as the other spouse regaining desire. Or if the couple say they argue a lot because of the sexual problem, we might ask them who would miss the arguments most if they stopped or who enjoys the arguments the most?

IV.   USING THE MILAN APPROACH IN INTERVENTIONS

As Palazzoli *et al.* (1980) speculate, the way in which the session itself is conducted may in itself be a major intervention. Questions provide the therapist with information; they also potentially introduce new information to the couple via the implicit connections certain questions may make. For example, a couple, June and Bill, who had initially completed some sexual tasks (non-genital and genital massage exercises) with great success, reported at the fourth session that they had stopped any form of sexual contact, according to the husband's resentful explanation, because of the wife's lack of interest following a row they had had about their 18-year-old daughter. Whilst exploring the patterns in this three-way relationship, it seemed clear that the husband was very close to the daughter and thought very highly of her, describing her as cooperative and easy going, unlike his wife. June seemed to feel excluded from and jealous of the relationship between her husband and daughter. During the series of questions, the female therapist turned to the husband and said "Do you think your daughter would be more likely to do the sexual tasks than your wife?" The husband replied rather matter-of-factly and in a somewhat unsure tone of voice, "No, I wouldn't say that", whilst his wife stared at him with disbelief. Such questions are potentially extremely powerful in challenging the family's beliefs and should not be disregarded as important sources of change. What will, however, be discussed here in greater detail is the deliberate and carefully formulated intervention given at the end of the interview.

We frequently positively connote symptomatic and other patterns of behaviour along with suggesting restraint from change. An example of such an intervention is that given to a couple who complained bitterly to us about each other, their endless arguments and lack of sex between them. During the final intervention, we said to them that their quarrelling and unsatisfactory sexual relationship had, over the years been useful in helping them to maintain more distance in their relationship. Such a distant relationship had been important for them because they had both suffered terrible losses, their elder daughter and both their fathers, and the risk would have been that if they had grown closer over the years they might have felt a lessening of the loyalty to those important relationships. Having defined their arguments and poor sexual relationship positively, we were then able to go on to say that we were not sure that it was safe for them to think about making any change at the present time for fear of upsetting their loyalties to their dead relatives. We went on to say that a colleague had suggested it might be helpful for *both of them together* to visit the graves of their daughter and fathers, but that we were less sure about this and thought they should only think about it. The suggested visit to the graves was a way of breaking the general pattern of distance between them as well as the specific pattern, established over the years, of mourning the deaths separately and covertly blaming each other and themselves for the death of the daughter. This latter pattern was expressed concretely by the fact that the wife had rarely gone to her daughter's grave whereas the husband visited his daughter's grave frequently to talk to her.

The couple cancelled their next appointment because they were going for a *joint* interview for jobs as steward and stewardess of a club. They left a message that "things are much improved" and that they were going *together* to their younger daughter's for Christmas.

Another intervention typical of the Milan approach is that of a prescription of a ritual or specific task for the family to undertake. Systemic reframings may introduce confusion by offering different meanings. As Tomm (1984) suggests, ritual in contrast may introduce clarity where there was confusion. It is interesting to speculate on the similarity between our use of sexual tasks and the use of ritual. Masters and Johnson used sexual tasks in order to reduce anxiety about sexual performance and to enhance sexual awareness and functioning. Hence a temporary ban on intercourse might cut across the vicious circle of anxiety about achieving an erection making erection less likely. Or a non-genital sensate focus exercise is a way of focusing a couple on learning techniques of giving and getting physical pleasure. Whilst we may at times employ these tasks for these reasons, our rationale for the use of them is usually more complex. For example, sometimes a request to do a sexual task is a way of putting a couple together and separating them from other family members; it is a way of implicitly affirming their status as a couple separate from others. Such a ritual has some similarities to the invariant prescription used by Palazzoli and Prata (1983).

Such a change occurred in the case of Don and Julie, who had been referred by their general practitioner because of Julie's loss of sexual desire. Julie bitterly told us that she was no longer interested in her husband because he ignored her all the time and was totally unresponsive to what she wanted. Don's view was that Julie was always nagging him about things she wanted him to do and he therefore withdrew into watching the television. It became clear that this sequence between them was also related to the couple's relationship with Julie's 18-year-old daughter, Mandy, a child from her first marriage. Julie and Mandy were close, and the more Don withdrew, the closer they became. Similarly, the more mother and daughter behaved in ways which indicated their closeness, the more Don felt excluded and withdrew even more. Though we could see the patterning of these relationships, we were unsure how accepting or rejecting the three of them would be of any attempt to alter the balance.

As is often the case for us, as a preliminary manoeuvre, in part to test the system's response to the possibility of change, we asked the couple to do a simple sexual task which involved them spending a small amount of extra time together privately. They did this successfully and the daughter was said "not to have noticed". We then instituted a series of similar tasks which required the couple spending small but increasingly frequent amounts of time together. All went well until we requested the couple to arrange a weekend away together, something they had never done throughout the entire time of their marriage, they said because of the existence of Mandy. Julie immediately said she could not possibly go away for a weekend because Mandy would find it impossible to remain in the house on her own. We gently challenged her on this and enlisted Don's support but finally said that though in our view it was important to do this we could see that she might be right and it might be far too risky at the present time both to leave her daughter alone and to risk her and Don being together for a whole weekend. When they returned for the next session, they both gleefully reported having gone away for a weekend and having enjoyed it enormously. Julie also reported with much surprise that her daughter had encouraged their plan, had arranged activities for herself while they were away and told her mother on her return how much she had enjoyed the weekend without them!

Prescribing tasks which put Don and Julie together and separated Julie and Mandy can be seen as rituals which clarified the relationships between the three of them. By enacting such rituals, the couple "informed" Mandy of a change in their relationship, that it was closer than previously, and Mandy behaved in ways which "informed" Don and Julie of her acceptance of this. We can speculate that, whilst Mandy might have been frightened to give up some of the closeness with her mother, she might also have been relieved to find herself less necessary to her mother and thus freed to get on with other aspects of her life.

Thus in much of our work, we make extensive use of systemic reframings, no-change prescriptions and sexual tasks which can be seen in part as rituals. But we also use a range of techniques derived from other approaches to family therapy as well as simpler interventions such as education, prescription of reading material and support of enhanced sexual exploration. The approach we choose is linked to our assessment of how easy or difficult the couple and other people in the context will find it to change and accept change, and how relatively autonomous the difficulties are. In assessing this, we use criteria such as the duration of the problem, the nature of the problem complained of, our evaluation of the couple's relationship generally, for example how clear or confused their communication patterns seem to be, how involved the couple appear to be in wider family relationships and the apparent degree of motivation for change.

With some couples, the degree of complexity of the problem and the level we should directly aim at is not always clear initially or may change from session to session. Where it is not clear, one strategy we often use is a split between the co-therapy pair, with one therapist suggesting a sexual task whilst the other therapist offers an opinion that the situation is certainly more complex than at first appears and that there may well be good reasons for the sexual difficulty and thus need for caution. When the couple return, we can then use the further information provided by their response to the intervention, for example whether or not they have completed the task and how this was or was not done. Where there seems to be a need to change our approach from session to session, we often continue to use such a split between the therapists, with one continuing to be hopeful about change and prescribing relevant tasks whilst the other continues to be pessimistic. This is an extension of the contrived team conflict strategies developed by the Cardiff group (see Cade, 1980).

V. CONCLUSION

When we began seeing couples with sexual difficulties, we initially assumed that we could use conceptualisations and treatment strategies developed by sex therapists such as Masters and Johnson (1970) and Kaplan (1974). Unlike them, however, we rarely seemed to see couples with straightforward sexual problems which we could usefully conceptualise and treat only at relatively simple behavioural levels. Rather, the sexual difficulties often seemed to be part of more general difficulties between a couple and often were indicative of problems in the wider relationship network as well. We thus found it helpful to use systemic formulations and, in the obviously more complex cases, paid relatively little attention to the sexual difficulties *per se*, often preferring to concentrate on their significance as distance regulators within the relationship matrix.

In the more straightforward cases, whilst we have still found it helpful to make a systemic formulation, our experience indicates that not all families have patterns which are so interconnected that an intervention needs to be addressed to the whole system in order to be effective. That is, interventions can be used which are aimed at changing directly only part of the pattern in the belief that some families are sufficiently change-accepting to adjust to any change occurring in sub-systems or indeed in individuals. Such a view echoes Erickson, quoted by Zeig (1980): "Family therapists think you have to change the family to change the kid. I say change the kid and let the family learn to live with him differently".

Applying the Milan approach to sexual difficulties has thus led to an increased awareness of the linkage of patterns of behaviour and relationships at individual, dyadic and systemic levels and to the possibility of intervening to disrupt the patterns at any of these levels (see Speed, 1984). This experience, together with finding the co-therapy relationship a viable alternative to working in teams, has led me to an increased confidence in the appropriateness of being flexible in approach to helping clients, whatever the problem presented.

Acknowledgment

I would like to acknowledge the contribution of my co-therapist, Roy Shuttleworth, in the development of many of the ideas presented here.

REFERENCES

Cade, B. W. (1980). Resolving Therapeutic Deadlocks Using a Contrived Team Conflict. *International Journal of Family Therapy* 2, 253–262.

Haley, J. (1980). "Leaving Home: The Therapy of Disturbed Young People". McGraw-Hill, New York.

Kaplan, H. S. (1974). "The New Sex Therapy: Active Treatment of Sexual Dysfunctions". Brunner/Mazel, New York.

Masters, W. H., and Johnson, V. E. (1970). "Human Sexual Inadequacy". Little, Brown & Company, Boston.

Palazzoli, M. S., Boscolo, L., Cecchin, G., and Prata, G. (1980). Hypothesising–Circularity–Neutrality: Three Guidelines for the Conductor of the Session. *Family Process* 19, 3–12.

Palazzoli, M. S., and Prata, G. (1983). A New Method for Therapy and Research in the Treatment of Schizophrenic Families. *In* Stierlin, H., Wynne, L. C., and Wirshing, M. (eds.), "Psychosocial Interventions in Schizophrenia". Springer Verlag, Berlin, pp. 237–243.

Speed, B. (1984). Family Therapy: An Update. *Association for Child Psychology & Psychiatry Newsletter* 6, 2–14.

Tomm, K. (1984). One Perspective on the Milan Systemic Approach: Part II. Description of Session Format, Interviewing Style and Interventions. *Journal of Marital and Family Therapy* 10, 253–271.

Zeig, J. K. (1980). "A Teaching Seminar with Milton H. Erickson". Brunner/Mazel, New York.

Part THREE

Agencies

Chapter 14

The Systemic Approach in a Mental Health Service

Laura Fruggeri, Daniela Dotti, Rossana Ferrari
and Massimo Matteini

I. INTRODUCTION

The research presented in this chapter took its initiative from a project which sought to introduce the intervention of psychotherapy in the public services while at the same time safeguarding the identity and character of those services. This research took place in Modena, Italy, within a public psychiatric service known as Servizio di Igiene Mentale e Assistenza Psichiatrica (Mental Hygiene and Psychiatric Assistance Service), more commonly known by the acronym, SIMAP.

A. The Social Service Context in Italy

One of the most important changes which took place in Italy some years ago in the management of psychiatric distress was the organisation of a social psychiatric alternative to the mental hospitals rendered obsolete by the passing of health reform legislation, and the reintegration of the patient and his psychiatric problem into the community and its social services. The law mandating psychiatric reform in 1978 was part of legislation reforming the national provision of all health services, and called for the establishment of so-called Local Sanitary Units (USL). These USL's are community agencies that provide a full range of health services to the public within a specified territory or catchment area.

Within a given USL, there are several SIMAP teams (each composed of 3 psychiatrists, 2 psychologists and 7–10 nurses) which are charged with caring for all problems related to the prevention, treatment and rehabilitation of persons suffering from psychiatric disturbances within a territory of about 60,000 to 70,000 inhabitants. The fundamental characteristics of the SIMAP's are that all services are free of charge; service is provided to anyone who requests treatment whether self-referred or referred by a doctor or another facility; the responsibility to deal with the full range of problems of a patient is accepted, implying a holistic approach not only to treat the psychological disorder, but all related problems in that patient's life. This final characteristic is an important one, as it requires the integration of all the public services available in order to address the client's need to resolve the full range of his

APPLICATIONS OF SYSTEMIC FAMILY THERAPY
ISBN 0-8089-1696-3

problems of housing, work, interpersonal relations, and so on, in order to arrive at an all-inclusive state of well-being.

II. SCOPE OF THE RESEARCH

The process of introducing psychotherapeutic interventions in the public mental health service was complicated by one important factor: that the clients traditionally did not come to the centres requesting psychotherapy per se, but rather looked upon these centres as a source of social assistance. The confusion was compounded by the fact that the 1978 legislation, based as it was on a radical philosophy of community social psychiatry, mandated the centres to perform this social assistance function whereas they did not explicitly require a psychotherapeutic service. Hence the services which the centres were providing at the time this research began, were the following: free psychopharmacological services, socio-economic assistance, bureaucratic certification of sanity, and emergency services. The development of these services had come about over time as a result of the interaction between those functions required of the centre by statute and those that had been historically requested by clients. Psychotherapy as an intervention was not among these functions, and it presented itself within this picture as new information (in the Batesonian sense) or as a change in the relational pattern of the "service-client" system.

By analysing the request/responses in terms of communicational exchanges and separating the two levels of communication (content and command), an important fact emerged. This was that the social assistance requests of the psychiatric clients such as requests for housing, work opportunities, medications, and financial assistance, were finding responses from the public psychiatric service *on the level of content*, as housing, work, medication, financial assistance and emergency services were made available. However, the *command* or *relational level* of the request was being ignored. The project to introduce a psychotherapeutic intervention into the public psychiatric service therefore consisted of the need to acknowledge, analyse and amplify the relational level of the communication between the client and service alongside acknowledgement of the content level of the request for social assistance.

The introduction of a psychotherapeutic approach came about through a process of separating and differentiating therapy from other interventions. The integration of various levels of interventions was seen as coming about primarily in a process that can best be described as the *acceptance* of the request on the *content level*, and *redefinition* of the request on the *relational level*.

A.   Social Responsibilities

A communicational analysis of the social assistance request which a client makes to the team of a psychiatric service (financial assistance, housing, job placement, etc.) reveals the two levels of the massage exchanged. There is often an apparent incongruity between the content of the client's request and the way in which the patient defines his relationship with the team. For example, a patient's request is made to a psychiatric professional; on the command or relational level the message also communicates something to the effect of, "I'm not the one who is asking for this housing; it's a force stronger than me (craziness, anxiety, aggressiveness, or other psychiatric symptomatology) that forces me to manifest this need". In this sense, the relational level of the message denies its content, thus denoting the request in paradoxical terms.

When this type of definition of the relationship is proposed by the client, three possible responses are available to the psychiatric team: *acceptance, rejection* or *acceptance-redefinition*.

With *acceptance,* the team perceives only the content level of the message; the incongruent relational level is ignored. This is the custom of the school of social psychiatry which is generally based on the linear hypothesis of social cause and effect regarding mental illness: "I'll find you housing because of your symptom; when you've got your place, I expect you to stop having the symptom . . ." The hypothesis in this situation is that when the housing problem is resolved, the other problems will be resolved as well. With acceptance, the team essentially perceives the symptom of the patient as justification for his intervention, and thus conveys the following message: "This help is being given to you, and I am getting involved because of your anxiety".

In this case, the response of the team reflects the relational context defined by the client: "I'll help you", qualified by, "I won't help you", that is, negation. What follows is of course a symmetrical escalation within the relationship; an endless and unfortunately unchanging game. The patient might communicate "What you have done for me is all right, but it is not enough; you did fairly well, but you've got to do more; the response of the team might be another job, a different type of job, hopefully more interesting and less stressful. The patient can't manage it, has difficulties; so more jobs, different jobs, frustration, impotence, pessimism of the team, veiled rebuke to the patient for his ingratitude; then the same response, this time stronger. At this point the team responds with hyperactivity, efficiency, etc . . . .

A *rejection* response made by the team to a client's request again emphasises only the level of content. In the client–team system, the relationship with the client becomes symmetrical. The team, however, is also becoming symmetrical with the definition of purpose of the institution which it represents (a higher level relational system).

The third possibility, *acceptance-redefinition,* offers an alternative so that the team can avoid the trap of a paradoxical directive set by the client. It consists of respecting the needs expressed on the content level and denied on the relational level and providing a solution which synthesises and incorporates both the opposing positions. The response might then be "I'll find you housing because you need it, and this will help you partially. The service will provide psychotherapy to help you with the problems resulting from your anxiety . . ." The separation of the two levels of intervention will encompass all needs by responding to them and not denying them.[1]

---

[1] The specific intervention which is typically social can be carried out by another service (for example, a social service); however, it is defined for the client as part of a unified program.

B. Pharmacological Responsibilities

The same team–client relational analysis is also proposed for the area of the pharmacological responsibilities. When the patient asks the team for a drug that will help him avoid anxiety, insomnia, depression, etc., he is asking to "change without changing". Drugs by definition (tranquillisers, antidepressants, etc.) reduce the perception of anxiety, enable the avoidance of the painful experiencing of the related situation and reinforce the defences in the categorical avoidance of the situation with its conflicts. Here, too, there are three types of feedback on the part of the team concerning pharmacological interventions: the first two, *acceptance* and *rejection*, focus attention only on the content level. The third possibility, *acceptance-redefinition*, instead, includes both levels.

The modality which uses *rejection* as a strategy is difficult inasmuch as it is symmetrical, especially regarding the responsibilities of institutions, i.e. larger context. *Acceptance* is exemplified in the following team response to the patient: "I'll give you a drug that will make your anxiety pass, calm you down and build up your morale . . ." The third possibility, *acceptance-redefinition*, contains an acceptance of the content of the patient's request (the drug,) but at the same time redefines them as only a partial instrument of intervention ("they will help you to feel a little better") and delimits their function in respect to the therapy ("they won't change you"). The team's redefinition of the therapeutic context is therefore maintained.

C. Responsibilities Related to Emergency Intervention

Emergency interventions, such as hospitalisation, sedation with drugs and home care, are characterised by the fact that the client or his reference group (i.e. the family or other significant social group) ceases to make any decision about his management. He is defined as incapable and incompetent, and he turns to a third party (the psychiatric team of the service) which takes over the decision-making functions regarding biological and social needs.

Emergency intervention brings into force the statutory duties and responsibilities of the social psychiatric service which include the proposal, validation and management of obligatory treatment. At that point the service becomes a social control agent whose primary function is to re-establish social equilibrium.

In his transaction with the team, in his urgent request, the patient sends out the following message: "Take care of me, I can't do it anymore by myself" (family members can also be the ones to declare the patient incompetent), qualified by, "I'm not the one who's asking, it's the anxiety that has caused me to make this request". Once again it can happen that the team *accepts* the request without being aware of the relational level of the message. This can result in a paradoxical response by the team which gives the message: "You will become autonomous, you'll get well, to the extent that I take responsibility for you". A pathological game is thus begun between team and client which does not have the internal rules that enable it to be broken up, because it is self-perpetuating. The most visible outcome is long-term hospitalisation.

The *rejection* response is symmetrical both in terms of the context mark (control) and in terms of the patient who can react with an escalation of symptoms: "You're not helping me, you don't see how sick I am, how much sicker I'm getting".

The *acceptance-redefinition* manoeuvre takes both levels into account. Emergency intervention is properly carried out if the team gives it a meaning of "pause", or "time out" or "moment of suspension" of the given interactional game within the family as well as the family-service system. The psychiatric team acts as a proxy for the patient and his significant others in the sense that it assumes a temporary and limited responsibility only for those functions which the patient cannot deal with himself and only for the duration of the emergency. In this way a temporal dimension is introduced as the understanding and resolution of the problems—the moment in psychotherapy when the patient will take for himself the responsibility for changing—is postponed to another time and context.

The case of Franca represents an example of *acceptance-redefinition* as a reply to a request for emergency service. Franca, aged 18, is diagnosed as suffering from a schizophrenic psychosis. She comes for her first contact with the SIMAP in an acute symptomatic state and is accompanied by her parents. The team conducts the session utilising a circular interview and gives an intervention aimed at the family relational game. The family reacts with a heavy disqualification: they request advice for a referral to a private therapist, seeing that the SIMAP is only a centre of a social assistance nature. The family departs, and after a brief sounding of private sector psychiatry, they return to the SIMAP, which by definition has to be always available. They report that Franca's condition has significantly worsened, and they declare themselves unable to deal with her situation at home any longer. The team decides to make a home visit and to talk to the patient in the presence of her family. During the home visit, the situation is extremely tense, as the team finds itself in the position to have to mediate between a social control intervention (involuntary hospitalisation) as requested by the parents, and an intervention strategically aimed at change. They decide to communicate to Franca in the presence of her family the following: "We understand that you do not want to worsen the burden your parents have in controlling and coercing you to behave . . . but at the same time we've understood from you how much you feel that it is dangerous at the moment to talk about beginning a therapy which could lead to changes. We have understood how much you and your family are in need of a respite from the grave tensions which have been created. We respect what you have been requesting through your behaviour, and interpret it as a request for temporary hospitalisation, even if involuntary".

With this intervention, the team accepted the request of the family, did not shirk its institutional obligations to provide involuntary commital in case of need, and redefined hospitalisation within the therapeutic context as a pause in the process of change that therapy would bring. In this way, hospitalisation does not represent an interruption or an alternative to psychotherapy, but it becomes incorporated as part of the whole therapeutic process. After Franca's hospitalisation, in fact, it was possible to continue a psychotherapy with the whole family.

III. BEYOND THE PSYCHOTHERAPEUTIC SETTING

The hypothesis which guided the second part of our research was founded on the assumption that psychotherapeutic interventions could be delivered also through a service classically defined as social assistance. Services such as home assistance, financial assistance, and other social welfare services, which are the typical avenues through which the service system remains in contact with the situations presented by the marginal clients, can be utilised to actualise a therapeutic intervention aimed at change rather than solely support or assistance.

Our objective to formulate, test, and verify specific operational hypotheses was supported by the theoretical debate which has been developing in the last few years within the field of cybernetic and systemic thinkers (Dell, 1981a, 1981b, 1982; Elkaim, 1981; Hoffman, 1981; Keeney, 1979, 1982a, 1982b, 1983; Palazzoli et al., 1980).

Consistent with the systemic-cybernetic approach model, the therapeutic system is analysed as a totally interactive and communicative ecosystem. This involves shifting the attention from the various elements that make up a therapeutic situation (the therapist, the patient, the patient's family, cultural considerations, the setting, context, interventions, etc.) to the relation between them inside a co-evolutionary process. Obviously, the above-mentioned elements are not all of equal importance, but what we wish to emphasise here is that none of them is therapeutically efficacious in itself. The capacity to bring about change is a characteristic neither of the therapist nor of the setting nor of the intervention, etc.: therapeutic efficaciousness is a bond connecting various elements.

New orientations in the systemic approach suggest the abandonment of the idea that the symptom is an expression of dysfunction, and the adoption instead of the notion that the symptom is the expression of the transition from one system toward new states; and the substitution of the concept of resistance to change with that of the coherence of a given system (Dell, 1982; Elkaim, 1981; Hoffman, 1981). These are rather stimulating positions; however, stopping at the concept of coherence of a system can generate a sense of immobility from the operative point of view if we do not add that this coherence, in systems with the designated patient, is characterised by repetitiveness of interactive patterns and rigidity of the descriptive maps of their behaviour, bearing in mind that according to the theoretical model adopted here, these two levels (behaviour and the world of ideas) cannot be separated but are reciprocally inter-related and influential. In this sense then, the so-called capacity to bring about change is linked to the possibility that this rigidity and repetitiveness will be broken down through the therapeutic relationship because the system will be reorganised on the basis of a new coherence.

The systemic-cybernetic model, which places the accent on relationships and patterns, offers the possibility of utilising for change what have been traditionally and perhaps are still considered contextual limitations to the realisation of psychotherapeutic intervention. The presence of diverse theoretical and operative orientations, or of different professional figures in a team, the mandate to take up all cases referred to the service regardless of motivation for treatment, the network of many cases, the obligatory relationship with other psychiatric structures, etc., are limitations from the viewpoint of relationship between a single team member and his patient; from the viewpoint of the ecosystem, these limitations serve as information which can be absorbed and used in the relationship. In this case, where for any reason it is impossible to effect traditionally agreed-upon psychotherapeutic intervention, the possibility of operating in a therapeutic sense is linked to the way in which the various elements that constitute the complex system of public service are inter-connected. The coordination of these service elements vis-à-vis the client's needs can in itself become an intervention toward change or be an avenue through which change can occur.

The aim is to identify strategies of intervention which, apart from their individual characteristics and qualities, are internally connected to the network of relationships and patterns of the client, in order to create relationships capable of preventing the repetitiveness of behavioural models or to break up the rigidity of the descriptive maps of the dysfunctioning group through the introduction of new rules which enable differentiation and therefore evolution.

Interventions on the social level, such as home care or a conversation at the centre, are in themselves neither therapeutic nor untherapeutic. The problem is to evaluate whether or not they are redundant with respect to the client, with respect to his epistemological premises or his relational pattern, or instead if they create differences and therefore information and complexity.

The following example illustrates the theoretical issues described above. Margherita, 42 years old, was referred to the service during hospitalisation in a psychiatric structure where she had been for several months, with a symptomatology described as "depressive syndrome with border line symptoms". After the sudden death of her husband, the patient abandoned all home and social activities; she spent her days in bed and stopped talking. Given the situation, her mother came to live with her in order to help with the house and take care of the children (a boy, 15, and a girl, 9). At the first meeting with the service, Margherita stated that she was absolutely incapable of doing anything; she walked like a robot and spoke of suicide.

Before his death, the husband had managed all social activities of the family as well as a great part of the household activities. After her hospitalisation, Margherita's brother took care of all problems dealing with the inheritance, while Margherita's mother became responsible for the house and children.

The patient has a sister and a brother living in the same city and a sister living in Brescia. All of them dutifully went to visit her in the hospital. Her records noted that the sister from Brescia felt that Margherita's living with her mother was harmful and proposed to ask the mother to come and live with her, leaving the job of helping Margherita face up to her responsibilities to the nearby brother and sister and the service. The brother did not agree, and animated discussion broke out on the subject. When questioned by the attending physician, the mother stated that she would remain at the house of her ill daughter for a while and she would then go to Brescia for a rest.

The case was discussed in a team conference, and a hypothesis about the family was formulated: the mother's (Maria's) transfer to the home of Margherita demonstrated the symmetry between the children to "have" the mother. In this picture, the symptom was useful to the patient, to reinforce even more the close bonds with her mother; to the children living in the same city, to have a privileged relationship with the mother because of Margherita's needs; to the sister from Brescia, to be able to ask the mother to go and live with her, justifying this as being for the good of Margherita; to Maria, who through the symptom of her daughter continued to "have" all her children, without defining the relationship with any of them.

After the hypothesis was formulated, what was the procedure to follow? Talks on an out-patient basis with the patient were impossible because even after discharge from hospital she did not get out of bed, and although she accepted visits, she refused to go alone or be accompanied to the centre. Talks with the family members were not proposed because the mother had a disqualifying attitude toward the team, and the sister from Brescia, who was offended because her advice had not been accepted, said she wasn't available.

Thus it seemed that home care was the only means of contact with the family, but such care had to be defined on the basis of the hypothesis formulated in order to trigger a process of change.

The following considerations were made: (1) To push for the separation of Margherita from her mother would have given the appearance of an alliance formed with the sister from Brescia and would certainly have started an escalation of symptoms. (2) If for the microsystem of mother–daughter, the greatest threat was separation, all of the activities proposed had to be defined as aimed towards the unity of the couple. (3) Home care could be interpreted by the mother as disqualification of her work, with the possible outcome either of exclusion of the team or of an increase in her active behaviour. (4) The team could substitute for her mother, re-creating the rigid relational pattern, with Margherita in a passive position. (5) Home care alone barely affected the position of brother who managed the entire economic situation.

In order for home care to bring about changes in relational patterns and to modify the family's way of seeing things, it had, in this case, to be redefined as help given to the mother to tolerate a desperate situation, with continuous positive reinforcement regarding her work. Reflecting this, stimulating Margherita to become active was redefined as a sacrifice for the mother and not as a step towards autonomy.

Margherita began to do more, and the mother started to telephone the centre not to complain about the nastiness of her daughter, but to ask for help. Regarding the son and therefore the economic problem, the mother was asked to ask him if he could continue to manage the difficult problem of the inheritance, and at the same time the neighbourhood social-worker was asked to find work for Margherita. Together with her initial improvement, the hiring of the handicapped in a local government department made the placement of the patient as an attendant possible.

Even though Margherita was accompanied to see about the job and to talk with her future colleagues, she denied its existence and continued to ask that a job be found for her. The next month she did not begin working, although her activities at home had greatly increased. We then decided to ask the government department as employer, to call the interested parties in order to press Margherita for a decision either to start work or to sign a statement declaring that she refused the position. At the same time, we asked the mother to be present at the meeting, with the message that she was the only one who could convince and help her daughter. The mother made a commitment to the personnel office of the department to help out in the placement of her daughter and even accompanied her to work every morning. This intervention confirmed the mother in the position of activity and Margherita in that of passivity, but the passivity of the patient this time consisted of going to work. Margherita ceased denying the existence of the job and started going to work.

Meanwhile, summer arrived, and the possibility that the mother might take a vacation alone (as well as the only chance that Margherita would have to try out living alone with her children) was brought up. The mother said that she was tired, that she couldn't go on any longer, but that she was afraid that her daughter couldn't manage by herself "all alone, and it's so hot!" A great sacrifice was then asked of the mother: not to go off on vacation, but to rest at her home because the team would do what it could to help the daughter, but it certainly wasn't up to the task. If it couldn't manage, at least it could call her, though unfortunately, it would be depriving her of the rest she deserved. The same message was carried to Margherita. Fifteen days passed during which the mother stayed at home, and Margherita, alone with the children, asked for help from the centre only twice. From then on, the situation has shown constant and gradual improvement.

Home care, like other interventions classically defined as "supporting", can thus be utilised to effect change. Defining support as something offered to the mother instead of the patient constituted a redefinition and a novel contribution to the system, although the rules are still respected. The nurses' behaviour with respect to the patient was based on the mother's indications, and therefore they were unthreatening to the mother–daughter dyad in terms of separation. On the other hand, establishing a relationship with the two women permitted both parties wider latitude for personal autonomy. The intervention of the social worker regarding job placement established the objective conditions for economic autonomy but did not deprive the brother of his relationship with the mother. The relationship which was established between the mother and the team, on the basis of the implicit rule that nothing would be done without her involvement, permitted the mother to leave Margherita for a brief period and permitted Margherita to attempt a relationship with the children for the first time without the presence of a third party (she had not even done this when her husband was alive).[2]

IV.   A METHODOLOGICAL PROPOSAL

The public service system over the years has had to develop complex and diverse operating strategies in order to respond to the complicated and heterogeneous requests of its consumers. Any attempt to modify this service system which does not take into consideration these complexities—those of the consumer's requests and those adapted as service strategies—risks to oversimplify the problem and produce new solutions which will not adequately respond to the far-reaching and wide-ranging nature of the request. For this reason, in our work we have attempted to articulate a mode of analysis and intervention which would render the public service therapeutic while remaining within the general contextual definition of the service with all its complex contingencies.

It is clear to us that the public service complex and its operating strategies can become therapeutic instruments aimed at change under the following conditions:

1) *If its interventions are read for their relational significance.* The intervention of a service is information which is introduced into the family system, and it becomes a part of the relational pattern developed over time within that system according to two possibilities: either the intervention can be integrated into the interactive pattern already existing, or else, through a process of circular causality it can bring about a new relational model. Evaluating which of these two possibilities will occur is the most fundamental part of the analysis. In the case of Margherita, home care could

---

[2] The authors wish to gratefully recognise the contribution of the nurses of SIMAP, Magda Carafoli and Lucia Rovandi, without whose cooperation and efforts this study would not have been possible.

have taken on any one of several meanings depending upon how it was introduced to the family and according to the subsequent interactional pattern that was established between the service and the family. For example, home care could have been interpreted as a disqualification of the mother's role or as a confirmation of the patient's passivity and helplessness, or as an alliance with the sister rather than as a push toward change in the system.

2) *If the services are coordinated among each other*. The team of a public service agency is composed of a variety of professionals who serve different functions and have differing competencies. In addition, in its entirety, the team is operationally tied to other services (for example, welfare assistance, etc.) outside of its own membership. It is essential that the interventions of every professional figure and of every service be coordinated among each other into a coherent therapeutic program that has been discussed in a team meeting. Every worker can play different roles or assist through different functions in the treatment of a patient according to a single plan of intervention which has been conjointly determined. In the case of Margherita, all services that were to be provided for the family, the home care by nurses, the psychopharmacological prescriptions, and the job-finding services of the social worker, had to be coordinated in such a way as to convey a similar and consistent message to Margherita and her family.

3) *If the team evaluates feedback received and recalibrates its own behaviours accordingly through time*. Margherita's refusal to accept the job found by the social worker was interpreted by the team as a signal not to push the separation of the mother-daughter dyad. Hence the job was redefined within a framework of the union of mother and daughter and not Margherita's individuation. The team must be able to analyse the reactions provoked by their interventions in the client system according to an evolutionary perspective which will permit it to identify the changes which occur, and if necessary change its own patterns of intervention in order to co-evolve along with their patients.

Acknowledgments

The authors are grateful to their colleague Dr. Sergio Pirrotta for the translation of this article. The research is divided into two parts: the first one was conducted by Daniela Dotti, Rossana Ferrari and Laura Fruggeri; the second one by Laura Fruggeri and Massimo Matteini.

REFERENCES

Bateson, G. (1972). "Steps to an Ecology of Mind". Ballantine, New York.
Bateson, G. (1977). *In* Brockman, J. (ed.), "About Bateson". Wildwood House, London, pp. 235–247.
Bateson, G. (1978). *In* Berger, M. (ed.), "Beyond the Double Bind". Brunner and Mazel, New York, pp. 41–64.
Bateson, G. (1979). "Mind and Nature". Dutton, New York.
Dell, P. (1981a). Some Irreverent Thoughts on Paradox. *Family Process* 20, 37–41.
Dell, P. (1981b). More Thoughts on Paradox: Rejoinder. *Family Process* 20, 47–51.

Dell, P. (1982). Beyond Homeostasis: Toward a Concept of Coherence. *Family Process* 21, 21–40.

Elkaim, M. (1981). Non Equilibrio, Caso e Cambiamento in Terapia Familiare. *Terapia Familiare* 9, 101–112.

Hoffman, L. (1981). "Foundations of Family Therapy". Basic Books, New York.

Keeney, B. P. (1979). Ecosystemic Epistemology: An Alternative Paradign for Diagnosis. *Family Process* 18, 117–129.

Keeney, B. P. (1982a). Not Pragmatics not Aesthetics. *Family Process* 21, 429–434.

Keeney, B. P. (1982b). What is an Epistemology of Family Therapy. *Family Process* 21, 153–168.

Keeney, B. P. (1983). "Aesthetic of Change". Guilford Press, New York.

Palazzoli, M., Boscolo, L., Cecchin, G., and Prata, G. (1980). Ipotizzazione, Circolarita e Neutralità: Tre Direttive per la Conduzione della Seduta. *Terapia Familiare* 7, 7–20.

Chapter 15

Toward a "Systemically" Organised Mental Health Centre

Alexander Blount

I. INTRODUCTION

This chapter discusses one attempt to use systemic epistemology to inform the entire array of clinical services and to organise the way those services are delivered at a mental health centre which was founded to serve the most seriously disturbed people in its catchment area. The discussion is concerned with both the rationale for the experiment which Crossroads represents and the present organisation of its clinical program. It is our belief that systemic epistemology allows us to analyse the institutional organisation of interactional premises/patterns in which systemic therapy is practised, thereby offering the possibility of creating a context in which this therapy can evolve and be refined.

There will be a brief description of the setting in which the program has developed. Then there will be an attempt to articulate the epistemology upon which systemic therapy is based. This is done to give a conceptual background and a language for talking about how systemic therapy makes learning or change possible. It will then be possible to show how the same basic approach is carried out in the very different set of relationships which make up a day treatment program. Then a greater level of abstraction will be attempted in showing how systemic epistemology has been used to structure the basic relating patterns between clinicians and clients (clinical procedures) and among clinicians (teams) in an outpatient department. Finally, the relationship of the agency to its larger environment will be discussed.

II. DESCRIPTION OF THE SETTING

Crossroads Community Growth Centre was founded in 1972 as an aftercare facility for people leaving the state hospital in Northampton and returning to the Holyoke/Chicopee community. Prior to the opening of Crossroads, there were no formal aftercare services available in the community. The name, with its implications of the coming together of both people and meanings, was originally picked to help locate the centre geographically for clients. The first site of the centre was on a corner which had traditionally been known as the "crossroads" of Holyoke. The determination on the part of the founders of Crossroads was to set up a program

APPLICATIONS OF SYSTEMIC FAMILY THERAPY
ISBN 0-8089-1696-3

which could engage clients who were unable or unwilling to participate in formal "psychotherapy". The flexibility and caring of the staff has been the major clinical resource of the agency from its earliest days. The continuity of having the same executive director since the beginning of the agency has helped to maintain a very low staff turnover rate.

In 1981, as Crossroads moved toward state mandated licensure as an outpatient mental health centre, the author was hired as Clinical Director. It was hoped that someone who had trained family therapists could develop a program which more effectively engaged clients with their social networks. Within six months the training program in systemic family therapy was started for all outpatient staff. For the next two years every staff member spent one full day per week on a treatment/training team engaged in live supervision of family therapy cases.

At the present time, the clinical program at Crossroads is made up of two major divisions: the day treatment program and the outpatient department. While there is a fair amount of overlap in function, we have generally conceived of the day treatment program as providing a bridge between the desocialised client and his or her social network and the outpatient department as working to solve problems in existing social networks.

The day treatment program staff consists of a director and seven line staff members. The program serves around 30 people, most of whom have experienced extended psychiatric hospitalisation. Almost all "program members", as they are called, enter the program while living at the state hospital or in a staffed community residence funded by the Massachusetts Department of Mental Health. Every program member has at least one other agency involved in his or her care, and most have two or three agencies involved.

The outpatient department presently has 12 staff clinicians and 6 interns. It takes as its mandate providing service to the most difficult individual and family problems in the catchment area. It serves primarily people who have experienced psychiatric hospitalisation, referred through the Department of Mental Health system, or cases of child abuse referred by the Department of Social Services.

The staff is organised into three teams. The teams are designed to have four staff members and two interns on each. The importance of the team's structure to the agency is described below.

III.   THE EPISTEMOLOGY

In constructing the program at Crossroads we have looked to the epistemology upon which systemic therapy was based rather than to the specific methods of systemic therapy itself. We have wanted to use those ways of thinking which are applicable to the therapist plus client system, the agency as a system, and the agency plus environment system. It is our hope that we can guard against using techniques which are uniquely applicable to therapist plus client system inappropriately in other systems.

We discuss epistemology, the rules for what counts as a fact and how facts are ordered into meaningful ideas, when we are discussing the organisation of the clinical services in an agency, because in systemic thought these are different perspectives on the same phenomena. Epistemology is the study of the ordering of premises in a particular setting. Agency structure is the organisation of behaviours or communication patterns in a setting. These are the same phenomena in any given instance. At any particular moment, the form of the act of communication and the form of what is being communicated cannot be separated. "Pattern of behaviour" is the concept used by an observer who is watching the pathways along which communication is travelling, i.e. the people who are communicating. "Premise of interaction" is the concept used by an observer watching the difference or information which is travelling along these pathways. For these reasons, the terms "patterns" and "premises" are used almost interchangeably in this discussion. We could also use the terms "epistemology" and "system" interchangeably.

We look for a language which can understand behaviours as meanings and vice versa. In this way we can study the epistemology/system that is a family, the epistemology/system that is therapy and the epistemology/system that is a mental health centre all in the same language. This allows us to set up certain patterns of interaction in the organisation which will become the meanings we want in therapy sessions and to set up certain meanings in our regular interactions with clients that will become patterns of behaviour in therapy sessions. We can use the notion that "epistemology" and "system" are words for different points of view on the same phenomena to help our client. I offer here a recapitulation of the particular formulation which Gregory Bateson (1972) uses, because its numbered levels of learning are particularly easy to transfer from the analysis of one sort of system to another. Where Bateson talks about Learning I, II and III, we will use the concept of premises at Level I, II and III. Change in premises at Level II, for instance, constitutes the phenomenon which Bateson calls Learning II.

Level I designates the premises/patterns which constitute the ongoing exchange between the system and its environment. For human beings, change in premises at Level I, i.e. Learning I, is the sort of learning which is usually being assessed by "learning" experiments in psychology. At time "A" you ring a bell and the dog looks at you with a blank stare. Several trials later, at time "B", you ring a bell and the dog salivates. At time "A" you ask Johnny for the capital of North Dakota and he looks at you with a blank stare. Later, at time "B", you ask for the capital of North Dakota and, he says "Bismarck". While we will discuss other levels of learning more extensively as we talk about our program, it should be remembered that Learning I is the most common form of learning. It is at Level I that the system has its greatest flexibility and potential for change.

At Level II, we find those patterns/premises which form the consistency of the system over time. They are the "character," or "identity" of the system. These patterns/premises consist of the generalisations, drawn from the system's exchange with its environment (Level I), which have been so consistent that the system has gradually come to be able to operate on them successfully without expending attention checking their appropriateness to each new situation. These premises have therefore come to be coded differently, to be part of the guiding structure of the decision-making process of the system, rather than to constitute a decision in any particular case. These premises/patterns are no longer correctable by trial and error in the usual sense. They are part of the "unconscious" of the system.

In organisations, these Level II premises/patterns form the formal and informal organisational structure and "culture". In families, they are the repeated patterns of interaction which are sometimes best distilled in those central interchanges called family rituals. They are the regularity in families over time, the homeostatic mechanisms. In individual human beings the Level II patterns in a particular situation are called "emotions" and seen over time are called "personality". Bateson (1963) said that what we call "emotions" are better described as the experience of and the signalling about the contingencies of relationship in a particular context. Change at Level II, i.e. Learning II, is the aim of the relationship structure and interactional methodology of most psychotherapies. This has been examined at great length elsewhere (Blount, 1976).

At Level III we find those most abstract premises about the fundamental nature of what relating is, what Bateson calls the "context of contexts" (Bateson, 1972). For our purposes it might be easiest to say that at Level III is coded the flexibility which a system has in regard to its Level II premises. Some flexibility at this level is required in families for individual development to occur successfully. In this way it is possible for a person to be one sort of person at one point and a very different person at another.

Inflexibility of Level II premises is experienced as the individual identity being the "ultimate reality" in a person's life. Therefore, the individual can control (and be to blame for) his/her social interaction. Causality is linear. Flexibility of Level II premises is experienced as the individual being a part of and being modified in interaction with a larger system. Influence is reciprocal. Blame doesn't work as a model. Causality is circular.

IV.   SYSTEMIC THERAPY AND SYSTEMIC EPISTEMOLOGY

Systemic therapy, especially as it is presently being practised in the "Milan method" (Palazzoli et al., 1978; Palazzoli, 1980), instead of attempting to promote specific Level II changes in a family, was designed to introduce flexibility of Level II premises, i.e. a change at Level III in the family. This flexibility is offered in three distinct ways: (1) Through the structure of the relating pattern invoked by the therapist and team, (2) in the premises of the messages given to the family, and (3) in the structure through which information is exchanged in the session. What is being attempted is a recontextualisation of the Level II patterns of the family. Through this recontextualisation, or increased flexibility at Level III, the regularities of family interaction become growth producing. The history or "identity" of the family does not change its form, but is put against a new background where it becomes the basis for transformation, morphogenesis, rather than rigidity, morphostasis.

The structure of the relating pattern invoked by the therapist and team is one in which the therapist "stands within" a larger system of people and meanings. The therapist is a living example that one can work within a larger tradition or set of meanings without losing one's coherence as a person.

The premises guiding the messages of the team can be understood as setting a new context in which the blaming nature of the Level II patterns of the family is no longer relevant. The team describes in words the Level II patterns of the family, but places its descriptions in the context of approval and support. If there are any problems in the ongoing development of the therapy relationship, the team willingly takes the blame. By doing so they enact the premise that taking the blame, or more properly owning one's agency in a particular difficulty, instead of tearing people apart, is an action done within a continuing pattern of benevolent relatedness. The ultimate coherence of the system in the face of any Level II changes which might develop is affirmed.

In the structure through which information is exchanged in the session, i.e. through circular questioning, is imbedded a model of nonlinear, reciprocal influence in family interactions rather than linear causality. Just as the regular patterns of interaction become Level II self-maintaining patterns/premises of the system outside therapy, the patterns of regular interaction in the session become part of the Level II premises of the new family-plus-therapist system. However, these premises, over time lead to generalisations at the most abstract level which are different from those upon which the family system had operated. They contain within them the abstract, unstated, "seed" of transformation. Information is exchanged through a structure which makes reciprocal influence rather than linear causality the only tenable model of interaction.

V. THE DAY TREATMENT PROGRAMME

The day treatment program utilises the Social Competency Development model to organise its programming. The model was created by Mark Spivak, Ph.D., in Jerusalem (Spivak et al., 1962; Spivak, 1977, 1967). The approach is remarkably similar to many of the methods of systemic therapy and provides, in addition, a carefully worked out way of organising the vast amounts of interaction time that are involved in day treatment.

The plan for getting through the day is based on a "social competency diagnosis" which analyses the next step in interactional "skills" which might be considered logical for each particular program member. The conducting of a full social competency diagnosis is done by the staff together and takes between one and two hours for each program member. The diagnosis is then the basis for building a program of groups and other experiences which organise each program member's day. Most groups are focused on such basic instrumental activities as menu planning, shopping, meal preparation, clean-up, woodworking, sewing and so forth.

The main difference between the social competency model and most models of day treatment is that the activities are primarily conceptualised as vehicles for enabling staff members to engage in relationships with program members, rather than as skills which program members need to acquire in order to go out into the world.

Spivak has four key concepts to describe the type of relationship which staff members try to create with program members: "permissiveness" and "support" on the one hand, and "nonreciprocation of deviant expectations" and "conditional manipulation of rewards" on the other. The former two terms are meant to describe an environment in which program members are encouraged to engage in the patterns of interaction which they do best rather than being told or pushed to act differently. The latter two terms describe the staff's attempts to respond in ways that transform these patterns, enabling members over long periods of time to begin to operate on different Level II premises. Conditional manipulations of rewards are designed to encourage program members to try new behaviours. Someone is offered free coffee for helping to prepare the coffee break. Nonreciprocation of deviant expectations is designed to create a situation in which a program member's usual ways of behaving can be defined as adaptive. The staff is constantly trying to catch program members in the act of being competent. In this procedure, all of the skills of "positive reframing" behaviour which are used in systemic therapy are relevant for the work of day program staff. A program member who will only sit in silence, for example, will probably find a staff member sitting beside him doing some kind of work, chatting to him. After a time, the program member is thanked by the staff member for making the work go more easily by keeping her company. While carried out in a casual way, this brief interaction was in all likelihood the result of careful planning by staff members and recurs in slightly modified form several times during the program member's day.

The practice of "permissiveness" is modified only by the necessities for protecting other people. The rule against violence is absolute. Not only is violence not permitted, it is firmly maintained that when the program is running correctly, it does not occur. This dogmatic assertion is designed to create problem-solving options in the event of a violent episode. If a program member pushes or provokes someone, both the member and his or her counsellor are called in by the director of the program. Instead of lecturing to the member, the director might say something like the following: "This is terrible. Violence can never happen at the day program. Somehow, Robert (program member) was put in a situation in which he was so frustrated he couldn't think of anything to do except hit. Now he has to miss a whole day at the program. While he is gone I want you to talk to the rest of the staff. Get ideas about what might make Robert so frustrated. When he comes back, I want you and Robert to meet and come up with a plan for what we can do to keep this situation from happening again and bring the plan to me." Structure of the relationship here invoked puts Robert within a set of rules for the common good represented by the director and at the same time keeps him from being isolated by his unacceptable behaviour. His "deviant expectations", that he will be isolated or ejected, are not reciprocated. He is joined to a counsellor in a problem-solving effort rather than isolated and blamed. At all times it is assumed that the program member's motivations, if not his behaviour, are excellent.

The Level II patterns which are enacted in this structure are designed to be corrective of the Level II patterns which the program member is used to experiencing. The program member, when he has encountered a situation which was frustrating in the past, has inevitably ended up feeling cut off and blamed because of his inability to understand or behave in ways that will reduce the frustration. He now initiates that sort of interaction when he encounters frustration. The intervention of the staff is designed to eliminate both the isolation and the blame which the program member usually elicits. The new Level II patterns imply, however, a different Level III form of what relating is. Just as systemic therapy intervenes at Level III to create flexibility within an experience of benevolent connectedness and reciprocal influence rather than an experience of linear causality and personal blame, the methods and structure of the day program, as seen in this example and the one below, attempt to foster the same sort of transition.

In one case, a program member punched female staff members on two occasions. There were many circumstances which led the staff to believe that the fact that both staff members were women was not coincidental. The first occurrence was handled similarly to the way described above. When this did not work, it was decided that greater specificity of meaning was needed. In discussions with the program member following the second incident, he was defined as a great protector of women. He was said to have been attempting to teach female staff how dangerous it was in the world for women and how much women should be on their guard, especially when working with mental patients. Following this discussion there were no further incidents of violence toward male or female staff members from the program member in question. The definition was developed by the entire staff and transformed the experience of the staff as well as the program member. Because the animosity and the fear on the part of female staff members dissipated, the entire Level II pattern was changed. The program member subsequently began regular visits with his mother. These had not been possible for years because of his threatening behaviour when visits were attempted. Of course, no direct link between these events can be proven, but the sequence was not surprising to day program staff members.

The day program serves as a bridge between isolated desocialised people and their social networks in two ways. The first way involves connecting people who have little or no contact with their families with a new set of relationships outside of the state hospital. This new social network develops and grows as the program member begins to find the ways of interacting at the day program coming more naturally and being more central to his or her life. The second way that the day program connects program members with social networks is one that has potentially dramatic implications for understanding the role of family relationships in the lives of the chronically mentally ill. The staff of the day program has found that as program members begin to change their interaction patterns and to function "better", their families suddenly become much more involved with them. Family members seem to "come out of the woodwork" even in cases in which contact between the family and the program member was not known to have occurred for years.

It is our assumption that the families of the most seriously desocialised, institutionalised people, are structured partially by steady state messages concerning the status of the identified patient. As long as no news of change is brought, all patterns are assumed to be as they have been in the past. It is the news of change, a difference that makes a difference, which can begin a process through which these families become more actively involved with the previously isolated member.

The day treatment program attempts to create flexibility at Level III while offering new patterns at Level II to clients. Just as in systemic therapy, the structure of relating patterns offered, the premises of the messages exchanged, and the way in which information is organised are all designed to create a model of benevolent relatedness which exists through any changes in immediate relating patterns. The difference between the day treatment program and systemic therapy is largely centred around the need of the day program staff to dramatically increase the intensity and complexity of messages which can be exchanged with a particular program member and then to focus this potential for intensity and complexity of exchange toward revivifying relationships with the program member's natural social system and constituting new social networks where the natural social system has atrophied beyond reclaiming.

VI.   THE OUTPATIENT DEPARTMENT

In the outpatient department there has been an attempt to structure the relationship and information exchange which constitutes therapy in ways designed to maximise potential for flexibility at Level III for both the therapist and the clients. This attempt has involved attending to the position of the therapist in relation to the client system at the outset of therapy, and the position of the therapist in relation to his/her network of colleagues in the agency.

A.   Clinical Procedures

The form that information takes is in fact influenced greatly by the "forms" that are routinely used in an agency. The forms at Crossroads are designed to evoke a problem to be worked on which exists within a defined temporal and relational context. The problem definition approach to structuring information was chosen because it seemed to be a good compromise between the definition of one person as sick and an evocation of process which is typical of systemic therapy. A problem-oriented definition allows us to engage systems which have identified one person as sick and still maintain the future flexibility for studying problematic process rather than problematic people.

Intake forms are designed to obtain the same demographic information on all members of the system as are obtained on the identified patient. The order of questions, however, clearly identifies the patient, thereby making sense to the members of the system who are involved in the initial interview. Besides asking for a clear behavioural definition of the problem which brings the system to therapy, the forms ask for the situation in which the problem is most likely to occur. This sets the assumption that problems are contextual. There is then a question about the history of the problem. This is distinguished from the history of the person. Medical and psychiatric information is elicited about the identified patient and subsequently about other members of the family. It is not uncommon for the intake person to be able to make a connection between a medical problem of a family member and the onset of the problem being discussed in the intake which the family has never made.

While we know that therapy begins from the first contact, we have found it helpful to "officially" put off the commencement of therapy for some time. Therefore, at Crossroads, no clients are accepted for therapy. All new clients after intake are accepted for the "assessment" only. This is a period of from one to four or more sessions in which there is an attempt to gather and organise information about the client's situation in ways that will make problem resolution most likely. Because we are involved in "assessment" rather than "therapy", we have had good success at involving other family members and people important to the client's situation. It has seemed much easier to get people to come to contribute to the assessment of a situation rather than to be involved in therapy. Once someone has participated in the assessment of a situation, we continue to be responsible to that person to deliver the outcome of our assessment. This determination on the part of the Crossroads clinician to be responsible to a broad network of people tends to engage people in solutions without defining them as being to blame for the problem.

The assessment stage and treatment proposal set a relationship in which it will be the clients who are the judge of the adequacy of the clinicians rather than vice versa. The willingness of the clinician to have his or her treatment process considered carefully by the client sets a particular pattern at Level II. It is possible to reverse roles later, maintaining the same pattern, to create a helping relationship for the client.

The point toward which the assessment period and the formulations of the clinician have been leading is the treatment contract. The treatment contract establishes the position of the clinician and the team in relation to the client system. It also establishes the form of the information about the clients upon which further treatment will be based.

The treatment contract is also a system of keeping Crossroads case records in compliance with the various licensing authorities which monitor outpatient mental health centres. It provides documentation of an initial assessment such as is required in an intake summary. It meets the requirements for a treatment plan. It includes the basic information necessary for a mental status report. It contains a diagnosis in the required format. Finally, it establishes open access of clients to their records and to the summaries which are kept about them. (See Figure 1.)

The treatment contract provides a tool for transition between models of problem etiology. Mental health regulating authorities operate on the same linear model as the client or clients usually do. It is a model of a problem or condition with particular causes manifested "in" a particular person. The treatment contract must meet the requirements of both the regulatory authorities and the client(s) that the information presented be adequate to explain the problem's etiology in their model. At the same time it must provide the basis for future work in a systemic model. The final statement which the client must sign is designed to force both the client(s) and clinician to begin their work within a systemic definition of problem development and resolution. If a clinician has not been able to offer a useful and workable systemic definition to a client by this point, the client will often ask the clinician to work harder to make these connections clear before he or she is willing to sign the paper.

Because the contract is routine and not undertaken because of any particular client's situation, people go through it without worrying that changes are occurring. Behavioural changes are not occurring, in fact, but information is being organised in ways that contain very different premises than the family has been enacting. These premises are contained both in the information which makes up the contract and in the different position which the therapist has taken in relation to the family. As these premises ramify in the therapy situation, learning/change becomes possible.

B.   Teams

The other major step which has been taken to organise the interaction patterns of Crossroads to support systemic premises has been the grouping of clinical staff into teams. The team has become the central organisational and administrative unit in the outpatient clinical program.

The most important aspect of the team is the way in which it represents a set of meanings which are designed to be helpful to our clients. It is our assumption that the way in which systemic therapy intervenes in the organisation of premises in families being treated, as was described above, through the way in which the thera-

NF-3
Revised 11/15/83

CROSSROADS COMMUNITY GROWTH CENTER, INC.
INITIAL ASSESSMENT & TREATMENT CONTRACT/PLAN

CLIENT (FAMILY) NAME: __Roger H._____

CASE #: _____

DATE: _____

Check One   (X)   Mental Health Services   ( ) Interim Services

Problem To Be The Focus Of Treatment: __Our goal is to alleviate Roger's inability to live__ independently without causing strain on Theodore and Margaret's (his parents) ability to live together harmoniously.

Other Problems Which Need To Be Considered: __Theodore's pattern of cyclical depressions__ seems to be temporarily alleviated but could return at any time. Theodore also has heart troubles and so stress is to be avoided.

Relevant History: __Theodore's cycles of depression led to the family's losing the ancestral__ farm and to Margaret's having to go to work. The stress between the couple was very great for many years. When it was Roger's turn to go to college, things went poorly for him and he ended up at home. For several years he spent summers picking apples and living in his car, and winters living at home fighting with his mother. He was finally hospitalized in a psychiatric unit for two weeks shortly before the first contact with Crossroads.

Ways In Which Identified Problems Impair Day-To-Day Functioning of Those People Affected: (Consider the following areas and add any that are relevant: appearance, orientation (time, place and person), speech, thinking, attention, concentration, memory, intellectual functioning, emotional state, special experiences & insight): __Roger: Rumination about things in his__ head, unable to hold a job. __Margaret: Difficulty maintaining order in the home without de-__ pression and anger. __Theodore: Difficulty with diurnal scheduling (sleeps during the day and__ stays awake at night, fear of disclosing his plans to family members. __Peter: Feels slightly__ depressed and guilty associated with his inability to help out his family. __Some social in-__ hibition. __Adam: Feelings of emotional distance from family members. __Sense of personal__ rigidity. __William: Sense of impending doom, foreboding, dread.__

What Specific Occurances Would Indicate Improvement Had Begun? __Roger would go to G. (thera-__ peutic community) and stay the time recommended by the staff. Margaret would be able to invite Roger home for a visit and the rest of the family would report she was relaxed about the visit.

Fig. 1.

What Specific Changes Would Indicate Treatment Contract Was Completed?__Roger would hold
a job for one year with no more than one month of unemployment and live in his own place.
Roger would be issued a key to T & M's house. This would indicate that Margaret was able
to feel trust in Roger's status as a person living independently. Theodore and Margaret would
not report extreme difficulty between the two of them to any of their sons.

Clinician's Formulation:_____
        Theodore's depression and economic failures, which have been matched by Margaret's
efficiency and economic successes, have helped to create the strong female-led family which
has been central to the continuity of the H. family over the years. His arguing with Margaret while at the same time not being a success, for years kept her strong. Recently,
Roger has given his father an opportunity to retire while still keeping Margaret strong by
taking over the role of arguing with his mother. Therapy must guard against the possibility
of drawing Roger's brothers away from their successful lives to fill the gap which might be
created by his improvement._____

Diagnosis of person most affected by problem. (This is required for third party payment of
fees)   Axis 1. (Primary Diagnosis)____309.24____2. (Secondary Diagnosis)____none____
3. (Physical Disorders)_____none_____4. (Severity of Psychological Stressors)
_____moderate_____5. (Highest level of adaptive functioning in past year)_____
                                        poor

Behavioral Treatment Plan:__Family meetings once every six weeks to monitor the progress____
which the family is embarked upon at the present time. These meetings will be more or less_
frequent as conditions warrant. Their main goal will be to prevent the family from attempting
movement so quickly that anyone is put under unnecessary or excessive stress._____

Medical Treatment Plan:___None at Crossroads. Roger is presently taking psychotropic medication prescribed by Dr. B. and will continue that treatment as long as he and his physician_
judge appropriate._____

Offered by: _____   _____
                        Clinician   Reviewing Psychiatrist

                   _____   _____
                        Reviewing Psychologist   Reviewing Social Worker

Accepted by: I certify that I have read this Treatment Contract and discussed it with a
clinician. The possible side effects of any prescribed medication as well as the possible
difficulties which a change (even an improvement) in the identified problems might cause
have been explained to me.

Signed: _____   _____   _____

           _____   _____   _____

Fig. 2.

pist "stands within" the larger group of people and meanings which the systemic team represents, can be available much more broadly in the clinic without requiring that every case be seen in front of a mirror. The team organisation is an attempt to make this structural configuration an experiential reality to clinicians in ways that will gradually help to extend these premises throughout the clinical work of the agency. We have made teams part of the Level II patterns of the agency. If it is true that the structure of interaction in the clinic will gradually come to shape the Level II premises of clinicians in their working lives, we hope that the team structure will provide the interactive process out of which innovations and refinements in our treatment can come.

VII.   RELATIONSHIP WITH LARGER SYSTEMS

Because Crossroads is only one part of a highly complex and well funded mental health service system which has developed out of the move toward "deinstitutional-isation" in Western Massachusetts, it is crucial that the agency use its systemic model to allow it to be innovative without isolating it from the larger system which it wants to support. To date, the "advances" or "refinements" in the Crossroads program have been met as often with skepticism as with support in the mental health system. Only by continually reminding ourselves and our colleagues that these efforts to set Crossroads on its former path are sensible, that they are motivated by a sincere desire to protect and help our clients, and that they should be encouraged until we can demonstrate that a new way is better, can we keep from taking part in a polarisation process that would reset the larger system by invoking its more funda-mental homeostatic mechanisms.

VIII.   SUMMARY

We have presented here an attempt to use systemic epistemology to organise an entire clinical program so as to reflect the premises/patterns inherent in systemic therapy. As in systemic therapy, there is a specific structure to the relating patterns of the staff. The team organisation in both the outpatient department and day treat-ment program is expected, as we all live in it, to become the Level II premises in the work situation. Designed into the team approach is the premise at Level III in which all of us work within a larger wisdom of the processes of the team. Secondly, as in systemic therapy, in order to support the ordering of premises described above, we have structured the flow of information. The forms and clinical procedures of the outpatient department and the social competency development model of the day treatment program are designed to create a context in which the negotiation of inter-actional reality, i.e. the step-by-step enactment of a model of reciprocal influence, is the basic feature of every clinical case. Thirdly, as in systemic therapy, the premises which inform the messages delivered between the agency and other systems, are part of a pattern of positively framed reciprocal influence. We catch everyone in the act of being helpful and competent, thereby invoking a formal relationship which can inform the reality of the whole system.

Having set the program in place and thought it through as best we can, none of us has a prediction about where it will take us. We assume that learning or change in all systems is similar to the processes we have observed in working with families, that sometimes things develop in a steady, "logical" fashion, but more often change is discontinuous and unpredictable. One can only set the context for positive transformation and stay involved the necessary length of time. We have set the context at Crossroads as best we can. We are aware that anything could change at any time. Our hope is that most of us will be here for the long haul to see what develops.

REFERENCES

Bateson, G. (1963). *In* Knapp, P. (ed.), "Expression of the Emotions in Man". International Universities Press, New York.

Bateson, G. (1972). Logical Categories of Learning and Communication. *In* "Steps to an Ecology of Mind". Ballantine Books, New York.

Blount, A. (1976). "Gregory Bateson and a Language for Psychotherapy". *Dissertation Abstract International* 37(1)B:450, Amherst, Massachusetts.

Palazzoli, M. (1980). Hypothesizing–Circularity–Neutrality: Three Guidelines for the Conductor of the Session. *Family Process* 19, 3–13.

Palazzoli, M., Boscolo, L., Cecchin, G., and Prata, G. (1978). "Paradox and Counterparadox: A New Model in the Therapy of the Family in Schizophrenic Transaction". Jason Aronsen, New York.

Spivak, M. (1967). Rehabilitation Club—A New Approach to the Treatment of the Mentally Ill in Israel. *Israel Annals of Psychiatry* 5, 219–221.

Spivak, M. (1977). Towards the Systemization of the Social Competency Approach to Rehabilitation Theory and a Definition. *Israel Annals of Psychiatry and Related Disciplines* 15, 289–299.

Spivak, M., Moore, K., and Stewat, T. (1962). Expert Social Interactional Approach to the Milieu Treatment of Schizophrenia. *Psychiatric Quarterly* 30, 484–502.

Chapter 16

Working Systemically with Disadvantaged Families and the Professional Network: Sharing is Caring but Meta is Better

Stephanie Christofas, Ann Goldsmith, Philippa Marx, Barry Mason and Philip Peatfield

I. FAMILY SERVICE UNITS

Family Service Units (FSU's) emerged as social work agencies during the war under the title "Pacificist Service Units". They were heavily influenced by the Quaker movement and staffed by conscientious objectors. They were located in the slum areas of large cities, and workers provided practical and personal assistance to families in distress.

After the war, the work continued and further units were established (see "Social Work Practice in FSU" in Miller and Cook, 1981). In those early days, before the development of welfare services offering a preventive service in the community, the FSU contribution was to provide practical and emotional support to families. The families referred presented many practical difficulties in maintaining an adequate level of material care (e.g. housing, money). These affected and were affected by relationship difficulties. The organisation was referred to under the title "Mop and Bucket Brigade", and the work was very much seen as a maintenance operation. Help would be offered until children grew older and the burden on families ceased to be as great. There was little anticipation that change would occur in any other way.

A. The Islington Unit

The Islington Unit was established in 1954. The main service offered was then described as family casework with multi-problem families. As the work developed, the unit established a role in "taking care" of families, with families and the professional network approving this development. Workers felt responsible for families on their caseload, and one would often be asked on the phone, "is this one of *your* families?" The worker "shared" the problems of the family. Dependencies developed in "caring" for the family, and the worker became enmeshed in the family system, thereby helping to maintain a homeostatic position by no longer being able to challenge the organisation of the system. Being a social worker in the unit was rather like being the performer in the circus who does the plate-spinning act. The art was to keep the maximum number of families spinning along, and to achieve this the worker would hurry from family to family to prevent them crashing to the ground. The professional network would assist rather like the audience at the circus, with urgent warnings to the worker as to which family was about to fall.

B. Changed Times

Social work in Britain has changed since the development of this style of work. The provision of more comprehensive preventive welfare services by local authorities has meant that a good deal of help is available to families from those sources. Practical and financial assistance is offered within a legislative framework, and advice and counselling facilities are widely available. Families can now achieve changes which were more difficult to achieve in the 1950's and 1960's.

In view of this we slowly came to the conclusion that it was no longer in anyone's interest for unit workers to be so close to families. The family might be more likely to achieve changes, and the worker might be less exhausted, if he then could maintain a meta position, an overview. We believed that we could only achieve this position if there was a consensus in our team about theoretical assumptions that informed our work, coupled with the introduction of live supervision of family work. We realised that if we could not establish some distance, this meta position, we would be in danger of continuing to offer unending support. Families would not change much and, if we kept supporting a few families forever, we could not take on any new referrals, so the network would also get a raw deal. In Islington, we slowly adopted family therapy in an attempt to alter this situation. Initially, this may well have been to give workers greater authority in the situations into which they had been drawn. To begin with we experimented with various theories and methods. For the last four years, however, we have used a systemic model based on the work of the Milan team.

There are five of us in the team, but with all team members expected to undertake administrative and organisational tasks apart from the therapeutic work with families, our resources are thinly spread. We work mainly, therefore, in pairs, with one member being the therapist and the other the live supervisor using video. We have not been able to devote the time for the entire team to work with one family. The combinations of pairs varies from case to case, but as we all meet twice weekly in team meetings, there is a reasonable degree of consistency in our practice.

The professional network (social service area teams, education, health) maintained an interest in the old caring model, however. We could not realistically expect anything else. We had many referrals from agencies who wished for someone to take care, or take control, of the family. We had been colluding with this, and sensed that we were often preventing change from taking place. We worried that if we stepped back, we would lose control. No one element in the circuit has overall control—each element effects and is affected by the other, whether the elements be the members of the family, or whether they be the family, the social workers or the professional network. Failure to understand this had led to the accentuation of redundant patterns of communication and the underestimation of a family's ability to realise its potential for change.

II. LEARNING A NEW APPROACH

Bowen (1966) has pointed out that families in distress are often characterised by the fact that more and more outsiders become involved. This is particularly true with disadvantaged families. In about 80% of the families that we see there are at least two other agencies that tend to be in contact with us about their concern for the family. The agency may be the educational system, the health system, the residential care system or the juvenile court system. It is therefore, extremely important when a family is referred to us that we consider where to draw the boundary to define the focus of our work. With disadvantaged families we have found that more often than not the system in focus tends to be the family plus therapist plus professional network system.

With many disadvantaged families, it is usual for one or more agencies in the professional network to have a strong belief that the problem exists solely in the *family* system. The network therefore, often has a stronger interest in our working with the family than the family itself. Indeed, if it was not for the power and status of the referrer, many families would choose not to have us involved at all. We have found that some families agree to come because they have fears about what the statutory authorities may do if they don't come, e.g. take the matter to court. We discovered it was important to address the relationship between the referrer and the family around the issue of referral in the first interview. One of the ways in which we do this is by asking family members and referrers what they see as happening if our work with the family is not helpful.

We now consider ourselves to be much clearer about such issues. When we first started to adapt some of the thinking of the Milan approach to an agency like ours, however, we experienced difficulties. The professional network, in particular, tended to experience our more neutral stance as "withdrawing", and this increased the potential for symmetrical relationships to develop. All the agencies with whom we had contact worked under considerable pressure and they resisted greater involvement with us. One of the Milan papers that particularly influenced us was "The Problem of the Referring Person" (Palazzoli *et al.*, 1980) and as a result, we decided that we would insist on the referrer attending the initial referral meeting with the family at the unit. For some people in the network this was something they could have done without, because it meant finding more time. We persisted in making this demand of referrers' as we believed that the family could gain a clearer understanding of the reason for referral and the difference between us and the referrer if both parties were present. The referrer's contribution to the initial interview is valuable for us as it provides information for them about the way we will work with the family.

We slowly developed a clearer systemic view of the referring person as the representative of the professional system. We began to recognise the importance of the initial interview in helping to sell the new way we were trying to work. By positively connoting the referring agency's ambivalence, for example, as determination and commitment to helping the family, we effectively made a statement about not being in competition with them; we made a statement about occupying different positions in the system; we were neither better nor worse. The effect of this was more positive feedback from the professional network and a more steady acceptance of our wish to have the referrer at the initial referral interview.

A. The Effect on Our Work

We continue to ask ourselves, when working with families and the professional network, how can we refrain from falling into relationships which bear a hallmark of competition, how can we avoid becoming symmetrical? How can we gain a view from above—a meta position—of the family plus therapist plus professional network system?

This can be illustrated by our work with the Jenkins family. The composition of the family is Jennifer Jenkins, aged 30, mother, unemployed; Deborah Roberts, aged 12, daughter; David Palmer, aged 6, son; and John Palmer, aged 2, son. The family were referred to us by the family health visitor via the social services area team because of her concern about the mother's ambivalent feelings towards the children. This was only a month after the case had been closed by the local authority social worker who had since moved on to another job. John had previously been on the Non-Accidental Injury Register after allegedly being physically abused, but his name had recently been removed. Not only did it appear significant that the health visitor was re-referring a month after closure, but Jennifer was also continuing to see a counsellor for individual help regularly and the GP was also closely involved. We formed an hypothesis that there was conflict amongst the professionals involved as to how concerned they should be about this family.

After having met the health visitor, the counsellor and the doctor, an initial referral meeting was arranged to take place at the unit. Only Jennifer and Deborah arrived with the health visitor for the session, for, as we were to learn, David and John were now being looked after by their father's parents, who lived across the road from Jennifer. James Palmer, the father, had also left Jennifer and married her younger sister. So we had a fairly chaotic, disorganised, enmeshed family with high professional network involvement. Although the family reluctantly agreed to the use of the video and live supervision, it was clear from Jennifer's manner in particular, that she didn't want to be there.

It was important as far as we were concerned that any feedback to the family should address its relationship to the network whose help, mother in particular, said was no longer needed. We decided that the competition was too much and sent the intervention to the family by letter. After positively connoting the family's reservations for being at the interview, and reframing the placement of David and John with their grandparents as a means of sacrificing a wish to keep the family together in order to keep the father involved, we moved on to address the network issue. We addressed it in the following way, moving on from the notion of mother's concern for her children by saying: "Concern is also important in another way—the concern the health visitor, etc., have for you, Jennifer, and the rest of your family. You say you don't want their concern, you say you don't need it. But why is it we ask, that you are failing to convince them of this? We are of the opinion that you need to do some further thinking on this important issue so that you are able to make the right decisions about the future of your family."

We weren't optimistic that the family would appear again and the appointment for two weeks later wasn't kept. We did hear from the health visitor, however, that Jennifer was less depressed. The family also failed to keep the next appointment and we thought that there was probably little further that we could do except have a meeting with the other professionals involved. The health visitor asked us to delay this idea whilst she contacted the family. When we spoke again, by phone, she felt strongly that what was needed was a home visit. She seemed exasperated with the family and us. From the information that she gave us, however, it was clear that decisions were being made in the family about its future. David had been moved with Jennifer's agreement, to his paternal aunt in Bristol and was going to school there. We decided as a result of this to write letters to the health visitor and the family. To the former we said that we had decided, as a result of further thinking, to abandon our idea of a meeting between the professionals involved as we now believed that the health visitor's idea about the way to proceed was the right one. A letter in a similar one-down tone was sent to Jennifer and Deborah to say that we would visit them at home.

At the home visit (no live supervision) it soon became clear that Jennifer, in particular, was less depressed. She appeared more competent and viewed the future more positively. The family had had no contact with the counsellor or the GP and only brief contact with the health visitor. It was agreed that no further purpose could be served by continued contact between us, although the option was made available to the family for the future. Jennifer also said to the social worker that if it made him happy he could call round!

A final letter was sent to the health visitor and the other significant professionals as well as the family. It was meant to be prescriptive for the family *and* the network:

Dear Health Visitor,

I visited Jennifer last week at home and had a long thorough discussion about the family situation and the help that they might or might not want from us or anyone else. It became clearer to me during the meeting that Jennifer likes to be in control about who she has help from and when she has help. There are things which Jennifer and Deborah need to work on at some time, things that they will need to be clearer about and I have said to Jennifer that we would be happy to work with the family. It was agreed between us that should she want to commit herself to doing some work, she could contact us at any time. That time may be next week, in three months time or never. She can decide, but we will be available. Jennifer likes to have the options whether it be with you, or her counsellor or her doctor. We think that these options should continue to be available, but would recommend the following, based on our work with families where similar situations have existed. We suggest that, apart from responsibilities to the children under 5, that you have (health visitor), the decision for having more extensive family help should, for the present, be left with the family.

Six months after the case had been closed by the unit, social services had had no requests from other agencies to re-open the case. The Jenkins family had been seen occasionally by the duty social work system concerning money problems.

Many families referred to us have children whose names have been placed on the Non-Accidental Injury Register. It is not uncommon for us to be asked such questions as, "Why are you keeping my child on this register?" The worker knows that he or she is only one of several people who have made such a decision. For the parents, understandably, the matter becomes a much more personal issue between them and the social worker.

III. THE IMPLICATIONS OF HAVING TO MAKE DIRECT INTERVENTION

As we are an agency which undertakes statutory work, wider systems such as the political and legal system have significant implications for our work with families. This is often in relation to child care law, concerning non-accidental injury to children, and care proceedings with children who are defined as beyond the control of their parents. In such circumstances, we see this request as information about the family's functioning.

In the preparation of a court report, we were able to link the discussions in the session with the written recommendation, to refer to these issues in relational terms rather than in the form of a firm conclusion. We wrote as follows: "Mrs S. has spoken about the difficulties of managing things on her own. Tom is aware of this and has shown himself to be concerned for her welfare. At the same time, he has shown himself to be resentful of the intrusion of men into the household who to him somehow seem to take over. Mrs S. thinks that Tom's getting into trouble is related to such men living with them and that Tom tends to speak in actions rather than words."

Workers who carry statutory responsibilities are in a different position to those who do not carry such responsibility. A relationship between a social worker and a family is rarely seen by either as an equal one, issues of authority and control being evident in all therapeutic relationships. When carrying statutory responsibility, the social worker's role is more overt, both in relation to the family system and the professional network system.

The difficulty for the social worker in trying to operate systemically is that issues which arise in the statutory process of power, control, and authority, are derived from a linear view of causality. This is most vividly portrayed in the court setting. An individual is brought before the magistrate. There is a precise definition of the reason for that person being there, and the court is asked to respond with a precise judgement. Using systemic thinking means using a different approach, whether this is on the telephone, in a case conference or writing a court report. We have had to move slowly and carefully in changing the way we have written reports. In court, it is not only the family who are participants in the process, but also the magistrates, the solicitors and the police.

IV. HANDLING INTERSESSION CONTACT

At a conference organised by the Family Institute, Cardiff, in 1982, Palazzoli made an important observation. She said that the person who contacts you between sessions is the person who feels the loser in the system at that time. This person could be either from the family or from the network. This is an important area for us, as the potential for intersession contact is considerable. With families who are involved with a number of agencies there are frequent contacts about the work that is going on.

What we now do, when we are approached between sessions, is to ask ourselves a number of questions. For example, how can this contact be seen as feedback from the last session? Why is this occurring now? Why is this particular person contacting us? How is this person a loser, and in relation to which system? Why is this person offering a coalition? These sorts of questions have been helpful in enabling us to move to a meta position. Indeed, as we have become more adept at using the model, we have found that the family has contacted us less.

There is also less intersession contact between us and other agencies in the professional network. When contact is made we might deal with it in the following way, for example: An education welfare officer phoned us to tell us that they hoped that we would impress upon Mr & Mrs Jones that their children should go to school on time more regularly. The meta message to us in these sorts of instances is "your approach is the wrong one". We would attempt to handle this by reframing the disqualification as concern. Asked what steps he had already taken to ensure the parents were aware of the school's concern, the education welfare officer said that visits had been made and letters written without any effect on the parents' attitude. We enquired whether any of the contact had included a request from the school for parents to come to discuss the matter with the head teacher. No request had been made. He then added, to our surprise, that this was something he could raise with the school, although the head teacher was somewhat reticent about direct contact with parents. We suggested that as he had more experience of this situation than us, we would leave the matter in his hands. We later learned that the parents had attended an appointment at the school and agreed with the school that they would try to get their children there on time. Although the school attendance issue remained a problem, the school felt that the parents were making some effort. Our work with the family continued. Near the end of our contact with them changes in the family enabled a resolution of the school attendance issue.

The rule for the worker in such instances is *don't get competitive*, for out of competition comes blame, and blame is indicative of linear thinking. We would seek to address the concern rather than chase the family.

V.   USING THIS METHOD WITH DISORGANISED FAMILIES

The unit has always worked with families that have been labelled as "disorganised" and this "disorganisation" presents us with various problems in our work as a unit. In the context of family interviews, it is extremely difficult to maintain a neutral stance when members of the family are dismantling the video equipment or sitting on a window ledge of a third-floor room. The worker is pulled to make interventions in order to "settle the family", with the consequent effect on the information coming out of the session. Additionally, if a family is presenting as not successfully managing its affairs, a consequent string of problems is evident. Rent isn't being paid and eviction threatened, bills aren't being paid and gas and electricity supplies disconnected, children aren't being got to school, money isn't available for spending on clothing and family members are inadequately clothed, and the distress of individual members is not being attended to because no other family member is certain of what action to take.

The temptation is very strong for the worker to intervene and accept responsibility for taking care of some of these problems. Indeed, members of the network may have expectations that the worker will accept professional responsibility for taking action to *protect family members from the effects of their form of organisation*. In using the Milan model we have had to look and see what functions the family's apparent disorganisation serves. This has helped us to work out more appropriate interventions, as we are not making our decisions and plans through anger, frustration and desperation that something must be done. *If organisation can be seen as information as to what the family system is, rather than being experienced as a burden on the worker, then more effective interventions can be made.* Indeed, we continue to undertake a variety of practical tasks on behalf of families as part of our work. We have found, however, that if undertaken selectively and carefully handled in relation to the therapeutic function, then this need not undermine one's meta position. For example, the agency can dispense cash assistance, but not perhaps, in the middle of the interview! The provision of live supervision has been an essential feature in managing this delicate balance.

A.   The Challenges of Working in the Home

Most of our work is carried out in the unit, but a significant proportion (40%) is carried out in families' homes. Initially, we ask families to come to the unit for sessions, so it is after they have not kept appointments that we consider visiting a family at home. In an initial home visit we would attempt to engage the family in coming to the unit for future sessions. However, if this is not possible and yet the family seems engaged in the work, we would be willing to continue at their home.

At times, also, families who have been involved in a series of sessions at the unit stop attending appointments. This often happens at a stage in the work when changes are taking place. If subsequent appointments are not kept, then a home interview may be offered and the issue of continuation/noncontinuation of work addressed. If the work is ended we hope to cease our involvement in a way that will enable the family to be comfortable about contacting us at a future time should they wish to do further work.

VI.   CONCLUSION

It is four years since members of this team began to adopt a systemic approach to their work. For the last two years, this approach has been taken on by all members of the team. To date, we have not embarked on any comprehensive evaluative or research studies, although this is something we have in mind for the future, so our conclusions are not scientifically based.

Over the last few years we have worked with a larger number of families. We no longer work with families for year after year after year. We usually work with a family for anything from six months to a year, or in some cases for one or two years. More cases are closed and the possibility of re-referral remains open, and is taken up.

We have managed to increase our input, without altering the types of families to whom we offer services. For us, this is very important. It would be a contradiction of the philosophy and ethic of Family Service Units were we to re-define the client population in order to fit in with our new work method. Agencies that refer to us, although experiencing some discomfort with our change of methods, continue to refer families who bring with them a multitude of problems. This is the best evidence we have that the services we offer continue to be relevant to the recipients and to the professional network.

REFERENCES

Bowen, M. (1966). The Use of Family Theory in Clinical Practice. *Comprehensive Psychiatry* 7, 345–374.

Davies, M. (1980). The Pre-School Child in Difficulty: A Systems Viewpoint. *Journal of Family Therapy* 2, 101–114.

Miller, J., and Cook, T. (eds.), (1981). "Direct Work with Families". Bedford Square Press, London.

Palazzoli, M., Boscolo, L., Cecchin, G., and Prata, G. (1980). The Problem of the Referring Person. *Journal of Marital and Family Therapy* 6, 3–9.

Chapter 17

The Application of Systemic Ideas and Techniques to a Child Care System: Always Arriving ... Never Having Arrived

Martin Little and Jane Conn

The Orford Road Centre[1] is one example of a setting in which systemic ideas and techniques have been used in the development of a new project and in providing a service to families with adolescents who are presenting problems in the community. It illustrates how the Milan model can be used to understand changes in the organisation and how the idea of a new project can arise. The staff of the Centre use the systemic model to provide a framework for viewing the rôle of the centre within its wider network and how they can organise themselves in relation to their organisational task. This led to a way of thinking and behaving about the work which has enabled the centre, as a new project, to support and complement changes which were already occurring in the larger system. As a part of this evolutionary process, the centre has developed an approach to problems with adolescents and found different ways of intervening in systems, that have an adolescent's behaviour as the focus.

Finally, the dilemma of a new project when it has achieved its organisational task but has become part of a system, is explored. It appears that a new rôle has to be negotiated with the host organisation or its own self-achieved redundancy accepted.

I. AN EXPLANATION FOR A SYSTEM ESTABLISHING A NEW PROJECT: THE ORFORD ROAD CENTRE

In 1978, a child care system in an Outer London Borough appeared to be going into a "runaway". It was predicted that the number of children in the care of the local authority social services department was going to increase by at least 25% in the next five years. The majority of these children would be in the 12–16 age range and would be placed in residential institutions. If this happened, it would be in

---

[1] The original name for the centre was the Children's Centre. It was changed to a more neutral label in òrder to shift the focus from children to families.

APPLICATIONS OF SYSTEMIC FAMILY THERAPY
ISBN 0-8089-1696-3

direct opposition to the local authority's policy of maintaining children in their families and in the community. It also represented a massive financial commitment, in excess of one million pounds per annum.

It meant that a potential credibility gap was likely to occur between the social service department and the politicians. Politically, it was unacceptable that such a large proportion of the borough's expenditure was being devoted to children, in particular delinquent and disturbed adolescents, and as the majority of the residential institutions were geographically located outside of the local authority, it would lead to an outflow of community resources. For the department, it questioned their ability to develop effective means of providing services to deal with the problems that adolescents presented to a child care system.

The idea of a children's centre was put forward. It would be a multi-faceted resource, combining the best practices of residential, day care and field work settings, and it would be situated within the community. At that time its task was to find alternatives to long-term residential care for children in the 12–16 age range. This concept was accepted by the politicians and came to be seen as the solution to the problem of adolescents in the child care system.

II. A CHILD CARE SYSTEM'S RESPONSE TO THE IDEA OF A CHILDREN'S CENTRE

Four years elapsed from the conception of the children's centre to its opening in May 1982. It was still being seen as the official solution to the adolescent problem by the politicians and the senior managers in the social services department, but the expected increase in the numbers of children in care had not occurred; these stabilised at the 1978 levels. The task of the children's centre was changed with the aim being to reduce the number of children in long-term residential care, thereby setting up the centre to spearhead changes in the child care system.

In the four years, other parts of the system had changed in response to the problem. These changes were having an impact. Residential units began to use a family therapy approach to work with families at the point of reception into care and successfully hold situations until alternatives to care could be found. Children in residential units were being rehabilitated to their families more quickly as decisions were being made to place them with substitute families or to help them achieve independence. No longer was it acceptable for children to be placed in residential settings and stay there until they were eighteen. Fieldworkers, also using a family therapy approach, were undertaking preventive work with families, so that placing children in care was not seen as an easy solution to a family's difficulties. There was an increase in the use of foster families. This resulted in any child, aged eleven or under, who was received into care, being placed with a foster family. This created space in the short-term residential units which were then able to concentrate on adolescents and achieve the work described above.

These were some of the changes that occurred in the child care system between 1978 and 1982. Where could the children's centre fit into it? It had a clear task defined by the organisation but it did not have a place in the child care system. It was viewed as an imposition which was experienced as a threat by some of the staff.

It was a challenge to an area of their work. Would the centre take it away from them and what would remain for them? Other staff saw it as the solution to all their child care problems and expected the centre to immediately remove the difficult adolescents who gave them headaches! Clearly the children's centre was not neutral but was a focus for many ideas and feelings about the future of children's services in the social services department.

This gave the centre a starting point and a rôle. By accepting the centre's place in the system as a centre of controversy, it was possible to take a "one-down" position to the rest of the system and define the centre's initial task as having to learn about the way the system worked. Through their discussions, the centre would begin to understand how it might support and complement the changes already taking place in the borough's children's services.

III. RECIPROCITY AS A STRATEGY TO PROVOKE NEW INFORMATION

When the social services department appointed the organiser to manage the children's centre, they were seeking someone with the necessary range of experiences and skills for the centre as they had originally envisaged it; they were seeking a person with a good knowledge of child care practice who had worked in residential, day care and fieldwork settings. They did not set out to appoint a family therapist, let alone a systemic therapist. In fact, family therapy was something of an anathema in a department with little understanding of it. Therefore the appointment of a social worker who was a systemic therapist was coincidental and introduced an interesting difference into the system.

It brought the children's centre an approach and skills which did not exist in the department but in which there was a growing interest. Consequently, there were many workers in the child care system who were willing to share their work, either through discussion or joining with the centre in exchange for learning about family therapy and how it might be used in their context. The centre evolved a staff support structure which recognised the needs of the workers and helped to evolve a shared ethos concerning the overall task of the centre. This enabled staff to present a coherent and unified approach to the work.

A minimum of one hour a fortnight with the organiser or deputy organiser was set aside to examine themselves in their rôle as centre workers and develop their identity as an integral part of the centre as a system. A centre-based training programme in systemic therapy was established. The centre recognised that the systems in which it was seeking to intervene were complex and were often emotionally very charged. Therefore, two or more centre workers would always be involved and have access to supervision. Later, as teams in line with the systemic model evolved, consultation was needed. Different ways are being tried to provide this at present. One of the major dilemmas facing the centre is the ability to find a sufficiently neutral position from inside the centre to obtain help when the work gets stuck; it may only be possible to obtain this by consultation from another agency. The staff group meets approximately every three weeks to discuss issues that affect the staff's working relationships. A fortnightly case discussion meeting is held to develop the practice of the centre in relation to its work with families and children. One half-day a month is set aside to focus on the work of the centre in relation to its internal development and the work as it interacts with the wider child care system.

These structures have become necessary for the centre to maintain its identity as part of a changing child care system, provide frameworks that enable the centre to continue to maintain a changing rôle and therefore an edge of difference in the wider system. This prevents the centre becoming homeostatic and ensures its ability to continue to challenge the redundant patterns that persistently emerge in the borough's child care system.

IV. THE PROCESS OF INTERVENTION BY THE ORFORD ROAD CENTRE IN SYSTEMS WHICH HAVE AN ADOLESCENT'S BEHAVIOUR AS THE FOCAL POINT

As there is no specific group of adolescents which would give the centre a clearly defined rôle in the child care system, the centre decided to try and intervene at any point in the system at which an adolescent was at risk of coming into care or could be assisted to leave care. The starting point for any intervention was seen to be the field workers and their team leader as they were responsible in the social services department for decisions made concerning children coming into or leaving care.

The first step in this process is the fieldworker telephoning the centre to discuss a family. As this is a voluntary decision, it defines the fieldworker and the team leader as needing help and places the centre in the rôle of helper.

Information is gathered to enable a hypothesis to be formed. This is done by tracking events seen as problems leading to referral, as defined by the referee, in order to gain a sense of their position in relation to the family system and other agencies. A date is then arranged for an initial discussion meeting (IDM). No further information is requested from the social worker until the IDM takes place.

The IDM is attended by a minimum of three centre workers—the organiser or deputy organiser who is responsible for the overall process of the meeting and the outcome in terms of the centre's further involvement, one worker who gathers the information (using a family tree as a visual aid) and another who records the information for the centre's records. Often the centre's teacher attends to provide an educational perspective. The aim of the meeting is for the centre to understand how the system has evolved through time and explore the relationship of the social worker and the team leader to other parts of the system at this point. Having obtained a view of the system, an intervention is made to the social workers to begin to test the centre's perspective and begin to include the centre as part of the field.

The interventions take a standard format—a consultation to the worker–family system, an offer of joint work, an assessment, the centre taking responsibility for the case or no involvement from the centre. Although the interventions can be categorised in these ways, each is designed to respect the team leader and the social worker as colleagues and confirm their place in the system.

A. Case Example

Mr. and Mrs. Smith had two sons: John, 14, who had been adopted in 1975 after a long-term foster placement; and Roger, 13, who was placed with the family for long-term fostering. For the past two years Roger had been placed in a residential therapeutic community, following a period of "seriously disturbed behaviour" and his foster parents had not been able to control him. The referral to the Orford Road Centre followed a case conference, in which Roger's return home was forcefully proposed on the grounds that the community could offer him no further help. The family agreed. The social worker considered this move precipitous, and in order to prevent the family's breakdown, she was mobilising as many resources as possible. There were also serious concerns from the educational psychologist as to whether Roger could cope in a mainstream comprehensive school.

Following an initial discussion meeting, the team invited the social worker and the family to come to the centre for a meeting. A summary of the thinking which led to the intervention and the subsequent work with the school system will give the reader a sense of how our work is done at the centre: As the team prepared their intervention, they were aware that to offer to meet with the family at this point would be a negative connotation of the family/social work systems, but that to have no further contact with any part of it would promote no climate for change. A further consideration was the anxiety expressed regarding Roger's re-entry into the education system. The centre's teacher's involvement was considered as part of a wider system intervention.

The intervention to the family/social work system: "We think you are fortunate to have such an experienced and caring social worker. In our experience, and in yours, as you have told us, this is not always the case.

"Mr. Smith, you understand the needs of adolescent boys and provide a practical, down-to-earth, caring for them, and your social worker understands and supports you in this.

"Mrs. Smith, you understand the emotional needs of your family, and receive support and understanding in this from your social worker.

"We see a family which is working very hard, foster parents who are doing a difficult job well—and at this point in time things are going well. However, your social worker is concerned for you, and rightly so. Because of the stressful period the family had, leading up to Roger's going away to school, she is concerned that your needs should be met now that Roger is home.

"Because of this, she has arranged for you to have an emergency service at your disposal, residential if necessary, and you are visiting there next week. The teacher from this centre will join the meeting you are having tomorrow to discuss Roger's educational needs, to see if there is any help she can offer."

To the social worker: "We can offer, with your agreement, an appointment for yourself and your team leader, in three months time so that you can tell us how the family is after this testing period, and whether there is any way you think we can help at that time."

The intervention was a further confirmation of confidence in the family and their ability to live together, and in the parents' ability to parent, while supporting the social work system in their decision to create a safety net for the family. It was further aimed at supporting the education system in providing a placement for Roger which could survive this transitional period.

In putting ourselves in a position of "not knowing" whether we could be of any further help to the social worker, her work and experience were not undermined. This was her case, and she was in control of any decision for further work with the family. The re-framing of the family system enabled her to take a fresh look at the system and her rôle within it. She also experienced the possibility of intervention from the centre's teacher as supportive, as her rôle in relation to the family and the pressure of her other work would not have led her to intervene in this way. By offering a further consultation to her and her own immediate support system, we were also providing a "safety net", and a message to Social Services that this was also a transitional point in their relationship with the family.

The intervention with the part of the education system involved with Roger's school placement was aimed at the interface between different subsystems within it (i.e. School Psychological Service and different parts of the school system itself), parents, Roger and social services. This has to be seen as a process over time, i.e. over a six-month period.

Initially this took place in the context of the meeting of the School Psychological Service and Social Services. The rôle of the centre's teacher was to positively connote the concern of both services, contribute to the discussion of choice of school from her knowledge, and gain the active agreement of both services to enable her to work with relevant school staff in consolidating Roger's place. The educational psychologist was able to accept this, as he could be part of the planning, and the social worker was also supported in her part of the decision-making process with the family regarding Roger's return home.

The next part of the process was identifying two key members of staff within the school who would be in a position to help Roger accommodate to a school routine while the school routine and other staff accommodated to Roger. One was his head of year, who was in a position of pastoral responsibility, and the other, the teacher with whom Roger spent most time. Further credibility was established with the school by the centre teacher's initially intensive involvement with Roger (three sessions a week), helping him adjust to a strange environment. Her work in walking around the school with Roger, establishing where different lessons were held, gradual introduction to subjects he found difficult, and in helping Roger to accommodate a staff/pupil relationship, provided a model which other staff could observe, and therefore it became possible for them to add to their own repertoire of skills. This was particularly important in relation to acceptance of punishment; by demonstrating that this could be achieved more successfully by questioning around the circumstances and allowing Roger time to assimilate this information, than by immediately engaging in conflict, she not only enabled key staff to use the same technique, but also found they were finding this useful in other situations!

Part of the work with the school system was to meet with all staff who taught Roger after two months in order to have the opportunity to share these experiences as a group and receive encouragement and thanks for the work they had done. By the end of the four-month period Roger was following a full school timetable, staff were accommodating his absence from games, and Roger had made two close friends. The school had also had some contact with Roger's foster mother, and had, after discussion with the centre's teacher, been able to maintain a neutral position when faced with the intensity of Mrs. Smith's anger or anxiety, enabling Roger to experience their acceptance of himself and his family context.

In addition to the intervention to the education system, three consultations were offered to the social worker and team leader over the six-month period. As both had been identified as important figures by the family, the team maintained this message by offering the consultations to them both, thus also maintaining a consistency of relationship to the work. The dramatic drop in anxiety between the first and second sessions, and even more so between the second and third, paralleled the apparent lessening of anxiety in the foster parents regarding their ability to make decisions and rear two sons.

The social worker structured her visits to monthly instead of weekly or fortnightly, when she would meet with the whole family with no separate contact with the mother. Concurrently, the latter's almost daily telephone contact with the area office lessened, and almost all contact was contained within the monthly visit. The social worker began to discuss with the family the possibility of her leaving the department at some stage, and the Smiths began to discuss the possibility of adopting Roger. At the end of the third consultation the team considered that to continue at this stage would have resulted in a struggle for ownership of the work. It was therefore mutually agreed that there was nothing further we could offer.

V. CURRENT POSITION STATEMENT

The centre's initial organisational task for its first year of work was to prevent the reception into care or facilitate a return home from residential placement for 12 young people in the 12–16 age range. The figure for children in this group placed residentially outside the borough since the centre opened in June 1982 has dropped from 154 to 59. This decrease reflects the changes in the whole child care system, both at the point of possible entry into care and in a reconsideration of the timing of the return to the community of those children already placed.

Referrals have come from every team in the borough, at an equivalent rate to their own child care referrals. The nature of referral, however, is changing. The consistent interest shown by social workers in the borough in working with families has been consolidated for the past year in a borough-wide course on working with families, facilitated by the centre organiser in conjunction with the Institute of Family Therapy. Forty social workers from field and residential settings (including residential provision for the elderly, day nurseries and education welfare officers) participated in this course, which proved to be a major intervention in the borough as a whole. This has created a working climate where social workers are enthusiastic in trying out their skills in family work. Current referrals, therefore, reflect those longer-term cases in which social workers are stuck, seeking direction, but not wishing to relinquish their rôle in the work. The main focus for the centre's recent interventions, consequently, has been to offer consultations to the family/ professional systems.

Within the centre, a system's view of the work is always taken; different techniques however may be applied in carrying out the organisational task, such as individual and group work, within a systemic framework. A range of techniques enables the centre to maintain an edge of difference. It is this edge that is often sought by referrers, and it is this that is difficult to maintain, as by the very nature of its use, the centre has established a niche within the social services system. In an attempt to maintain a perspective on this, the centre at times seeks external consultation. The centre staff is still learning how best to use this and in what circumstances.

The centre is now developing different and closer links with the wider borough network. The direct work provides a meeting point with different parts of the child care system. Further relationships are being established at different levels in relation to key groups within the borough, and a representative from each level of organisation within the centre links to counterparts in agency working groups. This facilitates a closer link to wider borough policy-making and child care resource provision and practice, with the inherent possibility of a more clearly defined relational position in the system.

The centre is now in a position from which its original organisational task is nearing completion, and it has become part of a changing child care system. It is in the process of having to re-define its organisational rôle, or accept that it will have achieved its own redundancy.

It is now in the process of testing out its own hypotheses regarding a useful re-definition of its rôle with regard to other changes within the borough. Consequently, the centre is always in the process of arriving—never having arrived.

Chapter 18

Instability and Evolutionary Change in a Psychiatric Community

Anna Castellucci, Laura Fruggeri and
Maurizio Marzari

I. THE OPEN CENTRE

With the advent of the Psychiatric Reform Law 180, which closed down the mental hospitals in Italy in 1978, the city of Bologna, as well as other parts of Italy, was forced to re-examine and re-organise its local psychiatric institution, the Roncati Hospital. One result of this process was the establishment of a so-called "open centre" whose function was the deinstitutionalisation and reintegration of the long-term patients into the community. The centre was staffed by 10 psychiatric nurses (now increased to 12), a head doctor, a part-time doctor and a psychologist, all of whom volunteered to be assigned to this new project. The staff was later supplemented by four additional professionals with socio-educational background. When it first opened, the open centre had 30 "guests", 15 men and 15 women, who had come from various wards within the hospital and who had been in the hospital more or less continuously from 10 to 20 years. A decision was made to call the clients "guests" and not patients because, as they had all been discharged from the hospital, they would be temporarily residing at the open centre en route to a permanent residence in the outside world. This allowed the team to define the centre as a "residential service" organisationally independent from the rest of the in-patient service of the psychiatric hospital.

The use of an ecosystemic analysis began to highlight the web of complex relationships in the wider system that contribute to the process of institutionalisation. To reverse the process and rehabilitate patients in the community involved more than the treatment of the individual. The effectiveness of the project had to be assessed in terms of its influence on the relationships in the wider system involved. But in order that the analysis of change, possible evolution and intervention not become merely a static description, we needed a conceptual framework which took the evolutionary process into account. We therefore used a model of analysis which included the dimension of time.

A. The Evolutionary Spiral of Time

For the guests, the centre brought back a sense of movement and change after years of forced immobility, when repression had been the typical response to any attempt at differentiation. In those years, drugs and electroshock therapy had been

Copyright © 1985 Grune & Stratton
All rights of reproduction in any form reserved

the standard treatment for any sign of psychiatric distress. The centre provided a different context, one which was meant to give the message: "Here begins the path leading to your independence", by allowing and encouraging subjective experience and stressing the importance of becoming an individual.

The centre enabled time to be measured by inserting the essential concept of stages into the life of the system as a whole. Any type of behaviour within that system can be described in terms of a process of movement towards the outside.

Within the centre, the adverbs of time gradually take on their own meaning, not only on the experience of each guest, but also in the comparison of one's own experience to that of others, and to the guest's past. The experience within the centre involves the interweaving of different aspects of time which converge on the centre itself. For example, the fact that a guest leaves provides confirmation for the other guests (and for the members of the team) that the entire system is moving in the right direction; it marks the passage of time in the developmental process of the system, and becomes an event which contrasts with other events within the system of the centre. Because of this, a process of review and adjustment is initiated not only for the individual, but also for the other sub-system and the centre as a whole.

Contact with the outside world and the time dimensions on the outside bring new information to this process and create a search for a new harmony between what is happening in the centre, the rhythms that measure out the events, and what is happening to each individual, the rhythms with which they experience the events. In the centre, every activity or behaviour is projected into the outside world in the spatial dimension, and into the future in the temporal dimension. The integration of some "guests" into the working world and the allocation of the first apartments were significant signs of the first stage of a break with the past.

The decision to hold meetings with the guests' families represents an important step in this evolutionary process. To begin with, the very fact that there is a mutual exchange between guest and family means the factor of time has been reintroduced. The concept of time inside the family meets with the internal time of the centre, which is quite different from that of the hospital. The new complexity of the context requires the definition of a different coherence within the system (Dell, 1982). This coherence enables the system to achieve a more complex state of equilibrium. The important task is to intervene in this complexity, respecting the times of all concerned, and by so doing, also respecting all the people concerned. The ability to wait becomes an essential requisite, in the awareness that each one has his own times of change while at the same time realising that the context itself will prevent stasis.

The chances of success of each treatment (defined in terms of rendering the guest independent) will depend on the extent to which the team succeeds in linking the internal times of the centre, those of the guests and the therapeutic team, to that of the outside world, the universal one which is measured out by the rhythms of the clock (Prigogine and Stengers, 1979).

To a system like the centre, and the families of the guests who undergo therapy, we could apply a pattern which bears a strong resemblance to the "dissipating structures" of Prigogine and Stengers (1979). They are systems seeking a new order arising out of disorder. The basis of this process of transition between two structures is "an instability arising from fluctuation". This kind of instability can be seen when an "external field", which functions as a source of energy, reaches a certain crucial dimension. "At this point, a point called 'bifurcation', the way lies open to various possible structures . . . the choice the system will make is an uncertain and unpredictable phenomenon" (Fivaz *et al.*, 1981a, pp. 64–65). The new coherence taken on by the systems of the guests' families cannot, in this view, be established beforehand by the therapeutic team.

It should be noted that at the moment when the centre was set up, the centre itself gave rise to a series of fluctuations in the various systems involved, beginning with the families. The next stage consisted of a constant verification of the state of the system subjected to those fluctuations. This verification should at every stage demonstrate which directions the systems preferred and which they ignored. If at the moment of its establishment, the centre was a destabilising force, it should not be assumed that this function remained during the whole process of the interaction, through all the inputs and feedback between the centre and the family systems and other elements involved: a careful examination of this interaction showed that things changed over time and that the initial fluctuation had been mostly reabsorbed. Keeping up the instability became more and more a task to be built up by concrete actions.

In every family system, changes proceed parallel to the introduction of new information brought in by the therapeutic team; this information flows into the system mainly through the setting up of concrete projects aimed at the departure of the guest from the centre: the fact of having a house at one's disposal and the practicable prospect of being integrated into the working world, represent starting points which will set off a process of instability in the direction of some new state of the family system.

A house and a job trigger a positive feedback loop which will bring change and evolution only if the temporal dimensions of each one of the subjects involved in the process are respected. This almost always takes a long time. The length is determined by the time taken by the fluctuation which arose in the system to build up a new order. Because of this, the main task of the therapeutic team is to keep up the difference and the instability, while at the same time being careful to analyse the messages and feedback which occur in the global system during this process. The therapeutic team functions as an "external field", in Prigogine's sense, and in every single case the intensity of the team must exceed a certain minimum level so as to allow the family system to evolve towards a greater complexity. This intensity must remain constant in the long term in contrast to the short transition times of the system. In particular, on no account should this intensity be changed during these transitions. As stated by Fivaz *et al.* (1981a), "This characteristic of constancy represents the systemic definition of the superior hierarchical position" (p. 66).

This same concept of "constancy" is one which brings us back to what Dell (1980a, 1980b, 1982) has maintained—that the optimism of the therapeutic team who refuse to be discouraged by an apparent stasis is the main and indispensable condition necessary to bring about change. The team's constancy is therefore necessary in any given treatment so as to guarantee respect for the temporal dimensions of the family and the guest. To become pessimistic has the effect of introducing an oscillation into the external field which will inevitably feedback to produce contradictory effects inside the system under therapy. Remaining constant does not mean standing still. If the system evolves, so will the therapeutic system. The "external field", which is a field of information, must remain constant and available for the successive variations which the family may show during the course of evolution. Because of this, any hypothesis will necessarily have to follow a spiral course, and no input of "new" energy will ever be the same as, or a mere repetition of, the previous one.

In order to encourage the growth of a new coherence in the family systems and in their modalities of interaction with the guest, it is necessary to start from the potential emerging from the individual members, so as to amplify the differences and introduce new behavioural patterns. The instruments of positive connotation and reframing introduce new variables which may endow the system with a different capacity to interpret the events and processes which bind them together. The therapeutic team can in no way attempt to "brainwash" or create a "cultural revolution" in the system. It can only show, through its work, that different solutions are possible and that the search for these solutions is not dangerous.

Amplifying the differences means only and exactly that; it does not necessarily mean that the best solutions can be achieved. In the absence of equilibrium in a system, randomness or chance can play an important role in encouraging the system to move in one direction as opposed to another. The so-called "ideal" solution is not "the guest returning home" nor is it "the guest living by him/herself". There exists an infinite number of solutions in between, most of which are not at all "ideal". In the process that leads toward independence, for example, symptoms and crises are quite common. Sometimes these crises can be seen as intermediary solutions or momentary states. In any case, any interpretation of these crises ought not be separated from the evaluation of the phase or the evolutionary moment that the process may have reached. Going back to the very beginning would mean creating a redundancy of *stuckness*, and would lose the incisiveness of the message of movement.

Our experience in the centre has demonstrated this last aspect with great clarity. The mistake of arbitrarily blocking a process is the simplest of epistemological errors which, as Bateson says, can be committed only as long as we are aware that we have actually committed it. To insert a crisis into the continuum of time, between the events "before" and "afterwards" makes it possible to receive important information, and to use different interventions. In other words, it becomes possible to act on the system as an "external field" in constant interaction with the system.

Symptoms often emerge when a fluctuation cannot be absorbed into the system by the usual means. It is at this time that the "external field" needs to be particularly intense and "therapeutic" and be the least supportive and comforting as possible. By continuing to work to create fluctuations in the midst of local disorders and within the again unstable limits of systems blocked by their own histories, the therapeutic plan of the centre can be seen as an attempt at "evolutionary therapy".

B.   The Guest as an "Unstable Limit"

From the very beginning of our work in the centre, the opening up of the psychiatric context from the institutional rules of the hospital to the deinstitutional assumptions of the open centre encouraged a regression from states of equilibrium that had been established in the guests' families over the years of hospitalisation. When our open system came into contact with these families, it created oscillation and instability through the very premises upon which the centre had been set up, i.e. the eventual departure of each guest from the centre and his/her reintegration into society. The guests, both as individuals and as a group, initially became a kind of shuttle between the centre and their families, within a larger movement which was inexorably directed toward the outside world and the future. However, at the same time, the guests continued to remain inside a psychiatric context, and felt tied to their relationships and patterns of the past. This new global system, far removed from equilibrium, was nonetheless connected and separated by the guests, who assumed the position of "unstable limit" (Fivaz *et al.*, 1981a).

For the guest, being an "unstable limit" can also mean undergoing a constant "tug of war" between the family and the open centre. Therapeutic intervention is thus strictly linked to the search for instruments and modalities of intervention which will break up the see-sawing rhythm between the old game and the possibility of change, growth and therefore autonomy.

The case of Gianni (37 years old, first admission to the mental hospital at the age of 16) is emblematic of this type of problem. Every time the team drew up a plan aimed at his re-integration into the outside world, Gianni himself or his mother (Gianni's only relative) would promptly shift ground and break up the plan. Gianni's inclination was to follow the plans worked out by the team, but at the same time, he felt impelled to prove to his mother that he loved her. These two things seemed to him to be irreconcilable, since in his relational context love for his mother was equated to need. Obviously Gianni was caught in a double bind: "I want to be independent to prove to you I'm a man" contradicted by "I want to be mad/ dependent to show you that I need you as a child would". In this situation, when Gianni went home for a visit, rows with occasional fighting commenced; when he did not go home, his mother would telephone and beg him to come home. His mother's contradictory messages to him became: "If you really love me, stay in the centre", but also: "Come home, because now, I'll be able to be your mother for the first time". They could not be together, they could not be separated.

The therapeutic team decided to take away any negative connotation from Gianni's separation from his mother. In order to do this, the separation between the two was redefined as an expression of Gianni's desire to help his mother: affection was made synonymous with the idea of living apart. This opened the way for a plan to develop the reciprocal independence of Gianni and mother as well as Gianni's own independence within the centre.

II. BIFURCATION AND THE AMPLIFICATION
OF FLUCTUATIONS

It became clear to us, from working with many of these cases, that it was important for the therapeutic team to discover the fluctuation which, in the course of time, spread out in the family system. These fluctuations can be seen as the "local disorders" described in the physics of non-equilibrium (Prigogine and Stengers, 1979). The return to acute symptomatology on the part of a guest could be seen in this light as a critical moment in the course of a process of change. It would therefore be considered as part of the phase of that change and interpreted as a request for greater support in overcoming the obstacles which blocked this process.

If the therapeutic team were to decide to call a halt and "start again from scratch" in the face of the acute symptoms, most likely there would be a precipitous entry into a loop without exit. In itself, the idea of being able to start again from the beginning is devoid of logic, even apart from the question of its effectiveness, for if we examine events in terms of a process evolving in time, a symptom which appeared yesterday will never be the same as one which might develop tomorrow. Since, through time, the context has changed or evolved, the meaning of the same symptom necessarily changes. With this view, the onset of acute symptomatology can be seen as simply another fluctuation within the system.

Fluctuations which develop in a member of a family system may either become extended into a bifurcation or be absorbed, according to the phase in which they occur, the concrete support available to the individual, or to the family member's own ability to overcome the critical moment. An example of bifurcation can be seen in the case of Gianni. At a certain moment, when the plan to render him independent was underway and the fluctuation which had been introduced into the family system appeared to be spreading out, Gianni found a job through the Labor Office. The interview with the head of the firm was positive, but the news that he was not to show up for work for another month and a half threw him into a state of anxiety. His mother, who on a previous similar occasion had remarked to the effect of "you see, he really can't work; he'll never be able to make it", this time did not give any disqualifying feedback: the process had moved along also as far as she was concerned. To be sure, Gianni was unwell, but in a different way. It was as if he had found himself at a central point of a bifurcation. On the one hand there was his job in the factory, and on the other were his symptoms: his habit of drinking and his requests to be hospitalised. For the team, amplifying the directive to integrate him into the working world meant a refusal of any attempt to go back on the plans worked out together.

In our experience at the centre, we discovered that an essential element which enables the amplification of the fluctuation is the possibility of realising plans in a concrete way. For example, the allocation of a house, together with an integration into the working world, may often prove to be turning points in the process of deinstitutionalisation.

The movement inside Anita's (35 years old, in the hospital for 10) family system denoted the persisting of continuing fluctuations, despite the apparent adjustment of the guest to the new global system (guest–family–centre). After a series of meetings in which Anita's mother repeated that Anita could not return home because of the strong disagreements with her sister (due to the fact that Anita did not work and spent too much money), Anita began to use the centre's programme as a threat towards her mother rather than as a real possibility for separation and autonomy. Anita's mother became ill, and Anita as well as her mother asked permission for her to go home for ten days. Permission was granted. The experiment seemed to work out fairly satisfactorily; she helped her mother, was able to sleep, but asked to return to the centre before the allotted number of days was up because she had physical symptoms. From that moment, that is, after she had demonstrated that she cared and was willing to care for her mother, Anita became genuinely more interested in the discharge plan and became actively involved in acquiring autonomy.

A different equilibrium thus seemed possible: the team decided to redefine the relationship between the three women, no longer in terms of money and work, but in terms of affection and caring. One of the steps in this process was noted by the positive response of the mother to Anita's pressure to handle her own money. Previously, in an analogous situation, she said to Anita: "If you want your money, I won't have anything more to do with you". The fluctuation was open, Anita began to oscillate: on the one hand, she worked successfully (she wove, handled her own money and participated actively in the life of the centre); on the other hand, her symptoms increased and she asked for help more often. The implicit messages to her significant systems were: "I'm doing my best to get out"—to the team; and "Don't worry, it's still going to be a while before I do"—to her family. The team decided to maintain the fluctuation which was already going on within the system, and to emphasise that, contrary to the past, Anita's symptoms would not impede her from continuing the process towards autonomy. This intervention was supported by concrete plans: in a situation that was already in transition, the search for a house functioned as an amplification of this flux and thus as a tool permitting further evolution. For Anita, a house of her own represented another step towards autonomy because having her own space would guarantee the potential for growth; whereas before there had been only two choices, namely "in the hospital" (and therefore dependent on the team) or "back home" (and therefore dependent on her mother). The house served as the concrete instrument for putting into practice the fundamental relational changes between Anita and her family.

A. The Constancy of the "External Field"

When faced with family situations in flux, a team risks the particular danger of "dancing" along with the family, or worse with an individual member of the family. This is an even more obvious trap in the case of the open centre which works with families while simultaneously housing a family member. Thus successful therapeutic function implies taking the position of a "constant external field", which means being constant in amplifying elements of change which are already present in one or more parts of the system.

The story of Anna represents an example of the constancy of the team as an "external field". Anna, a 20 years veteran of the mental hospital was one of the thirty original patients in the centre. The groundwork for her move towards autonomy was laid with occupational and psychotherapy, and equally important, family sessions in which the team intervened to alter the relational patterns and equilibrium of the family. When Anna was notified that she had inherited a sum of money, she stated that she wished to go to Rome and get her money; she asked the team and not the family to accompany her. Anna's important decision had deep repercussions on the relational equilibrium of the family. It was at this point that the function of "constant external field" on the part of the team became crucial. When tensions mounted and Anna began to fluctuate, that is to manifest difficulty in continuing on her plan, the team refused to permit her to go back on her decision and gave her concrete support in the realisation of her plan. Thus, when the inheritance arrived, the widening of fluctuations could no longer be reabsorbed by the proposition of the same relational system which in the past had required Anna to remain at the centre.

During that period of flux, the team had repeated, in concrete terms, its support of Anna's moves, without, however, neglecting the implications and feedback within the family system. The team thus accepted the messages regarding the wish for autonomy sent by the children as well as the messages regarding the inability to live together which the husband was sending.

Now Anna lives alone, works, has her own life and is no longer labelled by a psychiatric term. Her younger daughter is married and lives with her husband. There has thus been a process of relational restructuring which has not merely permitted Anna to be reintegrated into the outside world: fluctuation has permeated the entire system and has allowed the system itself to move to a new stationary state, a different provisional equilibrium.

One might ask if this new equilibrium is the best attainable, but the question itself is irrelevant, for the only answer to it is that this particular family system, in this particular phase, which is based on its own particular premises, has found a new relational modality among many possible ones, a modality which is different from that which was used in the past. From this point on, the family will undoubtedly experiment with new organisations and solutions which are more fitting to its own internal development as well as to its interactions with the external environment.

REFERENCES

Bateson, G. (1972). "Steps to an Ecology of Mind". Ballantine, New York.

Bateson, G. (1978). *In* Berger, M. (ed.), "Beyond the Double Bind". Brunner Mazel, New York, pp. 40–64.

Bateson, G. (1979). "Mind and Nature: A Necessary Unity". Dutton, New York.

Castellucci, A., Fruggeri, L., Bertoi, C., Bruni, I., and Venturi, A. (1981). Il Lungodegente a La Sua Famiglia: L'Analisi Sistemica in una Istituzione Psichitrica. *Psicoterapia e Scienze Umane* 3–4, 41–49.

Castellucci, A., Fruggeri, L., and Marzari, M. (1984). "Il Tempo del Cambiamento". Angeli Editore, Milano.

Dell, P. (1980a). The Hopi Parents and the Aristotelian Parents. *Journal of Marital and Family Therapy* 6, 123–130.

Dell, P. (1980b). Researching the Family Theories of Schizophrenia: An Exercise in Epistemological Confusion. *Family Process* 19, 321–335.

Dell, P. (1982). Beyond Homeostasis: Toward a Concept of Coherence. *Family Process* 21, 21–40.

Dell, P., and Goolishian, H. (1980). "Order Through Fluctuation: An Evolutionary Epistemology for Human Systems". Annual Scientific Meeting of the A. K. Rice Institute, Houston.

Elkaim, M. (1981a). Non Equilibrio, Caso e Combiamento in Terapia Familiare. *Terapia Familiare* 9, 101–112.

Elkaim, M. (1981b). *Cahiers Critiques de Thérapie Familiale et de Pratiques de Réseaux* 4–5, 8–9.

Elkaim, M., Golbeter, A., and Golbeter, E. (1980). Cartes, Territoires et Singulatés. Analyses de Transitions de Comportement dans un Système Familiale en Termes de Bifureations. *Cahiers Critiques de Thérapie Familiale et de Pratiques de Réseaux* 3, 18–34.

Fivaz, E., Fivaz, R., and Kaufmann, L. (1980). Terapie di Famiglie a Transazione Psicotica: Un Paradigma Evolutivo. *Terapia Familiare* 7, 63–88.

Fivaz, E., Fivaz, R., and Kaufmann, L. (1981a). Encadrement du Developpement: Le Point de Vue Systémique. *Cahiers Critiques de Thérapie Familiale et de Pratiques de Réseaux* 4–5, 63–74.

Fivaz, E., Fivaz, R., and Kaufmann, L. (1981b). Transazioni Disfunzionali e Funzioni Terapeutiche: Un Modello Evolutivo. *Terapia Familiare* 9, 113–130.

Hoffman, L. (1980). *In* Haley, J. (ed.), "Fondamenti di Terapia della Famiglia". Feltrinelli, Milano, pp. 355–387.

Hoffman, L. (1981). "Foundations of Family Therapy". Basic Books, New York.

Hoffman, L. (1982). A Co-Evolutionary Framework for Systemic Family Therapy. *Australian Journal of Family Therapy* 4, 9–21.

Keeney, B. (1979). Ecosystemic Epistemology: An Alternative Paradigm for Diagnosis. *Family Process* 18, 117–129.

Keeney, B. (1982). What is an Epistemology of Family Therapy. *Family Process* 21, 153–168.

Keeney, B. (1983). "Aesthetics of Change". Guilford Press, New York.

Palazzoli, M., Boscolo, L., Cecchin, G., and Prata, G. (1975). "Paradosso e Controparadosso". Feltrinelli, Milano.

Palazzoli, M., Boscolo, L., Cecchin, G., and Prata, G. (1980). Ipotizzazione, Circolarità e Neutralità: Tre Direttive per la Conduzione della Seduta. *Terapia Familiare* 7, 7–20.

Prigogine, I., and Stengers, I. (1979). "La nouvelle alliance". Gallimard, Paris.

Part FOUR

Consultation

Chapter 19

The Consultation Interview

David Campbell

I. INTRODUCTION

I am interested in the question: "How can family therapists help other family therapists who are 'stuck'?" I will discuss ways in which systemic thinking can be applied to a context in which one family worker seeks a consultation about his work from another family worker.

The Tavistock Clinic is a large out-patient clinic within the National Health Service which offers a full range of psychotherapy and consultation services to adults, adolescents, children and families. It offers training for psychiatrists, social workers, psychologists, child psychotherapists and remedial teachers, as well as other courses for professionals in the field.

Within the Department for Children and Parents, a group of family therapists have been practising for about 13 years, and a family therapy programme and a two-year training in family therapy were developed in 1975. Families come to the department with the usual range of emotional and behavioural problems from a catchment area which includes London and its environs. As a result of the work of the clinic, family workers in the area occasionally approach the programme to ask for help or consultation about their work.

The offer of a consultation interview is a response to a therapist or practitioner. In this chapter the thinking which underpins this work and the procedure which is used with these interviews is described. The ideas are illustrated with case examples.

II. A Theoretical Explanation

For the purpose of this paper I have defined *context* as a recognisable pattern of events, or ideas, which is created by an individual in interaction with his environment. Defining a pattern as context gives meaning to the thoughts and behaviour of the individual.

Ideas about context have proved helpful to me in my own practice of family therapy and I have applied some of this thinking to consultation interviews in the hope they may be helpful to other therapists. To begin, I propose a definition of family therapy as follows: it is a process of engaging a family to create a new therapist–family system and, by means of the newly created system, changing the context in which the problem behaviour has a predictable pattern and an acquired meaning.

APPLICATIONS OF SYSTEMIC FAMILY THERAPY
ISBN 0-8089-1696-3

This can be done in two ways: the therapist can address the context directly by offering alternative meanings to create new contexts or the therapist can address the behaviour directly by creating new patterns of behaviour which will have an implicative or upward force to create a new context (Cronen et al., 1982). Regardless of how the therapist conceptualises his work he will only create new contexts of meaning by introducing unpredictability into the system. This has the effect of shattering the connection between the behaviour and its context of meaning, since behaviour can only have meaning when it is seen to have a recognisable pattern. Pattern creates context; context equals meaning; and unpredictability is the enemy of pattern.

The therapist may attempt to introduce unpredictability in many ways: he can share startling or new information, he can be paradoxical, he can reframe family behaviour, or he can behave unpredictably. However, as the therapist attempts to introduce greater unpredictability into the therapist–family system, the family responds by incorporating the therapist's interventions into a new predictable pattern just as an amoeba ingests a particle of food. The therapist's move and the family's countermove are the first steps in the dance or the co-evolution of the therapist–family system. This process has been described by Keeney (1983). As the family places the therapist's interventions into their own context, the therapist will respond by placing that context within his own wider context or meta context. Each has a recursive or mutually interacting relationship with the other, and the process moves toward higher and higher orders of recursiveness. In other words, once the therapist has given an intervention, he is then viewing a different family system: it is a family system whose organisation now *includes* his efforts to introduce unpredictability.

As long as the therapist is able to see some pattern in the family's response to his interventions, he will continue to create contexts of meaning for his work with the family and continue to create interventions. And as long as he can do this he will be introducing unpredictability into the system and co-evolving toward wider, more inclusive contexts.

A therapist is really working with contexts at three different levels. Firstly there is the *family context*, which gives the family the meaning for its own behaviour—its history; the interactions around its own particular events. Secondly there is the *therapist's context* which includes such elements as personal background, other clinical experience, theory, agency relationships, etc. Thirdly there is the *therapist–family context* which is inclusive of the other two. This context is marked by the interventions of the therapists, the responses of the family, the therapists' responses to those responses and so on.

When you consider that each context attributes meaning to behaviour, it is no wonder that the therapist becomes confused by different meanings. The same event, such as an increase in symptomatic behaviour, might mean bad news for the family, good news for the therapist, or simply the first move in the game, depending upon which of the three contexts were used to provide the meaning for the event.

In the midst of a co-evolving system consisting of these three changing contexts, I take a rather kindly view of the therapist getting stuck. I see it as less an issue of the therapist's competence and more an issue of inevitability. There is an inevitable confusion of meanings or confusion of contexts. When a therapist attaches different meanings to the same behaviour, he has no clear idea of how to act in relation to the actions of the family. Confusion of contexts leads to the therapist losing touch with the interactive process of which he is a part, and he takes a linear view of his predicament: "I can't understand the family," or "The family won't respond to my interventions". He becomes paralysed and unable to act. He is unable to see his place in the co-evolving therapist–family system. Time stands still.

I think the way it happens is something like this: The relationship which develops between the therapist and the family, through the experience they share in therapy, triggers something in the therapist (McGoldrick, 1982). It might be something from his own personal life or from relationships at work. This triggering process leads the therapist to view the family more from his "own" context, which will be somewhat adrift from the interactions taking place in the therapist–family system. The therapist's thinking may become organised more by his own experience and less by the therapist–family system.

Tell-tale signs of this are the therapist falling back on a favourite hypothesis that has been used many times, or having no hypothesis because he has become confused by interference from his "own" context. Maybe it is vanity or maybe it is a need for constancy in the face of a system in perpetual motion, but we, as therapists, do tend to settle for using a familiar context with which to view the family's responses to us. Our behaviour with the family becomes part of a predictable pattern and we feel stuck.

This is where the consultation interview comes in. The consultant aims to identify the therapist's "own" context which makes him feel stuck, then he attempts to create a new context which gives meaning to both the appropriateness and the inappropriateness of the therapist's "own" context in relation to the family–therapy system. The process is actually the same as the process of therapy described above. The consultant, through a systemic interview identifies a pattern of behaviour connected, not to the symptom, but to "being stuck". This pattern will reveal a context, such as a symmetrical relationship with the mother, which is inappropriately attributing meaning to the therapist's observations. Then the consultant creates a new context by making an intervention to the therapist which addresses the symmetrical relationship in a systemic way. If this is done with proper exploration of the systemic meaning of the symmetry, the symmetry will *lose* its meaning and disappear or change its function (Bateson, 1974). This allows the therapist to move to a new, wider context which has included the therapist's troublesome "own" context, and thus to give new meaning to the family's behaviour and perhaps rejoin the co-evolutionary dance as a therapist rather than a spectator.

III. THE INTERVIEW IN PRACTICE

Some of my family therapy interviews are done as a member of a team (I am currently working with Mrs. Rosalind Draper and Dr. Caroline Lindsey). Since the consultation interview requires thinking simultaneously about many contexts, I ask my colleagues to observe the interview behind the one-way screen or at least discuss the case and help me prepare hypotheses for the interview.

When a request for a consultation comes to me I first want to know whether this worker wants to refer the case to me for family therapy, or to work alongside me with the family in order to develop his own skills, or to clarify the worker's own muddle in order to carry on working with the family. The other important issue to consider before the first appointment is: Where is the impasse located? Is it primarily to do with making hypotheses about the family, or about the worker's own agency, or about the confusion arising in the evolution of the therapist–family system? These considerations will affect the decision about whether the worker, the family or the agency (or all of them) are invited to the first session.

In the past when I invited the worker (with or without an agency colleague) and the family, I saw the worker beforehand to explain the way we would be working—to recognise the professional boundary which distinguished him from the family. However, I have recently been experimenting with other procedures. It may be easier to preserve one's therapeutic neutrality if the routine can be explained ahead of time on the telephone. Our team also likes to gather further information about the family or the background to the referral and we usually ask what the worker hopes will come from the consultation interview. But this can be done over the telephone and the information used to prepare hypotheses to be investigated in the first session.

The procedure that I use in the interview follows the guidelines for conducting systemic interviews laid down by writers such as Palazzoli *et al.* (1978, 1980), Campbell *et al.* (1983), Penn (1982) and Tomm (1984a, 1984b). Following the interview the team makes a formulation about the problem of "being stuck", and this usually leads toward a decision about the best way to deliver the intervention. In most cases I deliver the intervention to the worker and the family; however, in some cases it has proved more effective to send conclusions directly to the worker, allowing him to do what he wishes with regard to the family.

Two case examples are presented here which are based on the model of the consultation interview. They demonstrate the way such cases can be conceptualised and what actually happens in the consultation interview.

A.   Case Example I

Mr. B., a local authority field social worker, contacted our clinic to ask for a consultation about a difficult case. The Smith family had a 15-year-old son, Gary, who had been taken into the care of the local authority and placed in a children's home several years before. His behaviour was violent and destructive and he was moved in and out of several children's homes while Mr. B. and one of his colleagues attempted family therapy with the Smith family. When the two workers became "stuck" with the family, they discussed their work with a local family therapy support group who suggested that the family was too difficult to be treated in a social services setting and that they should be referred to the Tavistock Clinic.

In order to answer the initial question of whether the worker wanted a consultation for his own work or a referral for family therapy, one of my colleagues telephoned Mr. B. to gather more information. At this stage of the consultation our team has a standard set of questions which we ask of the referrers. We ask how the decision was taken to refer the family to us. We ask what events led to the idea of referral; who had the idea, what did colleagues and, most importantly, seniors or supervisors think about the referral; what did they hope to accomplish from the referral and what would be the effect on the network if the referral proved unhelpful?

It became clear from the telephone conversation that the two workers were disappointed that their support group was not able to offer more help and had suggested they refer the family elsewhere, and our team made a hypothesis that Mr. B. and his colleague were experiencing a confusion of contexts. In the context of being a family therapist, a message such as "It is impossible to do family therapy with this family; they should be referred", might be helpful, but the same message in the context of being members of a hierarchical family therapy support group might be construed as unhelpful because the support is not forthcoming and the therapist may feel disqualified by experts. If the context in which the referral is made is the hierarchical relationship of the support group, then an ineffective referral might be a means whereby Mr. B. could compete with the recommendation of the support team.

I was interested initially to explore this hypothesis as well as the relationship between the two workers, and I invited only Mr. B. and his colleague to come to the clinic for the first session.

The interview confirmed that there were rivalries within the support team, and to some extent Mr. B. seemed to want to defeat the experts at the Tavistock as well as within the support group. However, the interview led to a hypothesis which emphasised the way the context of the relationship between workers was being confused with the context of the aims of family therapy. It became clear that, of the two workers, Mr. B. was less experienced in family therapy but he was very keen that therapy should be successful lest he feel he had failed the family. His co-worker did not have the same personal investment in the case but wanted to work with the family to expand his experience as a family therapist. He seemed to accept that at the end of the day there may be nothing that could be done for Gary.

This information led the team to hypothesise that each worker saw the family therapy in a slightly different way and our message to the team was that it was not clear whether they were a team that was "stuck" in their efforts to change the family and help Gary, or whether they were a team that was slowly learning about the Smith family, building their skills as family therapists. If this were the case they would not expect to change the family but rather continue seeing them to learn just how difficult families can be and to learn about the way they work together as a team. I suggested they could discuss their working relationship and devise an interviewing method which took best advantage of their different perspectives and levels of experience. We would offer them a further consultation in about three months' time if they felt it would be helpful.

The aim of this intervention was simply to describe the two contexts in which we saw the co-workers working, i.e. the context of their relationship and the context of doing family therapy. The latter part of the message is an attempt to create a new context for their work—one in which they do not need to strive for change and one in which they can create a working relationship which includes their differences.

Mr. B. telephoned about three months later to ask for another consultation. He and his co-worker had had several family meetings which were disastrous and they did not know what to do. Our team made a hypothesis similar to the two previous hypotheses but focussed more specifically on the *therapist's context*. We assumed that there were conflicts in the hierarchical relationships between the two co-workers and also between the co-workers and their own agency which made it difficult for this team to clearly recognise the limits of what they were able to do for this family.

We decided to offer the next consultation session to the co-workers and the family because we felt we would be able to make a more powerful intervention if it were directed toward the entire therapy–family system. We divided this interview into two parts; for the first 20 minutes I interviewed Mr. B. and his co-worker to explore our hypothesis. I asked what they felt the family needed; to what extent were they able to provide it; how did they understand the reasons they could not provide all that was needed; what would have to be different for them to provide what was needed; would they ever tell the family they were unable to help; what would be the effect of this upon the line management of their agency; and finally some questions about their consultation with us: what effect has their contact with us had on their work with the family and what would happen if we were unable to provide what they wanted from the consultation?

It became clear from these questions that within the agency there were two different contexts for helping clients and confusion arose from the different meanings attached to Mr. B.'s behaviour. In the context of the relationship with Gary, Mr. B. had developed a close relationship with Gary and this was being reinforced by the family, Gary, the agency and Mr. B. himself. On the other hand, in the context of working with the family, whenever Mr. B. tried to reunite Gary with this family all hell broke loose and the family united in their condemnation of Social Services. In his declared attempts to do family therapy Mr. B. was undermined by Gary, who would lose an ally; by the family, who were ambivalent about Gary's return home; and by a beleaguered agency.

For the second part of the session I invited the family to join the co-workers. I explored the extent of Gary's troublesome behaviour; what attempts had been made to deal with the problem; and how each of them explained that the problems persisted. This helped bring the conflict to light. The family did not want family therapy but wanted a therapeutic home where Gary could be rehabilitated. Social Services had offered everything available and had run out of resources and Gary was very confused about his behaviour but seemed to want someone to talk to.

Our intervention was in the form of a letter sent to the family and the co-workers. It gave some possible explanations for Gary's behaviour based on our formulation of the family problem, then continued: "However, even if it is possible to eventually understand why Gary loses his temper, it may still be that there is nothing that anyone can do to control his temper and there may be nothing that Gary can do to control his temper himself.

"The social workers raised the question of what could be offered to the Smith family from Social Services. Our view is that what Social Services is able to provide is not what the family need. Unfortunately this is a time of limited resources and the family's needs simply cannot be fully met by Social Services. On the other hand, we have been very impressed by how Social Services have tried to help the Smiths and we have been impressed by the way the Smiths have continued to use Social Services even though they realised they might not get what they needed. We were particularly struck by the close relationship between Gary and Mrs. Smith and Mr. B.

"We recommend that Social Services consider ending their attempts to help the family with Gary's temper and accept that no one, including Gary, can do anything about it. However, Social Services might continue to offer support to the family as they go through this very traumatic time in their lives (for example, Mr. B. might continue to meet Mrs. Smith and Gary), and Social Services might help with practical problems such as finding a job for Gary."

The aim of this intervention was to address the different contexts in which the relationship between the co-workers and the family were viewed by different members of the therapy–family system based on the following formulation: the co-workers, for reasons already given, wished to succeed in doing family therapy but Mr. B. also wished to utilise an important individual relationship with Gary. This represented confusions between the co-workers which was dealt with in an earlier intervention, and confusions about the value of working with individuals or families.

The context in which the family seemed to view this therapeutic relationship was that Social Services did not provide enough but the family should continue to try to get what was needed from them. In addition Gary's individual relationship was viewed as something good and perhaps the most acceptable "ticket" to a continuing relationship with Social Services.

A follow-up telephone call several months later revealed that the co-workers felt that the consultant's view of the family was "right" and that Social Services decided there was not much they could offer the family, who were eventually referred to the probation service.

Therapists often feel "stuck" when they have lost sight of their own position in the interacting system of which they are a part. The interventions in this case were aimed at clarifying the different levels of meaning which come from different contexts, such as colleague relationship, agency values and relations with support group; and clarifying the contradictory nature of the therapist's behaviour within such a system.

B. Case Example II

A social worker, Mr. D., who was attached to a residential unit for disturbed adolescents, referred a family for consultation. The family consisted of two middle class parents, a younger daughter, aged 9, and a highly disturbed adolescent called Stephen. It became clear from the referring letter and our subsequent telephone call, that Mr. D. had been seeing the family for nearly a year on home visits and although he had grown close to the family, was frustrated in his efforts to change the destructive relationship between the parents and adolescent.

We invited the worker to bring the family to the first session. The family expounded a long tale of professional contacts which had failed to help their son, and the social worker described his efforts to get the family to see things his way and to make the best use of his supervisory discussions with his colleagues. We felt there was a powerful battle going on between the family, who attracted professionals and then made them impotent, and the worker, who was determined to succeed with the family in the eyes of his own agency. The first two sessions addressed the larger pattern of this symmetrical relationship.

We did this in the first session by joining the conflicting beliefs that the family seek further help, yet that they know no help will be effective. We supported the parents' differences while acknowledging they were united by seeking help and we addressed the conflict for the social worker of being a professional who was also a "non-professional", close member of the family. In the second interview, we attempted to reconcile the social worker's need to remain close to the family while at the same time express his disappointment and frustration and keep the support of his colleagues.

Following the second interview the family decided they would not attend further family therapy sessions at the clinic, and we decided to continue meeting the social worker on his own by focussing our hypothesis for the third session on the social worker's relationship to his colleagues in his agency. It seemed to us as though there were a symmetrical relationship between the family and unit to be more successful in caring for Stephen and thereby avoid the label of "bad parent". It seemed that Mr. D.'s role was to cure "bad parents" on behalf of the unit. If the family were to show signs of change, the effort of the professional team to cure them would be vindicated. The family repudiated his efforts, hoping desperately to place the blame somewhere else. Furthermore, if Mr. D. began to fail in his efforts it would jeopardise his position with colleagues since he would be seen as a bad "parent" and possibly tarnish the unit's reputation. To get out of this bind it would be natural for him in this context to turn toward other professionals—our clinic—whose expertise would make or break the case.

We then applied this hypothesis to our method of consultation and it became clear that we needed to make it possible for the social worker to see his work in a new context by pointing out the dilemmas he could not resolve while also supporting him to continue working as he was. During the fourth session Mr. D. said that although the family refused to come to further family therapy sessions, they were very interested to find out what went on between him and myself and had telephoned immediately after his last visit to the clinic. He also said when asked about his role that it was his responsibility to keep some hope alive. These two bits of information led us towards the following message at the end of the interview: I suggested that when mother telephones to ask about this interview, that Mr. D. tell the family that I had the impression that the parents had done as much as any parents could possibly do for a son and that Mr. D. could decide for himself whether it was better for his own work with the family that he agree or disagree with my view. He seemed greatly relieved by this and said he would write to me following his next meeting with the family.

Mr. D. telephoned a few weeks later to say that several members of his clinical team were interested to hear about his meetings with me and wondered if they might come to the clinic themselves to discuss their concern about Stephen. This was impossible for practical reasons and I therefore asked Mr. D. if he would like to speak to each of his colleagues and find out from them how each one saw the current problem with Stephen and what each would hope to learn from a consultation at our clinic. Then I met Mr. D. on his own.

Our hypothesis for this session was that Mr. D. was beginning to see his work in a wider context by seeing the limitations of his work in the face of the family's continuing despair. However, he may have wanted me as an ally so that his position in his clinical team was not weakened by his changing view of his work with the family.

We have found in such consultation interviews that if the consultation team is seen to be on the same level as the worker or his agency team, a competition can easily develop between the consultation team, the worker's agency and the family, with the worker placed squarely in the middle. The competition is important because it places the worker in the powerful position of being the central switchboard. He is connected to all of the competing sides and has the most to lose or gain through his association. But it is also important in this context that no one is seen to win the competition. If the consultation team were seen to be successful in helping the family, Mr. D. might lose his place with the family, the agency team might be thought useless and Mr. D. might be resented by his colleagues. On the other hand, if the consultation team were seen on the same level as the others and proved to be unhelpful, the judgement of the person who initiated the consultation would be called to question (and those who may have opposed it could say: "I told you so"), and the social worker's relationship with the family could be damaged by his alliance to an unsuccessful consultation.

The best way to avoid this pitfall is for the consultation team to comment on relationships in the worker/agency team–family system. This avoids the problem of being placed in a competitive position in which no one must be successful. In this case, our hypothesis was that Mr. D. was in a one-down position in relation to his team and we hoped to redress the balance by commenting on the relative positions of the members of the agency team in the context of their work with the family.

We addressed Mr. D.'s relationship with his colleagues by saying we felt there was no possible decision he could take which would prevent continued suffering for Stephen, and the unit and clinical team were right to pursue alternative diagnoses and alternative placements to help Stephen. We ended by saying: "We can see how you might feel that you have failed the family in the context of your professional colleagues, but as we see it you are in an impossible position, yet you have shown us today how you have managed to keep your goals clearly in mind".

During this session and the previous one, Mr. D. mentioned that these meetings had been helpful, and our plan was to have a longer break following this interview. Thus at the end he was invited to contact me in a "few months" if he felt he wanted to discuss Stephen and his family again. I did not hear from him again but coincidentally met him at a conference six months later. He told me that the problems with Stephen were still going on but the team was more united in the way they were approaching the family. He thanked me for the help and asked if he could refer another family at some time in the future.

The case highlights again the way the consultant must address the conflicts within different levels of the system. We began by looking at the symmetrical relationship between the worker and family, then moved to the relationship between the worker and the expectations of his colleagues, and finally included the request for consultation as a feature of that system. Although the consultation team is organised by the feedback it is getting from the family and the worker, a consultant, often with the help of a team, must endeavour to comment on his own position in the system he is a part of.

IV. CONCLUSIONS

The reader may have expected that a successful consultation interview involved the discovery and proclamation of a more useful hypothesis about the family system. In our experience, when professionals seek consultations because they are stuck, they have usually exhausted a supply of pertinent hypotheses about the family. Rather the problem seems to be, more often, that the worker has lost sight of his position in the system in such a way that *any* hypothesis about the *family* would be disqualified by higher level meanings which derive from the wider context which includes the behaviour of the worker, the agency, the health service, etc.

The aim of the consultation interview is to comment on the confusions which arise from working in systems in which behaviour has different meanings deriving from the different contexts from which the behaviour is observed. The consultant tries to lift the worker out of a more narrow context toward a wider context. In so doing new connections are made; the process of oscillation or recursiveness gets under way and the worker or therapist will see new alternative ways of behaving in relation to the family. One such way may be to prepare a new hypothesis and continue working with the family; another might be to refer the family to another agency; a third might be to end treatment. And there are many others.

REFERENCES

Bateson, G. (1974). The Cybernetics of 'Self': A Theory of Alcoholism. *In* "Steps to an Ecology of Mind". Paladin, St. Albans.

Campbell, D., Reder, P., Draper, R., and Pollard, D. (1983). "Working with the Milan Method: Twenty Questions". Occasional Paper No. 1, Institute of Family Therapy, London.

Cronen, V., Johnson, K., and Lannamann, J. (1982). Paradoxes, Double Binds and Reflexive Loops: An Alternative Theoretical Perspective. *Family Process* 20, 91–112.

Keeney, B. (1983). "Aesthetics of Change". Guilford Press, New York.

McGoldrick, M. (1982). Through the Looking Glass: Supervision of a Trainee's 'Trigger' Family. *In* Whiffen, R., and Byng-Hall, J. (eds.), "Family Therapy Supervision". Academic Press, London, pp. 17–37.

Palazzoli, M. S., Boscolo, L., Cecchin, G., and Prata, G. (1978). "Paradox and Counterparadox". Jason Aronson, London.

Palazzoli, M. S., Boscolo, L., Cecchin, G., and Prata, G. (1980). Hypothesizing-Circularity-Neutrality: Three Guidelines for the Conductor of the Session. *Family Process* 19, 3–12.

Penn, P. (1982). Circular Questioning. *Family Process* 21, 267–280.

Tomm, K. (1984a). One Perspective on the Milan Systemic Approach. Part I. Overview, Development, Theory and Practice. *Journal of Marital and Family Therapy* 10 (2), 113–125.

Tomm, K. (1984b). One Perspective on the Milan Systemic Approach. Part II. Description of Session Format, Interviewing Style and Interventions. *Journal of Marital and Family Therapy* 10, 253–271.

Chapter 20

Families and Multiple Helpers: A Systemic Perspective

Evan Imber Coppersmith

I. INTRODUCTION

"Who have you seen about your son's behaviour?"

"Well, he's eleven now, and he's really been a problem since birth. First, I talked to my family doctor. She sent us to a counsellor, who acted like it was our fault and so we quit. The school psychologist has tried working with him, but he's at a loss regarding what to do. Now he's in a special class for behaviour problems. The teacher uses rewards, so now he refuses to do anything unless he gets a reward. A policeman talked to him after he got caught shoplifting, but that didn't work. He's in a group at the clinic for disturbed children, but he misbehaves there, too. Recently, I called child welfare to see about putting him out for a while, though I doubt it'll do any good in the long run".

The brief exchange above illustrates the increasingly common problem of a family engaged with multiple helpers, either sequentially or simultaneously. This chapter describes applications of the systemic model to the particular problems posed by families and multiple helpers. Such problems if not addressed, may preclude therapeutic progress.

The work was initiated in a family therapy training program at the University of Massachusetts in a clinical seminar "The Family and Larger Systems". Specific Milan-style systemic elaborations of this work have been developed at the Family Therapy Program, Department of Psychiatry, University of Calgary, Alberta, Canada. The Family Therapy Program is tailored to deliver outpatient family therapy services and training in the systemic model. Several hundred families are either self-referred or referred by other professionals annually. Referral sources include the entire range of helping professionals.

II. DISCOVERING AND WORKING WITH THE "MEANINGFUL SYSTEM"

Work with families at the Family Therapy Program seeks to develop an understanding of the "meaningful system" or that configuration of relationships and beliefs in which the family's problems and issues make sense. Sometimes the "mean-

APPLICATIONS OF SYSTEMIC FAMILY THERAPY
ISBN 0-8089-1696-3

ingful system" is the nuclear family. Often, however, the "meaningful system" is more complex, including extended family, other helpers and the family therapist.

When family therapists are asked to describe their most difficult cases, they frequently point to those involving multiple helpers.

The original Milan team recognised the potential for professionals becoming part of the family's "meaningful system" and described this in "The Problem of the Referring Person" (Palazzoli *et al.*, 1980a). As early as 1969, Hoffman and Long addressed the issue, and more recently, a small but growing literature has developed highlighting the problem of the family and multiple helpers (Coleman, 1983; Goolishian and Anderson, 1981; Harkaway, 1983; Imber Coppersmith, 1982, 1983a, 1983b; Miller, 1983; Tomm, Lannamann and McNamee, 1983; Webb-Woodard and Woodard, 1983). Families and multiple helpers engage with each other for a variety of reasons and in a diversity of configurations.

III. EXPLAINING THE EMERGENCE OF THE FAMILY–MULTIPLE HELPER PHENOMENON

Our present culture supports the entry of multiple helpers, first by promoting specialisation which identifies a specific kind of helper for every aspect of a problem (e.g. legal, medical, educational, therapeutic, etc.) and second by deeming that helpers do their job well when they uncover a multiplicity of problems to address. Engrained cultural myths encourage professionals to adopt a deficit model of family functioning that sets them on a course of identifying more problems and more helpers. For instance, a family with a retarded child is often believed to need not only educational services, but therapy, as well. Single-parent families are generally thought to have more problems requiring more helpers (e.g. therapy, Big Brother, assertiveness training, etc.), when, in fact, more finances may be all the help that is needed.

A professional, with good intentions may enlist another helper due to her own confusion in a case, or lack of expertise. Rather than referring and backing out, the first helper remains involved, thereby developing a system of family and multiple helpers.

Families may engage multiple helpers because there has been a history of involvement with outsiders over several generations and thus it is a familiar way to conduct family life; i.e. it may have become a family tradition to have outsiders deeply involved in family affairs. Conversely, families who are separated from their extended families—those who could have served the function of helping to solve problems (e.g. immigrants or others who have left family far away; those with problematic cut-offs, etc.)—may engage multiple helpers to fill these roles.

Single-parent families may engage a helper in an effort to fill the gap left by the absent parent (see the case example below). Since helpers can never actually fill this gap, a pattern of enlisting more and more helpers often ensues.

Some families become involved with many outsiders in an effort to divert attention from internal family strife which is unacceptable and covert. The complexities involved in juggling relationships with several professionals comes to consume the family's focus. Such a relationship pattern requires that problems persist or recur so that outside contacts can be maintained.

One family member may engage an outsider in order to balance a countervailing alignment of another family member with an outsider, resulting rapidly in a family with multiple helpers.

A. Applications of the Systemic Model to the Problem of Families and Multiple Helpers

There are at least two major points in therapy when exploration of the family–multiple helper phenomenon is useful, and may, in fact, be essential.

(1)   *Assessment of the family–multiple helpers system:*
A therapist-facilitated interview

The first comes early in therapy, usually in a first or second session. Here, the therapist, utilising circular interviewing methods, seeks to discover who is involved with the family. In a vein similar to inquiring about extended family, the therapist inquires about outside helpers. Once it is established that the family indeed has other professionals in its sphere, the therapist seeks information regarding the relationship between the family and outsiders. Here the therapist is curious about fixed beliefs between the family and professionals, alliance patterns, configurations between helpers and the family that mirror family process, multi-generational involvement with outsiders, etc. Any particular question and its wording must be tailored to the actual family; however, some examples of questions to utilise include:

1. *"Whom do you think the outside help has helped the most? And then who?, etc."* This question yields information about alliances, as well as whether family members believe any help has helped anyone at all.
2. *"Over the time that your family has been involved with _____ (names of particular helpers), has it made the situation better or worse? For whom?"* Here the therapist and family begin to discover their views about professional involvement.
3. *"What would your mother, father, other extended family, etc. think about you working with professionals on this problem? Would he/she favour it or not favour it? Would he/she think it will help or not help?"* This question begins to inform the therapist and the family about issues of loyalty, and whether the family is caught between the views and wishes of extended family and helpers. This question can lead to an entire line of questioning regarding multi-generational involvement with professionals.
4. *"What do you think _____ (names of particular helpers) thinks about your family? What might he/she tell me about working with you? What would his/her advice be to me? How do you think he/she might compare you to other families?"* Here the family's perceived experience with professionals and their fantasies become available. Whether the family has had longstanding struggles or warm and cozy relationships with helpers frequently emerges.

Throughout this questioning process, the therapist must, of course, maintain neutrality towards the relationships between the family and outsiders. The therapist is not seeking to criticise these relationships, or imply their demise, but to assess their potential impact on the present therapeutic endeavour.

Several purposes are met by inquiring early on in therapy about the family–multiple helper relationship. The therapist will discover if she is one in a long line of outsiders who have resulted in no change. She may hear warnings, which, if not heeded, will lead to a familiar therapeutic stalemate. She may find out about special alliances that require symptom maintenance for their survival. She can elicit the family's fixed beliefs about the helping endeavour. The possibility of inviting one or more outsiders to a session may emerge.

With all of this information, the therapist is able to initiate an *unexpected* relationship with the family, one that does not meet their previous expectations of professionals and therefore facilitates the entry of new information into the system. Families with long-standing or repeated relationships with outsiders often develop reified modes of interaction with them that preclude change. The systemic therapist's use of unanticipated behaviour, ideas, opinions, tasks, rituals, etc. functions to alter rigid patterns both between the family and helpers, and within the family. She can plan for new ways to handle the difficult subjects. The family may, for instance, warn against inquiring about secrets, stating that prior helpers did so and "made things worse". The therapist can develop a mode of inquiry that does not replicate the prior failure, but still addresses the issue (Imber Coppersmith, in press). In addition, the therapist can begin to plan ways to involve the other helpers, whether through telephone contact, letters or actual sessions. Unplanned treatment triangles whereby helpers side with various family members, and struggle with each other, can be avoided, and treatment "partnerships" can be initiated (Imber Coppersmith, 1982).

(2)   *Assessment and intervention in the family–multiple*
helpers system: a consultant-facilitated interview

The second major point when examining the family–multiple helpers system is salient is when on-going therapy has stalled out. Either a case is proceeding with little or no progress, or earlier progress has not been maintained. At this point, a therapist will frequently seek consultation. If the family is one engaged with multiple helpers, then the consulting interview should be arranged to include as many of these people as possible.

It is important that a consultant, rather than the family's therapist, conduct this interview. The therapist is now part of the family–multiple helpers system, and her place in the system needs to be examined, along with the place of other professionals. In addition, professionals involved in a case tend to define their relationships with one another as symmetrical, and generally show resentment when the family therapist assumes a one-up complementary position by conducting the interview and defining him/her as "outside" the system.

The family's therapist generally organises the interview by inviting the family and other professionals. The therapist should make it clear to all the participants that this is a consultation which she is seeking. Care should be taken in order not to communicate blame or an aura of extrusion to any of the helpers. Rather, this interview is designed so that the family–multiple helpers system can learn about itself and make decisions based on new information.

The consultant conducts the interview according to the systemic model's principles of hypothesising, circularity and neutrality (Palazzoli *et al.*, 1980b). Preferably, a team is employed, using the full five-part session. A pre-session is held in which the therapist describes the case. The therapist then leaves and joins the family and any other helpers, while the consultant and team hypothesise. During the intersession, only the consultant meets with the team. The therapist and other helpers remain with the family, communicating in action the existence of this system. The focus of the interview is on the family–multiple helpers system. The consultant is curious about alliance patterns, about whether or not there are competing beliefs regarding the problem, its etiology, preferred locus of blame, appropriate solutions, views regarding the future, etc. Some examples of useful questions include:

1. *"Who of all the people here is the most optimistic that this problem can be solved? And then who? etc.".* This line of questioning may, for instance, reveal that the family members are very pessimistic about possibilities of solving the issue, but the assembly of helpers is quite optimistic and keeps trying harder. Or through questioning over time about optimism–pessimism, one may discover a pattern in which each new helper is warmly welcomed by the family, and gradually grows pessimistic until the point of getting a new helper. It may be revealed that no one is optimistic, that no one believes anything will change, but that all believe they must "keep trying".

2. *"Let's assume for a few minutes that this problem can't be solved. What do you think will be happening in (one, five, ten, etc.) years for _____ (explore the impact of this hypothetical future on individuals and various relationships between family members and helpers).* This question carries a certain power in its unexpectedness. Generally, if a family is engaged with multiple helpers, no one dares to entertain the possibility that a solution will not be found. Rather, people persist in trying harder, often adding new professionals. When the consultant briefly invites people into a reality of "no-solution", many relationships come into clear relief. Patterns of overinvolvement, alliances, beliefs about catastrophies, or conversely, beliefs about a normal future all emerge. It is not unusual for the family to believe there is a brighter future, both for itself and for the identified patient, than the assembly of helpers imagines, which frequently serves as an informative surprise to the family–multiple helpers system.

3. *"Let's imagine that all helping efforts were to stop".* This hypothetical question can be explored from a number of vantage points, such as, *"Who would be most upset?", "Who would be most glad?", "What impact would this have on _____ (individuals, various relationships)?", "Would _____ (name of identified patient or others) get better, worse, stay the same?".* This line of questioning regarding the cessation of help is as similarly unexpected as the question regarding no solution. Care must be taken during that portion of the interview devoted to this set of questions, in order not to communicate the opinion or belief that helping efforts should cease. The intent of the question is to create an unanticipated reality, and to enable the participants to draw a distinction between the effects of "help" and "no help" on individuals, relationships and whole family functioning. For instance, it is not unusual for a family and helpers to discover that people believe that "no help"

might result in improvement in the identified patient, but deterioration in other members, the marriage, etc. In a recent interview utilising this set of questions, the helpers were shocked to discover that all family members believed that professional help made the identified patient more stubborn, and that she would straighten herself out within five years without professional help! (For a full description of this interview, see Imber Coppersmith, 1983b.)

B. Case Example: Consultation and Intervention in a Family–Multiple Helpers System

A consultation was requested by a family ther.*pist for a case involving recurring school refusal by a 15-year-old boy. The case had an erratic history of slight progress followed by relapse followed by slight progress, etc. At present, the school guidance counsellor had called the therapist several times, urgently requesting that "more be done", while the therapist was following a course of backing off. Thus a treatment triangle existed.

The family consisted of a single parent, mother, Anne, age 39, the identified patient, Kevin, age 15, and a daughter Sue, age 13. The parents had been divorced 12 years. The father left following the birth of Sue, who was developmentally disabled. No one in the family has heard from him for 11 years. Mother described him as "irresponsible and alcoholic". Ann also came from a single-parent family, and described her own father as "irresponsible and alcoholic". Kevin had been an excellent student, until reaching adolescence, when he became "severely depressed" and refused to go to school.

The three members of the nuclear family, the family therapist, Mr. B., and the school guidance counsellor, Mr. Z., were present at the consulting interview. Since many helping efforts had failed, it was broadly hypothesised that the family and helpers were embroiled with one another, and that Kevin's symptoms functioned to maintain that involvement. The interview was utilised to gain details of the family–multiple helper system, and to inform this system about itself. The interview began with a discussion of the various efforts tried in the previous 15 months. The intent of this line of questioning was to discover the range of the family's involvements with helpers, their beliefs and attitudes towards help, how the helpers see the efforts tried, etc.

The family and the two professionals related example after example of slight improvement followed by a relapse of greater severity. A picture emerged in which every possible solution to the problem of Kevin's school refusal had been tried, including psychiatric care, anti-depressive medication, hospitalisation, individual therapy, structural family therapy, systemic family therapy and simply dragging him to school. Every solution worked briefly and then failed. Several salient issues and patterns emerged during the discussion.

1. Every helper engaged with the family was male.
2. Mother talked most to her own mother regarding each new plan.
3. Mother and the guidance counsellor were on a first-name basis. He called her frequently and stopped by the house. While evidently concerned about Kevin,

he was presently more concerned about Ann's well-being. He was usually the initiator of each new helping attempt.

4. Competing beliefs about the nature of the problem and its solution existed among the helpers. At present, the guidance counsellor believed that Kevin had a severe psychiatric syndrome and needed further hospitalisation; his superior (not at the interview and never having seen Kevin) believed Kevin had a "depressive–compulsive phobia" and also supported hospitalisation; the psychiatrist told the family that Kevin had a "depressive personality" and required medication; briefly, a belief had existed that Kevin was just a "bad boy", and during this period he was dragged to school each morning by a truant officer until mother and the school counsellor decided this was not a good plan. The family therapist conceptualised Kevin as being loyal to his father by acting irresponsibly, but was doing so in a "responsible" manner, since by not going to school, he helped his developmentally delayed sister and occupied his otherwise lonely mother. The most ferocious difference was thus apparent between the guidance counsellor, who wanted *action now*, and the family therapist who positively connoted Kevin's problem and prescribed "no change".

5. Mother vacillated with Kevin between supporting each new plan and then subtly expressing her doubts. In a similar vein, she would take Kevin's side and then quietly betray him and side with the outsiders.

Mother: I feel like I'm always in the middle between Kevin and whoever's involved with us.

Consultant: (to Sue) Whose side does your mother take more often?

Sue: She changes. I don't know.

Consultant: (to Kevin) What do you think?

Kevin: (sobbing) I'm confused. I'm confused.

6. Mother held a fixed belief that none of this would be happening if she were not a single parent.

The initial hypothesis was expanded. Kevin's symptoms were hypothesised to function to bring "helpful" men into this single-parent family and to keep the mother close to her own mother via discussions of the outside helpers' failed efforts.

The consultant explored what people believed would happen if all help were to stop, suggesting that at 15 or 16 years of age many youngsters decide to quit school. This was balanced with a line of questioning exploring the next intervention being suggested by the guidance counsellor, namely hospitalisation at the local children's hospital, a setting not previously tried. The consultant remained neutral towards both possibilities, and utilised the questions to draw a distinction between no help–more help and between normalcy–psychiatric patient. As might be expected, the two helpers split, with the guidance counsellor favouring hospitalisation and predicting a terrible future if all help ceased, and the family therapist favouring less help. Kevin believed he would do well in a few years "if everyone got off my back so I could think!" Sue preferred Kevin go to the hospital and "stop bugging" her. Most interesting was mother's response: "If all help stopped, I think he would pull himself together in about ten years. My brother quit school at 15, and now he's an engineer. So for a while he'd probably be a bum, but he'd get on his feet". Regarding the hospital, mother stated (looking at Mr. Z.): "Kevin would hate me if I make him go, but it might just be the best thing". The consultant hypothesised that the mother was caught between supporting her son and supporting the guidance counsellor, who was the primary adult male in her life. As a result, her messages to her son were duplicitous, and Kevin responded with increased confusion, thereby supporting the view that he was a patient. The periods of brief improvement followed by relapse were both a metaphor for the family's relationship to helpers and a way to insure that helpers remained in the family sphere.

Following the generation of the above information during the interview, the consultant and team met to design an intervention. Since the mother, in particular, had indicated that the most pressing concern was whether or not to hospitalise Kevin, and since this issue in all of its ramifications was symbolic for the family's entanglements with multiple helpers, it was decided to design an intervention that responded to this issue, potentially in a new way. The intervention was based on the hypotheses discussed above. In particular, the intervention was designed to target the vacillation of the mother between her son and outsiders. The intervention offered was a variation of the *odd days/even days* prescription, designed to separate in time the usual simultaneous mixed messages in the system regarding the efficacy of outside help. The team's view was that Kevin was the constant recipient of messages that "outside help was useful" and that "outside help was useless". These messages were set in a larger context in which men in general were seen as "necessary" and at the same time "irresponsible, useless, etc." Kevin, for his part, responded to these messages by appearing more and more confused, thus generating more helping efforts which continued to fail. The *odd days/even days* ritual also spoke implicitly to the struggle among the helpers for who had the "most correct" view.

Finally, family therapy was reframed as "consultation" in an attempt to block the triangulated pattern between the family, family therapist and guidance counsellor, and to imply the possibility that one can be "helpful" by listening to the family's ideas, rather than by giving advice.

C. Intervention

The consultant spoke to the mother: "You have let us know today that the most difficult issue you face presently is whether or not to hospitalise Kevin. I would like to suggest an experiment for you to do, designed, we hope, to produce greater clarity and help you reach a decision. We'd like you to divide up the week in the following way: On Saturday, Monday and Wednesday we want you to adopt the position that Kevin is going to the hospital. On those days, you should research everything you need to regarding hospitalisation. You can talk to doctors, you can talk to other mothers who have hospitalised their children, you can talk to people who have been to the hospital, you can talk to Mr. Z. about it and to your mother. On those days, we want you to regard Kevin as a patient, since that's what he will be, and we want you to talk to him *with conviction* about why you think it's a good idea for him to go to the hospital. You should do this regardless of how Kevin responds. Then on Sunday, Tuesday and Thursday, we want you to adopt the position that Kevin is a normal boy who has decided to quit school for a while and therefore no helping efforts are necessary. On those days you should take note of all the ways Kevin is just a regular boy. If any one calls you on those days to talk about help for Kevin—for instance, Mr. Z. or your mother—you should say 'Sorry, I can't discuss that today.' On those days, you should talk to Kevin *with conviction* about why no more help is needed, and that he's a normal boy. Then take Friday off and start again. We'd like you to do this for about three weeks or until you feel the issues have been clarified."

The consultant spoke to the family therapist: "We'd like also to suggest to you that no more family therapy be held for the time being, but that you be available to the family on a "consulting" basis. That is, the family should call you when they would like to have a discussion, for instance, when they feel this task is done and they want to talk it over.

Consultant: Yes.

Kevin: (*To Mother*) If you send me to the hospital, I'll run away.

Mother: (*To Kevin*) Today is Friday. Today is a "nothing" day. I'm not going to discuss it today! We'll talk about it tomorrow on the "hospital" day.

In this particular case, the intervention was punctuated in such a way as to address primarily the mother's involvement with multiple helpers and the ways in which the son's symptoms sustained this involvement. In other cases, one might address relationships among the various professionals, patterns that result in more and more helpers entering the family sphere, or the total family–multiple helpers system. The consultant can utilise a variety of systemic interventions, including positive connotation of the existing macrosystem, tasks and rituals. Frequently, the consulting interview is followed by a memo from the consultant to the family therapist, with copies sent to family members and the other helpers. Such a memo again defines all members of the family–multiple helpers system on the same level, is unexpected, and implicitly comments on the value of shared information, as opposed to secret alliances (see Imber Coppersmith, 1983b for a case example utilising memos).

IV. EFFECTS OF APPLYING THE SYSTEMIC MODEL TO FAMILIES AND MULTIPLE HELPERS

Applying the systemic model to families and multiple helpers has widened the conceptual base for understanding human problems. Just as family therapy initially provided a move away from individual blame concepts, so the family–multiple helpers view provides a move away from family blame concepts. The attempt here is not to blame professionals but rather to grasp the complexities that evolve when families and multiple helpers interact, and to design efficacious interviewing methods and interventions that promote family integrity and allow professionals to do their work effectively.

Family therapists who have been trained in this perspective report viewing and conducting their work differently. Initial or second interviews frequently contain a portion of time devoted to the family's past and present involvement with helpers. Stuck cases are reconceptualised to include a wider context. Former views of other helpers as "villains" or people to "take control of" are abandoned for a circular curiosity and understanding about each one's place in a macrosystem. The family therapist's appreciation of self as part of the system, rather than outside, is enhanced.

Some professionals who have been participants in family–multiple helper interviews have reported questioning and altering long-standing beliefs about the helping endeavour. The tendency to add more and more helpers has frequently been interdicted. A few have sought training in the systemic model.

The family–multiple helper schema aids the systemic therapist in initial engagement issues, hypothesis formation, understanding where a system might be stuck, conceptualising behaviour from a wide angle and generating interventions at the appropriate level of the system. It does little good, and may in fact, do harm, to continue to interview and intervene within the family if the "meaningful system" is the family and multiple helpers.

Acknowledgment

The author thanks Dr. Karl Tomm for his useful comments in the preparation of this manuscript, and for his support of a clinical environment that facilitates creativity and experimentation.

REFERENCES

Coleman, S. (1983). A Case of Non-Treatment of a Non-Problem Problem. *Journal of Strategic and Systemic Therapies* 2, 62–66.

Goolishian, H., and Anderson, H. (1981). Including Non-Blood Related Persons in Family Therapy. *In* Gurman, A. (ed.), "Questions and Answers in the Practice of Family Therapy". Brunner/Mazel, New York, pp. 75–79.

Harkaway, J. (1983). Obesity: Reducing the Larger System. *Journal of Strategic and Systemic Therapies* 2, 2–14.

Hoffman, L., and Long, L. (1969). A Systems Dilemma. *Family Process* 8, 211–234.

Imber Coppersmith, E. (1983a). The Family and Public Service Systems: An Assessment Method. *In* Keeney, B. (ed.), "Diagnosis and Assessment in Family Therapy". Aspen Publications, Rockville, Md., pp. 83–99.

Imber Coppersmith, E. (1983b). The Family and Public Sector Systems: Interviewing and Interventions. *Journal of Strategic and Systemic Therapies* 2, 38–47.

Imber Coppersmith, E. (1982). From Hyperactive To Normal But Naughty: A Multi-System Partnership in Delabeling. *International Journal of Family Psychiatry* 3, 131–144.

Imber Coppersmith, E. We've Got A Secret: A Non-Marital Marital Therapy. *In* Gurman, A. (ed.), "Marital Therapy Casebook". Guilford Press, New York, in press.

Miller, D. (1983). Outlaws and Invaders: The Adaptive Function of Alcohol Abuse in the Family–Helper Supra System. *Journal of Strategic and Systemic Therapies* 2, 15–27.

Palazzoli, M., Boscolo, L., Cecchin, G., and Prata, G. (1980a). The Problem of the Referring Person. *Journal of Marital and Family Therapy* 6, 3–9.

Palazzoli, M., Boscolo, L., Cechhin, G., and Prata, G. (1980b). Hypothesizine, Circularity, Neutrality: Three Guidelines for the Conductor of the Session. *Family Process* 19, 3–12.

Tomm, K., Lannamann, J., and McNamee, S. (1983). No Interview Today: A Consultation Team Intervenes By Not Intervening. *Journal of Strategic and Systemic Therapies* 2, 48–61.

Webb-Woodard, L., and Woodard, B. (1983). The Larger System in the Treatment of Incest. *Journal of Strategic and Systemic Therapies* 2, 28–37.

Chapter 21

In-Patient Hospital Systemic Consultation: Providing Team Systemic Consultation in In-Patient Settings Where the Team is Part of the System

Laura Nitzberg, John Patten, Marlene Spielman
and Richard Brown

Is family systems therapy possible in an in-patient psychiatric hospital? (Haley, 1975). This paper describes our application of a team approach based on a systems model to consultation within a psychiatric setting.

The psychiatric institution in which we work is affiliated with a major, prestigious medical school and is a tertiary care facility devoted to the training of psychiatrists and research. The medical care is superior and the staff is well trained and academic. Patients come from all over the country for evaluation and treatment. Family therapy has become more integrated into the program, and the director of the in-patient service is a family therapy researcher. Family therapy supervision and formal courses are required of the psychiatric residents. The hospital and senior staff tend to be psychoanalysts by training but many are increasingly interested in biological views. Although family therapy has become a more recognised and appreciated model, very few staff are trained in systems concepts and family therapy techniques. Psychoanalytic and biological models still predominate.

Three of the writers of this chapter are trained family therapists (at the Ackerman Institute in New York City) and supervise family therapy in the institution. The other writer is a psychiatrist with special expertise in psychopharmacology. Two of us are social workers who at the time of the pilot project worked on separate in-patient units. One is a child psychiatrist who supervises and teaches family therapy. Our interest in forming a team grew out of our familiarity with each other's work and philosophy of treatment in the context of a family therapy supervisor's group which meets regularly. Because of our common training, which exposed us to a team model, we become intrigued with the notion of applying the model and tailoring it to a psychiatric hospital. Because we were sensitive to the many unique characteristics of a psychiatric hospital which differ from family therapy agencies and other out-patient settings, we were cognisant of the importance of including a team member who was strongly identified with the medical model perspective. Therefore, we approached a colleague who was highly respected for his expertise in psychopharmacology and was also interested in systems theory and therapy.

We began our project by meeting regularly but informally to talk about theories of diagnosis and treatment. Ultimately our discussions focused on current treatment dilemmas in our own practice or in problems which we were supervising. Simultaneously we were receiving informal requests from staff social workers and residents for help on difficult family cases. We decided to approach these requests as a team rather than individually and to try to develop a model for consultation.

We wanted to avoid formally announcing our group to the institution at large for fear of being deluged by requests for help and for fear of being subsumed by a bureaucratic structure. We worried about a variety of institutional pressures and constraints: chart note requirements, statistical accounting and other hospital rituals. Therefore, we decided to maintain a low-key stance by not officially announcing our existence. Our informal status was helpful in that we were free to test our ideas because we were not controlled by the institution.

With each request for help, we met as a group to assess the origin and meaning of the request; in other words, we systematically scrutinised the referring context. We were immediately aware of a common theme which permeated the requests. In each situation, the case had become an enormous problem to the unit, and the family of the patient rarely had a good alliance with the hospital staff; in fact, there was an adversarial relationship between the staff and family. Also, the staff was extremely frustrated with the patient and in conflict with each other about the management of the case. These pleas for help impressed us as being immensely suitable to a systems approach because each problem was a complicated systems problem.

The hospital is divided into five distinct in-patient units, all of which have a different character. The units are very much like families, with clear personalities. A major part of our work was to try to understand the composition and nature of the system from which the referral came. We made a diagnosis of the system, with its hierarchies, coalitions and alliances, based on our previous knowledge of the unit as well as our observation during the consultation process. What was unique about our work as opposed to teams that consult only to families was that we were part of the system to which we were consulting. This fact proved both advantageous as well as disadvantageous. In some ways we were less threatening to our consultees because we were a known entity and had a history of personal and professional relationships with them. On the other hand, we were more threatening because when we became a team we developed a new and somewhat enigmatic identity which led to some suspicion and resentment.

In our numerous team discussions we paid close attention to the variety of feedbacks from staff (i.e. phone calls, corridor discussions, non-verbal cues) while formulating hypotheses and interventions. Members of the treating team attempted to make alliances with consulting team members for multiple reasons (including getting support or attempting to disqualify the consultation). In order to monitor ourselves, we designated one team member to communicate with the consultees. At times there was considerable pressure for one of us to intervene independently. Our group rule that no decision could be made without a team discussion provided a helpful safeguard.

When we were asked to help in certain situations we noted that the identified patient became the special child of the unit, and the longer the patient's length of stay, the more antagonism existed between the family and the staff. It seemed that there was a rivalry between the staff and the family. These cases reflected a certain bias by some staff to view the family as being evil or "toxic" with a recommendation to implement a "parentectomy" or "familyectomy". The problem with this approach was that chaos often resulted around discharge planning when the patient had to exit the hospital system and face the family and community again.

In these cases we found that our team, which had become a sub-system, could provide a view that was more objective than the treating system. Our distance allowed us some perspective so that we could identify the rivalries and tensions previously mentioned. We had frequent team meetings to scrutinise the systems to which we consulted. In our private team meetings, we discussed the dynamics of the families, the relationship of the family to the treating team, the relationship of the treating team to the consultation team, and the relationship of the consultation team to the family. These lengthy discussions were helpful in giving a systemic, or non-linear view of the problem. We were careful to reframe the problem positively for our consultees. The most important task in our work was to develop a good rapport with our own consultees and to maintain a non-judgmental demeanour which was not threatening or critical. Most of our meetings involved getting history about the presenting problem, the referring source, outside therapists as well as hospital staff, and family history. We also paid close attention to medical issues in the case and reviewed charts closely so as to be rigorous in our own diagnostic work. Our meetings were time-consuming and our belief in being exquisitely thorough had to be balanced against the urgent pressures our consultees faced on the units (i.e. external and internal pressures to discharge the patient as well as some serious medical deterioration that occurred in the patients).

In the cases we reviewed we became aware of the treating staff's dilemma. Because they used a linear model, they tended to get caught in the bind of being too rigidly focused on seeing the patient as a victim. In our consultation process, we changed the focus by our use of circular questioning (in gathering data about the patient, family and treating team) when interviewing our consultees. Our systems orientation was present in all our interactions with our consultees, although we never directly criticised the medical model.

In general, our consultations were limited to the key treating staff (i.e. the psychiatrist and social workers). We had a good rapport with our consultees but our effectiveness was limited because we did not have sufficient contact with other key people (nursing staff, units chiefs and other supervisors). Although we tried to make systemic assessments, our information was filtered through our consultees giving us only partial data. We were concerned that if we focused too much attention on ourselves (i.e. by having large staff meetings or scheduling rare meetings with unit chiefs) we would have limited our power. We were concerned that if we were to meet with very senior staff (i.e. the "grandparents" of the institution), we would force a direct clash with the proponents of a psychoanalytic model, thus potentially nullifying our power as consultants. We learned, however, that we should have interviewed all staff treating the patient, and we believe we would have been even more successful had we done so.

Another trend we noted was that at some point during every consultation, our consultees tried to seduce us to become the treating therapists in an attempt to relinquish their responsibility. While we empathised with their wish for relief, and while we sometimes struggled with our own grandiose, omnipotent wish to take over or rescue the treatment, we had to draw a line between doing treatment and offering consultation.

A. Case Example: "The Woman Who Wouldn't Stop Gagging"

We received a request for help from the resident and social worker on an in-patient unit. The patient was a depressed middle-aged woman with a complicated family situation who had a remarkable and irritating symptom of incessant, uncontrollable gagging. There was no medical explanation for this gagging phenomenon, and the staff found this symptom to be intolerable because they saw it as being willful, and the gagging precluded any talking psychotherapy. This request had originated in a group family supervisory meeting on that unit where this patient was being treated. That particular supervisory seminar concluded that this case was suitable for strategic approaches and that a paradoxical intervention was indicated. Even though, as previously stated, we had never officially announced ourselves to the institution, our existence had been noted and this seminar associated our team-style approach with the Milan group and equated our work with the use of paradox (Palazzoli et al., 1978). Although we appreciated being asked to consult, we were somewhat suspicious about the nature of the request since we believe that the Milan groups' approach is often distorted and that the word "paradox" has come to mean many things, many of which were never intended by our Italian colleagues. We hypothesised that we were being asked to prescribe a paradox so that we would be blamed if the meeting never occurred, and if it did take place, we would have to assume responsibility for the consequences of such a meeting.

We approached the case by meeting with the resident and social worker, who were genuinely eager for help in managing a very tricky family situation. The presenting problem was that of a woman in her fifties hospitalised for depression. The patient, normally a well-functioning person, had a life-long history of clear depressive episodes which often responded to medication and psychotherapy. She was married to a successful businessman (who was a VIP in hospital circles) who had never been directly involved in her treatment. He had always avoided family sessions. The couple had a son in his thirties with manic-depressive illness. This son was very close to this mother but was a terrible embarrassment to his father, who viewed him as being a failure and had contempt for his son's emotional illness, which he saw as weakness. At the time of the request for help, father and son were not speaking and in fact had had a recent violent altercation which resulted in bitter acrimony. The father had gone to the courts requesting an order of protection against his son, whom he claimed had threatened to kill him. The only person to whom both the husband and son would speak was the mother's psychiatrist of many years. This psychiatrist had unwittingly been catapulted into the role of family therapist (Palazzoli et al., 1980). Although he did not have meetings with the entire family, he relayed messages, gave advice and soothed heated tempers.

When we first met with our consultees, we learned about the patient's history and the family dynamics. The consultees seemed to have astutely assessed the family dynamics but had never had a family meeting with father and son present. Nor had they involved the patient's outside psychiatrist in the family meetings despite the important role he played in the system. Our hypotheses were the following: that the father was controlling the treating system as well as the family, thus making change impossible; that the son's manic-depressive episodes regulated the marriage; that the mother's depressive episodes helped negotiate the toxic mother-father-son triangle.

Our first intervention was to refuse to give a paradox since we believed we needed more data to make a systemic hypothesis. We urged our consultees to arrange for a family session. Just prior to the scheduled session, we received urgent calls from the unit's senior faculty, who was worried that we might do something dramatic in the family session and thus harm the patient, who was not getting better. We told the worried faculty that we simply needed more data.

Meanwhile, the patient's progress on the unit was negligible. Our team's medical expert reviewed the case and concluded that the patient's diagnosis of depression was correct and that the gagging was related to the depression, and he cited some references for the psychiatrist to read. He predicted that the gagging would vanish when the depression lifted (his prediction later became fact). Meanwhile family tensions were high, with father and son timing their visits to the hospital in such a way as never to collide. The patient's husband refused to attend a meeting with his wife and son present despite the attempts by the patient's outside psychiatrist to arrange such a meeting. The meeting never took place. Our next intervention (after refusing to give a paradox) was to enlist the outside psychiatrist's help. He came in for a session with the son and the patient. This session revealed valuable data about the family system. The psychiatrist believed that the patient's depressive episodes were temporally correlated to problems in the marriage which invariably focused on the couple's wayward son. Although the psychiatrist had never changed this disturbed family system, he had nonetheless stabilised the system with his role as mediator and supporter. His gentle, kind presence had cooled tempers and balanced the system. In our session he finally acknowledged his own feelings of helplessness and talked about his own sense of inadequacy with regards to improving the marriage.

Our third intervention was to meet with the family therapy seminar on the unit. We were cordially received and it was clear that some staff members were disappointed when we failed to deliver a flamboyant intervention. We had decided that not only was a flashy intervention not clinically indicated, we also felt we would undermine our effectiveness by appearing paradoxical. As one cannot be told to be spontaneous, we could not be told to be paradoxical. Instead, we carefully reviewed the patient's psychiatric history and framed it in the context of family and biological models. We reviewed the family's genogram and arrived at an hypothesis about the role of the mother's psychiatrist in that system. We recommended that the patient should continue to be in treatment with her psychiatrist, since he had clearly helped her function well in between depressive episodes. We also recommended that the couple seek marital therapy (we decided not to insist on a family meeting with the son present since such meetings were clearly too dangerous). All our recommendations were framed positively. Never did we label the husband's resistance negatively; we suggested that the marital therapy focus on the patient's depression since we saw a connection between the depression and the marriage.

We demonstrated by example how to approach the case from a system's framework. The treating staff had become obsessed with the notion of arranging a family meeting with the son and father present. By using a circular questioning we were able to elicit the family's dynamics without forcing the meeting which was clearly too dangerous to hold. The consultation gave support and direction to our consultees, who had been intimidated by the patient's gagging and the threat of violence between father and son. Our theoretical framework led us to include the patient's outside psychiatrist in our assessment of the family system. Including him in family sessions and discharge planning proved helpful to all parties. He also welcomed having an opportunity to talk about his own distress over the difficult chronic problem.

B. Discussion

Now we return to the original question posed at the beginning of the paper: is family systems intervention possible in a psychiatric hospital?

Psychiatric hospitals differ considerably from out-patient settings. This simple statement has profound implications. Hospitalised patients are usually more impaired or at least have had a long treatment track record, usually of failures. The hospitalised patients are the failures of out-patient treatment. They are the most visibly frail, medically ill and chronically suicidal. Hospital staff is drained by treating people with a poor prognosis. Each discipline tends to feel that their particular orientation is superior. When a patient does not respond, sometimes the family, patient or each other are blamed. On in-patient units tensions between modalities, sometimes irreconcilable, are commonplace and the tension can be helpful as well as destructive. Different views can promote a stimulating academic environment. On occasion, however, tensions can be so high as to cripple sound treatment decisions.

One of the ironies of psychiatric training is that in-patient units are staffed by beginning trainees. Lack of communication between supervisors can be problematic when the case is complex and there is an implicit or explicit difference of opinion either between supervisors or between the supervisor and the unit. Often the individual therapy is supervised by a supervisor with a psychoanalytic orientation and the family work may be supervised by a person with a family systems orientation. These tensions, although intellectually interesting, can be extremely anxiety-producing for an already anxiety-ridden trainee. The trainee is trying to treat a patient who may be very resistant and looks to the supervisor for practical advice and clear guidelines. Sometimes this clear advice is not forthcoming, however, and the trainee can be triangulated between supervisors. Also, the trainee may be working with a seasoned non-medical professional (i.e. social worker, nurse or occupational therapist) with years of experience and hierarchical status issues may interfere in the trainee consulting with the non-medical colleague.

Our team was unique in that it was composed of members with different professional backgrounds. It was essential for at least one team member to be clearly identified with the medical model. His presence gave us more credibility with the institution, and his expertise was invaluable. Also, as a team we had to openly discuss status issues and hierarchical issues.

Clinicians working in a psychiatric setting usually have inflexible belief systems about the models they employ in treatment, just as systemic family therapists models have their own belief systems. To imply that systemic models are better than other clinical models only invokes resistance, paralyses any useful consultation and produces no change in a traditional psychiatric setting.

By respecting and considering medical and individual psychological models, using that language and often devising interventions in the language of those models, we were far more effective. Privately the consultation team would talk and think in systemic terms, but publicly our consultations, although systemic, were translated into a more palatable language.

The Milan associates might say that one has to constantly interrupt and challenge a family's belief system on all levels to produce change. In our consultation process we do not try to change the whole hospital treating system, but rather try to produce one small change in the treating family system. Consultation requires a different and more minimal order of task than does family therapy.

Our team discussions were lively and thought-provoking and enriched our work at the hospital. Although our meetings were time-consuming, we made an impact on the systems to which we consulted. We feel that a team approach can be a useful addition to hospitals and play an important consultative role, different from traditional supervision, for difficult cases.

REFERENCES

Haley, J. (1975). Why a Mental Health Clinic Should Avoid Family Therapy. *Journal of Marriage and Family Counseling* 1, 3–13.

Palazzoli, M. S., Boscolo, L., Cecchin, G., and Prata, G. (1978). "Paradox and Counterparadox". Jason Aronson, New York.

Palazzoli, M. S., Boscolo, L., Cecchin, G., and Prata, G. (1980). The Problem of the Referring Person. *Journal of Marital and Family Therapy* 6 (1), 3–9.

Chapter 22

Consultations With Professional and Family Systems in the Context of Residential and Fostering Services: "In and Out of Care"

Caroline Lindsey

I. THE DEVELOPMENT OF A NEW CONTEXT

The work described in this chapter takes place in a Social Services Assessment Centre with residential provision. Traditionally, the Centre has been a resource for Social Services, education services and the court, to assess children at risk and their families with a focus on the questions: "Can this child return to live in his family and if not, where should he be placed?" Significant developments over the last ten years in the field of child care have led to changes in the way the centre is used.

The decline in numbers of the local population has led to fewer children going into care. (*Care* is the term used to describe the legal assumption of parental responsibilities by the local authority as a result of Care Proceedings.) There has also been an increasing emphasis on maintaining children in their families whenever possible. These developments, accompanied by evidence of the emotional damage produced by institutional care (Prosser, 1976), have led to closure of the majority of local children's homes. The need for financial economies increased the speed and number of closures. These closures, in turn, emphasised the need for more sophisticated attempts to maintain children at home. Fostering emerged as the most acceptable alternative to natural families when attempts at rehabilitation fail. During this time, family therapy became established in the field of child care in England. Training in family therapy in the Social Services, facilitated work with many families where care was an issue.

As a result there has been an increasing demand for family assessment whilst the child remains at home. Referrals of young children usually arise when it is difficult to resolve conflicts of interest over rehabilitation or permanent placement. Another change has been the increasing requests for help with fostering problems. Cases are referred for such problems as the imminent breakdown of a foster placement or conflict over access to the natural parents. Many families who are seen have teenage children, with problems of school attendance, delinquency, parental neglect, abuse or rejection, but now the consultation must also take account of the fact that they have often received family therapy before referral to the Centre.

APPLICATIONS OF SYSTEMIC FAMILY THERAPY
ISBN 0-8089-1696-3

The assessment team consists of the senior social workers, the educational psychologist and myself. As a psychiatrist and family therapist, I also act as consultant to the Centre and to Social Services. I have responsibility for my own work within the agency and have no managerial responsibility, unlike the social workers on the team who run the centre. The relationship with the staff of the centre and with referrers and families is affected by my dual role of consultant and team member. Although I am not a member of Social Services, I may be perceived as one by the family and referring agencies. This means that the relationship between members of the assessment team and the referring professionals has to be defined for each consultation. The Assessment Centre's consultative function has developed in response to the changing needs of the department. Whilst the consultants have no direct influence on its development, it seems that the application of systemic thinking and practice has influenced and has been influenced by the changing tasks of the Centre.

Over the last five years, the smaller context in which systems thinking is being applied has also changed. Previously the focus of referrals to the Assessment Centre by social workers was almost inevitably related to the consideration of reception into care and placement. Now, more commonly, the decisions about care have already been taken, because direct access to fostering is available in case of family breakdown. The consultation is often requested to consider the short and long term implications of the decision.

Previously, an approach to the Centre represented calling in "experts" in family therapy to help the social workers with the family work. Now, as a result of the expertise in Social Services, this idea may challenge the competence of the fieldworkers, and direct work with the family is therefore not always indicated.

Now whenever a social worker requests a family assessment, he is offered a team consultation for himself and his senior, sometimes including the area head. Since only a few of the cases social workers have to deal with are referred to the centre, one general hypothesis is that the referral may represent an attempt to resolve a problem in the professional/family system rather than the family system alone. The context in which systemic thinking is applied may consist of the social work team only, or may include the social work team plus family or foster family, or, thirdly, the social work team plus other agencies (e.g. foster care teams, schools and school units, etc.) involved in a conflictual relationship over the management of the family problems.

The meeting is defined as "a consultation" with the implication to the social worker that "the case remains your responsibility; the management decisions are yours; if the child is in care, you are the legally responsible parent", and with the implication that our role is not to become as involved as the social worker and not to take over the case. As a result the social workers' expectation that we will automatically work with their families, potentially excluding them because they seem to be unable to do the work themselves, is altered. In most cases, the task is to address the problem which the social worker is having in his own team or in his relationship with the client family, so that his work with the family can continue or not, in whatever way is appropriate. We recognise that in work with families, the tendency to lose control, to get "sucked in" to the system is a regular and inevitable hazard which may require consultation from outside the working team. In particular, in social work, the statutory demands compound the tendency to identify with a child or a parent and require roles to be taken which prevent the adoption of a neutral stance. The assumption of a metaposition by the consultation team may facilitate a systemic understanding of the role of statutory responsibility in a case and enable it to be positively connoted for the social worker.

II. THE APPLICATION OF SYSTEMIC THINKING

Before a consultation, an attempt is made to gather factual information about the case, so that a preconsultation hypothesis and related questions can be prepared. The hypothesis is usually in two parts: consideration of the family system and the family plus professional systems. For consultations within this context, hypotheses and questioning which focus on the relationship between social workers and the family have been most fruitful.

In the interview, circular questioning has proved invaluable in providing information to the consultation team and to the family/professional system. The questioning, without an intervention, may be sufficient to reorganise the social worker–family relationship so that change can take place.

The intervention is addressed to the professional team with or without a message to the family, or to the family and social worker. Key features of the intervention are a positive connotation of the family and professionals' contribution, attention to life cycle and developmental issues, the effect on those of family disruption and being in care, and a "no change" or "slow change" message.

In some cases, court reports are required. It is sometimes possible to ask the court's assistance in a reframing of parenting by a public statement. This is a powerful intervention, since the court is in a metaposition to both the family and the social work team, but it needs to be carefully balanced so that the family is not positively connoted at the expense of a negative connotation of the social worker.

The issue of the effect of the idea of "help" on the social worker–family relationship is particularly important with this group of families, who often have more professional "helpers" than relations and friends. A request, often by single parents, to a social worker for help may represent an attempt to replace an absent parent or spouse, maintaining a professional involvement in the family, thereby excluding others from taking on the role in the family. This is a working hypothesis which views this situation as leading to symptom maintenance.

For example, a mother said, "I can ring my social worker if I have trouble with my daughter over school. It saves me having to contact my ex-husband". This enabled the team to clarify that whilst an educational recommendation was required, a supervision order to carry it out was not appropriate.

The hypothesis that problem escalation, resignation of parental duties and disqualification of the "helper" may follow the social worker's response to a request from the family or more commonly from other professionals for them to be helped may be due in part to the family's perception that the social work role carries with it the known responsibility for scrutinising parenting. In some families, commonly amongst immigrants, social work involvement is tantamount to a definition of parental failure. The more helpful the social worker, the greater the failure.

For example, a grown up son of an immigrant family complained to Social Services about his mother's ill treatment of his eight-year-old brother. The investigation of the allegation resulted in reception into care, and he and his mother refused to consider his return. During the consultation, it became clear that the eldest son was "removing" his brother from home because he was no longer allowed to live there; that the boy wished to return but was torn by loyalty to his brother and the mother's "cruelty"—locking him in the house whilst she was at work—arose from her wish to safeguard him. The court was requested, with the social worker's agreement, to disclose to the mother the content of the report in which the social worker was described as having the duty to ensure that children were not cruelly treated. In this case, she had understandably mistaken the mother's protective parenting for cruelty. It was important to acknowledge the attempts that this mother had made to look after her child responsibly, to confirm that there was no evidence for the making of a care order and that the mother should continue to look after him. Alternative ways of managing holidays and after-school time could be offered to the mother. This restored the mother's authority and enabled mother and son to be reunited without loss of face. It also enabled the mother to accept the help of Social Services because it was offered within the context of her being defined as a responsible parent.

Other hypotheses address the issue of the effect of "help" in the form of statutory responsibility. One hypothesis is that, in families with a history of social deprivation, poverty and experience of care, a request for reception into care at a time of crisis may reflect an assumption that care is the only possible response that Social Services would make, rather than a wish for this course of action to be taken.

For example, a family requested that 14-year-old Mary be taken into care. Her mother, who was single and agoraphobic, had lived like a recluse with her daughter for years. Now adolescent, the girl had begun to rebel against their way of life by staying out. Her mother told Mary on several occasions that she would not have her back, and eventually Mary went to stay with her aunt. During the consultation with the social work team, we learnt that they were reluctant to receive her into care because of past failures with the family. During the family consultation, questions were asked about their relationship with Social Services. It emerged that the family believed that taking her into care would be detrimental to her development.

This led to a redefinition of the relationship between the family and Social Services, so that it was possible to ask the question, "How can Social Services help you to achieve your wish for Mary to be well cared for?" rather than, "Should they take her into care?" As a result the family was supported in finding a new home for Mary within the extended family.

Another hypothesis is that, in cases where it is recognised by the social work team and the family that reception into care is necessary, this action may not be taken because the social work team believe it is not helpful for them to hold statutory responsibility.

For example, there tends to be a sense of shame, guilt and failure involved in the reception of a child into care. When appropriate, the positive connotation of such a move for the family, child and social worker produces relief and facilitates constructive planning for the future.

A frequently used hypothesis is that deterioration in a reasonably stable family or foster family situation may be related to the recent or impending departure of a social worker. In contrast to the hypothesis above, that a request for a social worker may represent an attempt to replace an absent parent, the social worker here has usually statutorily represented a family member and his departure profoundly alters the child's family system.

Two general hypotheses apply to those families coming from poor and delinquent environments who have experienced frequent disruptions of care, separation and loss. Firstly, these experiences affect the emotional, social and cognitive development of the children, resulting in disturbance in their capacity to relate to adults and children, which may be understood in terms of developmental delay arising from deprivation. Secondly, the chances of change in those families are often limited. To be "on the side of no change" may be considered to be more realistic than paradoxical. But social workers have a societal responsibility to help children to change. Disappointment and a sense of failure in a social worker, foster or natural family and child may lead to deterioration as a result of the belief that if a child can be placed in the "right" environment, he will be able to flourish according to his potential.

For example, when a child from such a family is moved into a foster home, and fails to build stable relationships within a limited time, a loss of confidence in the relationship between social worker, foster family and child may lead to breakdown. In the intervention, it is useful to comment on the discrepancy between chronological and psychological age, and the effect of disruption on learning social skills. For example, the fostering task can be reframed as one of teaching the child how to relate, and the child's behaviour as being the only way he knows, rather than a sign of innate disturbance. The idea of the danger of too rapid a change takes the pressure off everyone involved and together with ideas of slow maturation, may allow time for growth.

When multiple agencies are involved, one hypothesis is that confusion over decision making and hence subsequent interventions is generated by the lack of definition of specific agency responsibilities for a family, i.e. the Education Authority has a responsibility to provide education in an appropriate form and Social Services may acquire responsibility (supervision or care order) to ensure that a child receives parenting which, among other things, will provide him with an environment in which his normal development can take place. Attempts made to ensure emotional development under the guise of school placement or to ensure provision of special educational needs by removal from home on a care order are often the result of a failure to define agency responsibility and may lead to unnecessary and untherapeutic statutory involvement in the lives of families.

For example, a social services team requested a consultation following a case conference involving multiple agencies. They had been asked, primarily by the Education Authority, to take a 15-year-old boy, John, into care, to enable him to be treated and educated in a residential establishment against his own and his parents' wishes, and they were reluctant to take this course of action. We suggested to the professionals that for years, professionals trying ro respond to the family's request for help had failed because of the great danger in altering the balance of relationships in the family. In order to provide education for the boy the authorities put themselves in a position in which they needed Social Services to take the child into care and the cooperation of the parents. Neither seemed possible to the conference members. One alternative was to reverse the educational recommendation and send him back to his school, alerting all agencies to the family's wish for John to be treated normally. If, subsequently, a breakdown occurred in the home, the family would have to ask for help voluntarily. The subsequent intervention to the family and their solicitor by the Social Services team was: they admired the solicitor for taking responsibility for securing the rights of his client to normal schooling despite the views of educationalists that special education was indicated, and recognised the failure of all the professional agencies to date to meet the requirements of the family for treatment of their son. Because of this recognition, the Social Services had decided that as the family wished, their son should be allowed to return to his school and to be treated normally.

III. THE APPLICATION OF SYSTEMIC THINKING
TO FOSTERING

The application of systemic thinking provides a framework for working with multiple systems. As a result, it has facilitated the development of work in the field of fostering, which always involves at least four systems: the foster family, the child's natural family, the Social Services team and the fostering section.

One recurrent problem is that foster parents are public parents; their parenting is always under scrutiny. This means that whilst they receive positive support for their parenting and are seen as experts, they must inevitably have an investment in "success" which affects their relationship with the child. The social worker has the ultimate responsibility for the child's placement but has no control in practice over the day-to-day parenting. The nature of his relationship with the foster parents is constantly affected by the balance of the need for scrutiny and the development of mutual trust about the quality of the child's care. The child, unless he is very young indeed, is caught up in conflict of experience, if not of loyalty, between his old and new systems. It is hardly surprising then, that foster placements come under threat of disruption, particularly when major changes occur in any of the systems, e.g. a foster parent's illness or unemployment, a social worker leaving, a natural parent remarrying or having another child, leaving or changing school or the onset of puberty. Access to natural parents may be one particularly important source of stress. There is often an acceptance that the child's behaviour is importantly influenced by his previous life experience but it is not always so easy to accept the idea that the way in which the foster family/natural family systems impinge on the child affect his behaviour as well as his experience of the relationship between his foster parents and his social worker. These hypotheses are utilised in examining differences in the functioning and nature of relationships in the child's natural family and foster family, e.g. the patterns of nurture, discipline and communication between parents, children, siblings and social workers, and provide information to all systems involved. Positive connotation of the child's behaviour in a disrupting foster placement can be framed in terms of loyalty and ties to the previous family; the understandable reluctance to take advantage of opportunities of which his own family is deprived. The "slow change" prescription is made on the basis of the inherent difficulties in leaving the past behind and acquiring a new family, including accepting the authority of the new parents. "Time" interventions are useful since the family and social worker always feel that they are working against time, to make up for lost time, with an official deadline of age eighteen, when children leave care.

For example, Jane at sixteen, had been in and out of care throughout her life. She had been finally rejected after stealing from her mother. A consultation was sought by her social worker, because after twelve months, the foster parents, an experienced, caring, sensitive couple for whom there was no question of foster breakdown, were worried that they were not succeeding in enabling Jane to communicate with them or to act her age. They described a cycle in which she moved closer to them and the other children in the family, joining in activities, appearing happy and contented, followed by an episode of staying out, stealing or truancy which resulted in her alienation and behaving as if she expected to be rejected. They were "afraid for her future".

Questioning was addressed to two main areas; one, the mutual expectations that the social worker and foster parents had of each other in relation to what could be achieved for Jane and their perceptions about her relationship to them; the second, with the assistance of the assessment centre's social worker, who had participated in earlier work with them, was about her experience in her natural family, which highlighted Jane's repeated experiences of rejection.

After this session, we took up the theme of development over time, since their preoccupation seemed to be with the absence of consistent results. We positively connoted the foster parents, social worker and Jane for coming. We understood that as experienced foster parents they knew how children mature at different rates. It must inevitably take a long time, if ever, before Jane could learn to communicate about things which went wrong and act responsibly all the time. But they were also conscious of the arbitrary time limit of eighteen years for the growing up process. They were being constrained to enable her to grow up within that time, although they all knew it was impossible.

Following the intervention there was a change in Jane's behaviour which brought relief to the foster family and social worker and helped Jane to feel that she had found a permanent home.

In conclusion, it seems appropriate to comment on the way that different systemic views held within our cultural context affect the work of social workers and the consultation team. For example, decisions about access to natural parents who are considered unable to have the permanent care of their children are affected by whether the professional belongs to the "permanence" school, committed to the idea that a child needs a stable family system in order to flourish, or whether he belongs to the "family rights school", believing in the pre-eminence of the natural family system. In working out the implications of these views for specific cases, it is often helpful to the social workers to disentangle their professional view, their personal beliefs and the stance of the Social Services management. Inevitably the consultation team members also hold personal views about these moral issues. Consultation is necessary to monitor the developing ethos of the team and to enable it to function therapeutically with these complex cases.

REFERENCE

Prosser, H. (1976). "Perspectives on Residential Child Care". NFER Publishing, Windsor.

Part FIVE

Training and Evaluation

Chapter 23

A Training Programme in Systemic Therapy: The Problem of the Institutional Context

Queenie Harris and John Burnham

I. INTRODUCTION

Family therapy is an approach to treatment stemming from a systemic episte-mology that views behaviour within the context in which it is embedded. However, using the context marker "family" imposes an unnecessary restriction upon the quest to achieve a more systemic view of how difficulties arise and persist in human inter-action. We share the views expressed by such writers as Palazzoli (1983) that viewing the organisation as a system has the potential of being a useful idea when working with the problems that occur in institutions. Difficulties encountered when intro-ducing family therapy training into the institutional context of trainers and trainees are examined in this chapter from a systemic view.

Our context is a regional child psychiatric unit. It has a multi-disciplinary staff providing a variety of treatment regimes. The clinic provides a teaching function for the disciplines of psychiatry, psychology, social work, nursing, and occupational therapy. The major teaching role serves psychiatry and is organised along traditional medical lines. Trainee psychiatrists gain their experience from working in different units on a rotational basis. This includes registrars from general psychiatry and senior registrars who have qualified and chosen to specialise in child psychiatry.

A. Introducing Family Therapy Training

It seems to us that the particular threat posed to an institution by the introduction of family therapy training is directly proportional to the rate, manner and timing of its introduction. To teach trainees to meet with the family as a first choice rather than as a last resort may be perceived as a method that is not only "dangerous" in itself, but also threatens other methods of treatment and other duties. In our case, concern extended outside the clinic and pressure was soon felt by the family therapy trainers from the organisers of the psychiatric training programme. The ultimate criticism is that family therapy is being taught to the detriment of a proper training in psychiatry. Attempts to discredit the method included comments like: "voyeur-ism"; "a flash in the pan"; "neglectful of important issues"; "dangerous as it ignores the individual".

APPLICATIONS OF SYSTEMIC FAMILY THERAPY
ISBN 0-8089-1696-3

If one thinks systemically then at least some part of every criticism is justified. Held (1982) introduces a useful reminder of this in saying that "Therapists must begin to perceive themselves as members of the systems in which they work and so as potential contributors to the 'resistances' that may emerge" (p. 40). An examination of the behaviour provoking negative responses, and moreover what it is about that behaviour that induces such responses, is likely to be more fruitful. The issue then concerns how to modify our interface with them to permit us to continue. Should these responses be viewed as sabotage or part of a natural homeostatic response? Issues such as use of time, resources, personnel, money and clinical material should be managed in a way that minimises rivalry and avoids the escalation of competition with other treatment approaches and training programmes.

II. STRATAGIES FOR CHANGE FROM WITHIN A SYSTEM

In our case, we responded by expressing to our critics that their criticism and accusations helped us to organise the family therapy clinic more efficiently. The training offered in family therapy continued to become a more structured formal teaching input in the clinic that became valued by the trainee psychiatrists, especially those on the general psychiatry rotation.

At first we agreed with the anxieties expressed by the general psychiatric training organisers about the need for "proper" psychiatric training, but our error was to continue to offer training in the same way as before. When we recognised this as a mistake we decided to withdraw all family therapy input for senior registrars on the child psychiatry rotation. We said it would become available when it was felt by the training board to be a necessary part of the overall training in child and adolescent psychiatry, in other words "when they were ready". This was a difficult decision to make, since we feared losing ground, but it was made easier since work in family therapy in the clinic had become established and could proceed without including senior registrars. Energy was invested in offering training to other professionals both inside and outside the clinic.

As new senior registrars in child and adolescent psychiatry wanted to become involved, they were told courteously that they must have the approval of their training supervisor in order to join. Registrars on the general psychiatry programme had learned of their colleagues' experience of family therapy in the clinic and expected this when they arrived. Their inclusion was requested and we agreed—though we permitted observational inclusion only—so that their training in psychiatry was not jeopardised. Two years elapsed and periodically senior registrars expressed their need for family therapy to be included in their training programme. Their course organisers came back with good reasons why these needs could not be met, according to their priorities for training. During this time, work in the family therapy service expanded with trainees from other disciplines both within and outside the clinic.

It was when the Royal College of Psychiatrists' accreditation team paid their triennial visit to the unit that a major shift became possible. This is a committee that monitors training in psychiatry in various institutions throughout the country. Their aim is to ensure that the college recommendations on training, which include experience in family therapy, are adhered to. The visit provided a forum that enabled the psychiatric trainees to express their need for training in family therapy at a higher level. The feedback in the form of recommendations from this team, together with the support from other professional colleagues in the institution, resulted in a formal request being made for training in family therapy. People responsible for organising their training programmes were reassured by their perception of our programme as rigorous and derived from a sound theoretical and conceptual framework.

Four systemic principles were probably the most important in the process of gaining acceptance for training in family therapy: Firstly, the concept of circularity, whereby each behaviour is seen as part of a circuit of interaction, enabled us to see our part in the escalating symmetry between ourselves and the establishment. Secondly, positively connoting the criticism and doubts of the organisers of the psychiatric training programmes towards family therapy training ensured that our withdrawal was not viewed negatively. Thirdly, we suspended the family therapy input to trainee psychiatrists until the organisers considered that it was an essential part of their curriculum, i.e. "until they were ready". Fourthly, we established and maintained neutrality by not adopting a superior stance over other approaches used in the clinic.

In retrospect it seems that the creation of family therapy training made a difference in the established psychiatric training regime. The establishment's initial response to this information was to diminish the difference by casting doubt on the validity of family therapy. We, by viewing these responses in a linear fashion, i.e. that the establishment was rigid and resistant, acted in a way that completed the negative feedback loop, thus decreasing the likelihood of the acceptance of family therapy training. Therefore, suspicion, criticism, and doubt should be anticipated as a natural systemic response to something new. Positively connoting such reactions diminishes the likelihood of their continuation.

The need to consider context in resolving the issues outlined above, altered our perspective in other areas of work.

III. THE TRAINEES CONTEXT

One of the courses our programme offered ran for 20 weeks with a group of eight people of various disciplines and from different agencies. They attended the family clinic for one-half day per week. The first term was mainly taken up with what is common to many courses—videotape presentations, lectures on theory, role plays of family interviews and viewing "live" interviews conducted by the course leaders. The second part of the course was kept relatively less structured in order to be able to respond to the training system as it developed. In this second term the focus turned to presentations of case material by the trainees from their own agencies. Such cases are usually those with which the trainee feels at an impasse and wishes to have some new view, strategy or solution offered.

The type of approach selected to analyse case presentations is usually a reflection of the underlying theoretical framework of the training programme (Beal, 1976). Various ways of approaching these issues have been proposed, including role-play or sculpting of the family (Whiffen and Byng-Hall, 1982; Andolfi and Menghi, 1980;

Behr, 1977; Sigal, 1976), and group discussions with solutions suggested by the group. In some instances attention is focused on the therapist's own family of origin (Braverman, 1982; Horn, 1982; Whiffen and Byng-Hall, 1982).

Our orientation is usually to discuss cases in terms of the family/therapist suprasystem. This helps the trainees to think systemically about their behaviour with families as well as focusing on specific techniques. Trainees were becoming familiar by now with the techniques of hypothesising, circular questioning (especially in relation to families) and so on, but we wanted to broaden their awareness of the systemic epistemology. An opportunity to do this arose during the first case presentation by a team of therapists working together in the same agency and will be discussed further.

A. Our Initial Approach

The problem of the trainee's institutional context is a familiar one to us on courses at all levels. Trainees are often full of enthusiasm after a session, only to return the next week in a despondent fashion with such statements as "They (their agency) wouldn't let me do it. They're very resistant to change". Often on past courses our response had been to accept the trainee's punctuation and therefore to devise strategies to overcome this resistance. Occasionally they worked, in that particular instance, usually they did not generalise, i.e. the relationship between the trainee and their agency was not recalibrated. There was no second order change.

In retrospect, this was an error which can be explained according to the difference between the two diagrams in Figure 1a and 1b. Figure 1a illustrates our interventions that tended to be based on the mistaken premise that the course and the trainee were change-oriented and therefore "good", or "progressive" and that the employing agency was "homeostatic", or "bad", and "resistant". Therefore we created in our thinking and consequently our action an artificial distinction between the course (including the trainee) and the employing agency.

While some agencies tend more towards homeostasis than others, we consider that responses such as doubt, questioning and caution are not necessarily manifestations of one-sided resistance (cf. de Shazer, 1983). Instead "resistance" should be con-

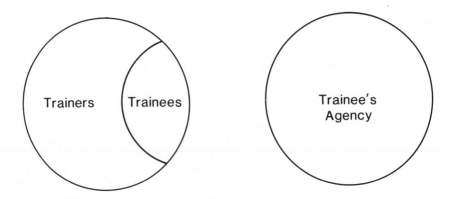

Fig. 1a.   Our initial position in relation to the trainees and their agency.

The "Training Triangle"

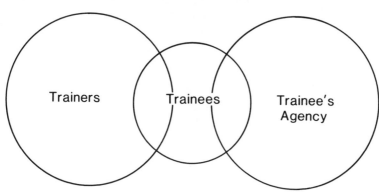

Fig. 1b. A more "correct" systemic view of the "training triangle" showing the connectedness of the trainers, trainees and trainees' agency.

sidered as a description of a relationship or a change in a relationship. In other words our neutrality was lost in forming a coalition with that part of the institutional system that showed itself to us, i.e. the trainee against the rest of the work system. It is very easy to be seduced by trainees who adopt your model, practise your techniques and so on, into thinking that they are "good" and the agency is "bad". We may have been showing them how to think systemically at the "micro" level but certainly not at a "macro" level, which naturally includes the behaviour of all the sub-systems involved.

B. Moving to a Meta-Level

Case Example 1

A solution to this problem came spontaneously during the course described. Trainees had been asked to present problematic case material from their own agency in the second term. The first presentation was made by a team of two (a social worker and a charge nurse). They worked in a psychiatric hospital for adolescents some 60 miles from our centre. They presented a case with which they had been working for some time.

Early in their presentation they indicated some disagreement between them about how they should handle the case relative to accepted procedure in their agency. We had the idea that we could work on this case by viewing these professionals as a "couple" presenting with a problem about their relationship on four levels: 1) with the case itself; 2) between the workers; 3) between the workers and their agency; 4) between the workers, their agency and the course.

Conceptualising the situation thus, we decided that the other trainees should form a team to interview this professional system in a similar manner to the way in which we had interviewed families. This interview would be observed by the trainers. Simultaneously this presented a potential solution to two other problems encoun-

tered in training, namely: when trainees are struggling to grasp and apply the concepts of systemic thinking in broader terms than the family, i.e. the professional
networks, including their own; when trainees are not working with families under
the live supervision of the teachers.

C. The Interview

To make the connection between all four levels of system, we set in motion a
procedure that we continued to use throughout the rest of the course. We shall refer
to the trainees presenting a case as the "C" group and the trainees conducting the
interview as the "I" group. Each session was organised into intake, interview, intervention, mid-session discussion and post-session discussion.

(1) *Intake*

The "C" group gave sufficient information in order that the "I" group could,
separately from the "C" group, hypothesise about the function of the "problem" in
the supra-system that consisted of the worker, their agency, the case and the course.
The trainers followed the same format.

(2) *The interview*

The process of interviewing was based upon the ritual described by the Milan
team and the methods advocated in Palazzoli *et al.* (1980). The questions would
relate initially to the problem the "C" group were experiencing with the case. The
enquiry then proceeded to include other levels of system. Some of the most useful
questions (including some from the trainers!) asked in the first case were: "Which
member of the "C" group was most keen to come on the course—did one have to
persuade the other?"; "What was the attitude of the rest of the unit staff to these
two coming on the course—who was the keenest—who had to take their place while
they were attending the course?"; "Did they have meetings with the rest of the staff
to share the knowledge from the course—who received this feedback most enthusias-
tically?"; "Which part of the usual unit procedure did they find most difficult to
follow since they came on the course?"; "What was the relationship like between
them now as compared with before they came on the course?"; "What did each of
them think the other members of staff thought about the course?"

(3) *Mid-session discussion*

The "I" group then took a break to decide separately what intervention should be
made to the work system as represented by the professional "couple". Thus far the
"I" group had to think systemically in broader terms than family systems and act
sensitively; unlike a role play, these were real issues. Further, they had the
opportunity to interview a *real* not simulated sub-system of the agency system—the
"C" group had all the information that was necessary—unlike a simulated family.
Finally, they had the task of devising an intervention to this system from which they
would be able to obtain feedback. This was in essence then a genuine systemic interview and intervention.

(4) Intervention

The "I" group made an intervention which was followed by the trainers' intervention. At this stage (perhaps naturally) the trainers' opinion was taken as the "real" intervention.

(5) Post-session discussion

A rule was established that the intervention was not discussed until four weeks later; isomorphic with the feedback time commonly allocated to a family system. Most trainees seemed to respond positively to this system of interviewing and being interviewed since everybody had a turn in either role and the group was small.

D. The Outcome

In the above example, what emerged from the questioning was that the charge nurse was the most keen to develop as a family therapist. He had attended our introductory course, immediately enrolled for the intermediate course and persuaded his social work colleague to join him. The unit was keen for them both to come and set up a meeting each week so that they could share their new-found knowledge with the rest of the staff.

The charge nurse became keen to establish his position as a family therapist and, thinking that he would improve his neutrality, began to miss various staff meetings. He considered that the information he might hear from the staff or be required to give them about the particular family might threaten or weaken his neutral position with the family. His partner, the social worker, was more cautious about casting off her usual "role" and decided to continue attending the regular meetings. Thus the couple began to "split", and the effects began to spread through the rest of the unit; the referral rate dropped and a negative feedback loop was formed. This had the pragmatic effect of diminishing the concept and practice of family therapy in the unit, probably to the frustration of the "couple" and the dismay of the other staff members.

Viewed systemically the trainers felt that the unit had been threatened with a "runaway" situation, i.e. that the changes proposed by the family therapists reverberated through the unit's usual pattern of work. The unit was threatened with revolution not evolution and responded homeostatically to diminish, if not exactly extinguish this threat. Viewed in this way we can punctuate the sequence of events to implicate both the agency, the trainees and the trainers. Performing this exercise (interviewing the trainees as a system) enabled us to see the connection between the three sub-systems of what might be called the "training triangle" or "training suprasystem".

The intervention that we made of necessity had to include all three subsystems and went as follows: "Naturally, we as trainers are pleased when trainees are dedicated to study and work hard at the course material, do the reading and so on. What has impressed us most about you as a team is the way in which your individual qualities are so complementary to one another. You, Derek, have the drive and initiative to push this new method of working in every way that you can. Mavis recognises the need for caution and to maintain good relationships with other staff members who take on your duties while you are doing this course, and they encouraged you to come. (Derek begins to nod at this point!) This complementarity is good and necessary for the steady growth of family therapy in your unit.

"What we recommend is that you both, within the next week, go to the consultant in charge of the unit and ask her to decide with which cases you can do 'pure' family therapy and those with which she would prefer you to work in the usual way. You should say that we recommended this".

This intervention was based on our hypothesis, confirmed during the interview, that the "couple" were in a rigidly complementary relationship to each other. Derek's attempts to persuade Mavis to abandon the usual procedures of the unit in order to become "pure" family therapists increased her insistence that they had other responsibilities to the unit and vice versa. The final part of the intervention was designed to minimise the symmetry that we saw developing between the consultant of the unit and the trainers.

The feedback from this intervention that we heard some four weeks later was that the "couple" had as they described it "put the brakes on" (we had thought they were in a "runaway" situation) in the battle over becoming exclusive family therapy practitioners. The unit had responded by becoming more receptive to the ideas that they did present; thus there was a co-evolutionary process between the new information (in the form of a change in working practice) and the existing work system. The relationship between the two workers also improved.

Case Example 2

One of the reasons that we have not called this chapter systemic "family" therapy can be demonstrated by reference to our second example of a trainee interveiw. Three probation officers who are members of a team working in a divorce conciliation service presented a problem to the "I" group. The interview was conducted according to the format already described and revealed the following information: the agency and their colleagues were in full agreement with them attending the course; the particular problem that they presented was their relationship with solicitors who "lost out" in legal fees when the divorce conciliation team were successful in resolving custodial disputes before the case came before the court; and in general, their team was confused about using a method called "family therapy" when they were working with clients who were ceasing to be families. They expressed their disappointment that they were only able to use some of the techniques and not the model.

The trainers' intervention began by stating: "Your team is not doing family therapy, and you should stop trying to do family therapy. What you are doing is a systemic approach to divorce conciliation."

The intervention continued by suggesting that they routinely send a letter to the solicitors of their clients informing them of the way in which the team worked and trusting that the solicitors would cooperate in this as it had been found to be the best way of helping divorcing couples to come to a less painful way of separating, both for adults and children.

Information from the divorce conciliation team was gained through follow up discussions after periods of one month and one year. The letter to the solicitors had not been used per se but they reported that it had led them to include other professionals in their hypotheses about the maintenance of the custodial dispute. The most marked change had been effected by our statement that they were not doing family therapy. They referred to this as a professional revelation in that it had helped them to make the shift from technique to approach.

On reflection, a hypothesis common in all of these trainee interviews was the enthusiasm of the trainees to show the trainers that they were introducing a systemic way of working into their own context immediately; the message that they may have implicitly received from the trainers, underlined by the short duration of the course, was "hurry up and be systemic, you don't have long to go!" Therefore it is understandable how some trainees adopted what might be called the "missionary position" in preaching a systemic "gospel" to their agencies. The "problem" of the cautious response of their colleagues perhaps provided to the trainers a justification for the trainees' "failure". "I did my best, honestly, my colleagues just don't see the sense of it like I do!" The trainers may then have increased their efforts to enable the trainees to "be" systemic and so on.

Some trainees have reported, as do many families, that the interviewing process itself helped them to view their own situations more systemically. The questions prompted answers that made new connections between their "new" behaviour and attitudes since beginning the course and the emergence of the apparently "unreasonable" and the "nonsystemic" behaviour and attitude of their colleagues and network. They found both positions, being interviewed and interviewing, to be valuable experiences. The task of interviewing fellow trainees was found to be taxing and stimulating both intellectually and emotionally since it was not a simulation.

IV. SUMMARY

We have examined the kind of problems commonly brought by trainees for discussion on courses from a systems perspective and suggested a strategy for dealing with these problems that may be termed "agency of origin" as an alternative to the "family of origin" approach. It allows trainees the opportunity to conduct systemic interviews and deliver interventions to a system other than a family system. It facilitates the concept of systems thinking and therapy rather than family therapy alone. It gives the trainees valuable experience in working as a team. And it presents the trainers with a novel way in which to observe the progress of trainees during a course that does not include the live supervision of the trainees' work.

The removal of the context marker "family" from the term "systemic family therapy", marked an extremely important shift for us in our thinking, and therefore our action. It enabled us, and we think also our trainees, to achieve a more systemic position from which to examine the problems that confront us in our institutional context, our clinical work and the training process.

REFERENCES

Andolfi, M., and Menghi, P. (1980). A Model for Training in Family Therapy. *In* Andolfi, M., and Zwerling, I. (eds.), "Dimensions of Family Therapy". Guilford Press, New York, pp. 239–259.

Beal, E. (1976). Current Trends in the Training of Family Therapists. *American Journal of Psychiatry* 133, 137–141.

Behr, H. L. (1977). Introducing Medical Students to Family Therapy Using Simulated Family Interviews. *Medical Education* (U.S.A) 11, 32–38.

Bloch, D. A., and Weiss, H. M. (1981). Training Facilities in Marital and Family Therapy. *Family Process* 20, 133–146.

Braverman, S. (1982). Family of Origin as a Training Resource for Family Therapists. *Canadian Journal of Psychiatry* 27, 629–633.

de Shazer, S. (1983). The Death of Resistance. Unpublished paper, Brief Family Therapy Institute, Milwaukee.

Heath, A. W. (1982). Team Family Therapy Training: Conceptual and Pragmatic Considerations. *Family Process* 21, 187–193.

Held, B. S. (1982). Entering a Mental Health System: A Strategic Systemic Approach. *Journal of Systemic and Strategic Therapy*, Spring 1982, 40–50.

Horn, D. (1982). Family of Origin Technique. *Canadian Journal of Psychiatry* 27, 616.

Kniskern, D. P., and Gurman, A. S. (1980). *In* Andolfi, M., and Zwerling, I. (eds.), "Dimensions of Family Therapy". Guilford Press, New York, pp. 221–238.

Palazzoli, M. (1983). The Emergence of a Comprehensive Systems Approach. *Journal of Family Therapy* 5, 165–177.

Palazzoli, M., Boscolo, L., Cecchin, G., and Prata, G. (1980). Hypothesizing, Circularity and Neutrality. *Family Process U.S.A.* 19, 3–12.

Rubenstein, J. S. (1982). Learning Objectives in Family Therapy Training. *Canadian Journal of Psychiatry* 27, 556–558.

Sigal, J. J., and Levin, S. (1976). Teaching Family Therapy by Simulation. *Canadian Mental Health* 24, 6–8.

Sugarman, S. (1981). Family Therapy Training in Selected General Psychiatry Residency Programs. *Family Process* 20, 147–154.

Whiffen, R., and Byng-Hall, J. (eds.), (1982). "Family Therapy Supervision: Recent Developments in Practice". Academic Press, London.

Chapter 24

Training in Systemic Thinking for Professional Workers

Rosalind Draper and Peter Lang

I. THE CONTEXT FOR TRAINING

The City Centre was established in 1979 as a small private centre in London to provide a setting for the development of systemic ideas and their application in family treatment and professional development. A group of four therapists worked together on a regular basis, for one day a week, critically applying the methods emanating from the Milan Centre for the Study of the Family.[1] In their work the City Centre team had in mind the warning given by Haley (1980): "Therapists should study the work of the Milanese group carefully and examine its social context before attempting to replicate their approach" (p. 247).

Referrals came from other agencies such as general practitioners, social services departments, a pastoral foundation and churches. Families who came to be seen at the centre represented a cross-section of social groups living in and around London. The problems and symptoms they came requesting help with were those well known to family workers: e.g. bulimia nervosa; marital stress and breakdown; some adolescents with school problems; family members suffering psychotic delusions; young adults, particularly those aged between 20 and 30 trying to separate from parents; suicidal attempts; adults with compulsive symptoms.

Whilst working with these families the team received repeated requests to have their work observed and then to provide a training programme in systemic therapy using the theories described by the Milan group. These requests came from experienced professionals in either pastoral counselling or social work. We selected trainees who had already taken part in a minimum of two years of training courses in family therapy. They were familiar with interviewing different sizes of families and different members of families. The aim of the course was to provide those participating with a conceptual framework, tools and methods which would facilitate effective work with families in their agencies. (Trainees treated families with live supervision.)

At the beginning of the course we tried to clarify the relationship between the agency setting and the training setting, and the task of the agency from which trainees came. We sought to avoid some of the pitfalls arising from trainees applying methods and actual interventions used in a training setting in their normal working

---

[1] In 1983 the City Centre ceased to exist due to members' family commitments and relocation.

APPLICATIONS OF SYSTEMIC FAMILY THERAPY
ISBN 0-8089-1696-3

life without careful attention to the different contexts. These pitfalls were like those aptly described by Boscolo and Cecchin (1982) when trainees seemed to apply "a bit of kit therapy" (p. 163). Some training exercises are described in this paper.

Our trainees reported considerable success in their work with actual families, but whether successful or unsuccessful in the work with families, trainees nonetheless seemed to be in a "heads, I win; tails, you lose" bind in their normal work settings. They were encouraged by the agency to come to a course in which they would learn new and, hopefully, useful ideas which would enhance the work of the agency. Simultaneously trainees reported that new ideas were thrown out when tried. Our experience of these phenomena was consistent with that of Haley (1975). Hierarchies were threatened as trainees challenged the views of their supervisors with suggestions of different approaches to work. Confusion increased, both for the trainees and work colleagues, as they tried to accommodate to each other. Referring agencies became alarmed as they discovered that the families they had referred were being treated in ways which they did not understand.

As course tutors we tried to gain a more comprehensive systemic perspective. We saw the trainees coming to our centre as not dissimilar to the family coming from a referring person—their home agency—to be changed. We saw the importance and necessity for the home agency to preserve its own order and organisation and efficient running whilst at the same time wishing to be innovative. We set up an exercise to clarify the communication and patterns of behaviour taking place between the two systems, namely the training institution and the home agency. We emphasised the definition of the course as training and thus defined the exercise as one of those "five-finger exercises" necessary when looking at any work being done. The principles in this particular five-finger exercise were:

1. What is the nature of the particular systems on whose interaction we focus?
2. What are the definitions of the system as seen in a) their image; b) their publicity; c) their actual work; d) their funding; e) their sponsoring authority?
3. What is the position of the person or persons in focus in each system with which they are involved?
4. In what ways do all the participants in the drama come together to preserve the status quo, limit new learning and thus attempt to control possible evolution?
5. What strategies will facilitate development and evolution satisfactorily?

The exercise consisted of the following stages:

1. Each of the trainees made a brief statement of their work setting; the task of the agency; the management, supervisory and support structure. Each trainee described his position in the agency and the freedom and restrictions "imposed" on the work which he is able to do.
2. The remaining members of the training group then formulated questions to the person who had described his agency, on the basis of their hunches. These questions aimed to try and elucidate information about the person's position in the system at work and the expectations of the work system of the training course.
3. Group members then discussed possible areas of difficulty for a particular trainee at work whilst on the course and then together devised possible strategies for handling these.

Common themes emerged from this exercise. Most frequently trainees were seen by their colleagues and managers at work as creative, imaginative and able. Usually they had been sent on a training course at about the time when they had become dissatisfied with what they were able to do whilst simultaneously being branded difficult by colleagues. They were at the same time prized and a problem. The course was a way of keeping them in the job. "We value you, don't leave. The course will make your staying here worthwhile, especially if you bring back what you have learnt". The investment of agencies sending people on the course was very high, more especially since most trainees were paid for by the agency. However, this brought about an escalation in the game of colleagues and managers saying bring back to the agency the new learning from your course:

What emerged was that all these communications were simultaneously operating, together with some further complications. Thus we had found that trainees suffer considerable stress. As Lynn Hoffman (1981) points out: "The length of time a person is allowed to rest at either end of two incompatible poles could have something to do with the degree of stress he would experience" (p. 116). For "when incompatible demands are being made on the individual almost simultaneously . . . one might expect some kind of shift, cut off or breakdown" (p. 116). The agency sends someone to learn. The trainee then gets new ideas and begins to think that this is the best way to work. The "teachers" feed into this pattern by their own hubris and encourage the worker to go back to the agency and try to get it to work in a particular way.

It is important to give trainees some understanding of the contradictions implicit in their position and thus hopefully increase their ability to work more effectively as well as learn more fully and freely. First, and this was paramount, both tutors and trainees took an attitude to the training that new ideas were not to be seen as ultimate truths, handed down as a sort of new decalogue to supercede all other ideas. We were all to place ourselves under the arch of Bateson's (1973a) definition of "wisdom" as "a sense of recognition of the fact of circuitry" (p. 119). Ideas are part of an interconnecting network of ideas; they never encompass the whole; they are never complete or ultimate. Rather, as Hofstadter (1980) has put it, "the process by which we decide is an act; . . . truth is too elusive for any human or collection of humans to attain fully" (p. 695).

A second strategy addressed the issue of context: Ideas which were put over in a training session may or may not have relevance to a context in which trainees were working. Every aspect of the training course should thus receive critical evaluation from each trainee, carefully weighing the possible implications of using new-found approaches at work. Central to this point, we established that none of the trainees should attempt to do family therapy, since this was not part of their work in their home agencies. Rather, they should critically apply a systemic and circular view of events to their work. Thus, the tutors reaffirmed the primary loyalty of each trainee to his own agency and the work which he had chosen to do within it. As Palazzoli (1983) put it, "Avoid imposing and teaching" the systemic model "in an abstract fashion" (p. 169).

Each trainee should therefore continue to work in such ways as his agency required. Perhaps once a week, or at some other interval, there might be a limited period of time when other members of the agency might work with the trainee, critically applying such bits of learning to actual work with families within the agency context. These sessions should be repeatedly evaluated in the most rigorous fashion, always employing a degree of scepticism. Trainees and their agencies could feel free to continue to use such ideas as seemed to be effective, but should report to us those notions which had been counterproductive or useless to aid our increasing learning.

This approach introduced the element of time into the main area of simultaneous messages in the network. In the home agency there should be a time to keep things the same, a time to explore how new ideas from a course might be; a time to be different, a time to be the same. In the training centre: a time to do things the tutors are teaching, a time to be critical and teach the tutors from your experience in your own agency. By introducing the possibility of doing different things at different times, trainees were freed from the negative effects of simultaneous messages, they could then respond positively to only one injunction at a particular point in time.

As tutors of trainees using the techniques described in "Paradox and Counterparadox" (Palazzoli et al., 1978) and in "Hypothesising Circularity and Neutrality" (Palazzoli et al., 1980), we had to clarify what trainees now wished to know and be able to do more fluently and effectively.

The tutors developed another ritual procedure for arriving at this definition. Each participant should briefly introduce a case with which he is currently working, including a description of who was in the family, what was the defined problem, who else was involved, wider family and other professionals, length of involvement and frequency of meeting. This was followed by a short review of video tape of the families, together with a description by the trainee of his hypothetical understanding of the way in which the behaviour and communications of those involved fitted the functioning of the system in focus. The remaining members of the trainee group were then to question the trainee presenting, about what skills he was using in the video tape presentation and also what skills he would like to develop. The trainee group and presenter would then engage in a negotiation, mutually defining aims for future development of that trainee.

This ritual was repeated for each trainee. Its usefulness consisted of the trainee group doing the questioning, taking every bit of behaviour and communication of the presenter as information. The way in which the presenter talked about the case, the video tape of the work, etc., were all seen as aspects of his present competence and understanding and naturally highlighted areas ready for development. The questioning of the presenter enabled him to see himself, as it were, from the outside. The double experience in this exercise of seeing in another both things you know and can do and also things you would like to do was instructive. Not only was the group learning about developing questions which enabled the questioner to make connections for himself, but the very process of asking questions develops links and makes connections for the person questioned. Thus we began the process of establishing that therapist behaviour, like other behaviour, is part of the recursive process.

In deciding what skills needed developing, tutors asked trainees to define the specific purposes of particular skills with the overall aim of enabling the therapist to show interest, warmth and care whilst remaining neutral to a family system. Whilst accepting the family system the way it is the therapist also wishes to work with it, so that the system itself may make its own next discontinuous leap. In this sense the skill is aesthetic: "Artistic skill is the combining of many levels of mind—unconscious, conscious and external—to make a statement of their combination. It is not a matter of expressing a simple level" (Bateson 1973b, p. 439). An effect of these rituals was that the group of trainees and the tutors had arrived at an agreed and clarified definition of the task of the group, namely to work together in developing the necessary flexibility for these people to be able to function effectively in their own agencies.

The tutors were given authority for the structure of the timetable and the definition of how to tackle tasks. Agreeing and clarifying the work of the trainees and of the tutors as both engaged on a joint task reduced the negative effects of the false distinction between teacher and taught, enhancing the training programme as a setting in which both tutor and trainee are repeatedly testing the usefulness of theories and applying a critical faculty to the methods of one particular approach in order to ensure the recognition of the essentially unique nature of the rules and nodal points of any system. Thus both tutors and trainees work together in relation to the development of a circular epistemology which always stands at a higher level than any of the participants in the pursuit of recognising differences between systems and differences within the same systems over time.

The rituals were also a way of developing a team of trainees that could work co-operatively for the period of the training course on the task of repeatedly developing a circular systemic view of problems, families and agencies. We saw teamwork as essential and addressed this repeatedly.

Tutors found that trainees became more ready to do new things and to try out different actions (e.g. asking clients provocative questions such as "when you are dead, how long will they take to forget you?"). Our experience confirmed that as reported by Palazzoli (1983): "The fact of having the same model and the same orientation towards agreed-upon objectives, requires and produces a type of elastic solidarity which can be compared to that of different organs of a living body" (p. 170).

The establishment of an agreed structure for a theory and reading seminar proved particularly important. The first hour of every session with the tutors included the presentation and discussion of one or more seminal papers in the development of ideas associated with the model. We agreed that session-by-session one or two papers would be required reading by all participants. One trainee would briefly present the main thrust of a paper. The discipline of presenting the main thrust focussed the trainees' discussion on the relevance and usefulness of the ideas. This brief presentation was followed by a description of ways in which the ideas being examined could enlighten or enhance work with a family by enabling trainees to gain a more circular view of previous success or failure.

All reading in the theory seminars was related to concrete work and a discussion of the "so what" of any learning. Exactly how could this be used? How could we guard against misapplication in a work context? During the course trainees would report back on the way in which they had used ideas from their reading in their work in the home agency. Throughout the course, the tutors were cautious to take up a neutral stance in relation to ideas being discussed in the theoretical seminars. At times they would expand upon points being made in a paper as the tutors understood them, but they always attempted to allow the ideas to stand in their own right and rather than attempt to defend the ideas, to challenge trainees to apply critique to the usefulness of the ideas for their work. In this sense we always used a double-pronged approach. The first was usually to get trainees to look at families with whom they were working in the light of the paper being discussed. For example, when discussing Bateson's paper, "Double Bind, 1969" (Bateson, 1973a), trainees engaged in an orgy of double-bind spotting in a particular family's communication pattern. This was a purely theoretical and orienting exercise. The second prong was usually facing the hard question of the "how" of applying the ideas being discussed and relating it in rigorous detail to the idiosyncracies of a particular family.

As tutors, our previous experience of case discussions had convinced us that these could often be unhelpful to learning. For example, the person presenting the case would often flood the team with detailed data about the case, what they had been doing, their various hypotheses, etc. This often had the unfortunate effect of reducing the number of possible new ideas which a team might produce because they had already been hooked in to the presenter's modes of thinking. At the same time as requesting help, the presenter would repeatedly advance reasons why certain suggested courses of action could not be followed. The presenter would tenaciously hold on to his own ideas, often no matter how persuasive the suggestions emerging from the team discussion were.

We tried to use a structure similar to that of a family interview for this case discussion time and found it enabled the presenter to gain a fuller, fresher view than that held previously. We made a rule that data would only be given in case discussions by the presenter in answer to questions from team members. We had heard members of the Milan team say that allowing family members to interact in the presence of a therapist may be interesting, but that circular questioning was a more helpful intervention, because it introduced differences of information both for the family as well as the therapeutic team. Thus, the family did not continue in those old tracks which were the very conditions within which the symptom remained perpetuated. Similarly, therefore, in a case discussion the process whereby team members questioned a presenter immediately introduced differences and information for the presenter. The process involved three stages:

1. Questions by the team to the presenter, of basic information: who in the family? seen by whom? for how long? for what family problem? leading to what problem for the presenter?
2. Questions by the team to the presenter based on their ideas and hunches about the systems under scrutiny. These systems included the family, the family and presenter/presenter's agency, the family and other professionals and the presenter and other professionals. The presenter would silently observe the discussions producing the hypotheses on which the questions to him were based.
3. Discussion by the team members of strategies for handling the situation. This was observed silently by the presenter, who participated only after the team had arrived at three or four possible approaches. Then, when participating, the presenter was encouraged to be critical, assessing with care how and whether any of the suggestions made could be used in the work setting.

II. FAMILY TREATMENT

When undertaking the treatment of families who had been referred to the City Centre, we employed those procedures which had been developed and described by the Milan group in Palazzoli *et al.* (1980). The team of trainees became a therapeutic team; from among them, one was chosen to be the interviewer of the family.

The task for the interviewer was to gather information by the use of circular questioning based on such hypotheses as the team had discussed before the session. The team behind the screen were allocated slightly different roles within the framework of the main task, namely acting "as observers interrupting the session when necessary, making suggestions and hypotheses" and "participating in the discussion concerning the intervention" (Boscolo and Cecchin, 1982b, p. 157). The roles allocated were those of researcher, recorder, non-verbal monitor and hypothesis confirmation monitor.

The researcher was always to remain less directly involved in the process of therapy, commenting from time to time on the relationship between the observers and the interviewer and monitoring the development of the work from session to session. The recorder was to keep notes of the hypotheses and pre-session discussions, the areas of questioning, the information gathered and the highly fruitful discussion taking place after the family left. The non-verbal monitor particularly looked for indications of alliances and patterns in family interactions at the analogic level: "We draw up a written statement of behaviour as observed, taking into account spontaneous behaviour as well as reactions prompted by our interventions, trying to connect and classify them, so as to bring into evidence the most salient data" (Palazzoli *et al.* "First Session of a Systemic Family Therapy." Unpublished paper. Centre for Study of the Family). Our experience accords with that of the Milan team that the family game may more easily be observed at the analogic level.

Finally, one member of the team monitored the circular connections being made as evidence in support of pre-session hypotheses as supplied by the family. This distribution of roles in the team varied from family to family, but once established remained constant for each family the team was working with.

III. WORKERS' PRACTICE AFTER THE COURSE

A long enough time has not yet elapsed for a thorough assessment of the usefulness of the training programme. Nonetheless ex-trainees were asked to do an interim assessment of the ways in which their experience in training had effected their practice. Ex-trainees were asked to consider the effect of the training experience on their work with families, their management of relationships with referrers and other professionals involved with families, and their management of their position in their home agencies. Workers reported that their work with families had developed significantly using learning from the training programme. Most workers were able to use elements of the Milan approach and achieve good working alliances with families. As far as can be judged in the short term, workers described themselves as "doing less and acting less frequently", and families as discovering more of their own strengths and acting for themselves. This has been particularly valuable in social services setting where the effects have meant less demands by some families on the social work staff.

Workers reported that they continued to encounter repeated difficulties when working with referrers and the wider network involved with a family. This they saw as an aspect of their work that needed further development and experience. Though still encountering problems, the ritual five-finger exercises we had used during the training course were being constantly employed by these workers to gain further understanding of the tangles they got into and to devise strategies to help manage such situations. Ex-trainees described the value of accepting and supporting the role of other professionals involved with the family rather than trying to threaten that role.

What is striking is the way in which ex-trainees have gained new support and recognition in their at-home agencies. Each worker has been given new responsibilities and been able to work more freely in a systemic way. At-home agencies have now encouraged and demanded extending systemic approaches to their work. One agency has established a long-term pilot project approaching adoption and fostering from a systemic Milan-type perspective and given a team responsibility for developing this. Other agencies have given large slices of time to teams of workers to use such an approach.

These conclusions are necessarily brief and tentative. A longer term follow-up is necessary to ascertain anything more conclusive. A more detailed study of exactly what has been useful and what has hindered ex-trainees will need to be conducted before any certainty of assessment can be gained. A final limitation to our critique is that it is based on self-report. In time the view of management and the whole agency from which the trainee came would need to be sought in order to gain a more systemic picture of the effect of the course programme.

REFERENCES

Bateson, G. (1973a). Style, Grace and Information in Primitive Art. *In* "Steps to an Ecology of Mind". Paladdin Books, London.

Bateson, G. (1973b). Form, Substance and Difference. *In* "Steps to an Ecology of Mind". Paladdin Books, London.

Boscolo, L., and Cecchin, G. (1982). Training in Systemic Therapy at the Milan Centre. *In* Whiffen, R., and Byng-Hall, J. (eds.), "Family Therapy Supervision—Recent Developments in Practice". Academic Press, London.

Haley, J. (1980). "Leaving Home". McGraw Hill, New York.

Haley, J. (1975). Why a Mental Health Clinic Should Avoid Family Therapy. *Journal of Marriage and Family Counseling* 1, 3–13.

Hoffman, L. (1981). "Foundations of Family Therapy". Basic Books, New York.

Hofstadter, D. R. (1980). "Godel, Escher and Bach—An Eternal Golden Braid". Penguin Books, Harmondsworth, Middlesex.

Palazzoli, M., Boscolo, L., Cecchin, G., and Prata, G. (1980). Hypothesising, Circularity and Neutrality: Three Guidelines for the Conductor of the Session. *Family Process* 19, 3–12.

Palazzoli, M. (1983). The Emergence of a Comprehensive Systems Approach. *Journal of Family Therapy* 5, 165–177.

Chapter 25

When Learning is the Problem: An Example of the Milan Approach Applied to a Family Therapy Course

Paula Boston and Rosalind Draper

I. INTRODUCTION

The application of systemic thinking to teaching a course in family therapy is presented from our perspectives as teaching supervisor (R.D.) and one of the two course teachers (P.B.). We were faced with the prospect of planning a course for students of family therapy whose previous learning experience had been problematic. We began to conceptualise teaching in a different way.

The family therapist works to facilitate a problem family's capacity to move from redundant and ineffective solutions towards an ability to create and use new options. Our task was to help family therapy students develop a wider repertoire of theoretical constructs and therapeutic tools. We believed that some of our knowledge about the process of facilitating family change could be applied to the teaching system itself. We wanted to adapt certain clinical skills, particularly from the Milan way of working, to enable a change in the group based on our belief that learning had become "the problem".

We based a great deal of our current thinking on the works of Bateson (1973) and the Milan Associates (Palazzoli et al., 1978). One of the most relevant contributions towards our thinking as teachers was the notion of the stochastic process of learning described by Byng-Hall et al. (1982) who linked that idea to training family therapists. They state that a trainee can actually select new clinical information (to expand their stochastic storehouse of family therapy skills) when it is seen as safe, rewarding, effective and when there is an opportunity for consolidation. A slightly different slant to the same process is given by L. Allman (1982), who says that play, schematic learning and reflective abstraction are needed for epistemological transformation of trainees.

Bradford Keeney (1983) has written extensively on the process of epistemological transformation. A central theme relevant to this paper was in his quotation of Pask's theory which states that the learning situation of teacher and student is one of co-learning and co-evolution. Although meaningful data is different for each, the selection of new information and its consolidation occur recursively, for both students and teachers. In addition to wanting to help students to develop their clinical skills,

APPLICATIONS OF SYSTEMIC FAMILY THERAPY
ISBN 0-8089-1696-3

we hoped to add to our knowledge about teaching. In that vein, this paper is about learning as a problem and learning about learning.

II. CONTEXT

We believe in the importance of understanding and marking context. For our purposes, we defined the larger context as the overall organisation, and the smaller context as the class/teacher/supervisor system within it. The larger context, the organisation, has two main functions, one is to provide a wide range of psychological services to clients (individuals and families) and consultation and training to local agencies. The other is to train postgraduate specialists.[1] One specialisation is a two-year advanced training programme for family therapists who want to develop their skills and are likely to become trainers of family therapy. Trainees treat families as part of the course (supervision groups, one-way screen, video, etc.). Within the second year, some students also become teachers of family therapy courses offered by the clinic.

The smaller system included a family therapy group that was beginning its third year and had different teachers for each year. The course participants were social workers, team leaders and area heads from the local borough. The course had been taught in its first year by a highly respected senior staff member of the organisation. It was then taught in its second year by a family therapy programme trainee. This experience was not seen as positive. Poor attendance became a crucial issue, which frustrated both student and teacher. The group, now labelled "rebellious", was to continue for a third year, taught by two other family therapy trainees.

The structure of the sessions and team work in the Milan approach has been described elsewhere. Similarities to the model included our hypothesising process, use of a team and adaptation of many fundamental concepts which will be demonstrated in the body of the paper.

The teaching system was made up of three sub groups: the teachers and students, the two teachers themselves, and the teachers and supervisor. The feedback which organised our teaching passed from the teachers/students (1) to the teachers (2) who discussed the teaching with the supervisor (3), and this discussion produced feedback which was taken back to the teachers and students sub-group (1). Since we met our supervisor once a fortnight, the feedback process occurred over this two-week interval, which raised some interesting problems such as the fact that an idea which seemed appropriate in one sub-group at one time might no longer seem appropriate two weeks later in the context of a different sub-group.

The system of two teachers in the classroom compensates in some ways for not having a "live" observing team. One teacher monitored and introduced "different" information (akin to the team introjecting a new theme to the therapist for questioning), while the other teacher taught.

---

[1] Tavistock Clinic, Sheldon Programme, Advanced Programme in Family Therapy, 120 Belsize Lane, London, England.

During the months from July 1983 (the end of second year) to January 1984, three primary hypotheses shaped our thinking and interventions. These were not mutually exclusive. There was an evolutionary process that suggests that at different times, some ideas appeared more relevant than others.

III. HYPOTHESIS ONE: ATTACHMENT

There seemed to be the rule in the group that learning required an amount of attachment between teacher and students. The group had remained attached to the first teacher. They demonstrated their attachment to her by behaving badly to the second teacher. The second teacher remained attached to his hierarchy as a second year family therapy student by behaving in a less competent manner than his predecessor. That is, a trainee must show some need of supervision to support the complimentary relationship of student/supervisor. Because there was a perceived change in teaching/learning competence, the first teacher remained attached to both the class and the second teacher. Thus, it appeared learning could not take place with the second teacher because it would violate the rule that attachments are both fixed and necessary for learning.

(1) *Episode*

To deal with the problem, the "handover" meeting scheduled by the second teacher at the end of his tenure included both himself, the new teachers and the original teacher. The fact that the group wished to include the first teacher after a year's work apart suggested that the attachment was strong indeed.

Students alternated between indignation about their loyalty to the first teacher and then self-degradation and guilt about it. The students were verbally negative and dismissive about the second year's course. The teacher showed his frustration and depression at the end-of-year review. There was a demand for the teacher "newcomers" to present their authority in a way that clearly was then to be defeated by the group. Arms were crossed and scepticism conveyed by the tone of questions asked by the students about the experience of the new teachers and their plans for the next course.

A. Intervention

Based upon the hypothesis about attachment, several responses formed an intervention. The group's attachment to the first teacher was addressed. The new teachers said that they did not see this strong feeling for the first teacher as a problem in the way that the group did. This strong feeling was an understandable reaction to having had such a good experience, indicative of a capacity for real attachment. We shared their respect for her as an exceptional teacher: "It was an impossible act to follow". The obvious was declared: "Trainees are never of the stature of their teachers". One of us remarked that some day the group might resolve their feelings about the loss of the first teacher enough to be able to go ahead and learn anyway, and the other teacher remarked that it was probably too soon to consider such a possibility.

We further defined ourselves as people who were less likely to be so involved in their social service work because of our "foreign" backgrounds. One of us did have experience in child care placements, but it was relevant to the U.S., and the other did know Social Services, but only in another geographical area. Therefore, we could only really offer ourselves as "resources" for them to use as was helpful. We were not experts in their agency work. Then, we asked them questions about what family therapy information would be most useful.

The group's original teacher joined the meeting. It was not clear as to who was to stay. The third-year teachers made the choice to leave, saying that the old group had some important history to which they needed to attend. The learning context was marked as different by moving the impetus of responsibility for learning away from the teacher and epitomising the stance of neutrality. The notion of time was introduced in a multi-level way. The idea of mourning the loss of an attachment as a process that occurred over time was presented and then a message not to change too quickly was added. An analogic counter-paradox to this no-change statement was added when the third-year teachers got up and left early.

B. Feedback

During the discussion between third-year teachers and course participants, the tone of the dialogue became more relaxed and animated. Shortly thereafter, both past teachers reported to the new teachers that the group expressed optimism for the future class, and there had been a good job in "joining".

(2) *Episode*

Support for the attachment hypothesis was gained in another sequence of episodes. An ordinarily benign request from the original teacher about having an observer in the class caused confusion among all concerned about the decision-making process. Informal chains of communication were activated and boundaries crossed.

C. Intervention

In retrospect, we saw an intervention had developed. When we laughed together with the class about the degree of confusion created by the request, we positively connoted the event as being useful to students as an example of systems in action. The teachers shared their confusion about the levels of requests and most appropriate response. We clarified the requests and who appropriately should respond. As teachers, we said we would need some time to develop the best solution in our own structure, and would let them know our decisions at the next meeting. In two weeks, the class had made decisions appropriate to their level and we had come up with a solution to the request for observation: We let the observer view videotapes of the class.

D.   Analysis

Humour was used to defuse any anxiety and was positively connoted as a learning situation for everyone. To use the episode as a systemic learning event rather than see it as linear behaviour supported the stance of neutrality. The need to consult the supervisor affirmed the position of student as well as teacher, which also did not challenge old attachments. The use of time by the teachers' sub-system demonstrated that an inherently paradoxical attachment could push a system into a more creative solution. The result was that each level of request was answered more appropriately. The students were relieved of the task of reminding the hierarchy that trainee teachers were less competent than their own senior staff because the teachers would be showing more of their work, and the relationship of teacher to supervisor became a clearer "attachment".

IV.   HYPOTHESIS TWO: DEFINITION

Learning was a problem because of issues of definition. Contextual confusion had made it impossible for anyone to be clear about what was to be learned, so no learning could take place. If it was learning about Social Service family work, it became more like supervision, which had not been requested by the Social Service hierarchy. If learning was more theoretical, social workers felt it unrelated to their actual work. So the teacher could be neither expert in social services, nor expert at family therapy. And students could not learn in either case.

(1)   *Episode*

The second hypothesis arose out of the realisation that the expectations for the class and motivations for participation had become unclear. Students presented themselves as being knowledgeable about family therapy, but had difficulty responding to rudimentary questions. They were not heavily invested in theoretical concerns. It was impossible to ascertain what material had been covered. The class had presented the paradox of only two ways of learning (theory or practical application), and neither one was feasible. Some circular questioning was done around the area of knowledge sought by them and materials used, i.e. if we were to talk about "structural" family therapy, how would that affect your case work? What would have to happen to make the Social Service organisational structure more or less significant in class? It became clear that at that point in time, theory was too abstract and their own case material too threatening to the structure of the class.

A.   Intervention

We realised we had to develop new ways of combining theory and practice at numerous simultaneous levels. As detailed later, a piece of fiction was used as case material and different family therapy orientations were presented in class (see Appendix). Finally, the teachers stressed the fact that only the students could make decisions about relevance of class material to their outside work.

B. Analysis

Exercises were chosen to shift the context of the class from one of struggle and/or boredom to one of stimulation and enjoyment. We took a neutral stance about the applicability of the learning so they would decide if it had any relevance to their real work.

C. Feedback

Consequently, the group became much more actively engaged in discussion and demonstrated an increased application of theory to other situations.

V. HYPOTHESIS THREE: GROUP COHESION

The notion of group cohesion among social workers is a valued commodity in Social Services, both for external political reasons and mutual internal support. In a clearly defined hierarchy (them/us), group cohesion is not threatened and people are free to learn as individuals. But if people are free to learn as individuals, individual capacities are more obvious and an internal hierarchy of competence develops. If a hierarchy of competence develops, the rule of group cohesion is broken and individual learning must be inhibited by issues of group cohesion.

(1)   *Episode*

The third hypothesis was supported by information from the onset and continued to be the most systemically useful over time. On the "handover" meeting mentioned earlier in this paper, the students defined themselves as being "uncommitted" and attendance reflected this. We as teachers were asked to force them to attend regularly and be committed to readings. The new third-year course got off to an interesting start. They had realised that six of the eight members were unavailable for the first session, so they cancelled it themselves. This behaviour was understood to mean that they had attached themselves together enough to avoid a beginning class with only one or two participants, but their movements towards the new teachers was nil. At the second meeting, half of the membership attended. The ones who attended appeared somewhat ready for a guilt-evoking inquest about absent members by their new teachers.

A. Intervention

It was agreed that the topic of attendance merited consideration. We presented our dilemma in this way. We had a well prepared agenda to exchange with the class about the course outline, but felt it was unfortunate that only half of the participants had input. The question was posed about whether we should save the outline for next time and penalise those present and exclude absent members or repeat the process next time, and bore those who had been there. The group's responsibility in running the class was supported, and finally, they agreed to take on the obligation of filling in absent members.

Then mechanisms related to attendance were explored. A ritual was developed. We took the position that we would not be cancelled by the non-attendance since we needed to be there anyway, and would always be able to make use of the time ourselves. But, we could better tailor our teaching to the number of participants if advance notice were given.

B. Analysyis

The major aspect of this response was the avoidance of the teacher/student battle over attendance. We effectively neutralised our investment by being their regardless of their participation. The problem of attendance was shifted from being our problem we could not solve, to one they as a group could respond to. The primary intervention was that learning could continue independently of whether or not the group was cohesive.

C. Feedback

The response to the notion that we would be available to whoever wanted to use the time was to have someone laugh and say they would love the consultation time and would sabotage others' efforts to attend class when they had a particularly stressful case. The ritual around attendance was partially carried out for approximately three sessions, each time with a slightly different form of confusion around it. The ritual became redundant because attendance was actually good, and not pursued further at that time.

VI. CONCLUSION

We feel the Milan method provided a useful foundation and adaptable guideline in the training of family therapists. One of the most influential basic premises for us was "context as matrix of meaning", i.e. that the rules governing relationships were based in context. Attention to context allowed us to plan whether to behave in a way that maintained a contextual integrity (behaving like teachers rather than family therapists) or at times to assume a strategic position (to redefine ourselves as resource people rather than teachers). Our adherence to the teaching context provided reminders that our goals had to do with increasing individual skill level and not provision of systems therapy. The use of the method was a means to this end and had to be tailored to fit the classroom.

Another contribution to our experience was the usefulness of assuming a neutral position. Every "systemic course" has members who are at different points of incorporating or rejecting the exposed concepts. Undoubtedly someone represents a "psychoanalytic" perspective that can appear dogmatic. In our case, this view was given equal validity and then framed as presenting an opportunity for the group to work on psychoanalytic–systemic semantics.

Neutrality as a platform may have been particularly useful for relatively inexperienced teachers who might have tried to compensate for professional stature by an over-zealousness.

Appreciation of "systemic time" was also useful to our work. We noted the time span needed for the system to react and reorganise to certain interventions, which influenced our thoughts about subsequent interventions. Discussion with the often centred around the juxtaposition of different systems time and the accommodation process. Over the course, the teachers slowed down their input and the supervisor students seemed to require less time for consolidation of ideas.

We found the description of relationship positions, complimentary or symmetric, facilitative to understanding the process of teacher/student, teacher/teacher, teacher/supervisor, etc. interactions. For example, at one point we found the teacher/teacher system had become too symmetric. Our antidote was to deliberately become more complimentary with each other.

An important contribution of the Milan method at the level of basic premise is that of an appreciation of the value and discipline required for careful thought. The development and testing of systemic hypothesis was cognitively taxing, but gave us structure from which to act. We agreed with the defined difference between information and data, and felt supported in seeing analogic communication as equally important. Arms crossed during a break was data but arms crossing in response to a discussion of a Social Service case was seen as information. It had become relevant to a hypothesis about reactions to class material as affected by external roles. In many ways, it furthered our thoughts about teaching.

This experience of the approach, as a way of enhancing a student's systems capacity to learn and as a tool to increase teaching skills, could be applied to other training programmes. The Milan approach has already moved from the specific area of family therapy to work with networks and organisational systems. Training of organisational consultants or group therapists may find potential benefit in this way of working.

People sometimes have to be reminded of their own basic "truths". This course experience allowed us to remember our belief in the creative potential inherent in paradoxical situations. It is hoped that the students in the class have gained some sense of that part of the experience as a foundation for their future work with families.

VII. APPENDIX: A SPECIFIC TEACHING EXAMPLE

As presented earlier, one of the positions the teachers found themselves in was the difficult one of finding organisationally safe enough case material (see second hypothesis) while still making theoretical concepts relevant and applicable. Kafka's *Metamorphosis* was used as a piece of fiction which beautifully conveyed the notions of symptom development and the family as a mutually related and reactive system.

The sudden change of Gregor into a "dung beetle" was the presenting problem, and material in the fiction about family members provided background information. The class was divided into three therapy groups and each group was assigned a systemic family therapy orientation (structural, strategic, Milan). They were to present their conceptualisation of the case, their use of the history, and an intervention which would be representative of their assigned school of therapy. They were to meet this family at a point in the story prior to Gregor's fate being sealed.

It was hoped that in this exercise, certain fundamental premises could be conveyed either directly or indirectly. The use of a rather unusual presenting problem enhanced the freedom to understand the symptom systemically, rather than easily resorting to previous ideas about symptom causality. The neutrality, as it were, of the symptom provided more freedom to think. It is presumed that other forms of symptomology, i.e. bed wetting, would have more easily aroused a debate about psychoanalytic or physiological explanations.

In addition to actually providing case material for theoretical appreciation which enhances the consolidation phase of learning, the metaphor of *Metamorphosis* was used to convey ideas about systems' change over time and the metamorphosis of family therapist, and the experience demonstrated that mutually beneficial solutions can develop from what appear to be inherent deadlocks.

The combination of humour and learning, maximisation of complimentarity can be nicely illustrated. The group responsible for presenting the orientation of the Milan group set up a role play. One of the teachers was requested to play Gregor in his dung beetle state. A teacher could not ask for a more "one down position" and gamely played a beetle. The presenting group did a very good job of circular questioning of the family. In the subsequent discussion, the teacher was able to develop the need for awareness of analogic communication because the non-verbal dung beetle had actually provided a great deal of information in the role play. This led to an exchange about ways of dealing with non-verbal clients, and other very relevant and generaliseable questions about family therapy skills.

Acknowledgment

The authors would like to acknowledge the important contribution to the thinking of this paper made by the other course teacher, Gerrilyn Smith.

REFERENCES

Allman, L. (1982). Aesthetic Preference: Overcoming the Pragmatic Error. *Family Process* **21**, 43–56.
Bateson, G. (1973). "Steps to an Ecology of Mind". Paladin, St. Albans.
Byng-Hall, J., de Carteret, J., and Whiffen, R. (1982). Evolution of Supervision: An Overview. *In* Whiffen, R., and Byng-Hall, J. (eds.), "Family Therapy Supervision: Recent Developments in Practice". Academic Press, London, pp. 3–14.
Kafka, F. (1983). "Metamorphosis and Other Short Stories". Penguin Books, Harmondsworth, Middlesex.

Keeney, B. (1983). "The Aesthetics of Change". Guildford Press, New York.

Palazzoli, M. S., Boscolo, L., Cecchin, G., and Prata, G. (1978). "Paradox and Counter Paradox: A New Model in the Therapy of the Family in Schizophrenic Transaction". Jason Aronson, London.

Palazzoli, M. S., Boscolo, L., Cecchin, G., and Prata, G. (1980). The Problem of the Referring Person. *Journal of Marital and Family Therapy* 6, 3–9.

Chapter 26

Evaluating the Milan Approach

Bebe Speed

I. INTRODUCTION

While a number of teams are currently evaluating their use of the Milan approach, aside from individual case studies demonstrating effectiveness, there have been no reports of any rigorous quantified investigations. Some information is available on the work of the Milan group themselves. Prata (personal communication) reports that of the 15 families written about in "Paradox and Counter Paradox", 13 showed significant changes whilst two remained unchanged. Prata is continuing to undertake phone call follow-ups on all the families seen by the group since 1967 but none of this data has yet been published. Tomm (1984) cites Cecchin (personal communication) as having said that the Milan team find improvement in approximately 68% of their families, which is comparable with other published studies of outcome in family therapy (see Kniskern and Gurman, 1980). It is worth noting here that the families seen by the Milan team were those who would be recognised by other family therapists as being some of the most difficult. A figure of 68% improvement on follow-up is, therefore, particularly significant. Palazzoli and Prata (1983), working together since the group split up in 1980, have given some preliminary results on their research into the use of the invariable prescription. They indicate that of the 19 families they had treated or were still treating, all of whom had identified patients who "represented extremely serious, discouraging cases (six presenting patients with chronic infantile psychosis, ten presenting chronic schizophrenic patients, and three presenting acute delusional patients)", 10 out of 19 showed substantial improvements.

Tomm's group in Calgary are also evaluating their work, comparing outcome data on families treated using Milan therapy with that on families treated with different approaches. Tomm (1984) does not cite improvement rates *per se* but does comment, "while the improvement rate remains the same, the changes reported in the presenting problem occur with fewer sessions using the Milan approach compared to our previous more directive interactional approach. The average number of intakes that could be handled by the same number of staff increased by 25% for the four years after introducing the Milan systemic approach" (p. 270).

Groups at the Charles Burns Clinic, Birmingham, the Royal Hospital for Sick Children, Edinburgh, The Department of Clinical Psychology, Exeter and the Cardiff project team at the Family Institute are some of the British groups who are evaluating their use of the Milan Method; but again; no data is so far available as work is still in progress. Currently, the Cardiff study has reached the stage where the

APPLICATIONS OF SYSTEMIC FAMILY THERAPY
ISBN 0-8089-1696-3

interviewing of families is nearly complete but the data has yet to be collated. The Cardiff work will, however, be used to illustrate some of the issues with which this chapter is mainly concerned, that is, the epistemological and methodological problems encountered in attempting to evaluate a Milan approach to therapy.

II. THE WORK OF THE CARDIFF PROJECT TEAM

This team set out four years ago to use a Milan approach with the more difficult families referred to the Family Institute. The development and functioning of the team has been documented in greater detail elsewhere (Speed *et al.*, 1983). Six months after clinical work began, and consistent with normal agency practice, a decision was made to follow-up all families seen and a more detailed follow-up design was proposed than that normally used at the institute. By following up families we wished to see whether there had been any changes following therapy, whether any changes during therapy had been maintained or not and how any such changes or lack of them might be correlated with therapy.

A research design was finally agreed and abbreviated versions of three of the four forms used appear in the addendum. *Form 1* was to be completed by the team prior to the follow-up interview and covered the team's view of the therapeutic strategies used, what, if any, changes were thought to have occurred and how the former might be related to the latter. *Form 2*, again to be filled in by the team, recorded factual information about the family, how it was referred, family composition and the problem as seen by the referrer, the family and the team. This form also recorded information of use to the researcher whose task was to interview in person all family members (apart from young children) who had been involved in therapy. *Forms 3 and 4* were for the use of the interviewer when seeing the family and a separate *Form 4* had to be completed for each family member. (Form 3 is not displayed in this chapter.) *Form 4* addresses questions to each family member concerning issues such as the way in which the referral was made; the client's thoughts and feelings about the process of therapy, about the therapist and about the team; the client's view about changes which may have occurred both in the problem and in relationships both within the immediate and extended family, and how any such changes might be related to therapy and so on. For the sake of standardisation and comparison, the questions were the same for each family, except for question 25 on *Form 4*, which allowed the team to fill in specific questions related to a particular family.

III. PROBLEMS IN EVALUATING THE MILAN APPROACH

A. Epistemological Problems

A number of commentators have questioned the applicability of traditional scientific methods to outcome research on systemic family therapy. Tomm (1983), for example, queries the use of a non-cybernetic lineal way of thinking to questions of outcome when our work is based on a cybernetic epistemology. How can we look for A causes B sequences, i.e. that therapy causes change, when our epistemology directs our attention to recursion and feedback loops? Furthermore, cybernetic epistemology suggests that the researcher or therapist is part of the process of research or therapy and, therefore, it is erroneous to assume that therapy or research can be done in an "objective", scientific way.

Though adhering to a holistic view in principle, it is nevertheless clear that we cannot grasp all the information available about a family and the therapeutic process at the same time, much less describe it. What is described is a punctuation, a partial description of highly complex processes. Similarly, the process of doing therapy is a series of punctuations; as Cecchin has indicated (personal communication), the hypothesis (and related intervention) is a punctuation which rescues the therapist from the chaos of overwhelming information and enables the therapist to make decisions and act. Thus too with outcome research; a particular research design is one possible punctuation among many. The questions which are asked will partially determine what information is obtained, so in that sense research can never be truly objective. But it is possible within the epistemological framework of circularity to accept that therapy may be one influence on the family system, which interacted with other influences, which then reacted back on the therapy and other influences in such a way that over time change occurred. Therefore, it seems reasonable to try to measure change and to look for connections between therapy procedures and such change, but only if it is borne in mind that therapy is one of the many different influences impinging on a family at any point in time.

In support of such a view Gurman (1983) advocates the use of standard research procedures in follow-up studies of therapy based on systemic approaches on three grounds: "First, that they are the only ethically responsible means presently available by which we can assess the efficacy of our work and study the factors influencing therapeutic outcome; second, that despite the very brief history of research in family therapy, these research models have already provided data of immediate practical relevance to clinicians, patients and policy makers alike; and, finally, that traditional research methods and designs are far more compatible with systemic thinking than some observers have suggested" (p. 229). The project team at Cardiff arrived at similar conclusions. Whilst aware of the limitations of standard research procedures they were all we had, and it seemed more worthwhile to at least attempt outcome research despite these limitations than to do none at all.

B.   Methodological Problems

(1)   *Effectiveness criteria—what to measure?*

Different outcome studies select different criteria to measure the effectiveness of therapy, from the more simple criteria of symptom improvement to more complicated criteria of improved general functioning of individuals and improvement in the quality of family relationships. As Gale (1979) and Frude (1980) argue, a number of measures of effectiveness are likely to be more reliable.

Prata (personal communication), in following up all the families seen by the Milan team since the beginning of 1967, asks three standard questions: 1) How is the patient now? 2) Has anyone else had psychological problems in the family? and 3) Has the family sought help anywhere else? In the Cardiff project research, as will be seen from questions 22 and 23 on *Form 4*, we also ask about the family's view of the status of the problem both when therapy ended and at the point of follow-up. Apart from the standard questions, Prata asks questions specific to each family derived from a careful reading of the family's file prior to the follow-up phone call. Similarly, we also devised specific questions for each family to be written on *Form 4* against question 25 for the use of the interviewer. Though question 25 is defined as "specific questions to indicate status of problem", in practice "status of problem" was defined widely to include questions aimed at eliciting information about any changes in the family relationships regarded by the team as linked with the symptomatic behaviour complained of. For example, one couple was asked whether the husband could now go out alone (one of the presenting symptoms). But they were also asked did they differ more, the same or less in their decisions about their child since therapy ended, as well as other questions aimed at eliciting information about changes in their marital relationship.

Questions 26 and 27 on *Form 4*, asking if any other problems have arisen in the immediate or wider family since therapy ended, is similar to Prata's second question. This is necessary information because a client may report disappearance of the presenting symptom but substitution of another, either in the client or another family member. Question 28, asking if the family has sought help elsewhere with the original or other problem, is similar to Prata's third question. A family may report that the original problem has improved but in answer to question 28 reveal that it has remained sufficiently a problem to have taken them elsewhere for help.

Seeking treatment elsewhere once family therapy has ended can be seen as a more objective measure of successful or unsuccessful outcome than family members' more subjective estimates of improvement. For example, a family might report relatively small improvements in the problem but indicate that they have not sought help elsewhere. This might be particularly impressive with those families who came to therapy with long histories of previous treatment. For example, in one of the project follow-ups, the husband reported substantial improvements in his symptomatic behaviour (psychosomatic pains) whilst the wife was considerably more equivocal. They both, however, reported that the husband now visits the GP "very rarely", a considerable change from his previous pattern of visiting the GP, usually weekly, over a three-year period prior to therapy.

(2)   *Effectiveness criteria—how to measure?*

One way of measuring effectiveness is to ask the client(s) their opinion about what, if any, changes have occurred. This apparently simple procedure initially posed us a dilemma; using the Milan approach we had adopted a stance of discovering, accepting and positively connoting family patterns and frequently recommending that the family should not change for the time being. How could we then ask questions about change at the point of follow-up when this could risk revealing that we had been trying to promote change after all? Prata feels that they avoid this dilemma by asking how things are now, how is the identified patient now, rather than asking about change *per se*. But we wanted to ask more specific questions aimed at eliciting information about particular changes and it thus remained for us problematic.

We finally decided that the inconsistency would be removed if the questions, including those about change, were posed by an independent researcher. The family could then see this person as potentially neutral about change, more-or-less disinterested in whether changes had or had not occurred for them as a family. The researcher's interest in the possibility of change would be explicable as a wider interest in the relationship between therapy and outcome which could be seen as a legitimate general concern beyond the boundaries of any one particular family. (An additional advantage of using an independent researcher is that it should avoid a family attempting to re-engage, which might be more likely to happen if the family's therapist or a member of the team did the follow-up. It is, however, interesting to note that Prata, who introduces herself at the beginning of the telephone follow-up as either the family's therapist or a member of the team behind the screen, reports few problems with families attempting to re-engage. She feels this is so because the follow-up call is presented as part of the centre's normal procedure in ringing for news of all families after a period of time.)

In retrospect, it is less clear that asking directly about change was the difficult issue we first supposed it to be. For example, many families, at least at a conscious level, seek therapy because they want change. Therefore, it would not necessarily appear illogical to enquire about change even if the family had been advised against it by the therapist or the team. Additionally, 18 months at least had elapsed between the last interview and the follow-up and, arguably, families would have evolved to a point where questions about change, even if asked by the therapist (though in a neutral way), would not matter.

Relying on client reports is also problematic in that such reports may be fairly reliable over quantifiable data, for example weight maintenance in the case of anorexia or numbers of outings in the case of agoraphobia, but they become more problematic when commenting about an individual's improved general functioning or about improvement in the quality of family relationships generally. For example, a question such as "Do you argue more, less or the same since therapy ended?" cannot be so objectively assessed by family members. Additionally, "We argue more" might be viewed as a negative development by some family members but seen as a mark of improvement by others and/or by the therapist.

Assuming that family members view things differently, we decided it would be more reliable to interview all family members who had been seen in therapy. Whilst many of the comments made to the researcher by different family members echo each other, some do not and there is then the additional problem of interpreting sometimes conflicting statements from different family members. For example, in one family, the wife reported that the problem, severe arguments between herself and her son, was the same at the last appointment and at the point of follow-up, whereas the husband rated the problem as improved. Assessing the meaning of these comments was not helped by the son's response. He was reported to be "immediately antagonistic to follow-up and refused contact".

The reliability of family members' comments is even more an issue if elucidated by a therapist or team member, rather than a relatively independent researcher, because of the potential biasing of data in the way that information from the family is interpreted. Information from the referrer of a family might be seen as potentially more reliable. Such a procedure was not built into the Cardiff research though we may decide to approach referrers for information when a family refuses follow-up.

Such a source of information is also problematic, however, because of the way in which some referrers are caught up with the family and family-plus-therapist system (see Palazzoli *et al.*, 1980). There may, for example, be rivalries between the different professionals involved which may influence the referrer to give or withhold information in particular ways.

(3) *Relating changes to therapy*

Even if we can establish that changes have occurred, how can we know that these are related to the family's involvement in therapy? One way of assessing this and one used by the Cardiff team is to ask the family's opinion of the reasons for any change (see questions 29, 30 and 32 on *Form 4*). But again, as with the reliability of a family's perception of the occurrence of change, there are also problems with the reliability of the family's opinion about links between changes and therapy. Tomm (1984) encountered this particular difficulty and comments that "When a major transformation has occurred the family generally does not attribute it to therapy. They tend to associate it with non-therapy events and often do not even remember the triggering intervention" (p. 269).

Similarly, Frude and Dowling (1980) in their follow-up study found that a greater number of clients reported improvements in the original problem than reported that family therapy had been helpful. They comment that this "raises the intriguing possibility that there is positive reluctance among some clients to attribute improvement to therapy. . . . in many of the strategic cases paradoxical injunction was used and in such cases we might expect symptomatic change to occur and to be recognised by the client but *not* to be recognised as an effect of the specific treatment. Thus the evidence obtained is in line with this theoretical prediction and underlines the special problems associated with the status of clients' reports where paradoxical methods have been employed " (pp. 159–160).

How can a family's denial of the link between therapy and change be explained? One possibility is that such a view is sometimes correct, i.e. that therapy actually had very little to do with any changes which occurred. A further possibility is that family members may not be aware of the connection between therapy and change. A cybernetic view would suggest that an intervention could have triggered changes in family members' behaviours which then in turn triggered further changes; and amidst this welter of changes, the family can only remember that somehow everyone stopped quarrelling, say, and account for change in that way. Of relevance here is the notion that family members may not have pre-existing categories which would help them to perceive the relationship between what happens in this type of therapy and change. In contrast, clients involved in, say, individual psychotherapy are more likely to have expectations that change will occur via insight and the relationship with the therapist. Such expectations will probably be congruent with what occurs and they are therefore more able to explicitly identify links between therapy and change.

It is also possible that a potentially key ingredient of Milan therapy, that is, putting the family into a position via the systemic prescription of wishing to prove the therapist and team wrong, would lead the family to deny any link. Unlike Tomm and unlike our experience in some cases, Prata (personal communication) reports that families often remember the therapy and the prescription "as if it were yesterday". She further reports, however, that the family member spoken to is often angry and eager to tell Prata that the team was quite wrong in its opinion and eager to prove this by triumphantly detailing changes which show just how wrong the team was. One implication of this is that the family change in order to prove the team wrong and, given such a stance, the family would be most unlikely to admit that therapy had been at all helpful.

What of the reliability of client reports where changes are positively linked with therapy? In our experience, this does sometimes occur; for example, in one family the father said therapy had helped because of "decisive bits of advice". Naturally, it is more tempting simply to accept such a positive link made by a client since it is in "our favour", as it were, but we cannot do this at the same time as wishing to query as "inaccurate" negative correlations between therapy and change suggested by other clients.

Using clients' views of the links between therapy and change in outcome research is, then, problematic, particularly so if the very nature of the therapeutic approach influences clients to be less likely to attribute change to therapy. How otherwise can changes be more reliably related to therapy procedures? One possibility is to use therapists' rather than clients' views of any such link, but these are not necessarily any more reliable than family members' views.

A further possibility and, according to Gale (1979) a pre-requisite of adequate outcome studies, is to use a "control" group which either receives no treatment or different treatment from the "experimental" group. Though attempts were made by the Cardiff team to arrange such a control group, for various reasons, this was not possible. Though a control group would have been more satisfactory, we neverthe-less thought it legitimate to proceed without one, arguing that the families seen in the project were, as it were, their own control group. Many of them had had prob-lems for many years and/or had had multiple previous treatments and/or presented with severe symptomatic or relationship difficulties. Therefore, if change occurred during or after family therapy, it was at least a serious proposition that such change was likely to be partially correlated with the treatment received.

IV.   CONCLUSION

The main epistemological and methodological problems associated with evaluating the Milan approach have been reviewed. There are of course other problems, parti-cularly methodological ones, which have not been considered, for example: a) eluci-dating what specific aspect of therapy was potent; b) decisions concerning the timing of follow-up and what differences a variable time gap makes to outcome findings; and c) how to satisfactorily define what the therapy consisted of.

In concluding, I want to mention two issues which have surfaced directly from the work of the Cardiff team. The first issue is that the researcher has been unable to interview a number of families, sometimes because the family has moved and is untraceable but sometimes because the family refuse to be interviewed. During the pilot study when we used phone calls, none of the nine families refused to talk to us. It is therefore necessary to consider whether the various advantages of using an inde-pendent researcher and being able to question all family members using a detailed questionnaire (which was thought to be too time-consuming and off-putting a prospect for the family by phone) outweigh the disadvantages of the lack of information about those families who refuse a face-to-face follow-up interview.

The second issue is that conforming to a particular therapeutic approach in order to suit research criteria may itself result in biasing outcome. A therapist, because of such constraints on spontaneity and creativity, may perform less effectively, resulting in poorer outcome results. One of our team members particularly felt the "mental and emotional straitjacket" of being required to heed other team members' comments of "but it's not systemic" and related a number of his therapy failures to this therapist variable. Thus the very act of attempting to measure the effectiveness of therapy may, by placing constraints on what can be done, paradoxically result in rendering that therapy less effective.

Acknowledgment

I would like to acknowledge the participation of my team members, Brian Cade, Phillip Kingston and Philippa Seligman in the therapeutic work underlying the research discussed in these pages, and the further contribution, both by them and by Neil Frude of University College, Cardiff, to the research design. Thanks are also due to Dave Locke of the South Glamorgan Institute for Higher Education in doing the follow-up interviews.

REFERENCES

Frude, N. (1980). Methodological Problems in the Evaluation of Family Therapy. *Journal of Family Therapy* 2, 29–44.

Frude, N., and Dowling, E. (1980). A Follow-up Analysis of Family Therapy Clients. *Journal of Family Therapy* 2, 149–161.

Gale, T. (1979). Problem of Outcome Research in Family Therapy. *In* Walrond-Skinner, S. (ed.), "Family and Marital Psychotherapy: A Critical Approach". Routledge and Kegan Paul, London.

Gurman, A. (1983). Family Therapy Research and the "New Epistemology". *Journal of Marital and Family Therapy* 9, 227–234.

Kniskern, D., and Gurman, A. (1980). Clinical Implications of Recent Research in Family Therapy. *In* Wolberg, L., and Aranson, N. (eds.), "Group and Family Therapy". Bruner Mazel, New York, pp. 217–223.

Palazzoli, M. S., Boscolo, L., Cecchin, G., and Prata, G. (1980). The Problem of the Referring Person. *Journal of Marital and Family Therapy* 6, 3–9.

Palazzoli, M. S., and Prata, G. (1983). A New Method for Therapy and Research in the Treatment of Schizophrenic Families. *In* Stierlin, H., Wynne, L. C., and Wirsching, M. (eds.), "Psychosocial Interventions in Schizophraenia". Springer Verlag, Berlin, pp. 237–243.

Speed, B., Seligman, P., Kingston, P., and Cade, B. (1983). A Team Approach to Therapy. *Journal of Family Therapy* 4, 271–284.

Tomm, K. (1983). The Old Hat Doesn't Fit. *Family Therapy Networker* 7, 39–41.

Tomm, K. (1984). One Perspective on the Milan Systemic Approach: Part II. Description of Session Format, Interviewing Style and Interventions. *Journal of Marital and Family Therapy* 10, 253–271.

ADDENDUM

Form No. 1

(To be completed by the team *before* the interview but *not* given to the interviewer.)

1. and 2. Family name and research number: _____

List here the number
of times each strategy
was used

3. Particular team strategies used:

a. Stating the process in the family and
positively connoting it. _____

b. Stating the process in the family, positively
connoting it and explicitly recommending that
it continue for the time being. _____

c. Telling a story or other analogy. _____

d. Split team message. _____

e. Giving a ritual task. _____

f. Split team message, a task and a no-change
prescription. _____

g. Giving a task to monitor behaviour. _____

h. Stating the normality of responses to crises
and stages of development. _____

i. A statement by an eminent/expert colleague. _____

j. Unconscious fantasy (usually in I.P.) about
what may happen to others if symptom not
maintained. _____

k. Other. _____

4. Which of the above strategies seemed most effective in bringing about the
change?

5. Team's estimate of outcome of therapy immediately after the last interview, as
compared with the situation at the time of the first interview.

Better		The same		Worse
1	2	3	4	5

6. The team's opinion of what the family will say about whether things are better, the same or worse, at the point of follow-up, compared with the situation at the time of the first interview.

Better		The same		Worse
1	2	3	4	5

Form No. 2

(To be completed by the team before the interview and handed to the interviewer.)

Many of the questions on this form cover factual information such as: family's name, address, research number; occupations of husband and wife; date last seen, number of interviews, follow-up due; name of therapist. The other questions are:

3. Source of referral: (9 possibilities specified including self-referral, on recommendation of various specified professionals or directly by those professionals.)

9. Family members seen in therapy:

Name	Relationship to I.P.	Age (at time of referral)

10. Family composition: (11 possibilities specified including married/unmarried couple, with/without children; divorced/separated couple, with/without children; reconstructed family, single and so on)

12. Problem(s) as stated by referrer (whether the referrer is a family member or somebody else). (11 possibilities specified including psychiatric, criminal or delinquent behaviour, violence, sexual deviation and dysfunction, drugs, the referrer, marital or other relationship problems)

13. State which problem was seen to be the main one by referrer

14. Problem(s) as stated by family by end of first interview. (Same possibilities listed as under question 12.)

15. State which problem was seen to be the main one by families

16. Problem(s) as seen by team in retrospect. (Same list as in questions 12 and 14.)

17. State which problem was seen to be the main one by team

Form No. 4

For use of the interviewer and to be completed in relation to each family member interviewed. (N.B. specific questions in Section 25 should be completed by team before the interview.)

1.–4. Family name, individual's name, research number, follow-up date.

5. What was the problem(s) which took you to the Family Insitute?

_____

Questions 6 and 7 enquire whether the family was referred by someone, the client's view of why this was and who most thought referral was a good idea.

Questions 8–11 ask whether the meetings at the institute were understandable, embarrassing, upsetting or uncomfortable in other ways and were each rated as below:

Most of the time		Some of the time		Hardly at all
1	2	3	4	5

Questions 12, 13, 14 ask open-endedly what were the most/least useful aspects of the meetings and what the client thought of the therapist.

15. Did you think your therapist:

	Completely:	Moderately:	Not at all:
a. Understood the family situation?	_____	_____	_____
b. Sympathised with the family?	_____	_____	_____
c. Was helpful to the family?	_____	_____	_____
d. Was competent?	_____	_____	_____
e. Was as direct as you would have wished?	_____	_____	_____
f. Was equally fair to all members of the family?	_____	_____	_____

Questions 16–18 ask for the client's opinion about what the therapist was trying to do; what the therapist's view of the problem was thought to be and whether he/she was thought to have focused on a particular family relationship.

Questions 19–21 and 36 elicit the client's view of the use of a team; why the therapist was thought to have one; the client's impressions and feelings about the team and whether it would have been helpful or not to meet the team.

22. Immediately after your last appointment at the Family Institute, was the problem you went there with:

Better   The same   Worse
   1   2   3   4   5

23. Same question as 22 but enquires about status of problem now in comparison with at first appointment.

24. Have any important events happened in this family or in your wider family since you last went to the Family Institute? (e.g. births, deaths, marriages, move of house etc.).

25. Specific questions to indicate status of problem: (to be completed by the team before the interview; usually about five questions).

26. Have any other problems arisen in your immediate family since you ended at the Institute?

   a) YES   b) NO

   If 'YES' what are they?

27. Same question as 26 but enquires about wider rather than immediate family.

28. Have you sought help with any problem(s) (old or new) since you ended at the Institute?

   a) YES   b) NO

   If 'YES' what are they?

29. If changes have been existent in the answers given to questions 22, 23, 24 and 25, ask: How would you explain those differences?

30. If the Family Institute is not mentioned in response to question No. 29, ask: Do you think that contact with the Family Institute had anything to do with these differences?

   a) YES   b) NO

   If 'YES' in what way did it have anything to do with these differences?

31. Were there other agencies involved either at the time you were going to the Institute or since?

   a) YES   b) NO

   If 'YES' what agencies?

32. Do you think that those other agencies had anything to do with the differences you have referred to?

a) YES   b) NO

If 'YES' in what ways did they have anything to do with those differences?

Questions 33, 34 and 36 ask whether or not the client would return to the Insitute if the need arose and the reasons why; whether or not the client would recommend the Institute to anyone else, with reasons, and whether the client has any further comments.

Part SIX

Discussion

Chapter 27

Twenty More Questions—Selections from a Discussion Between the Milan Associates and the Editors

Luigi Boscolo, Gianfranco Cecchin, David Campbell, and Rosalind Draper

I. EDITOR'S INTRODUCTION

We wanted Luigi Boscolo and Gianfranco Cecchin to be a part of this book, so in February 1984 we travelled to Milan and spent a weekend with them discussing some of the issues raised in the book. From many hours of conversation, we have selected parts of the discussion which we think the reader may find helpful.

We do not think of the comments as though they are definitive statements, nor should the reader. Rather they are ideas which have been taken out of their original context and edited with a view to enhancing the reader's experience of the contents of the book.

We found it difficult to organise this chapter, because the discussion itself was a rambling, circular process. However, we found that punctuating it under headings helped us to organise our own thinking and the reader may also find them helpful.

We would finally like to thank Luigi and Gianfranco for generously sharing themselves and their ideas in such a way that made this chapter possible.

II. BASIC CONCEPTS OF THE MILAN APPROACH

Eds.: I think one of the aims of the book should be to help people develop tools they can use to understand their place in their own system. If we can shed some light on that, it will be easier for people to apply this method in their own settings.

G. C.: The Milan approach has developed two basic ideas. One, that without context there is no meaning. The meaning of action and behaviour is only given by the context. The second is, when you observe a system you become part of it. You are part of the context but at the same time you have to examine yourself as though you are outside the context. This is a self-reflexive position.

APPLICATIONS OF SYSTEMIC FAMILY THERAPY
ISBN 0-8089-1696-3

When we started 10 years ago, we tried to describe the system and how to change it. What was the nodal point? Now I think the emphasis is on the therapist, the person who is watching the system. What is happening to him? What is he doing? The way he connects with the family is now more important.

Eds.: How would you describe what actually happens to the therapist when one works within different levels of context?

G. C.: In a simulated family when a person becomes part of a certain context, i.e. the created family, he becomes part of that context and belongs to that context. This person cannot express certain feelings and may be inhibited by the system to say certain things or even to think certain things. When the role play is over, this person becomes himself again and can say all those things that he couldn't say during the session. He could not say he was angry with the therapist, or angry with the partner even if he felt so. There was a constraint and he could not do it. This is a very good example of how changing context already changes your ability to formulate a hypothesis and to observe a system. You can observe much better outside the system. When you are inside the system, you must limit your understanding. So it is part of the theory that once a system is defined it constrains the members' thinking and action, but it is only defined in the first place out of the constraints upon the observer.

When you become part of a system you begin to cut down possibilities, you are constrained, when you are outside you can develop your ideas. Of course you cannot be there too long because when you become part of an observing group you become part of that system too. When you are part of a system you are constrained but it is impossible not to be part of a system, so it is impossible not to be constrained. You have to hold these two positions all the time.

L. B.: We share Bateson's simplest definition of a system: "a system is any unit structured on feedback". He gave this definition while talking about cybernetic epistemology, that is an epistemology which tends to see the relationship between observer and observed as one which is structured on feedback. To be an observer is a self-reflexive position. Being aware that you are in a self-reflexive loop is a tremendous advantage. This is what we see with our students. They feel much better when they understand this position. Especially in countries where there is socialised medicine, in institutions where they are doing therapy, they are always in a double bind. For example: in an institution organised by the state to take care of handicapped people, you may decide to confront them about their position of being handicapped, but at the same time you have to obey the institution that tells you to take care of the handicapped people, which confirms their position. So it is a permanent contradiction.

Eds.: So the first rule is to appreciate the self-reflexive nature of your position.

G. C.: Yes, because as a worker you must obey both the larger system which says take care of them and you have to obey the patient, who says you have to cure me. If you obey both injunctions, you are out of a job. So the question is how to keep your job by not doing it? *That's a contradiction.* How to keep a salary by not doing a job and by not doing it you do it more correctly. *That's a second contradiction.* If a therapist has a real experience of doing that, I think he is liberated; he has freedom to act.

L. B.: Any system or subsystem is simultaneously in a relationship with at least two subsystems. The worker is in a relationship with the client and the task is to change the client, but at the same time he is in a relationship with the institution which might have different aims. For parents, for example, being a parent with their children might be in conflict with the grandparents in their relationship with the parents. So one of the dilemmas one usually finds any time one acts is that when one acts and thinks, he has to act and think in two systems simultaneously. That's what creates difficulty for an individual: if you scold your children it is not good for your parents and vice versa.

Eds.: What you are saying is that it's a dilemma you have to appreciate.

G. C.: When you appreciate it you can use it. You can use it to apply these two levels to your interventions.

Eds.: I want to ask a question about theory. Since your paper, "Hypothesizing, Circularity and Neutrality" (Palazzoli *et al.*, 1980), how has the relationship between the hypothesis, interview and intervention evolved?

L. B.: Since we wrote that paper we have come to realise more and more that the most effective questions are the hypothetical questions and the questions about future solutions. Also at the time we wrote the paper, most of the questions were ones in which we asked a person to describe the relations between two or three other people, which are questions related to phenomenology, i.e. people describe behaviour. More recently, we have been asking what people *think* about behaviour. These are what we call explanatory questions. These are questions about the hypothesis the person has about their own behaviour.

Eds.: Do you find that you're making different types of hypotheses about the family system?

G. C.: We found that we were making similar hypotheses. This made it difficult to collaborate because after a while you see similar things and they look very good. You become affectionate toward one hypothesis and you can demonstrate it all the time.

L. B.: When we began our training we created the setting of an observer group and when the observer group met the therapy group and shared their hypotheses, we saw they were different hypotheses. These differences helped to prevent us from marrying our hypotheses.

G. C.: For example, three years ago we were looking for what was the most important marriage in the family; we were always talking about bonds in the family and the confusion between generations. But now we are looking for what is the premise, the basic idea that keeps the family going. For example, there may be a premise that you have to be happy all the time and that no one can be aggressive or that no one can separate. We would make a hypothesis about this premise.

L. B.: Or that there must be one in control and the others must be controlled.

G. C.: Yes, the basic problem in life is how to control and you see all relations in terms of this dichotomy, either you are on the top or you are on the bottom. If you work on this hypothesis, then you see that all the other marriages in the family become secondary to that. Another hypothesis is about symbiosis: If you love your parents, you cannot leave home.

L. B.: Another premise is about the concern to be loyal or disloyal in the family.

G. C.: Or the theme of justice. Somebody is trying to cheat you all the time

L. B.: The Milan approach tries to change the world view, the premises. You can operate at the higher level of premises even while you change behaviour at a lower level if you have in mind the higher premises. If you don't have the premises in mind, then you are only at the level of the single behaviour.

G. C.: If you work at a lower level something will happen at the higher level. But if you are *aware* of the premise at the higher level you have much more subtle ways of provoking the change, such as making reflexive questions.

L. B.: What is primary in our work is to think at the level of the basic premise of the family. Then when we act, we act at different levels. The most important thing is our thinking about the basic premises of the family.

When you talk about the premise of the family, it's just as important to think about the premise of the therapist, because every therapist has a premise. A structuralist has a premise that there is a normal family which has clear boundaries between members of the family.

G. C.: But a clearly defined hierarchy in the family is only one of the many solutions that a system may find in the history of its stochastic process of organisation but it is not the *right* premise. It is one of the premises which the culture organises in a certain period.

L. B.: A behaviourist has a premise that symptoms are related to anxiety. The premise cannot but have a powerful effect on the therapy. The therapist will finish therapy when he has reached the goal which is established by his basic premise about therapy. Very often we are not aware of the premises of the therapist.

G. C.: If you are a systemic therapist you believe in your premise, which is circular epistemology; the one that Brad Keeney describes (Keeney, 1982). This gives you much more freedom to act than the premises we just described. With your premise you create a tension between your premise and the premise of the family, which can create such a tension that the family has to change their premise.

L. B.: Another important point is the way we terminate therapy. We often do it abruptly. We terminate when we see the system on the verge of major change and when we see a major change, the team discusses this and if the team agrees, then we terminate therapy. In this sense we are consistent with the premise we talked about before. We say we will finish therapy because we do not see any psychiatric problems; of course there will be difficulties, but they will find their own solutions. We give a message to the family that they will find solutions; we step out and in this way we have respect for their solutions. We avoid introducing a map of what we think is normality and this frees the system.

III.   THE THERAPIST'S POSITION IN
THE SYSTEM

Eds.: What can therapists do when they get feedback from the family that they are not helping the family to change?

G. C.: The question is wrong because if you have a circular epistemology you should be indifferent about whether you achieve change or not. People come to you because that is your job and you start to work with them with these methods. What happens is totally unpredictable and one possibility is that there is no change whatsoever. If we had an effect all the time that would be bad for us. It would not be ecological in the larger sense. It may be good that sometimes we don't have any effect, and that some families resist very well. Perhaps they have some premises that we cannot reach; perhaps the family is too advanced for us to understand. It can even be *good* for us because we will have difficult cases to study and *good* for the family because they may be part of a larger context in which it would be very dangerous to change.

Eds.: One of the most difficult problems for a therapist is being part of a client's therapeutic system as well as his statutory system. An example might be working therapeutically with a client who is called to court, and you are asked by the judge to give an opinion about the client's statutory problems.

L. B.: Many times a judge will ask you (in an adoption case for example) for an evaluation and at the same time he asks you to do something to help this youngster and construct a support system, which are two contradictory requests. He responds to his position. You can conclude that the position of the judge and that of the mental health professional can be paradoxical, and the worker may not be able to do anything. This is very important because people in this context often think that they can do something. If they decide it is impossible for them to do anything, this is a therapeutic position. If there is not the awareness that nothing can be done, then any movement creates *more* pathology because of this network of paradoxical relationships. The analysis of this position that you cannot do anything introduces a *clarification* into the system; otherwise if this is not clarified, it perpetuates what Laing calls mystification.

Eds.: If you were to write a letter to the judge saying I'm happy to do a report although I'm in an impossible position because if I say 'A' it will affect the child and if I say 'B' it will affect the court . . .

G. C.: You can't say that to the judge because he's part of the court system and he will act to protect the interests of the court.

L. B.: But the judge himself is connected to the request he made for a report. When you have to make a decision about adoption or fostering you are called to be part of the construction of the system. You are one of the people who are building the system. You can't stay outside.

Another aspect of this paradoxical relationship is that the therapist may be called to give an expert opinion about what should happen to a child, and that at the higher context no one really knows what to do, but in a lower context, one has to make a decision. Therefore in the higher context your opinion cannot be accepted as trust-worthy or expert.

Eds.: When you challenge people to think like this there is another paradox. People say they only want to be family therapists and not systemic thinkers.

G. C.: Family therapy is a kind of limitation to a systemic thinker. If you think all intervention should be systemic family therapy then you miss opportunities to make other kinds of interventions at other levels, such as home visits, meeting teachers, individual therapy, hypnosis, etc. All these techniques are part of the ecological pattern. Whether therapy is good or not depends on the context you create around it. For example, giving medication can be good in certain situations and bad in others. In therapy you work to create a context in which *whatever* you do becomes effective.

One of the basic actions of systemic therapy is the positive connotation of the symptom. It is effective because you are in a context where the symptom is *bad*, something to be cured. An institution says symptoms are bad, they will cure them. So you try to introduce another opinion. But if the idea is to change the paradigm, and eventually the whole institution believes that symptoms are *good*, you create an impossible reflexive loop.

The institution will collapse if it loses the ability to create differences.

G. C.: For example, if you were to reach a point in the wider culture in which everyone believed that symptoms were functional in terms of family relationships, then if a child had a problem, the family and the therapist might believe the problem was in the *family*. They would go home, feel guilty, exaggerate their care of the child and he might get crazy. Then one day somebody might say this child's problem is an organic syndrome. They resolve the problem; the child gets better; the parents are liberated; the teachers know what to do, etc. It is a higher level context to discover organicity. It's a higher level of functioning. In that case it's a change.

Eds.: What ideas are helpful for people wanting to identify the feedback patterns they are working in?

G. C.: We have found simulation is a very good exercise. A therapist interviews a simulated family and is called out after a brief time. The observing group must not say what *he* did wrong, but what the *family* did to make the therapist helpless and empty-headed. That's a tremendous experience to see how the empty-headedness of the therapist is due to the activity of the family. Then you see there was a look, a movement, or some area that the therapist needed to explore if he wanted to remain the therapist, but he didn't do it. At that moment he feels like leaving the room, or he starts a conversation; not therapy, but a conversation. It is very important to become aware of this. To learn how not to be a therapist paradoxically is the way to see the tremendous possibility of becoming a therapist. This is always about moving back and forth—the recursive process.

L. B.: This exercise can also have the effect of creating a much more positive context for work among colleagues. Another thing is that when someone makes an observa-tion during discussion, we don't allow others in the group to say I don't agree with you. A word like agreeing implies there is something that is truth and something that is not. You're wrong, I'm right.

G. C.: Just as with a family in which you say you understand that their solution to ↙
the problem for the moment is what they are doing; also for the therapist being
helpless or in a double bind is at the moment the only possible solution to having to
obey different injunctions, for instance, from an institution and from an individual.

L. B.: We see that trying to analyse these injunctions is so difficult the therapist
often becomes paralysed. To get out of this paralysis you must act. It does not
matter what you do; you just *do* something and watch the feedback.

Eds.: Yes, it's not possible to think your way out of the paralysis, but action creates
some feedback.

L. B.: Then you must take into account circularity. By appreciating the recursive
process between the action and the feedback you enter into a co-evolutionary
process. While you appreciate you are part of the co-evolutionary process you avoid
being paralysed.

G. C.: The establishment will always be the establishment. It will never be a systemic establishment. That is impossible—it is a contradiction.

Eds.: Any institution has a linear function. Some of the contributors are trying to
establish family therapy teams in their agencies and are struggling not to lose sight of
the fact that they are a part of an oscillating process and cannot act in isolation.

L. B.: What is important is to think of analysing yourself as part of the system—
what we call a systemic analysis—then you act and as you do, you observe the feedback of the way you are acting. Through this process you will find that all different
techniques can be useful. So you go into a state of permanent revolution in order to
get out of the dilemma of freezing in the system. For instance, a group of our
trainees decided to start work with a group of chronic schizophrenics. One hypothesis is that the chronicity of patients is maintained by the therapist. So they gave
messages (I don't know exactly how): "We are doing this work with you now, but if
the situation would change, the service which we create for this task will disappear".
Because the premise is that the service creates the patients. They create a service for
these patients with the idea that this service will end when the patients get out.

Eds.: That's a neat double bind, because you're telling them that the institution will
change if anything happens to the relationship between the patient and therapist. So
for the clients to keep the institution the same they have to change in relation to the
information from the therapists.

G. C.: So the institution says you define yourself as a chronic patient. But we have a
law on a higher level that tells us we should change; we cannot be a chronic institution, so we want you to help us to change. It's turning things around: instead of
trying to help the patient to change, we are saying, "We [the institution] are the
patient. You must help us to change because we may become chronic therapists".
Similarly, in therapy we sometimes ask children how can we help the parents to give
up being parents. They cannot give it up, but in six months they have to give it up
because we are to change something—an interesting intervention.

IV. CONTEXTS AND CONTEXT MARKERS

Eds.: What is happening when therapists feel confused about the context in which they are working?

G. C.: When you accept the higher context that you have to be paid by somebody to be a social controller, and they tell you you should be there to do therapy and help people you are in a double bind. So you accept that you cannot help them. For example, you can say, "I cannot help you, you have to stay in this institution for some time; there is nothing you can do; you have been defined as sick. I am interested in what happened to you when you were defined this way". You react to the patient with a curious attitude: "But I cannot do anything because the decision has already been made by you, the family, the institution. Let's not talk about help, I am doing research". Then the therapist feels better and probably the patient also because he doesn't have to act out. So we are very optimistic. No matter where you are working, there is always something you can do to change the context. Something you can do to create the implicative force to change the context. Like in this case the context is totally repressive and controlling. You can create some curiosity: "While you are here in the hospital there is no problem, but when you go home, that's a problem. Probably if you take more medication everybody will be happy. You will go through this period without everybody suffering so much".

Eds.: What's the difference between a context and a context marker?

L. B.: The context marker is created by interaction. It is imminent, a part of the system. But you need the lower level context with an implicative force to keep feeding the strength of the context marker. The context marker comes from the outside, such as "I am a doctor, I will set up a hospital to control people". But this context marker must be fed by all the community who keep saying you need to control people, and they give explanations as to why people should be controlled and then you get a recursive loop.

The therapist is using the shifting of context markers to give different meaning to what is happening. If you preserve this kind of freedom you can act much more powerfully. If the context marker of the therapist is a linear one, i.e. "I am here to be nice to you because you are a poor suffering person", you cannot be very helpful with this one context marker. It doesn't change the epistemology of the system you face. Or if your context marker is: "I am here to re-organise your life because you screw it up so much, so you, Mother, must be a mother". At this moment you have the context marker of being an organiser. The aim of a systemic therapist is to be able to utilise different context markers. Often a systemic approach gets accused of creating cold therapists isolated from context; intellectual therapists who don't get involved. This myth results from the idea that as an observer you are outside. People think this is being in a "meta" position. But it is better to think of the process in terms of being "there" and then "out of there". This is much more alive.

When the family come for therapy, they may have the context marker that, "We have tried to solve the problem and have failed so you give us advice". The therapist says, "I am not going to tell you, you have to find your own solution" and then there is a new context marker. Sometimes you can reach a situation in which neither side accepts the other, and you can have an escalation of negativity and the therapist feels helpless and cannot understand anything. Then you come out of this craziness by introducing a context marker, "I am the therapist".

Eds.: How would you describe the way different context markers evolve?

G. C.: It happens sometimes that people come and say, "I don't want therapy, just give me medication". That's the context. You cannot say "Who is more upset when you are crazy, your mother or your daughter?" because they say, "don't give me that talk, just give me medication".

If you go to a pharmacist and ask for sleeping pills and he says, "Do you sleep better when you are alone or with people?", you say, "You are a pharmacist, give me the medication, shut up". If the pharmacist tries to be therapeutic, it's totally out of context.

G. C.: Another example is in the context of love, anything that happens is love. So when the husband says to the wife, "You idiot, you are so stupid", she says, "He loves me because he is able to tell me these things. He is free to tell me because he loves me". But if this continues, there is eventually a point at which the word "stupid" becomes a context maker itself. It is no longer marked by the context of love. There is a change of implicative force. The word "stupid" acquires the force to create its own context. Suddenly the wife begins to say this is not love: "He married me in order to persecute me because he's a bastard". Therefore everything that happened in the past acquires a new meaning: "A year ago when he gave me a present, he was trying to put me down". Everything changes meaning because the context marker changes.

When you are confused, and you are totally destroyed by the family, sometimes you use the context marker, "I don't understand anything here. I am the therapist, I am the one who is going to tell you what to do, and how you *do* that. Because that is the only thing we can do". And then you come out of the craziness by introducing this context marker temporarily.

Another context marker is to say "I am confused, I will go out behind the one-way screen to see what they say". You create the context marker that the people behind the screen are more important and the fact that you are confused doesn't mean anything in the therapeutic process.

When we say the context is *there*, it's not true. It's *co-created*. Sometimes we cannot change the context because it is too powerful. It is at a higher level: cultural, practical, institutional, and you as a therapist have no influence.

The context is fixed by a lower level with implicative force which reinforces the first level, but there is the possibility that the implicative force can become so powerful that it changes the higher context. There is always this duality.

You as a therapist can do something about this movement. When you say, "It's not sickness, it is love. Probably you shouldn't come here because we are therapists, but as long as you continue to believe it's a sickness you should continue to come", that introduces a powerful change of context.

To be able to accept your position as a social controller or as being controlled by your institution, you need to have a larger context in your head. To see it and accept it introduces a small difference which will have an implicative force on the higher organisation. If you face it directly you get lost. You cannot change the higher context just because you don't like it. You cannot change people symmetrically but only through implicative force. One aims to change the context marker so the meaning of what you are doing has an effect on the higher level.

Eds.: (We asked both Dr. Boscolo and Dr. Cecchin to describe some piece of recent clinical work which they felt reflected their current thinking. In our opinion, Dr. Cecchin's case is useful in understanding this issue of context markers.)

G. C.: I am thinking about a case of a lady who has been an alcoholic for many years. She is about 55 and has three teenage children. The husband is a business man in an upper middle class family. When she drinks it is a disaster. Everyone has to care for her. They have to go out at night and look for her in the bars and bring her home; they take her to hospital. Everyone is desperate. One son is obsessive about studying, one daughter is obsessive about being promiscuous, and another daughter is a nice little girl to her father—different behaviour but extreme for all of them. So they came here and spent half an hour talking about how terrible mother is when she drinks. Then she denies it and they accuse her of lying. Everybody cares a lot about her; no one can leave her alone.

When I went back into the therapy room after discussing it with the team, I said, "We understand now the terrible things that happen when you drink. But we are interested in when you are sober. Tell me all the terrible things that happen when you are sober. It must be terrible for you when you are sober since that leads you to drink".

Then she started to get emotional and she talked about all the terrible things her husband did to her in the last 15 years. Once she had to give up a child when she was pregnant because the husband didn't want it; he had not wanted to sleep with her for the last 10 years; the children mistreat her all the time; and when she is sober she has to be the typical wife looking after everybody. But when the others in the family discussed these things they said, "but you should have seen her yesterday when she was drinking". They tried to bring it back to the drinking. I said we are interested in sobriety.

Then I left the room and when I came back in I said, "You have been in therapy for a long time and everyone has been trying to help you not to drink. We in our hearts are not able to tell you not to drink even though this is the most logical thing to say, because we are sure it's worse for you when you are not drinking, so we don't know what to say because to tell you to keep drinking is also crazy. When she drinks, it's much worse for everybody, but when she doesn't drink, it's much worse for her. So we don't know what to say. Come back in a month".

So in a month's time on the day of the session, the husband phoned up saying, "We cannot come because something happened, my wife is sick". So we gave them another appointment in two months time.

They came back and they were very quiet. I asked, "What happened?" and the son said, "It's perfect. She doesn't drink any more". "Since when?" "Since the last session that we missed". The story was that she drank off and on until the day of the session, when she drank herself to the danger point—"hitting bottom". At that point she felt she was dying and she decided not to drink anymore. Everyone said, "Life is fantastic. If it would only go on like this it would be great". And then I tried not to talk about the drinking, but to talk about the behaviour of the son and daughters, and to get the parents to talk about the children just to kill time, and not talk about drinking too much. And then without making an intervention, I said we would meet in another month.

They came back in a month and everybody was angry. "What happened?" "She started to drink again". "How much?" It turned out she never drank herself to death again but was drinking aperitifs, Campari, wine, but never getting drunk. Everybody was watching her, suspiciously, saying, "It's going to happen again". She said, "Absolutely not". I asked what she had been doing during the day and she had been acting the part of the good wife, bringing her husband coffee in bed, then going out for the day and helping a friend who worked in a clothing shop. She was playing at being a good wife but not believing it was the right thing to do.

Then when I discussed this with the team we used the idea of Bateson (1973), that the problem in drinking is the issue of control. She said she was controlling herself, and the others said she wasn't controlling herself. So I started asking other members of the family about the issue of control. It came out that the boy is studying too much; the daughter is always playing around with boys; and the father said, "I never buy a bottle of whiskey, because I know if I buy it I will drink it in two days. So I never buy it".

So our final intervention was: "We understand one thing about this family and that is that you are so close, so united, in order to resolve one main issue, that issue is how to control yourself. No one can control themselves. The father cannot control his drinking of whiskey. The son cannot control his desire to study, the daughter cannot control her promiscuous behaviour and the little daughter cannot control her concern about the family. One thing we understand is that mother is the only one who can control herself. She can drink some aperitifs and not get drunk. How does she do it? With the help of her whole family. You have done a good job of helping her control herself.

"Now we will give you a prescription. Next month the whole family should spend their time trying to help the father control himself. Now that mother is doing well you can help Father because he needs your help". The Father burst out in laughter. His daughters went up to him saying "Now we'll look after you". The mother was very happy. We said, "That's for next month; after that we'll all get together and try to help the son to control himself and another time we try to help the daughters".

The idea was to take the idea of control and apply it around the family not just with the alcoholic. . . . That seemed to be a good idea, introducing sobriety as a change of context marker; then giving a prescription of everyone helping father not mother, and giving a positive connotation of her drinking.

L. B.: In the first session when you talk about sobriety, I think you introduce a new reality. So you also had the effect of introducing new maps. Probably the system cannot get unstuck without someone outside introducing a new way of perceiving this behaviour.

G. C.: This case describes all the things we've discussed: introducing a new context marker: sobriety; making reflexive questions by finding out the details; then looking for the premise. Everyone was concerned with the issue of control.

V.   CONTEXT AND STATUTORY
RESPONSIBILITY

Eds.: Both enthusiasts and critics question whether this approach can be used when they have statutory responsibilities for curing a client. The dilemma they feel is that they are trying to satisfy the court and also be therapists for their clients. Do you think there is an ethical dilemma?

G. C.: The therapist's dilemma is that as an agent of social control he should tell a client to stop stealing but as a therapist, he understands why it is impossible for the client to stop at the moment.

In this position the therapist might say, "I am trying to obey the *judge* and I am also trying to help *you*. The judge thinks you can be cured so I must find a way to tell you not to steal. When the judge told you, you did not listen; when your parents told you, you did not listen; now I am supposed to tell you in a more efficient way. That's why we are meeting. But let's leave that for a moment and go back to why it happened, how did it start, what has been the effect on your family?" (These can be investigated with circular questioning.)

After a while you say, "I can tell you to *stop*, but I can also see the reasons why you *do* it, so I am in trouble. What can I do now? Can we meet again perhaps in two weeks? I hope you don't steal in those two weeks but if you do, please warn me so I know what to tell you. See you in two weeks".

Eds.: But implicit in that is a difference between doing therapy and telling someone to stop stealing.

G. C.: Exactly, that is very good. You respond with this statement to the two levels/contexts—where you are the social controller paid by the judge and also where you want to be a therapist—which is about trying to introduce in a person the self-healing capacity—where it is his decision to stop not the decision of the judge. You play at both levels.

Eds.: Is there an ethical problem when the therapist is working in two contexts, in one of which he is required to obey the judge?

G. C.: A confused therapist would show the effect of the contradictions if he told the client, "Stealing is not a problem; it is a problem that you have got caught and are so stupid". Or perhaps the therapist would say, "I think you should go on stealing for another month"—a paradoxical prescription—but then the therapist gets into trouble because there is too much difference between the official position of the therapist and what he prescribes.

One way out is to say to the client, "I am here to tell you to stop stealing but it is very difficult because officially you can tell the judge that although you have been sent for psychiatric help, therapy takes time and for the moment you cannot be cured". That is the official position of therapy, but to the client, you say, "I cannot tell you to stop". There is no contradiction; the therapist is no longer in a dilemma.

But the idea that the therapist has to be honest or has to fit a certain ethic can lessen the possibility for him to be therapeutic. Honesty is part of the context in which we understand the information.

In a difficult situation like this, you give the patient a chance to help you by relating to this dilemma. One way out of the dilemma would be for the client to say, "Forget it, I refuse therapy and will go to jail". This is a very clear, simple solution. The other is to stop stealing. The patient who goes to jail is much better than the one who accepts therapy because the thief who accepts therapy tries to manipulate in some way; but if he says, "I want to go to jail; therapy is not for me", this is already a very honest thief.

In the context of the family you might say stealing is a generous act, but in the context of society, it is a very nasty act. So practically, the therapist is saying both "steal" and "don't steal". "Stop stealing because the judge has told you and me, but don't stop stealing because it is a moral action". The client is caught between the two moralities. The therapist introduces a conflict which can be resolved by the client. The client can give up stealing if the therapist recognises his moral action for the family.

VI. CHANGE AND CO-EVOLUTION

Eds.: How do you see the process of change occurring? What can a therapist do?

L. B.: According to Prigogine and Stenger's (1977a, 1977b) ideas about systems, a system is in continuous fluctuation. During these fluctuations, when the impact on the system goes beyond certain parameters, the system will reorganise at another level, but we never know where the oscillation starts. It can start any place. In terms of family therapy, for instance, the oscillation can start in relation to a behaviour that the therapist is not very much aware of. And this can be the beginning of a change. So, Prigogine says, the therapist is just a facilitator.

In conducting the session we are mostly in the domain of *thinking* but in the intervention we give prescriptions and we are more in the domain of *behaviour*. There is a recursiveness between behaviour and thinking and thinking and behaviour. In our therapy we are always oscillating between these two limits—thinking/behaviour: behaviour/thinking.

L. B.: The introduction of time is important here. At the moment in time that you do something, you cannot at the same time do something else. So for instance, when I am a therapist with the family, the moment I ask questions I'm interacting with the family. I cannot at that moment be the observer of myself interacting with the system but the next moment I might be the observer, so there is always the oscillation.

One of my conclusions is that many therapists ignore the concept of time. I am more and more obsessed about time now, in the sense that things get into a muddle when we do not take time into consideration.

G. C.: Another position I find very interesting is "being the therapist" and "not being the therapist". If you accept the idea that you can only be a therapist some of the time, that is an improvement. Most of the time you are not a therapist, most of the time you are a supporter, a social controller; you organise society around certain concepts. But sometimes you can be a therapist, which means being able to introduce into the system the self-healing capacities. As long as you are a social controller, social worker, or supporter, you are not producing the self-healing capacity. You are just confirming the client's dependency on the system and you. But one should accept that most of the time one is not a therapist.

If a therapist can accept this idea, he can be very effective because he says, "I will wait for the right moment to do something, meanwhile I'm a social controller, or an educator".

Eds.: But aren't you also suggesting that at some point the oscillation actually comes together so that you are a social controlling agent with a systemic view?

G. C.: Exactly. I think the novelty is that you can be a social controller, give medication, even give electric shock and have a systemic view. In the past it seemed like a systemic therapist just had to do family therapy, which is ridiculous. Paradoxically, a systemic therapist can decide not to do family therapy. If you have the concept "I have to be a therapist", you use the verb *to be*. "I am a therapist, therefore I cannot be a social controller, so I get confused". It is an epistemological error to have *to be* a therapist.

In systemic theory you are not "something", you are "someone in this moment" in relation to the context, who has acted in time. So if you introduce the concept of time you can say, "I am the therapist now but tomorrow I will be the social controller".

So one must be very decisive, yet knowing nothing about what you're doing. If you say, "I'm very sorry I can't act because I have to know more", you create an impossible situation. You never know enough to act and you keep looking, proving, you can never act decisively.

L. B.: Introducing time liberates you from the verb *to be* because whenever the therapist says "I am", he is stuck. If the therapist says, "I am systemic", this becomes a straightjacket that stops him from being a therapist.

Eds.: How does the way clients use the verb *to be* stop the therapist using the process of oscillation?

G. C.: For example, if a woman says the problem is that "my husband is too cold", then the issue of warmth is important. If you are not warm it is a disaster.

If the therapist asks the question, "Why do you have to be warm?", and there is an answer, then you see that it is not a fixed premise. By asking these questions you see how rigid the premise is. When you ask why does it have to be warm, you see whether it is a fixed premise or whether the relationship can be warm *and* cold. If your relationship is only warm, obviously you are limited.

You begin to believe in small action. You do something, you wait for feedback, then you act again. What you do is decisive because you are introducing a definition.

Eds.: (*The following case of Dr. Boscolo's includes an example of a systemic approach to a rigidly held premise.*)

L. B: A couple was referred to us from a private hospital. The husband, a manager, was about 45 and the wife about 40. At the beginning of the session I was asking questions about names, ages, etc. I asked the husband if they were married and he said, "Yes" and I asked if they had children, and he said, "Yes, one child of a year and a half". Then when I turned to the woman and asked her, she gave me her name, but she said, "This is not my husband". Then the husband looked at me and said, "This is the problem. For a year and a half she has been saying I am not her husband and that our child is not our child". At this point in the session I asked questions like this: "This person who thinks he is your husband" or "This person who thinks she is not your wife" just to be neutral.

The information from the first session was that she became depressed four years ago and the husband related this depression to her father's death. She was very attached to her father and when he died she attempted suicide. She also has a sister who was also attached to her father. The husband is an only child and *his* father also died four years ago, shortly after *her* father died.

What was interesting was that this was a couple that had been married a long time—six or seven years—and all of a sudden after her depression and attempted suicide she said she wanted a child. The husband agreed and then when she became pregnant, she started to feel good; she was normal. As soon as she had the child, she became depressed and was diagnosed as having a post-partum psychosis. She started to deny the child was her child and that the husband was her husband. So the husband called his mother, who came every day to look after the child and his wife. This had been going on for one and a half years.

Towards the end of the session I asked what she expected in coming here and she said, "I expect nothing". And she gave the impression she wasn't at all interested in the therapy. This lady was very lucid and clear; she didn't appear psychotic, and her only delusion was that the man was not her husband and the child was not her child, and she said also she felt dead inside.

I asked them to bring his mother, her sister and the child to the next session. The child was very sweet, very normal, and it was interesting the way he moved. Most frequently he went to father. When he went to the mother, she ignored him. The intervention we made for the second session was this: "What we see is that Mary says this is not her husband and this is not her child and there are others who say she is a wife and she is a mother. What we think is that if she has these convictions they must have some relationship to something. She might be getting a message from somewhere in the family that she must not be a mother and she is not a wife. Yet all of you are saying this is a mother and this is a wife. This is what we don't under-stand. Therefore we think that there is an indication for therapy but we're going to see you only under one condition, and the condition is that, Mary, you keep your conviction of not being a wife and not being a mother. Because if you were to start to have doubts about your conviction it could become very risky." She asked, "Risky for whom?", and I said "We don't know. But if we begin therapy and you tell us you begin to have doubts about these convictions, we will stop therapy because we will only do therapy if you keep this conviction".

The hypothesis is that her behaviour is consistent with what is happening in the system since her father died. The mother-in-law became very close to her son and this was a very important marriage, so her idea that she was not a wife and not a mother was very consistent. The reason why we say we will only do therapy if you keep this conviction is that she put the therapist in a paradoxical situation. She said, "I'm not interested in therapy" and she was saying "I'm here but I'm not here", so this message had the effect of taking the therapist out of the paradoxical situation, by saying "I only do therapy if you keep thinking this way".

In the third session our intervention was: "The last time we asked your mother-in-law, your sister and your child because we were interested to see what kind of a child was this who had one person saying, 'I am your father' and another person saying, 'I am not your mother'. We were very shocked that this child was a normal child. We couldn't believe that we would see a normal child. The idea that we had about why this was a normal child was that in the house he has a man who defines himself as a father, and two women. One is defined as mother and the other as a grandmother. But how come this child has a good relationship with the women and is a normal child? We think this is related to the fact that both of you women have a very clear relationship with the child. You, Mary, defined as a mother, we don't know whether you are or not, but if you really were a mother, you are a very good mother because it is like you have given your child to be adopted and then you have stayed out. We know that if a woman gives a child to another woman to be adopted and then stays out the child will be normal. And the other woman, the grandmother, is very good too because she doesn't try to tell the child 'I am your mother". That's why we think the child is very normal'.

As we gave this intervention, Mary began crying. She had had a frozen face for a year and a half but this made a very big impact on her. Then we offered a fourth session and the husband came and said his wife didn't feel like coming. At the end of the session we gave the intervention in a letter. We gave it to the husband and asked him to take it home and give it to his wife. The letter was addressed to his wife. In the letter we wrote: "Today we have seen Mr. X (the husband) and our impression is that he is confused, and we would like, if you want to come next time to help us, to help *him* get out of his confusion". That was the last session. We will see what happens.

The formulation that led us to that intervention was that the intervention of the first and second session caused the mother to get alarmed. She said, "I don't want to go", so we made the intervention that he was confused in order to try to connect again with her by asking her to come and help us.

We are very curious. If only the husband comes to the next session, then we will work with the husband and eventually show him how he has been confused by all these women; with the aim of breaking the very rigid pattern this system has developed over time.

The most important thing in this case is how to engage a member of a family who communicates by saying, "I have this conviction . . . I don't agree to be here . . . I don't agree that I need to change". This puts the therapist in a paradoxical position. In order to engage a family member in this situation, the therapist has to respond with a paradoxical message.

VII. TRAINING

Eds.: Teaching people to think systemically is a different activity than teaching people to do therapy. Would you comment on that?

L. B.: We show our trainees how to do family therapy during the first year but tell them they will not have enough experience to do family therapy at our centre until the second year. So from time to time during the first year when we enquire about the work which they do in their own agency, we put the student in a context in which he has to think not just imitate, and we are saying, "You do not have to do what you do here in your own work setting. Your work is context-dependent".

G. C.: We teach the students to think by creating a simulated family and telling the student he has to make five mistakes, for example, with neutrality. We don't try to teach them to do it right, they should make some mistakes so we can learn. We feel if we do not make some mistakes then we can't think, so it's only through the contradictions that you learn, not through learning how to do something. The traditional way of teaching is to teach how to do something so every time you do it, you have to bring out the contradiction in what you do. It's a double edge.

Eds.: What is the aim of the observing groups? Are they observing the way the therapy team works or are they observing the way the relationship between the family and the therapy team develops?

L. B.: The task of the therapist and therapeutic group is to do therapy. The observers observe the interaction between the three subgroups: the family, the therapist, and the therapeutic group. This is very important from a training point of view because the people who are in the observing group can more freely observe the therapist, especially how he responds to the family analogically and verbally. If you are in the position of therapist or therapeutic group, you are bound to see the family rather than the therapist.

Eds.: Some of the more enthusiastic teams are attempting to be consultants to other members of their own professional contexts in their own agency. What do you think about that?

L. B.: I think it can be done. It can be extremely useful in the context of that service, but there is a problem of consensus. If one of the members of staff asks for a consultant at a particular time, there should be a consensus and then this can be very effective.

When the team or a group or a member of the staff, by consensus, allows one or two colleagues to be a consultant, this creates for that moment a different position for the person who is the consultant. Usually the ideas the consultant has are related to the position that the system decided to put him in at that moment. That is why the consultation is also a difference.

One possible solution to this problem is one found by some of our trainees in Modena, where the first person who is involved with the case sees the family either in the institution or at home and reports what he has observed to a team. He introduces information to his team. They discuss and give a message to the therapist in terms of what they observe about the therapist/family system. They found this solution was very effective. They found even workers without much experience can get involved with the case and do very good family therapy.

Eds.: How are you used as consultants to the trainees once they go back to their own agencies?

G. C.: One example is a group that trained here and came back a year later. They said they felt pretty good about their work and they discovered that everything they learned during the training was totally useless. It was paradoxical; they said what we did was useless and even though they came back to us they could not ask us for any help because what we offered was useless. It looks like a statement of disappointment but the feeling they had was very positive and they wanted to come back. So our way of training seems to help people become more independent. We are not creating a dependent relationship. We do not go on with them for years. They disappear.

G. C.: It is interesting that when we offered the opportunity for people to come for supervision after training, we expected an enormous number of requests, but we have had very few. But the people who are working in their own context may say, "It's better if we don't see the Milan team again".

L. B.: I think when we got stuck, the students came to our rescue. When we were with Selvini and Prata we were a closed system. The students opened up this system. When we call ourselves systemic therapists, and not family therapists it is because of the students.

G. C.: Also, in Italy when they closed the mental hospitals there was a state of confusion and people were looking for something to find a solution. In a country which is already well organised, it's almost impossible to penetrate with systemic ideas.

L. B.: In Italy there were so many ideas in the field of psychiatry; individual, psychodynamic therapy, small groups and the anti-psychiatry movement, the students were already prepared to think at different levels of systems. My impression is in the United States people think more on one level. The psychiatrist doesn't see the different levels such as the political level. The psychiatrist thinks of himself as an expert trying to cure an illness. This restricts his field of observation and his hypothesis. In Italy we find the cultural milieu more open.

VIII. EVALUATION

Eds.: What is your view of research as a systemic thinker?

G. C.: We say we never know whether it is our intervention that brings about some change in the system. We can only observe that in a certain number of families, certain things happened. We like to *think* it is because of our intervention, but we can never demonstrate it.

Eds.: Why bother to do it?

G. C.: That's a good question. In certain contexts this service is required.

Eds.: If you are working in a context in which you have to justify your work in order to get government funding, then you have to do evaluation in that context even though you know from an epistemological point of view it is impossible.

L. B.: Also, evaluation is always biased. For example, if you have the bias that a normal family is one in which the children have to separate after the age of 18 years, you are going to see normal families as ones who change in this way. But you may have a bias, like I have, that it is not necessary for a family to be normal or functional, it is not necessary that the son and daughter have to go out and get married. A daughter can decide to stay at home all her life if there is a consensus in the family. Results are always biased. I think all follow-up studies have to take into consideration the bias of the one who does the follow-up and the bias of the one who hears about it.

My impression is that in Italy they bother less and less with follow-up studies.

G. C.: Follow-up must be an Anglo-Saxon idea.

REFERENCES

Bateson, G. (1973). "Steps to an Ecology of Mind". Paladin, London.

Bateson, G. (1979). "Mind and Nature: A Necessary Unity". Dutton, New York.

Elkaim, M., Prigogine, I., *et al.* (1982). Openness—A Round-Table Discussion. *Family Process* **21**, 57–70.

Keeney, B. (1982). What is an Epistemology of Family Therapy? *Family Process* **21**, 153–168.

Keeney, B. (1983). "Aesthetics of Change". Guilford Press, New York.

Maturana, H. P. (1975). Organization of Living—Theory of Living Organization. *International Journal of Man–Machine Studies* **1**, 313–332.

Maturana, H., and Varela, F. (1980). "Autopoiesis and Cognition: Realization of the Living" Reidel Press, Boston.

Palazzoli, M. S., Boscolo, L., Cecchin, G., and Prata, G. (1980). Hypothesizing–Circularity–Neutrality. *Family Process* **19**, 3–12.

Pearce, W. B., and Cronen, V. E. (1980). "Communication, Action and Meaning" Praegar, New York.

Prigogine, I., and Stenger, I. (1977a). New Alliance, 1. From Dynamics to Thermodynamics—Physics, Gradual Opening Towards a World of Natural Processes. *Scientia* **112**, 319–322.

Prigogine, I., and Stenger, I. (1977b). New Alliance, 2. Extended Dynamics—Towards a Human Science of Nature. *Scientia* **112**, 617–653.

Contents of Family Therapy : Volume 1

The first volume in the Complementary Framework
of Theory and Practice series, edited by Arnon Bentovim,
Gill Gorell Barnes and Alan Cooklin.

PART III—PRACTICAL ISSUES

Contents of Family Therapy : Volume 2

The second volume in The Complementary Frameworks
of Theory and Practice series, edited by Arnon Bentovim,
Gill Gorell Barnes and Alan Cooklin.

INDEX

action, meaning and, 6
adolescent behavior, interventions, 173, 176–79
adolescent in-patient unit, 119–25; admissions, 119, 120; case example, 121–23; circular questions in, 122–23, 124; context, as a concept in, 120–21, 124–25; intervention in, 121; neutrality in, 120; organization, 119–20; referrals, 119–20, 124
agency setting, 5; context factor, 6
anomaly, 74–75, 76

Batesonian theory, 11, 24, 31, 33, 38, 151
belief system, 3; interpersonal, 26
behavior: linear view, 25; "reasons" vs. "causes," 24–25; showing vs. being, 2; systemic hypotheses vs. common sense schemas, 24–25
biology, hierarchy, as a concept in, 18–19

case example: adolescent behavior, 177–79; adolescent in-patient unit, 121–23; consultation, 63–67, 196–201; context, 15–16; context/consultation relation, 14–15; family service unit, 166–67; on hypothesis formulation, 27–31; in-patient hospital service, 216–18; mental health service, 141, 143–44, 185, 186–88; multiple–helper system, 208–11; psychiatric nursing team, 115–17; sex therapy, 128–29; social service agency, 90–92
causality, 24–25
change, 142; co-evolution and, 285–89; conditions for, 5, 15–16; evolutionary feedback and, 19; hierarchy, as a concept and, 18–19; hypothesis, as a

concept and, 23–24; recognition of, 92
child care centre, 173–80, 221–27; assessment, 222; case example, 177–79; circular questions, 223; consultation, 221–27; context, as a concept, 222; hypothesis formulation, 222, 223–25, 226; interventions, 176–79, 223, 225, 226, 227; legal factor, 221, 223; organization, 173–76, 179–80; referrals, 176, 179, 221–22; time factor, 226–27
child guidance clinic, 97–105; context, as a concept in, 97–99; evaluation of results, 103–4
child psychiatric unit, training programme, 231–40
circular questions (questioning), 2, 33–45, 77, 79, 153; in adolescent in-patient unit therapy, 122–23, 124; categorical context, 41–42; category difference, 39–41; in child care centre consultation, 223; conservative effect, 37; descriptive, 35–37; evaluation, 44–45; explanation, 43; for exploring differences, 38–39; generative effect, 37; in in-patient hospital service, 215, 217–18; interaction centered, 44; interpersonal perception, 44; interventions and, 36; interviewing and, 43–44; with multiple-helper system, 205; person oriented, 43; problem definition, 43; in professional training centre, 246, 247; reflexive, 35–37; in sex therapy, 130; tactical, 36; temporal context, 42–43; temporal difference, 41–42; theoretical basis for, 37–39; triadic, 36; types of, 39–43, 40
circularity concept, 12–13, 23, 279; in interviewing, 33–45
clarity, in social systems, 74–76, 79
client selection, 16–17
co-evolutionary process, 59